THE EARLY LIVES OF MELVILLE

Nineteenth-Century Biographical
Sketches and Their Authors

Norman Melville

The first reproduction of the Eaton portrait of 1870: an engraving in *A Library of American Literature,* compiled and edited by Edmund Clarence Stedman and Ellen Mackay Hutchinson (New York, 1888–1890), vol. VII, facing p. 464. (Photograph courtesy of Professor James A. Sappenfield.) Stedman's son Arthur, who later became Melville's literary executor, made his initial acquaintance in an interview to arrange for use of the portrait in that anthology.

THE EARLY LIVES
OF MELVILLE

Nineteenth-Century Biographical
Sketches and Their Authors

MERTON M. SEALTS, Jr.

The University of Wisconsin Press

Published 1974
The University of Wisconsin Press
Box 1379, Madison, Wisconsin 53701

The University of Wisconsin Press, Ltd.
70 Great Russell St., London

Printed in the United States of America
For LC CIP information see the colophon
ISBN 0-299-06570-7

Eleanor Melville Metcalf's recollections of her grandfather, first printed in Raymond M. Weaver, *Herman Melville: Mariner and Mystic,* © 1921, and reprinted in her *Herman Melville: Cycle and Epicycle,* © 1953, are printed here with the permission of her sons, David M. Metcalf and Paul C. Metcalf, and with the concurrence of Sidney A. Burrell (for the estate of Raymond Weaver) and of Harvard University Press. Frances Thomas Osborne's "Herman Melville through a Child's Eyes," first printed in the *Bulletin of the New York Public Library,* 59 (December 1965), © 1965, is reprinted here with the permission of Mrs. Osborne and the New York Public Library.

For R. M. S.
   M. M. S. (1876-1946)
   D. H. S. (1879-1974)

—and for Pixie (1954-1973)

Contents

Illustrations

ix

Preface

Sooner or later, the dedicated student of Melville will feel the need to go behind even the best of his secondary sources, such as Jay Leyda's indispensable *Melville Log* (1951, 1969), and examine complete primary documents. Besides Melville's own writings he will consult the observations of friends and relatives who knew the man and what he did—and who had their own ideas about what sort of being he was. Some of the most important of these documents are the least accessible: Elizabeth Shaw Melville's memoranda concerning her husband, only partly in print; J. E. A. Smith's biographical sketch of his old friend, incompletely exhumed from the Pittsfield *Evening Journal* by Mrs. Melville in a rare pamphlet of 1897; Arthur Stedman's various fugitive essays about the man he served as literary executor. Even if one faithfully takes notes on these and other materials, as we used to do, or makes electrostatic copies, as we do now, he still faces the scholarly tasks of analysis, interpretation, and comparison—chores which have been duplicated and reduplicated as researchers individually consulted these sources at different times and with different purposes in view.

For some years, as my own collection of notes, copies, and partial analyses grew larger and the complex interrelations among various contemporary accounts of Melville gradually became more apparent to me, I have had the idea of editing the key documents in a single comprehensive volume, both to satisfy my own curiosity about what these records and their recorders have to say and also to share my resultant findings with others interested in Melville. A good and useful edition must do thoroughly what I had previously done only in part: establish the texts, set forth their basis and authority, furnish genuinely helpful notes and commentary, and—last but not least—index the entire study in order to make it readily usable as well as readable. These have been my goals in *The Early Lives of Melville.*

The organization of the book is in keeping with these objectives. The introductory chapters survey the basis and authority of the most important nineteenth-century biographical sketches of Melville, written either during his lifetime or immediately after his death by persons who knew him directly. The contemporary documents which follow include (1) short articles on Melville from four contemporary reference works published between 1852 and 1890; (2) six retrospective essays of 1891–1892; and (3) further reminiscences of Melville by his wife and two of his granddaughters. Chronological arrangement of these documents and also of those related materials printed in the Appendices has made it possible to show with a minimum of explanation and annotation the genesis and transmission of certain ideas about Melville as well as the evolution and development of the major biographical essays by J. E. A. Smith and Arthur Stedman. A chronology and an index of proper names conclude the book.

All quotations from individual volumes of Melville's published works not otherwise credited are from The Writings of Herman Melville, the Northwestern-Newberry Edition, edited by Harrison Hayford, Hershel Parker, and G. Thomas Tanselle (Evanston and Chicago: Northwestern University Press and the Newberry Library, 1968–   ). Unless otherwise noted, documentation of other materials cited by date or by the short titles indicated below will be found in the following publications:

Letters   *The Letters of Herman Melville.* Edited by Merrell R. Davis and
William H. Gilman. New Haven: Yale University Press, 1960.

Log   Jay Leyda. *The Melville Log: A Documentary Life of Herman Melville, 1819–1891.* 2 volumes. New York: Gordian Press, 1969.

Asterisks (*) have been used throughout this volume to call attention to erroneous dating in source materials; for the correct dates, see the Chronology.

For their kindness in making various items available for study and publication I am indebted to the four granddaughters of Herman and Elizabeth Melville, to Messrs. David and Paul Metcalf (sons of the late Eleanor Melville and Henry K. Metcalf), to the Ferris Greenslet Trust, and to the staffs of the Berkshire Athenaeum, the Boston Athenaeum, the Fogg Museum and the Houghton Library of Harvard University, the Metropolitan Museum of Art, the Newberry Library, the New York Genealogical and Biographical Society, the New-York Historical Society, the New York Public Library (Astor, Lenox, and Tilden Foundations), the Wisconsin State Historical Society, the libraries of Columbia, Harvard, and Yale Universities, and the Memorial Library of the University of Wisconsin-Madison. In assembling materials over the years I have benefited first from the financial assistance of Lawrence University and more recently from that of the Research Committee of the Graduate School, the University of Wisconsin-Madison; during the summer of 1970, when I established the texts of the several Lives, I received a grant-in-aid from the American Council of Learned Societies. Special thanks go to Warren Beck, William H. Bond, John C. Broderick, Sidney A. Burrell, C. E. Frazier Clark, Richard Harter Fogle, Barry Gaines, Donald Gallup, Harrison Hayford, Carolyn Jakeman,

Richard Colles Johnson, Kenneth A. Lohf, Duane Macmillan, Jean R. McNiece, Joel Myerson, Robert G. Newman, Hershel Parker, Norman Holmes Pearson, Walter B. Rideout, M. Douglas Sackman, James A. Sappenfield, Stuart C. Sherman, Mary Stevens, and G. Thomas Tanselle, who have all helped in various ways, and to Ruth Mackenzie Sealts, who has been a virtual collaborator from the beginning. For all the assistance and encouragement thus given me by individuals and institutions I am grateful indeed.

Merton M. Sealts, Jr.

PART I

Records and Recorders

A Man of the Time:
Melville in the
Biographical Dictionaries

PROLOGUE: "THE UTTER UNSATISFACTORINESS OF ALL HUMAN FAME"

Book XVII of Melville's *Pierre* (1852), satirically treating "Young America in Literature," reveals to the reader for the first time that the title character of the book is something of a writer for "magazines and other polite periodicals. His magnificent and victorious *debut* had been made in that delightful love-sonnet, entitled 'The Tropical Summer' " (p. 245). Despite Pierre's youth and immaturity and his scanty output as a writer, editors and publishers have proposed a collected edition of his fugitive pieces; young ladies have sought his autograph for their albums; "Lyceums, Young Men's Associations, and other Literary and Scientific Societies" have invited him to lecture before them; the proprietors of magazines have requested his portrait. Such fruits of literary fame were thoroughly familiar by 1852 to Melville himself, who had begun his literary career six years before by writing of his own Tropical Summer in *Typee* (1846). Editors and publishers, autograph-seekers, and lecture committees had all made their applications to him as well as to Pierre; the proprietors of magazines had asked for his own picture. In 1851, while Melville was working on his sixth book, Rufus Griswold's *International Monthly Magazine* had mentioned his name in promising its readers a series of portraits and biographical sketches of contemporary authors, and at the same time Melville's friend Evert Duyckinck, who with his brother George had just taken over *Holden's Dollar Magazine,* requested both a daguerreotype and an article for their rival publication. Melville replied in a letter of 12 February 1851 that he was "not in the humor to write for Holden's Magazine" and would not send a daguerreotype for publication "even to you"; indeed his portrait and biography appeared neither in *Holden's* nor in the *International.*

That Melville had this exchange in mind when he wrote Book XVII of *Pierre* is obvious enough; what is surprising is the difference in tone between his letter to Duyckinck and Pierre's response to "a joint editor of the 'Captain Kidd Monthly'" who had made a similar request of him: "To the Devil with you and your Daguerreotype!" As Melville's narrator observes, "Pierre had an ugly devil in him sometimes, very apt to be evoked by the personal profaneness of gentlemen of the Captain Kidd school of literature" (p. 254). Otherwise, the real and the fictional episodes have much in common. Since "almost everybody is having his 'mug' engraved these days," Melville had written to Duyckinck, "this test of distinction is getting to be reversed; and therefore, to see one's 'mug' in a magazine, is presumptive evidence that he's a nobody." Pierre's private reasoning is along the same lines: in an age when everybody's portrait is published, "true distinction lies in not having yours published at all. For if you are published along with Tom, Dick, and Harry, and wear a coat of their cut, how then are you distinct from Tom, Dick, and Harry?" To these words the narrator appends his own observation: "Therefore, even so miserable a motive as downright personal vanity helped to operate in this matter with Pierre" (p. 254).

As Pierre refuses to supply his portrait for publication, so also does he decline to furnish various petitioners with "the materials wherewith to frame his biography," and again personal experience must have been in Melville's mind as he wrote. In dealing with Pierre's would-be biographers he is at first light and playful: these "zealous lovers of the general literature of the age" point out to young Pierre that in the event of "any sudden and fatal sickness," his last hours would be "embittered by the thought, that he was about to depart forever, leaving the world utterly unprovided with the knowledge of what were the precise texture and hue of the first trowsers he wore"; indeed, these solemn representations did "touch him in a very tender spot, not previously unknown to the schoolmaster"! But Pierre becomes "the more bewildered and pained"—and Melville himself the more serious—when "other and less delicate applicants" bombard him with

> their regularly printed *Biographico-Solicito Circulars,* with his name written in ink; begging him to honor them and the world with a neat draft of his life, including criticisms on his own writings; the printed circular indiscriminantly protesting, that undoubtedly he knew more of his own life than any other living man; and that only he who had put together the great works of Glendinning could be fully qualified thoroughly to analyze them, and cast the ultimate judgment upon their remarkable construction.
>
> Now, it was under the influence of the humiliating emotions engendered by things like the above; it was when thus haunted by publishers, engravers, editors, critics, autograph-collectors, portrait-fanciers, biographers, and petitioning and remonstrating literary friends of all sorts; it was then, that there stole into the youthful soul of Pierre melancholy forebodings of the utter unsatisfactoriness of all human fame; since the most ardent profferings of the most martyrizing demonstrations in his behalf,—these he was sorrowfully obliged to turn away.

And it may well be believed, that . . . he had not failed to clutch with peculiar nervous detestation and contempt that ample parcel, containing the letters of his Biographico and other silly correspondents, which, in a less fero-
cious hour, he had filed away as curiosities. It was with an almost infernal
grin, that he saw that particular heap of rubbish eternally quenched in the
fire, and felt that as it was consumed before his eyes, so in his soul was forever killed the last and minutest undeveloped microscopic germ of that most
despicable vanity to which those absurd correspondents thought to appeal.
(pp. 255–256)

Melville himself had not taken so dim a view of the rewards of authorship at
the beginning of his own literary career. While enjoying the initial success of
Typee he was pleased to compare himself with Byron, who also "woke one
morning and found himself famous" (*Letters,* p. 42), and on returning to England in 1849 he reflected with some satisfaction, wry or otherwise, on his
change of fortune since first arriving there ten years before: "*then* a sailor, *now*
H.M. author of 'Peedee' 'Hullabaloo' & 'Pog-Dog'" (*Log,* I, 325). But as he
undertook *Moby-Dick* in 1850 and 1851 he was increasingly conscious of a pro-
gressive inner development that seemed to be approaching its climax. In the
light of what he was then attempting he looked back with distaste on outward
events, on his earlier books and the kind of reputation they had brought him,
and even on fame itself. "I did not think of Fame, a year ago, as I do now," he
wrote to Nathaniel Hawthorne in June of 1851.

All Fame is patronage. Let me be infamous: there is no patronage in *that.*
What "reputation" H.M. has is horrible. Think of it! To go down to posterity is bad enough, any way; but to go down as a "man who lived among the
cannibals"! When I speak of posterity, in reference to myself, I only mean
the babies who will probably be born in the moment immediately ensuing
upon my giving up the ghost. I shall go down to some of them, in all likelihood. "Typee" will be given to them, perhaps, with their gingerbread. I have
come to regard this matter of Fame as the most transparent of all vanities. I
read Solomon more and more, and every time see deeper and deeper and un-
speakable meanings in him. (*Letters,* pp. 129–130)

Convinced like Pierre of "the utter unsatisfactoriness of all human fame,"
the Melville of 1851 was no more likely than his disillusioned young hero to respond favorably to Biographico-Solicito Circulars appealing to "that most despicable vanity."

THE EARLIEST LIVES OF MELVILLE

On 14 August 1852, little more than a year after Melville had written Hawthorne on the vanity of fame, Evert and George Duyckinck reprinted in their
New York *Literary World* (XI, 100) the first biographical sketch of him, taken

from a new compilation brought out by the publisher Justus Starr Redfield. Redfield's publication, *The Men of the Time or Sketches of Living Notables,* is a biographical dictionary of 564 pages adapted for the American market from an English work of the same title issued earlier in 1852 by the London firm of David Bogue. In the words of the American Preface, the English volume had been "used, where available, as a basis, but in almost every instance with corrections or amendments. Other and important information has been supplied to a considerable extent from original sources. . . . The plan pursued with the American biographies has been to verify, in every practicable case, the statements of fact from the most authentic sources" (p. 4)—presumably the subjects themselves. This "American portion" of the book was of special interest to the Duyckincks, long exponents of cultural nationalism, whose review in the *Literary World* takes particular note of those American names such as Melville's "which are now, for the first time, biographically displayed—ripe pippins on the tree of knowledge which have somehow escaped the industriously-aimed efforts of Dr. Griswold" (XI, 100).

To anyone aware of the perennial infighting among the New York *literati* of the day, the Duyckincks' barb at their old rival Griswold would be unmistakable, then and now. Griswold, notorious today for his malicious biography of Poe, was known in his own time not only as editor of the *International Monthly Magazine* but more significantly as compiler of *The Poets and Poetry of America* (1842), *The Prose Writers of America* (1847), and *The Female Poets of America* (1849). The *Literary World*'s review of *The Men of the Time,* "testing" Redfield's compilation by quoting several of its sketches in full, singles out that of Melville as "one of the latest biographical pickings" among Americans previously unnoticed by Griswold, printing it under the seemingly inevitable subheading "THE AUTHOR OF 'TYPEE.'" This brief but "matter-of-fact account," as the *Literary World* called it, is the direct or indirect ancestor of the many biographical sketches of Melville that were to appear in the sixty-nine years between 1852 and 1921, the year in which Raymond Weaver's *Herman Melville: Mariner and Mystic* became the first book-length biography. Although later biographical dictionaries and encyclopedias supplemented this first Life of Melville by providing additional material about his later career, the basic information given in *The Men of the Time* was long regarded as standard; whether or not Melville actually "visited London" during his first voyage, as the sketch asserts, remains an open question even today.

Given the priority of this brief article as the earliest Life of Melville, it is unfortunate that no scholar has been able to penetrate the anonymity of Redfield's contributors and establish its authorship. With the "American biographies" generally, according to Redfield's Preface,

A mass of valuable matter, in this large portion of the volume, is now for the first time submitted to the public. The interest taken in the work by those whose relations to public affairs have enabled them to aid in the completeness of the collection, has exceeded the expectations of the Publisher, who takes this opportunity to return a general acknowledgment to the different persons throughout the country to whom he is indebted for important contributions. (p. 4)

The words just quoted, which have their counterpart in many a similar reference work, scarcely reveal how Redfield and his staff had actually prepared the individual biographies: whether through direct application to the persons concerned, by Biographico-Solicito Circulars, or through dependence on intermediate agents for the necessary material. The laudatory review in the *Literary World* throws no light on this significant point beyond repeating Redfield's own statement, though the Duyckinck brothers may have known enough about either his methods or the subjects concerned to be confident that the particular sketches they chose for quotation in their review were essentially accurate.

With regard to the long paragraph on Melville, the Duyckincks had a basis for assurance in their personal acquaintance with both Melville and his family and their direct familiarity with his first six books, five of which had been extensively covered in the *Literary World* since it began publication in 1847. Obviously believing that Melville's writings generally, with the exception of *Mardi* and *Moby-Dick,* were essentially autobiographical, they struck out once more in their review of *The Men of the Time* at those who had questioned his veracity as a story teller, remarking that this account of his life "will show that his various romances rest on a more substantial basis than has been sometimes supposed" (XI, 100). Evert Duyckinck, the elder brother, had known Melville since 1846, when as editor for Wiley and Putnam, Melville's first American publishers, he had been introduced to "the author of 'Typee,'" and soon came to number both Melville and his brother Allan among his friends. In 1847 Melville began writing for the *Literary World* and its humorous satellite *Yankee Doodle* while the Duyckincks continued to foster his growing reputation by publicizing his books in their columns; his most recent contribution had been "Hawthorne and His Mosses," appearing in two issues of the *Literary World* during August of 1850. A year later, while both brothers were visiting Melville in the Berkshires, Evert Duyckinck "said a great deal for Redfield" as a potential publisher of *Moby-Dick* (*Log,* I, 420); Melville's final decision, however, was to give it to Harper and Brothers, who had brought out the American editions of *Omoo, Mardi, Redburn,* and *White-Jacket.* Now in 1852 the *Literary World* was praising Redfield's *The Men of the Time* for including American authors unnoticed by Dr. Griswold, and soon the Duyckincks themselves would be directly challenging Griswold's several compilations with their own two-volume *Cyclopaedia of American Literature* (New York: Charles Scribner, 1855).

In view of Melville's unwillingness to cooperate even with the Duyckincks when they had proposed to publish his portrait in *Holden's* early in 1851, it

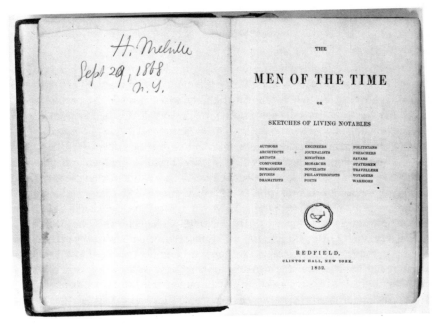

Melville's signature opposite the title page of *The Men of the Time* (New York: Redfield, 1852), which he acquired on 29 September 1868. From the author's collection.

seems doubtful that he would have been any more responsive if applied to directly by either Griswold or Redfield for a biographical sketch; his surviving copy of *The Men of the Time* was not acquired until 1868 (see illustration). But since Redfield did in fact print such a sketch, one which the Duyckincks evidently accepted as authoritative, it may well be that some other knowledgeable person had consented "to aid in the completeness of the collection" by furnishing—or at least verifying—information about him. The most likely informant would be Allan Melville, who as a New York attorney customarily handled his brother's negotiations with American publishers and who probably knew Redfield himself as well as their mutual friend Evert Duyckinck. Although no documentary evidence has been turned up that would either confirm or rule out this possibility, there is an analogous situation involving the Duyckincks' own account of Melville in their *Cyclopædia of American Literature,* to which Allan Melville apparently did contribute information, as surviving manuscript material indicates. Moreover, there had been an abrupt estrangement in the previously friendly relations between Melville himself and Evert Duyckinck since the publication of *Moby-Dick,* as suggested by the handling in *Pierre* of such "gentlemen of the Captain Kidd school of literature." In November of 1851, reviewing *Moby-Dick* in the *Literary World*, Duyckinck had taken Melville to task for his "piratical running down of creeds and opinions" in a book where "the most sacred associations of life" were "violated and defaced"; in the following February, when Melville returned to Pittsfield from a brief visit to New York that probably included a meeting with Duyckinck, he was moved to cancel his subscription to the *Literary World* in a brief note to its editors. The pages of *Pierre* treating "Young America in Literature"–Duyckinck had been a leader of the "Young America" movement–and "Pierre, as a Juvenile Author, Reconsidered" have been characterized by Perry Miller as "a private letter to Duyckinck" in which Melville "works off his long-concealed resentment against the sublime condescension of Young America."[1] In return, the *Literary World* for 21 August 1852–the issue following that which reviewed *The Men of the Time*–treated *Pierre* as "a literary mare's nest," condemning its dubious morality, its "supersensuousness," and its general unintelligibility (XI, 118–120).

During the next two years, a period in which their relations with Melville remained cool, the Duyckincks were formulating plans for a new publication of their own that was intended to eclipse the labors of Griswold as a connoisseur of American letters. First *Holden's* and then the *Literary World* had ceased publication; Evert Duyckinck had assumed the literary editorship of an Episcopal magazine, the *Churchman;* then in the spring of 1854 he and his brother were mailing out their own Biographico-Solicito Circulars to living American authors for their projected *Cyclopædia*. The professed design of the work, according to the editors' Preface, was "to bring together as far as possible in one book convenient for perusal and reference, memorials and records of the writers of the country and their works, from the earliest period to the present day," the primary concern being historical rather than critical. "The study and practice of criticism may be pursued elsewhere," the Duyckincks observe: "here, as a matter of history, we seek to know in general under what forms and to what extent literature has been developed . . . on American soil" (I, v). The *Cyclopædia* is organized in terms of chronology, with due attention paid to the time and place within which each writer flourished. Given the compass of "two royal octavos," how should the editors allot their space in order to carry out these objectives? "It was considered," they explain, "that, under any principle of selection, the story should be as briefly told as possible; being confined to the facts of the case, with no more comment than was required to put the reader in ready communication with the author, while matters of digression and essay-writing should be carefully avoided. The lives of the authors were to be narrated, and their best works exhibited in appropriate extracts" (I, vii–viii).

In dealing with Melville's life and writings in the light of these announced principles the Duyckincks faced particular difficulties. The close personal relationship of earlier years had not survived Melville's disillusionment with the Young America movement in general and his particular resentment of the handling of *Moby-Dick* and *Pierre* in the *Literary World;* on their side, though the Duyckincks must have recognized the cutting personal implications of Books XVII and XVIII of *Pierre,* they had already poured so much critical capital into Melville's literary achievement over the years that they were now in no position to renounce their entire investment. Meanwhile, though they appear to have been out of direct touch with Melville himself between 1852 and 1856, when something of the old sociability was resumed just before Melville's departure for the Mediterranean (*Log,* II, 523-525), there was evidently continued contact with his brother Allan, who had remained a resident of New York City. The first three paragraphs of the *Cyclopædia* article on Herman Melville (II, 672), which deal at length with the distinguished family background of the Melvilles, were set in type directly from a manuscript apparently furnished by Allan Melville (see Appendix A below). Separated from these initial paragraphs by Herman Melville's signature in facsimile is a résumé of his life and works up to 1855 (II, 672-674), accompanied not by his portrait, in the manner of most of the longer biographical sketches, but rather by a line drawing of his residence in Pittsfield. The article then concludes with an extract from Chapter 14 of *Redburn* (II, 674-676)—the same passage quoted in the *Literary World*'s review of that work in 1849—as an exhibition of Melville's writing at its best.

This survey of Melville's career reaffirms the Duyckincks' long-standing view that he "kept more closely" to "the range of personal observation and matter-of-fact description" in his more successful works "than was generally supposed" (II, 673). Enlarging upon this point, as in their earlier review of *The Men of the Time,* they cite here the corroborative testimony of another Pacific traveler, Lieutenant Henry A. Wise, as evidence of Melville's "fidelity" in *Typee* and *Omoo;* they likewise praise *Redburn*—its "lurid London episode" excepted—as "a witty reproduction of natural incidents" and *White-Jacket* as "a vivid daguerreotype of the whole life" of a man-of-war, its description "everywhere elevated from commonplace and familiarity by the poetical associations which run through it." Even in *Moby-Dick,* singled out as "the most dramatic and imaginative of Melville's books," there are "purely descriptive passages" on whales and whaling in which "the details of the fishery, and the natural history of the animal, are narrated with constant brilliancy of illustration" (II, 673). Here too Melville had been faithful to fact:

> Just at the time of publication of this book its catastrophe, the attack of the ship by the whale, which had already good historic warrant in the fate of the Essex of Nantucket, was still further supported by the newspaper narrative of the Ann Alexander of New Bedford, in which the infuriated animal demonstrated a spirit of revenge almost human, in turning upon, pursuing, and destroying the vessel from which he had been attacked. (II, 673-674, note)

Conversely, despite the announced intention of the Duyckincks to eschew critical pronouncements in their *Cyclopædia* they single out for specific disapproval not only "the latter portions" of *Mardi*, where a less matter-of-fact Melville, "embarrassed by his spiritual allegories, . . . wanders without chart or compass in the wildest regions of doubt and scepticism" (II, 673), but also the whole of *Pierre*, whose "conception and execution were both literary mistakes." By seeking in *Pierre* to evolve a passion "morbid or unreal, in the worst school of the mixed French and German melodramatic," Melville had left "the track of his true genius" (II, 674).

Although *Moby-Dick* escapes the strictures expressed about *Mardi* and *Pierre*, the relatively brief paragraph concerning it lacks the enthusiasm apparent in the Duyckincks' discussion of the "natural incidents" and "pleasant, easy narrative" of his earliest books. After the experiment of *Mardi*, they observe,

> Mr. Melville, who throughout his literary career has had the good sense never to argue with the public, whatever opportunities he might afford them for the exercise of their disputative faculties, lost no time in recovering his position by a return to the agreeable narrative which had first gained him his laurels. (II, 673)

Doubtless they had hoped for something more "natural" after the publication of *Moby-Dick*, as the more agreeable *Redburn* had followed *Mardi;* instead, Melville had given them the loathsome *Pierre*. But in 1849 Melville was still living in New York—a member of the Duyckinck circle, and now he is in Berkshire: "In this comparative retirement," the article suggests, "will be found the secret of much of the speculative character engrafted upon his writings" (II, 674).[2] Some of the magazine work appearing since *Pierre* seems more encouraging: "Cock-A-Doodle-Doo!" is one of Melville's "most lively and animated productions," and both "Bartleby," as "a quaint, fanciful portrait," and *Israel Potter*, as a "reproduction" of the adventures of "an actual character of the Revolution," have met with "deserved success" (II, 674). In other words, these writings are akin to the "true genius" of Melville's first works, and if he shows the "good sense" exhibited in *Redburn* and *White-Jacket* his future writing will continue in that same vein.

The only wholly new material in the Duyckincks' essay is the genealogical information with which it begins; these critical observations on Melville's various books echo or recapitulate what the *Literary World* had already said of them while the treatment of his years as a sailor is basically a shortened version of the earlier account in *The Men of the Time*. The following parallel passages tell their own story.

The Men of the Time (1852)	*Cyclopædia* (1855)
When about eighteen years of age, he made a voyage from New York	In his eighteenth year he shipped as a sailor in a New York vessel for Liver-

to Liverpool, before the mast, visited London, and returned home in the same capacity. . . . About a year after his return home, he shipped on board a whaling-vessel, bound on a cruise to the Pacific, to engage in the sperm-whale fishery. Having been out about eighteen months, the vessel arrived at the port of Nukaheva, one of the Marquesa islands, in the summer of 1842. The captain had been harsh and tyrannical to the crew; and, preferring to risk his fortunes among the natives, than to endure another voyage on board, Mr. Melville determined to leave the vessel. . . . Accompanied by a fellow-sailor, he separated from his companions, intending to escape into a neighboring valley, occupied by a tribe of friendly natives. But, mistaking their course, after three days' wandering, the fugitives found themselves in the Typee valley, occupied by a warlike race, taking their name from that of the valley. Here Mr. Melville was detained in a sort of indulgent captivity for about four months. His companion shortly disappeared, and was supposed to have been murdered by the natives. He had long given up all hopes of ever being restored to his friends, when his rescue was effected by a boat's crew from a Sydney whaler. Shipping on board this vessel for the cruise, he arrived at Tahiti the day the French seized the Society islands. . . . Several months passed in the Society and Sandwich islands afforded Mr. Melville opportunities for observing the effect produced by the missionary enterprise and foreign intercourse upon the native population. For some months he resided at Honolulu

pool, made a hurried visit to London when he arrived in port, and returned home "before the mast." His next adventure was embarking, Jan. 1,* 1841, on a whaling vessel for the Pacific for the sperm fishery.

After eighteen months of the cruise, the vessel, in the summer of 1842, put into the Marquesas, at Nukuheva.

Melville, who was weary of the service, took the opportunity to abandon the ship, and with a fellow sailor hid himself in the forest, with the intention of resorting to a neighboring peaceful tribe of the natives.

They mistook their course, and after three days' wandering, . . . found themselves in the barbarous Typee valley.

Here Melville was detained "in an indulgent captivity" for four months.

He was separated from his companion, and began to despair of a return to civilization,

when he was rescued one day on the shore by a boat's crew of a Sidney whaler. He shipped on board this vessel, and was landed at Tahiti the day when the French took possession of the Society Islands. . . . From Tahiti, Melville passed to the Sandwich Islands, spent a few months in observation of the people and the country, in the Sandwich islands. The frigate United States, lying at that port, offered the safest and quickest passage home, and Mr. Melville shipped aboard as "ordinary seaman," and arrived at Boston in October, 1844, after a homeward cruise of thirteen months. He thus added to his knowledge of the merchant and whaling service a complete acquaintance with the inner life on board a man-of-war. (pp. 350–351)

and in the autumn of 1843 shipped at Honolulu as "ordinary seaman" on board the frigate United States, then on its return voyage, . . . reaching Boston in October, 1844. This voyaging in the merchant, whaling, and naval service rounded Melville's triple experience of nautical life. (II, 672–673)

Although the Duyckincks modified the spelling of one proper noun, changing "Nukaheva" to "Nukuheva" (the form used in *Typee*), and added a slightly inaccurate date—1 January 1841—for the beginning of Melville's second voyage, their principal alteration, in the fashion of experienced editors, was to condense and sharpen the story of his life at sea as *The Men of the Time* had told it. In the process, however, they removed every qualifying "about" with which their anonymous predecessor had carefully hedged his chronology, just as Melville himself had previously done in *Typee* and *Omoo*. *The Men of the Time* says only that having first gone to sea when "*about* eighteen," Melville embarked again "*about* a year after his return home," and that following a Pacific cruise of "*about* eighteen months" he reached the Marquesas Islands "in the summer of 1842," spending "*about* four months" there among the natives. With respect to Melville's second voyage, at least, the 1852 account follows his own lead. He had published *Typee* as the narrative of "a four months' residence" in the Marquesas Islands though in fact he had been in Nukuheva for no more than four weeks in all—specifically, from 9 July to 9 August 1842. In his later writing he remained committed to the exaggerated figure, plausibly explaining in *Omoo* that "No journal was kept by the author during his wanderings in the South Seas; so that . . . precision with respect to dates would have been impossible" (p. xiv) and reaffirming that "in the summer of 1842" he had been "detained in an indulgent captivity" among the Typees "for about the space of four months" (p. 3).

Although various reviewers had already expressed reservations about Melville's general credibility as a writer of travel-books, no one either challenged the purported length of his stay among the Typees or worked out the actual chronology of his years in the South Pacific until the present century, when a number of scholars—notably Charles R. Anderson in *Melville in the South Seas* (1939)—finally documented his wanderings and separated the diverse strands of first-hand observation, appropriations from other travelers, and outright literary invention in *Typee, Omoo,* and *White-Jacket.* Meanwhile, the later nineteenth-century biographical dictionaries and encyclopedias continued to repeat the inaccurate dates given either in *The Men of the Time* or by the Duyckincks. As for Melville's earlier voyage, which had taken him to Liverpool in 1839 when he was nearer twenty years of age than "eighteen" or "about eighteen" as these earliest Lives had asserted, later reference works were to translate their phrasing into a flatly erroneous "1837." The narrator-hero of Melville's fourth book, *Redburn: His First Voyage,* who also sails to Liverpool, neither specifies a year nor reveals his own age, saying only that he was "but a boy" when he first went to sea (p. 3); William H. Gilman, the first scholar to uncover the details of Melville's own Liverpool trip, judges the young sailor to be "about fifteen."[3] Stressing the differences in age, physical appearance, and character between Redburn and Melville himself, Gilman aptly observes that knowing the facts might have deterred biographers "from taking *Redburn* as autobiography thinly veiled"[4] and so accepting Redburn's visit to London—an episode which "has interested both literary critics and biographers for a century"[5]—as an experience of Melville's own.

Taken together, the Lives of 1852 and 1855 thus set the pattern for treatments of Melville in reference works for many years to come—until his death in 1891 and even beyond. Both *The Men of the Time* and the Duyckincks' *Cyclopaedia* stress the relation between his personal experience and direct observation and the subject matter of his first six books, partly in reaction to those contemporary critics who had questioned the authenticity of *Typee* or doubted that "Herman Melville" was more than a pen-name for some already experienced writer. Whoever wrote—or revised—the sketch of Melville in *The Men of the Time* was careful to see that it embodied no overt challenge to the credibility of either *Typee* or *Redburn* by giving precise dates. The Duyckincks, by contrast, were either unaware of possible discrepancies or determined, in their commitment to Melville's supposed factual "fidelity," to minimize them, as suggested both by their handling of *The Men of the Time* in their review of 1852 and by their adaptation of its sketch of Melville to the purposes of their own *Cyclopaedia* in 1855, where the dates are given without qualification. The *Cyclopaedia,* moreover, went further than *The Men of the Time* in the direction of literary criticism, despite the insistence of its editors that their objective was historical rather than critical, to express a clear preference for Melville's earlier and more matter-of-fact narratives as against *Mardi, Moby-Dick,* and *Pierre,* with their "speculative character." Authors of those later nineteenth-century sketches of Melville that mingle critical comments with their biographical data and listings of his publications and their dates reflect tastes not dissimilar to those of the Duyckincks.

Throughout Melville's remaining years, as the later Lives reveal, the received picture of the man remained very much as the Duyckincks had rendered it: that of an essentially autobiographical writer—one well advised, in anything he might still publish, to keep to "the track of his true genius" rather than risking another *Mardi* or *Pierre.* Not until well into the next century, when modern scholarship began to investigate the objective records of Melville's life apart from his books and to recognize the extent of his wholesale borrowings from literary sources even in his supposedly direct transcriptions from personal observation and experience, did the encyclopedias respond with a noticeably different approach to either the man or his works. But until such findings as Anderson's and Gilman's could be made and disseminated there was little basis for challenging the nineteenth century's ready identification of the man with his writings: Melville "*talks* Typee and Omoo," wrote his friend N. P. Willis in 1849, "just as you find the flow of his delightful mind on paper. Those who have only read his books know the man—those who have only seen the man have a fair idea of his books" (*Log,* I, 320).

As we have now learned, Melville himself viewed his work from a perspective far different from that of Willis or the Duyckincks. Aware of his own inner growth, he identified as the important period of his development not the years spent on shipboard or wandering in the South Seas but those devoted to exploring what in *Mardi* he called "the world of mind." "Until I was twenty-five," he told Hawthorne in 1851, "I had no development at all" (*Letters,* p. 130). Though Melville clearly intended *Mardi, Moby-Dick,* and *Pierre* to win a different kind of "reputation" for their author, these efforts on his part seemed merely willful aberrations to those convinced that the success of his first book had determined his "true genius" once and for all. For Melville's own generation he remained "the author of 'Typee,'" and by that label, among men of his time and for posterity, he was identified in the encyclopedias until the present century.

SCISSORS AND PASTE: THE LATER LIVES

The contemporary biographical sketches of Melville which followed those published by Redfield and the Duyckincks, though adding some information, or misinformation, about his later life and writings, contributed little to an understanding of either the man or his works beyond what had already been said in print by the mid-1850's. Articles about him continued to appear regularly in encyclopedias and biographical dictionaries even after *The Confidence-Man* (1857) marked the end of his professional career as a writer of fiction, but in many cases the persons responsible for their compilation and printing were evidently little concerned with the accuracy and dependability of the information they dealt with. If the various sketches of Melville published between 1855 and his death in 1891 are a fair sample of how reference works were put together in the nineteenth century, one must conclude that original research or even verification of existing material was the exception rather than the rule. The essential tools being scissors and paste, the inevitable result was that an error appearing in one publication was all too likely to be multiplied by expropriation in others. A survey of representative later sketches, beginning with those appearing in successive editions of *The Men of the Time,* will illustrate the point.

Redfield's British counterpart David Bogue enlarged his second London edition of *The Men of the Time* in 1853 by incorporating sketches of various Americans from Redfield's New York edition of the previous year. In Melville's case he brought the Redfield account up to date by adding two new sentences about *Pierre,* quoting without identification of source from the Duyckincks' unfavorable review of that book in the *Literary World* of 21 August 1852 (XI, 118-120):

> His latest production is "Pierre, or the Ambiguities," an unhealthy mystic romance, in which are conjured up "unreal night-mare conceptions, a confused phantasmagoria of distorted fancies and conceits, ghostly abstractions, and fitful shadows," altogether different from the hale and sturdy sailors and fresh sea-breezes of his earlier productions. It met with a decided non-success, and has not been reprinted in this country. (p. 312)

The London edition of 1856 published by Bogue (p. 547) and those of 1857 and 1859 published by his successor W. Kent & Co. (pp. 526-527) reprinted the account as it stood in 1853 except for very minor changes. In New York, however, Redfield retained the original sketch of 1852, unaltered, in his "Fourth Edition" of 1856 (pp. 350-351).

The first major reworking of *The Men of the Time* after 1853 took place in 1862, when a new edition "thoroughly revised" by Edward Walford, an Oxonian, was brought out in both London and New York by the firm of Routledge, Warne, and Routledge. Its sketch of Melville (pp. 543-544), shorter than what the earlier editions had carried, is marked by several unaccountable misstatements such as these: Melville "was educated in the State of Massachusetts"; while in the Pacific he "disembarked at Loukabisa"—i.e., Nukuheva; in 1847 he "married and settled as a farmer." The inaccurate wording of this sketch is repeated with only minor changes in the editions of 1865 (p. 586) and 1868 (p. 575). An "eighth edition" of 1872, revised by Thompson Cooper, introduces a few more alterations in the account (p. 674); the ninth edition of 1875, also prepared by Cooper, extensively expands and revises it (pp. 718-719), combining material from the previous editions with new and strange information. According to this version, Melville's father was "a merchant in Boston"; Melville himself while in the Pacific "deserted with a comrade at Nakahioa, one of the Marquesas Islands"; in 1860 he "undertook a new voyage round the world, and after his return was for a time employed in the Customs House in New York; but subsequently retired to his farm in Massachusetts, where he now resides."

This catalogue of errors could easily be extended by citing other reference works of the period which are no more accurate than *The Men of the Time* in its later revisions. Mistakes in the dates of publication of Melville's books are especially common, even in otherwise reliable volumes. One article reports him as having served "in the U. S. frigate *Constitution*" rather than in the *United States;* another gives "A Chapter in the Life of a Young Sailor" as the subtitle of *Redburn;* still others credit him with writing "The White Jacket," "Toby Dick," "Peter," and "The Piazzi Tales"—all inaccurate renderings of actual titles—and *The Refugee,* which was an 1865 reprinting, by T. B. Peterson and Brothers of Philadelphia, of *Israel Potter* with an unauthorized change of name. How could such egregious oversights creep into standard reference works, especially when earlier sketches had listed Melville's writings by their correct titles and given their place and date of publication without error? Apparently some compilers were not even accurate copyists. Such errors as "Loukabisa" and "Nakahioa" in *The Men of the Time,* which probably derive from a clerk's misread handwriting, should certainly have been noted and corrected by an editor or proofreader before the books were published. Locating Melville's father in Boston rather than New York and then assigning Melville's own schooling to Massachusetts could be the result of confusing different generations of the family; these mistakes too should have been caught before they reached print. Melville himself, through letters to the Petersons and to the New York *World,* had protested mistitling *Israel Potter* as *The Refugee* (*Letters,* pp. 287, 304), but apparently he cared less about correcting similar errors in published reference works even when direct application was made to him. On receiving one such request, in 1873, probably from M. Laird Simons, who was preparing the 1875 revision of the Duyckincks' *Cyclopaedia,* Melville replied concerning "the Article in question" that "I dont remember anything in it which it would be worth your while to be at the trouble of adding to or omitting or amending" (*Letters,* p. 241).

The garbled account of Melville's later career in Simons' revision of the *Cyclopaedia* (Philadelphia: William Rutter & Co., 1877; II, 636-639) and in other biographical works of the period comes in part from contemporary misreporting of his travels of 1860. In that year he embarked as a passenger aboard the clipper ship *Meteor,* commanded by his younger brother Thomas, for what was projected as a voyage round the world, but he left the ship at San Francisco and returned home by way of Panama. The erroneous statement that "In 1860 Mr. Melville sailed again on a voyage round the world in a whaling vessel" appeared the following year in *The New American Cyclopaedia: A Popular Dictionary of General Knowledge,* edited by George Ripley and Charles A. Dana (New York and London: D. Appleton and Company, 1861), at the conclusion of its article on Melville (XI, 370-371). Repeated in editions of 1866 and 1872, this same statement or variants of it also will be found in such other reference works as the London, 1872 edition of *The Men of the Time* (p. 674); Francis S. Drake's *Dictionary of American Biography, Including Men of the*

Time (Boston: James R. Osgood and Company, 1872, p. 615; Boston: Houghton, Osgood & Company, 1879, p. 615); and at least two revisions of *Chambers's Encyclopaedia.*[6] The misstatement in *Chambers's* caught the eye of Mrs.
Melville, who made a note of it in her family memoranda; as she rightly observed, "This voyage to San Francisco has been incorrectly given in many of
the papers &c of the day." At least one private correspondent, a former whale-
hunter named Leonard G. Sanford, was moved to inquire of Melville himself
in 1886 about this most recent voyage. "No, I did not go a voyage round the
world in 1863," Melville wrote in reply, adding with evident amusement that
"The Cyclopedias are not infallible, no more than the Pope" (*Letters,* p. 283).

Melville's absence from Rufus Griswold's literary surveys of the 1840's was
not overlooked by later compilers when revised editions of two of Griswold's
anthologies were prepared in the 1870's: *The Prose Writers of America* by
John H. Dillingham (Philadelphia: Porter & Coates, 1870) and *The Poets and
Poetry of America* by Richard Henry Stoddard (New York: James Miller,
1873). Stoddard's collection (pp. 630-631) introduces seven of Melville's poems from *Battle-Pieces* (1866); Dillingham's (pp. 665-667) provides a biographical and critical notice of Melville followed by extracts from *Typee* and *Omoo.*
In view of the old rivalry between Griswold and the Duyckincks, culminating
in his devastating review of their *Cyclopaedia* in the New York *Herald* in 1856,
it is ironic that Dillingham silently cribbed most of his biographical information
and even his critical comments about Melville from the Duyckincks' article of
1855. An exception is his final paragraph, a representative nineteenth-century
judgment of Melville's talents:

> Herman Melville is an original thinker, and boldly and unreservedly ex-
> presses his opinions, often in a way that irresistibly startles and enchains the
> interest of the reader. He possesses amazing powers of expression: he can
> be terse, copious, eloquent, brilliant, imaginative, poetical, satirical, pathetic,
> at will. He is never stupid, never dull; but alas! he is often mystical and un-
> intelligible,—not from any inability to express himself, for his writing is pure,
> manly English, and a child can always understand what he says,—but the
> ablest critic cannot always tell what he really means; solely from his incorri-
> gible perversion of his rare and lofty gifts. (p. 666)

But here again Dillingham was borrowing without acknowledgment, this time
from a widely quoted article on Cooper, Dana, and Melville originally published
fourteen years before in the *Dublin University Magazine,* 47 (January 1856),
47-54, and reprinted shortly thereafter in the United States by *Littel's Living
Age,* 48 (1 March 1856), 560-566.

The *Dublin* article, frequently excerpted in later studies of Melville, also provided, in this same striking passage, the concluding observation in a major
nineteenth-century reference work far more influential than Dillingham's revision of Griswold: S. Austin Allibone, *A Critical Dictionary of English Litera-*

ture and British and American Authors, 3 vols. (Philadelphia: J. B. Lippincott & Co., 1854–1871). Allibone's magisterial volumes, widely consulted over the years, helped to fix critical judgments of books and authors for a long time to come. His treatment of Melville (II, 1264–1265) is not primarily biographical, though it begins with a brief sketch of his early life drawn, like Dillingham's, from the Duyckincks' *Cyclopædia.* Allibone's real concern is to illustrate and document the critical response to Melville's successive books from *Typee* to *The Confidence-Man* through a still-valuable collection of more than two dozen brief extracts and citation of other publications relating to the man and his works—all of them scrupulously identified.

In 1888 the first biographical sketch to be accompanied by a portrait of Melville himself was published anonymously in *Appleton's Cyclopædia of American Biography,* edited in six volumes by James Grant Wilson and John Fiske (New York: D. Appleton and Company, 1888), IV, 293–294. The portrait is a line drawing based on a photograph made in October of 1885; beneath it is a facsimile signature. The article itself briefly covers Melville's family background, his voyages to Liverpool and the South Pacific, his marriage, his residence in Pittsfield and later in New York, and his appointment to "a place in the custom-house." Following the pattern established long ago in the Redfield volume of 1852, the author of the sketch concentrates on *Typee,* working in details drawn directly from the book, including a brief quotation, to illustrate its "remarkable vividness." There is no discussion of the later works, which are merely listed by title and date (with some minor inaccuracies) through *Clarel* (1876); clearly Melville remains primarily "the author of *Typee*," as in the 1850's. Whose judgment is expressed here? Through what channels did Melville's portrait and signature come into the hands of the editors? No unqualified answers to either of these questions can be given on the basis of available evidence. According to the *Cyclopædia*'s Preface, "The signatures are for the most part in the collection of some six thousand American autographs in the possession of the senior editor" (I, vi). Melville had written to Wilson years before in connection with a lecture engagement in Chicago in 1859 (*Letters,* p. 192); more recently he had been in correspondence with two other men listed among the "chief contributors" to the fourth volume, Edmund Clarence Stedman and Richard Henry Stoddard (IV, vii–viii). As recently as 20 January 1888 Stedman had asked Melville, in another connection, where the best engraved portrait of him might be found; Melville replied on 29 January that to his knowledge none had been published (*Letters,* pp. 285–286), but he subsequently agreed to let Stedman make an engraving—not of the 1885 photograph but of the portrait painted by J. O. Eaton in 1870. Whether Stedman, Stoddard, Wilson himself, or some other individual provided the portrait, signature, and biographical sketch of Melville for the *Cyclopædia* is still undetermined.[7]

Arrangements for copying the Eaton portrait of Melville were handled for Stedman by his son Arthur, who called at the Melville home for this purpose, probably later in 1888. "The interview was brief," he remembered, "and the interviewer could not help feeling, although treated with pleasant courtesy, that more important matters were in hand than the perpetuation of a romancer's countenance to future generations; but a friendly family acquaintance grew up from the incident, and will remain an abiding memory." The steel engraving made from the portrait is reproduced as the frontispiece of the present study from its first appearance in *A Library of American Literature,* edited in eleven volumes by Edmund Clarence Stedman and Ellen Mackay Hutchinson (New York: Charles L. Webster & Co., 1888-1890), VII, facing p. 464; volume VII also reprints Melville's story "The Bell-Tower" and three poems from *Battle-Pieces.* It was Arthur Stedman who prepared the brief notice of Melville included among the "Short Biographies" in the concluding volume of the anthology (XI, 454). There are several mistakes in this account, including a familiar error undoubtedly derived from some earlier reference book: the statement that Melville "voyaged round the world in 1860." When the younger Stedman wrote the "Short Biographies," as his father later explained to a complaining correspondent, "he obtained, in the case of living authors within reach, his materials from their respective selves,"[8] but in view of the obvious errors it seems unlikely that he applied for such information to Melville. In later years, as their acquaintance ripened, he gained Melville's confidence, being designated his literary executor on Melville's death in 1891.

"A HERMIT'S REPUTATION"

"If you know that fine writer, Melville, why not write his life?" This was the question posed in 1883 by W. Clark Russell, the English novelist of the sea, to an American correspondent, Augustus Hayes, who wrote short stories for the magazines. Russell did not know Melville himself or even whether he was still living (*Log,* II, 806), but he did know his books—"the best sea stories ever written," he called them in his letter to Hayes, by "the greatest genius your country has produced." The world ought to be told "as much as can be gathered of his seafaring experiences and personal story" (*Log,* II, 784). Hayes showed Russell's letter to a writer for the New York *Herald,* who published an excerpt in his column. If quoting Russell was intended to test the attractiveness of his suggestion to prospective American readers and publishers of a Life of Melville, as it may well have been, the results were evidently not encouraging. Although Melville's reputation in England seems to have been continuous, his name and his books were no longer familiar in America during the Gilded Age, where even in New York there were said to be professional authors who supposed him to be long since dead.

Russell himself was in no position to undertake the research necessary for a biography, but he did what he could during the 1880's to celebrate Melville's writings. In the *Contemporary Review* for September of 1884 he praised not only *Typee, Omoo,* and *Redburn* but also *Moby-Dick,* which he regarded as Melville's "finest work." After Russell's essay was reprinted in expanded form in *In the Middle Watch* (1885), published in New York by the Harpers, Melville acknowledged his praise in a letter delivered by their mutual friend Peter Toft, an artist who had "accidentally discovered" Melville in New York (*Log,* II, 799). Russell's reply, dated 21 July 1886, expresses his pleasure in learning "from Mr. Toft" that Melville was "still hale and hearty." "Your reputation here," he assured Melville, "is very great. It is hard to meet a man whose opinion as a reader is worth having who does not speak of your works in such terms as he might hesitate to employ with all his patriotism, towards many renowned English writers . . ." (*Log,* II, 801). Since Melville had been receiving similar-ly flattering letters from other English admirers, James Billson and J. W. Barrs, he had some confirmation of Russell's gratifying remarks about his fame over-seas. In 1888, with Russell's permission, Melville dedicated to him his *John Marr and Other Sailors,* printed for private distribution to a few chosen friends; Russell responded in 1889 by dedicating *An Ocean Tragedy* to Melville and again praising him unreservedly in a Chicago weekly, *America.* "I know not if the works of the author of 'Omoo,' and 'Typee,' and 'Redburn' are much read and esteemed in the United States," Russell wrote in his article, "but I am sure there is no name in American letters that deserves to stand higher for beauty of imagination, for accuracy of reproduction, for originality of conception, and for a quality of imagination that in 'Moby Dick,' for instance, lifts some of his utterances to such a height of bold and swelling fancy as one must search the pages of the Elizabethan dramatists to parallel" (*Log,* II, 813).

Among Melville's own countrymen there was no contemporary voice to speak as glowingly of his achievement as Russell had done in England. As for a possible biography, apparently the first suggestion from his own side of the Atlantic that the Life of such an author was deserving of book-length treat-ment came later in 1889 from Alexander Young, contributor of the "Here in Boston" column of the Boston *Post* under the pen-name of "Taverner." After proposing that "some of our enterprising publishers would find it in their in-terest to reprint 'Omoo,' and 'Typee,'" Young added that "I do not see why the author's life should not find a place in the American Men of Letters series" (*Log,* II, 817). Young himself, an antiquarian who at the time of his death was writing a book on "Old Boston," devoted a later column primarily to Mel-ville's grandparents, Major and Mrs. Thomas Melvill, and their home on Green Street in Boston as an old friend recalled it, concluding with a reference to Melville. In the parlor of the house, this unnamed friend remembered, were "many curiosities," among them

a glass ship, fully rigged, modelled after the fashion of some celebrated French vessel, which was the delight of his young eyes; and, under a glass cover, some very precious tea—a part of that veritable tea which was thrown overboard when the American people resisted "taxation without representation." Major Melville [sic] was one of the sturdy band who, dressed as Mohawk Indians, assisted in throwing the tea into the water; and when he returned home the specimen referred to was shaken out of his high boots and preserved as a valuable relic. For his display of patriotism he was given a lucrative office in the custom house which he retained for some years. One of his six daughters became engaged to a young lawyer, who was long devoted and sincerely attached to her; but her early death prevented her union with one who was afterwards revered and honored as Chief Justice Shaw, whose daughter subsequently became united to Herman Melville.[9]

As we now know, Herman Melville spent the summers of 1827 and 1829 with his grandparents in Boston. He long remembered the glass ship, which figures prominently in *Redburn;* the Melvill and Shaw families carefully preserved the Major's vial of tea following his death in 1832.[10]   When Melville married Elizabeth Shaw in Boston's New South Church on 4 August 1847 it was Young's father, Rev. Alexander Young (1800-1854), its Unitarian minister, who performed the ceremony (*Log,* I, 255). Nothing has been discovered to indicate a subsequent personal relationship between the minister's son (1836-1891) and the Melvilles, but it is evident from this and other references in "Taverner's" column that he maintained a Bostonian's interest in members of the Melville and Shaw families.

Although no Life of Melville was to appear "in the American Men of Letters series" until 1950, when Newton Arvin's biography was published as part of a twentieth-century revival of that project, another Bostonian, Horace E. Scudder, may have recalled "Taverner's" suggestion on assuming the editorship of the *Atlantic Monthly* in 1890. On 14 October 1890 Scudder wrote to George Parsons Lathrop, Hawthorne's son-in-law and author of *A Study of Hawthorne* (1876), who had been an associate editor of the magazine, suggesting two possible subjects for a "miniature American men of Letters" series that Lathrop might handle: "Fitz-Greene Halleck & Hermann Melville, especially the latter" (*Log,* II, 826). Lathrop, who had corresponded with Melville when preparing his book on Hawthorne (*Log,* II, 745), replied from New York that he believed Melville to be still alive and at work in the New York Custom House (Melville had in fact resigned at the end of 1885), but

very much averse to publicity. He is an excellent subject, however. I don't know of any unpublished material that I can get, relating to him. If I could find time I might go down to the Custom House & unearth him, & perhaps get at something. . . . A capital article could be made about him, even without any new material. There is enough in the *Study* & references of Hawihorne's, to suggest a picture of their friendship in Berkshire; a picture nowhere I think very clearly outlined. But I mean that Melville himself, any way, would furnish forth a good & interesting article. . . . (*Log,* II, 826)

Scudder's response was discouraging.

> I can't help thinking that there must be some good material in the subject, though probably it would be better still if Melville would only let go of life. So much more frankness of speech can be used when a fellow is apparently out of hearing. What you say of his aversion to publicity makes me pause. I hate the whole business of making papers on living men, when the appeal is not to the interest of the men as writers, or artists, or publicists or what not, but to a petty interest in personal details.
> On second thought therefore, I believe we had better wait for our shot at Melville, when his personality can be more freely handled. (*Log*, II, 826)

While Melville, with his aversion to publicity, was still alive but aloof in New York there would be no full-length Life written of him in America, as Russell and Young had proposed, or even a biographical article of the sort that Scudder had in mind for the *Atlantic*. Russell's pronouncements from England and those of Henry S. Salt, who wrote on Melville in the *Scottish Art Review* in 1889, drew less of a reaction in this country than other remarks from abroad by the Scottish poet and novelist Robert Buchanan, who after a visit to the United States in 1884 accused the New York literary community of neglecting Melville, "the one great imaginative writer fit to stand shoulder to shoulder with Whitman," in Buchanan's words, on the American continent. So Buchanan wrote in a footnote to his poem "Socrates in Camden," contributed to the London *Academy* of 15 August 1885, which praised Melville fulsomely along with Whitman. This "sea-compelling man" who raised Leviathan from the deep and

> whose magic drew Typee,
> Radiant as Venus, from the sea,
> Sits all forgotten or ignored,
> While haberdashers are adored!

So Buchanan charged in the poem; his accompanying note explained that while he was in America he had "sought everywhere for this Triton, who is still living somewhere in New York," but "No one seemed to know anything" of him (*Log*, II, 792). Returning to the attack four years later, Buchanan was more specific in his account of the circumstances. His "very first inquiry" in America had been for Melville, he asserted in a note to his "Imperial Cockneydom," written for the *Universal Review* of 15 May 1889.

> There was some slight indication that he was 'alive,' and I heard from Mr. E. C. Stedman, who seemed much astonished at my interest in the subject, that Melville was dwelling 'somewhere in New York,' having resolved, on account of the public neglect of his works, never to write another line. Conceive this Titan silenced, and the bookstalls flooded with the illustrated magazines! (*Log*, II, 787)

To literary New Yorkers the jab at Stedman would have been unmistakable—especially if they realized that in 1884 he and Melville had been near neighbors on East Twenty-Sixth Street: Stedman at No. 44, Melville at No. 104. Whatever Stedman's exact knowledge of Melville may have been in 1884, he had certainly been aware of his existence two years earlier, when the founding members of the Authors Club, Stedman among them, had offered Melville membership. In 1888, Ernest Rhys, another Briton then visiting Stedman, was told that Melville, "living only a few doors away," had "a hermit's reputation, and it was difficult to get more than a passing glimpse of his 'tall, stalwart figure' and grave, preoccupied face" (*Log,* II, 956). In these words Rhys was not only recalling the occasion but also quoting one of Arthur Stedman's later articles in which the phrase "tall, stalwart figure" is applied to Melville. Buchanan's story and its repetition in America obviously struck a sensitive nerve with the younger Stedman, who did not become a visitor in Melville's residence until some time in 1888. When the old tale turned up once again in the New York *Times* following Melville's death in 1891,[11] Stedman was moved to comment tartly in print that the complaining Buchanan was merely a literary adventurer who "apparently 'sought everywhere' except in the one place where all of Mr. Melville's contemporaries made their search when they had occasion to visit him—the City Directory."

But Buchanan was not the only contemporary figure to charge neglect of Melville by the American public and especially by his fellow writers in New York. That Melville's name "would not be recognized by the rising generation" was granted by the New York *Commercial Advertiser* in an article of 14 January 1886. "Although his early works are still popular," the paper continued, probably meaning "still popular" among older readers, "the author is generally supposed to be dead." Nevertheless, "he is not very old—sixty-five—and his rather heavy, thick-set figure and warm complexion betoken health and vigor." In recent years

> he has done nothing in literature. For a long while he has been in the custom house as inspector, and is dependent on his salary. . . . He has, indeed, been buried in a government office. . . . He is a genial, pleasant fellow, who, after all his wanderings, loves to stay at home—his house is in Twenty-sixth street—and indulge in reverie and reminiscence. (*Log,* II, 796)

Edward Bok, the young editor of the *Ladies Home Journal,* was even more pointed: "There are more people to-day," he wrote in 1890, "who believe Herman Melville dead than there are those who know he is living."

> And yet if one choose to walk along East Eighteenth Street [*sic*], New York City, any morning about 9 o'clock, he would see the famous writer of sea stories—stories which have never been equalled perhaps in their special line. . . . Busy New York has no idea he is even alive, and one of the best informed literary men in the country laughed recently at my statement that

Herman Melville was his neighbor by only two city blocks. "Nonsense," said he. "Why, Melville is dead these many years!" Talk about literary fame? There's a sample of it! (*Log,* II, 827)

Bok's paragraph, syndicated in his newspaper column and reprinted both in *Publishers' Weekly* and in the Boston *Literary World,* provoked a variety of comments. Alexander Young was led to reflect in the Boston *Post* on "the difference between Boston and New York in regard to appreciation of literary men": in Boston, he insisted, "an author of Melville's genius and reputation would not be allowed to lapse into obscurity simply because he had ceased to write."[12] In New York, according to the *Critic,* "the friends of Mr. Herman Melville have been annoyed" by the publication of Bok's paragraph. "Mr. Melville, it is true, has gone out very little since the death of his son, some two years ago," the *Critic* conceded; "but in literary circles in New York it is by no means unknown that he is a resident of this city, and an employee of the Customs Revenue Service" (*Log,* II, 828). As this inaccurate report suggests, the *Critic*'s information on Melville in 1890 was scarcely up-to-date. It was then nearly four years since Melville had left the Custom House; if the loss of a son had affected his social life it was more likely the death of Malcolm in 1867 than that of Stanwix in 1886. Actually there had been many deaths of relatives and friends during the New York years. Melville's wife, as one of her granddaughters recalled, "had been in mourning so often for members of her family" that whenever her grandchildren appeared in black hair ribbons "she changed them to bright colors." When the family first returned to New York in 1863 Melville had resumed his visits to Evert Duyckinck, continuing until Duyckinck's death in 1878, and was seen occasionally with such writers as Alice and Phoebe Cary (*Log,* II, 676-677), but he seems never to have sought companionship among the younger generation of authors and editors.

According to Arthur Stedman, who knew both Melville and Whitman as well as other writers of his father's generation and his own, Melville, in spite of his "hermit's reputation," was always "an interesting figure to New York literary circles." Making this point in his obituary notice, Stedman went on, with Buchanan's slur at his father obviously in mind, to cite the invitation extended to Melville—"among the very first"—to join the Authors Club. Stedman was correct; in fact, according to Charles De Kay, secretary of the Club, Melville had at first accepted but later declined the invitation because, in De Kay's words, "he had become too much of a hermit" and "his nerves could no longer stand large gatherings" (*Log,* II, 781). Another member, Brander Mathews, recalled, however, that "the shy and elusive Herman Melville" actually "dropped in for an hour or two" at one of the Club's early meetings when "all the men of letters residing in or near New York" were invited (*Log,* II, 784). But in 1890 the elder Stedman, still one of the Club's moving spirits, acknowledged to a friend his disappointed surprise that

> I never yet have been able to get the members to take an interest in Melville—
> one of the strongest geniuses, & most impressive *personalities* that New York
> has ever harbored. *He* ought to be an honorary member. He is a sort of re-
> cluse now, but we might perhaps tempt him out. (*Log*, II, 823)

Frank Jewett Mather, Jr., writing in 1919, asserted that shortly before Melville's death Stedman "managed a complimentary dinner for him and with difficulty got him to attend it" (*Log*, II, 831)—though such an event is unrecorded
by other writers on either Stedman or Melville, Mather presumably had the
story from Stedman himself. Both Stedman and his son were genuinely drawn
to Melville during the final months of his life; both evidently remained sensitive
to the old charge that he had been ignored by New York writers, Stedman included. The implications of Arthur Stedman's rebuttal to this charge in his
obituary notices were not lost "in literary circles," as a paragraph in the Springfield, Massachusetts, *Daily Republican* of 12 October 1891 (p. 4) clearly attests:

> Herman Melville's separation from his fellow-authors was voluntary, and
> not due to their neglect, as has been said. He was one of the first to be in-
> vited to join the Authors club at its founding in 1882, but he declined. Few
> literary men and women in New York knew him; one of the few, naturally,
> was Edmund C. Stedman, whose friendly acquaintance no recluse even would
> willingly forego.

Along with the Stedmans, Melville's other New York friends and visitors during his last years included Dr. Titus Munson Coan, an old acquaintance who
"visited him repeatedly," and Oliver G. Hillard, who found that though Melville
was "eloquent in discussing general literature" he would not talk about his own
writings (*Log*, II, 787-788); Peter Toft had the further impression that he
seemed to hold them "in small esteem" (*Log*, II, 799). Melville in fact told Hillard that he owned none of his early works, and Oscar Wegelin reported delivering copies of them to Twenty-Sixth Street that Melville had ordered from the
bookshop of John Anderson, Jr. (*Log*, II, 826-827). Besides visiting Anderson's
shop Melville, still an omnivorous reader and a wide-ranging walker, browsed
also in that of Francis P. and Lathrop C. Harper (*Log*, II, 794) and in at least
two libraries, the Lenox and the New York Society (*Log*, II, 768, 771, 823,
825, 831-832). As for literary talk, he reminisced uneasily about Hawthorne
with Hawthorne's son Julian in 1883 (*Log*, II, 782-783) and more openly with
Theodore F. Wolfe, probably somewhat later;[13] there are records of both inter-
views in print, but nothing to suggest further discussion of Hawthorne with
George Lathrop for the *Atlantic*. Other acquaintances who were not professional writers included George Brewster, whom he knew through his Albany connec-
tions the Gansevoorts and Lansings, and George W. Dillaway, a lawyer, both
New Yorkers who were present at Melville's funeral along with Coan, Arthur
Stedman, and members of the family. In 1885 he made a last visit to Pittsfield,

where according to his old friend J. E. A. Smith, poet, journalist, and historian, he "did not evince the slightest aversion to society, but appeared to enjoy the hearty welcome which it gave him" there.

From the testimony of a number of these men it seems evident that Melville's seclusion, though deliberately cultivated as Arthur Stedman insisted, was by no means impenetrable. "He never denied himself to his friends," Dr. Coan asserted; "but he sought no one." Coan traced the cause of his withdrawal not to any particular event so much as to "his extremely proud and sensitive nature and his studious habits," both of which had been evident when the two first met as early as 1859 in Pittsfield. Though Peter Toft found "much in common" with Melville and termed him "a delightful talker when in the mood," he thought him "abnormal, as most geniuses are," and felt that he "had to be handled with care." Hillard had no such reservations, however; "With the few who were permitted to know him, he was the man of culture, the congenial companion, and the honestest and manliest of all earthly friends." Melville, it appears, selected his own intimates and correspondents as time and occasion suited him. On at least two occasions he wrote letters of thanks to men who had spoken favorably in public about his work: W. Clark Russell and J. W. Henry Canoll (*Log,* 796-797). When he declined an invitation it was invariably with the utmost courtesy. An illustration is afforded by his letter of 5 December 1889 to Professor Archibald MacMechan, who had written him from Halifax, Nova Scotia, proposing a correspondence and seeking "some particulars of your life and *literary methods* . . . other than given in such books as Duyckinck's dictionary" (*Log,* II, 817). In a regretful refusal, after citing his advanced age and long service "as an outdoor Custom House Officer," Melville explained that "I have latterly come into possession of unobstructed leisure, but only just as, in the course of nature, my vigor sensibly declines. What little is left I husband for certain matters as yet incomplete, and which indeed may never be completed" (*Letters,* p. 291). His unspecified reference was of course to at least one more volume of verse to follow *John Marr* (1888) and to the prose work then in progress that he would call *Billy Budd, Sailor.* But both *John Marr* and *Timoleon* (1891) were privately printed, *Billy Budd* was still undergoing revision at the time of his last illness, and neither the public nor even his friends had reason to know that to the end the "hermit" was actively writing.

Following Melville's death on 28 September 1891 there was a flurry of renewed interest in both the man and his works that continued into the next year and beyond, both at home and abroad, though Weaver's full-length biography was still thirty years in the future. The New York *Sun, Times, Tribune,* and *World* and the Boston *Journal* and *Evening Transcript* carried obituary notices within a day or two of his passing, editorials and extended critical appraisals soon followed, and by the end of December 1891 some thirty notices or longer articles had been printed or reprinted in at least eighteen American newspapers and four magazines.[14] With respect to purely biographical materials the most informative of these articles were written by three men whose fugitive contributions are collected in the present volume: Arthur Stedman, Titus Munson Coan, and J. E. A. Smith. All three not only knew Melville but spoke with authority about particular phases of his career, such as his life in the South Seas and in Pittsfield and his dealings with various publishers. Their essays provided more new information than any other publications since the *Cyclopædia* of 1855, when the Duyckincks had said far less of what they knew about the man behind the writings than they had done in private correspondence. None of the three was moved to bring out the book that Russell and Young had called for, but the younger Stedman, who had charge of Melville's literary affairs after his death, arranged for new editions not only of *Typee* and *Omoo,* as "Taverner" had suggested, but also of *White-Jacket* and *Moby-Dick.* As an Introduction to the first of these volumes, *Typee* (1892), Stedman printed the brief Life of Melville that had been evolving, with Mrs. Melville's suggestions, in his earlier articles. Meanwhile, Coan, also with Mrs. Melville's help, had published at least one shorter piece of his own, and Smith, working independently in Pittsfield, had turned out a serialized biographical sketch and accompanying editorial on Melville for the Pittsfield *Evening Journal;* in 1897, after Smith's death, Mrs. Melville arranged for a partial reprinting, in a thirty-one page pamphlet, of Smith's account.

Remaining to be examined here is the substance of each of these Lives, considering the particular interests, the special authority, and in some instances the characteristic biases of its author. Although these men tell us more about Melville than those who had written of him during his lifetime for the various dictionaries and encyclopedias, the Duyckincks included, they perhaps reveal still more of themselves and the conventions of their day. For an even closer glimpse of their subject we must turn to the reminiscences of Melville's family —not so much Mrs. Melville's memoranda, which are almost entirely factual, as the vivid recollections of two of his granddaughters, written long after the event but still instinct with the presence of the living man. They too are included in this volume.

The Biographers of the Nineties

JOSEPH EDWARD ADAMS SMITH (1822-1896)

On 8 August 1851, writing from Arrowhead, his friend Melville's home in Pittsfield, Evert Duyckinck reported in a letter to his wife in New York on the events of the previous day. A "pic nic on the mountains" had been planned by the "kind and inventive genius" of Melville's neighbor Sarah Huyler Morewood of nearby Broadhall, the old farmhouse formerly the property of Major Thomas Melvill, Jr. Her guests were driven into a barn by a sudden shower, however, and mounted into the hayloft, "dislodging the hens" and settling themselves comfortably in the hay while rain pattered on the roof. Mrs. Morewood "had a poet in the company and his poem too," and as "the flattered author . . . sat thoughtful on a hay tuft" his poem was read aloud "with emphasis" by Melville, who interjected such compliments as "great," "glorious," "By Jove that's tremendous," and so on. "Perhaps the most noticeable incident," Duyckinck continued, was

> a gathering of the exiled fowls in a corner who cackled a series of noisy resolutions, levelled at the party. "Turn em out! " was the cry. The author impelled by the honor of his poem charged fearlessly, scattered the cuties of the pit, clasping the most obstinate bodily and "rushing" her a rapid descent below. This was the ludicrous side. On the other, the Poet was a thoughtful sensible man and was our pilot to the Ashley Pond or Washington Lake which we reached at last after an endless ascent by the side of steep gorges, on the summit of the Hoosac, looking back to the distant sublimities of cloud & mountain of the Taghconic. (*Log,* I, 420–421)

Mrs. Morewood's picnic was the first recorded meeting between Melville, then thirty-two, and the poet of the company, a young man of twenty-nine named Joseph Edward Adams Smith, known to readers of the *New Englander* magazine as "Godfrey Greylock." His "stout MSS in heroic measure," as Duyckinck called it, was entitled "On Onota's Graceful Shore: A Ballad of the Times that Tried Men's Souls"; it is included in Smith's *Souvenir Verse and Story* (1896). Over the next few years a lifelong friendship was to develop between the two writers.

Smith's earlier life is summarized in a newspaper account first published in 1894 and reprinted at the time of his death in 1896 by the *Berkshire Evening Eagle:*

> Joseph Edward Adams Smith was born in Portsmouth, N. H., February 4, 1822, and his father removed to Bangor, Me., while he was a child. After a three years' course at Gorham seminary, he entered Bowdoin college, in 1840. What had all the symptoms of an advanced stage of consumption, as the doctors pronounced it, sent him home in his junior year. Outdoor exercise and amusements apparently cured him, and he returned to college, to be again sent home for the same cause. He got better and entered the law office of Appleton, Allen & Hill, of which the late Chief Justice John Appleton was senior partner. In less than two years the old troubles re-appeared in a new form, affecting his head, so that when he found himself in Boston (where his father had removed) in charge of Dr. Woodbridge Strong, a noted physician of the old school, he did not well know how he got there. Dr. Strong, however, at once saw that the diagnosis of the Maine doctors was all wrong, the lungs being perfectly sound, and that the trouble was chronic bilious dyspepsia, so deeply seated as to be almost as dangerous as consumption, the danger of death or insanity at an early day being imminent. Six months of heroic treatment, however, effected a permanent cure.
>
> He began to write for the press in the Clay-Polk presidential campaign of 1843, composing words for music about the same time. In Boston, and afterwards in Berkshire, he devoted himself to the same line of literary work, the lyrical work predominating for the first two or three years. In 1847 he spent a year in Lanesboro, where his father, Edward Smith, was building the Briggs Iron Works. There he fell in love at first sight with Berkshire life and scenery, began to write about them for Boston papers, and continued to do so, residing by turns in Boston and in Pittsfield where his father's family had their home after May, 1848. This led to the writing and publishing, in 1852, of "Taghconic, the Romance and Beauty of the Hills," a little volume descriptive of Berkshire scenery, with tales whose scenes were laid in it. It was published over the nom de plume of "Godfrey Greylock," which was not, as George William Curtis surmised, an imitation of Washington Irving's "Geoffrey Crayon," but originated as follows: The New Englander, a new literary journal, was about to be started in Boston—about 1850—and the publishers proposed to herald their first number by posters announcing a story by Grace Greenwood and a poem by a writer of note. The poet failed them at the last moment because of illness, and Mr. Smith, whose writings over the name of "Greylock," were known to the publisher, was persuaded to contribute a poem instead. It then occurred to the publishers to make their poster alliterative

and putting Godfrey before Greylock they had it: "Story by Grace Green-wood and a poem by Godfrey Greylock."[1]

Before Smith met Melville in the Berkshires he had once called on Melville's aunt, Miss Priscilla Melvill of Boston, who was "very fond of her handsome nephew" and "proud of the fame which he had suddenly won" by his books, though "she did not quite approve all of them";[2] Melville in turn probably knew of Smith through the poet's Pittsfield sponsor Mrs. Morewood. Whether the two writers saw one another again before late December of 1851 is not revealed in surviving records. There may have been another meeting during Duyckink's visit in August when he and Melville attended "a general gathering" at Broadhall, although Smith's name does not appear in Duyckinck's subsequent account to his wife; she had previously received from him, as an anticipation of what Mrs. Morewood's hospitality might offer, a recent clipping from the Boston *Evening Transcript* headed "A Petit Fancy Dress Party in Berkshire" that her husband identified as "written by the Smith known as 'the mad poet.' " It was "all about Mrs. M[orewood]'s family," with further reference to "Miss Hetty Huyler [a sister] engaged to said Smith."[3] Both "the mad poet" and the Melville family were among Mrs. Morewood's guests on Christmas Day as listed in her letter of 28 December to George Duyckinck. Melville was "more quiet than usual" on that occasion, she remarked, adding that though the Morewoods both liked him his "opinions and religious views" troubled her husband. "It is a pity that Mr. Melville so often in conversation uses irreverent language," she continued; "—he will not be popular in society here on that very account—but this will not trouble him" (*Log,* I, 441). Melville, she noted, was already at work on a new book; this was *Pierre,* begun while the first reviews of *Moby-Dick* were still coming in. Smith too had literary work in progress. In 1852, as Godfrey Greylock, he was to publish his *Taghconic; or Letters and Legends About Our Summer Home,* a volume aptly described by Melville's mother as "a sort of guide book of our beautiful County of Berkshire." As she explained, a few of its chapters had been written by "some of the gifted ones around us," such as Sarah Morewood and Melville's future brother-in-law John C. Hoadley, but "Herman has not contributed one line, tho often requested to do so" (*Log,* I, 461).

Declining to write for Smith's book did not exclude Melville from the pages of *Taghconic,* where he appears as "Herman Mellville" in references to his "strong-lined portrait of Captain Ahab" and his friendship with Nathaniel Hawthorne; there are also allusions to both Melville and Sarah Morewood in Smith's account of the celebrated Balanced Rock near his former home in Lanesboro (see Appendix B below). In his later writings Smith was to enlarge on these various topics, first in the revised 1879 edition of *Taghconic* (see Appendix C below) and later in the biographical sketch of Melville he published after Melville's death in 1891, where he calls attention to use of the Balanced Rock in *Pierre*. Smith's comments on Melville's friendship with Hawthorne—and particularly their first meeting in 1850—are dependent on second-hand information, as he was careful to acknowledge in the 1879 *Taghconic,* and there are several now-notorious errors in his statements there and in the biographical sketch. With his abiding preference for "the simplicity, vigor and naturalness" of Melville's earlier works, Smith came to think in later years that an "excessive intimacy" with Hawthorne was "a misfortune" to Melville, holding that their "philosophical seances" in 1850 and 1851 had a "disastrous effect" on his subsequent writing. Recalling the hostile reception of *Pierre* in 1852, he agreed that its condemnation had been justified; even among the greatest authors, as he put it, there are writings such as *Pierre* "to which oblivion would be the best charity." Even so, he acknowledged the "keen and just thoughts scattered here and there through the book, and at least a score of pages of local interest which we of Berkshire could ill afford to lose." In short, *Pierre* to Smith was "simply a freak of genius, and should have been so regarded by the world."

During 1853, as Smith correctly remembered, Melville turned from the composition of full-length books to short stories written for magazines and published anonymously, though their authorship appears to have been something of an open secret at the time. In 1854 Smith began on a supposedly temporary basis what became an eleven-year term as editor of the *Berkshire County Eagle.* He may already have contributed occasional items to the paper,[4] and its passing notices of Melville's recent writings may therefore be his.[5] Another article possibly by Smith is a column of "Pittsfield Portraits" that briefly describes Melville: "a stalwart, earnest resolute looking man . . . unassuming, but very popular" (*Log,* I, 479). Later references to Melville during Smith's editorship are almost certainly from his own pen, since the terms of his engagement with the paper left him in charge of all of its non-political writing. The *Eagle's* obituary article of 1896 explains the arrangements:

> In December, 1854, Henry Chickering and Henry A. Marsh, having just bought the Berkshire County Eagle, he was engaged to edit it, until the term of Mr. Chickering as executive councilor expired which would happen in a few weeks. Mr. C. was, however, re-elected and Mr. S. continued with the paper, in an indefinite way, for eleven years, ending in 1865, always expecting to close his connection with it in a few weeks, the end of which never came. There is a curious fact in connection with the beginning of this long service. In purchasing the Eagle Mr. C. intended to make it the leading Whig organ of the county. Mr. S. was so well known for his radical anti-slavery sentiments and his connection with the Free Soil party that he was required to promise not to write anything of a political character for the paper. The Kansas-Nebraska iniquity [1854] and the position of the Whig party in regard to it, soon, however, rendered that restriction needless. Mr. Chickering was still always the controlling political editor and wrote a majority of the political articles, but little else.

It would be interesting to speculate on the part Smith's political opinions may have played in his conversations with Melville and his other Pittsfield friends; if the Morewoods were troubled by Melville's unorthodox religious views, how did they respond to Smith's "radical anti-slavery sentiments"? Certainly there is no political coloration in his published references to Melville, either in the years before the Civil War or in his later biographical sketch, which in retrospect stressed for its Pittsfield audience the "touch of Berkshire" that Smith was pleased to detect in the works written at Arrowhead and celebrated "the great joy" of Melville's Berkshire days, his excursions through the local countryside. Smith permitted himself more latitude in the sketch, for what the *Eagle* had reported at the time was mainly Melville's comings and goings and some notice of his current publications. Beginning in 1855, when Melville was ill first with rheumatism and later with sciatica, the paper took increasing notice of the state of his health, as in its report of a Morewood-inspired "fancy dress pic nic" in September: Melville, "just recovering from a severe illness," came only as a spectator, though Smith himself was costumed as "a 'Friar of Orders Grey'" (*Log*, II, 507). As Smith's biographical sketch was to say, Melville "often, and sometimes very closely, modelled incidents in his stories upon real ones in his own experience," but if Smith saw reflections of Melville's illness in "I and My Chimney" (1856) and of the "pic-nic *en costume*" in Chapter 24 of *The Confidence-Man* (1857) he did not draw the specific parallels in print. Of *The Confidence-Man* Smith had little to say publicly, either on its appearance or later, but he liked Melville's earlier writing for the magazines—especially those pieces with a Berkshire setting. He reviewed the collected *Piazza Tales* in 1856 as "decidedly the most readable" that "our fellow citizen . . . has published since Omoo and Typee"; he particularly commended the opening sketch to local readers "for its description of familiar scenery" (*Log*, II, 515). A subsequent article in the *Eagle* mentioned four illustrations for "The Bell-Tower" that an artist had recently sent to Melville (*Log*, II, 517, 519); in later references, including the biographical sketch, Smith commented briefly but not always accurately on other stories and sketches.

A conversation with Melville that Smith vividly remembered took place during the summer of 1856. Its subject was an article originally published in the *Dublin University Magazine*, "A Trio of American Sailor-Authors," that *Littel's Living Age* had reprinted in its issue of 1 March 1856—the same article whose comments on Melville, quoted in part by the *Eagle* on 8 August, were also to be used in after years by John B. Dillingham and S. Austin Allibone as well as by Smith himself in the biographical sketch. While Melville was reading the article, Smith recalled, he had

> looked up to say, "Well, it is pleasant to read what those fellows over the water say about us!" And he was greatly amused when he found the critic, thinking that his name was altogether too fine for common use in America, concluded that it was a pseudonymn.

If Melville was "sensitive to the praise of these reviews," Smith inferred, "so also he must have been to the censure." After he had sailed for Europe later in 1856 the *Eagle*'s notice of his departure mentioned the issue of Melville's name as well as the state of his health:

> Mr. Melville much needs this relaxation from his severe literary labors of several years past, and we doubt not that he will return with renovated health and a new store of those observations of travel which he works [writes?] so charmingly. The literati of Europe will also have the opportunity to learn that Herman Melville is the real name of a man, and a real man all over. (*Log*, II, 525)

Smith's paper took no notice of Melville's return to Pittsfield in May of 1857, although it was mentioned in the rival *Sun* (*Log*, II, 579). On 19 June the *Eagle*, after quoting an appraisal by the London *Saturday Review* of his latest publication, *The Confidence-Man*, added only an unenthusiastic one-sentence comment: "We need not say to those who have read the book that as a picture of American society it is *slightly* distorted" (*Log*, II, 580); the biographical sketch does not even mention it. Though Smith evidently did not know that in 1857 Melville was already thinking of a possible appointment in the New York Custom House, he was well aware that his friend wished to be freed of the burdens of farming. On 24 June 1857 the *Eagle* accepted a running advertisement offering Melville's house and land for sale; its conventional phrasing sounds more like Smith's than his own: "For situation and prospect, this place is among the pleasantest in Berkshire, and has other natural advantages desirable in a country residence" (*Log*, II, 580). But though the western half of the farm was sold in July, the desired appointment in New York was not to be secured until 1866,[6] and in the fall of 1857, as an alternative to another winter at his desk, Melville began his three rather unrewarding seasons as a traveling lecturer. The *Eagle* carried nothing on this development until the fall of 1858, when Smith announced and later reviewed Melville's Pittsfield lecture on the South Seas. Its material, he reported, was "pleasant and instructive," "enlivened with incidents of personal adventure," and "written in the style of Mr. Melville's best books" (*Log*, II, 596, 597). When in the later biographical sketch Smith returned to the subject of Melville's lecturing he had little firm information to go on; his statement there that besides Pittsfield Melville also lectured "in New York, Philadelphia, Montreal, St. Louis, San Francisco," and "intermediate cities and towns" was flatly wrong with respect to Philadelphia, St. Louis, and San Francisco.

In the *Eagle*'s next reference to Melville, on 31 May 1860, Smith announced his departure aboard the *Meteor* "for a voyage round the world, in pursuit of relaxation, renewed vigor, and, we hope, material for another charming volume on sea-life" (*Log*, II, 618); he said nothing, then or later, about the projected book of poems that Melville had completed before sailing. On 8 November 1860 Smith reported what Melville had written home to his wife: that his health had not profited as much from the voyage as he expected and that he would be returning from San Francisco via Panama (*Log*, II, 628, 630). But the *Eagle*'s hope "that Mr. M. will reach us in the full vigor of health that used to distinguish him" proved to be ill-founded. During the next two years Melville again sought to avoid the rigors of wintering at Arrowhead, going instead to Boston and New York in the fall of 1861, as the *Eagle* duly noted (*Log*, II, 643), and moving into Pittsfield village in November of 1862. While returning to the farmhouse he was thrown from his box wagon and "very seriously injured," according to the *Eagle* (*Log*, II, 655); Smith, who had accompanied him, was also thrown to the ground but was less severely hurt. This accident, according to the biographical sketch, "had something to do" with Melville's decision to leave Pittsfield permanently for New York in 1863, "and also with other changes in his life" during his later years.

Restoration of Melville's health, the *Eagle* had said on 10 December 1863, was the purpose of Melville's removal to New York (*Log*, II, 664); in the biographical sketch Smith advanced a number of additional considerations: Melville had been obliged to give up farming at Arrowhead; he was unable to live there during Pittsfield winters; the local schools were inconveniently distant for the Melville children; New York's libraries were superior to Pittsfield's. Smith was unwilling to accept Arthur Stedman's suggestion in the New York *World* that "dissatisfaction with the village schools" was the sole issue, nor did he think that Melville intended "forsaking literary work," though he conceded that there may have been some "intimation" of a possible appointment in the Custom House. Still another factor, Smith added, was Mrs. Melville's inheritance of a "moderate fortune" after her father's death in 1861; this money made it possible for the Melvilles to buy "the very pleasant and convenient house" to which they moved in New York. "Furnished like the old home at Arrowhead, to suit the tastes of its occupants, with its rare and story telling engravings and with Mr. Melville's curious library which had been so gathered that he was its soul, 104 East 26th street became a very attractive and satisfying home for people like Mr. and Mrs. Melville." Evidently Smith knew the house from his own visits there; in 1864 he had married, and in 1865, "after closing his connection with the Eagle," in the words of the obituary notice, he "spent some months in New York and Boston."

On Smith's return to Pittsfield he was engaged by a committee of local citizens to write the history of the town, an assignment which, like his editorship of the *Eagle*, continued far longer than originally envisioned. "An unexpected wealth of material," according to the later account of Smith's career, extended the time to ten years, and as a result he was forced "to eke out the town's appropriations for the work by acting as the local correspondent for the Springfield

Union, preparing the first extended catalogues of the Athenaeum library and cabinets, and other similar work." The ultimate product of Smith's historical writing was his two-volume *History of Pittsfield* with its "aggregate of 1243 octavo pages": the first volume to appear, published in 1869, covers the period 1734-1800 and its successor, published seven years later, deals with the years 1800-1876. To the *History* Melville contributed a reminiscent sketch of his late uncle, Major Thomas Melvill, Jr., that was "written subsequent to 1871," according to Smith, and "furnished in his old kindly spirit, and with the same love for the town which he always manifested. All his intercourse regarding it was marked by his old frank, friendly and considerate manner—not one whit changed." When a resident of Pittsfield, Smith was to suggest, Melville had "modelled himself as a 'gentleman of the old school' upon the pattern of his Boston-born and Parisian-bred uncle, the democratic aristocrat" Major Melvill.

In the first volume of the *History* Smith quoted a portion of Melville's sketch of his uncle and paraphrased other parts of it (I, 399–400); in his 1879 revision of *Taghconic*, his contributions to an 1885 *History of Berkshire County*, and in his biographical account of Melville himself he again drew upon the sketch. During 1871, while still engaged with the *History*, Smith was apparently instrumental in securing certain of Melville's works for the newly established Berkshire Athenaeum. The Athenaeum had been founded earlier in that same year when the Pittsfield Library Association, for twenty-one years a private organization, became incorporated under the new name as a public library; on 25 October, Smith wrote to Allan Melville thanking him "for the volumes of your brother's works rec'd by the Athenaeum" and expressing the hope that portraits of both Herman Melville and Thomas Melvill, Jr., could be obtained for the *History* (*Log*, II, 720). Allan Melville died in the following year, however, and the *History* went to press without either portrait. Its principal reference to the Melville brothers was in a paragraph about Arrowhead (pp. 7-8), then the summer residence of Allan Melville's family, that Smith was also to draw upon in his later writings including the biographical sketch. This paragraph, much quoted by later writers on Melville, includes several misstatements: besides giving 1852 rather than 1850 as the year in which Melville purchased Arrowhead and rendering inaccurately the title of "I and My Chimney" it makes the first of Smith's two legendary additions to the Melville canon, "October Mountain"; the second was to follow in 1879 when Smith asserted, in the revised *Taghconic*, that before meeting Hawthorne Melville had published a review of *The Scarlet Letter*. The biographical sketch corrects some but not all of these errors.

To characterize the relations between Smith and Melville during Melville's years in New York is difficult in the absence of surviving correspondence or other relevant documents. The biographical sketch, composed when the metropolitan papers were stressing the "hermit's reputation" Melville had acquired in the city, is specific only about his final visit to Pittsfield in 1885, when, as Smith recalled, "he did not show even the changes which time commonly works on men in the number of years which elapsed" since he had left for New York. "Perhaps his manner was a little more quiet than in the old time," Smith conceded; "but in general society it had always been quiet," and "his conversation had much of his old jovial, let-the-world-go-as-it-will spirit." That communication between the two families had been maintained over the years is suggested by Smith's handling of Melville's "seclusion from society in New York, so far as there was any seclusion." He mentions Melville's "ill health and the exhaustion which follows it," which for a time "robbed his spirits of some of the old elasticity," and he recalls correctly that "death followed death" among the Melvilles' "relations and dearest friends in such rapid succession that there was scarcely a year when the family could be said to be out of mourning." Smith appears equally knowledgeable in his later reference to the circumstances of Melville's own death "after a lingering and painful illness of several years, during which he manifested heroic fortitude, and patience, and also a considerate regard for those who attended him which commanded their admiration as well as their gratitude"; in this instance his language may well reflect that of a recent letter from Melville's widow, since he himself had apparently not gone to New York for the funeral. As for Melville's writings during the years in New York, Smith obviously knew *Battle-Pieces*, but there is no discussion of *Clarel* in the biographical sketch, where references to Melville's other privately printed poems of his last years seem to derive from Arthur Stedman's articles rather than the volumes themselves.

When Smith came to write about Melville during the month following his passing he was not himself in the best of health, and during his own last years his life was said to be "shadowed by care and poverty, for in business affairs he was an infant."[7] A writer for the Springfield *Republican* was to recall his "somewhat pathetic appearance" as he passed along the streets of Pittsfield, "his neck wound in a white kerchief, if the day was a bit chilly—cane in hand and a little basket of books on his arm." Everyone recognized him as "Uncle Joe," and all Berkshire knew him at least by reputation. The local community, said the Pittsfield *Sunday Morning Call*, had been with him "a life study, and one which he thoroughly mastered and continued to be master of almost up to the time of his decease"; the neighboring *Republican* added more specifically that Smith was both "thoroughly in love with Berkshire" and "certain that the natural beauties of the county had much if not everything to do with the production of so many famous men, poets and scholars in those highlands." What Smith had to say about the place of Berkshire settings in Melville's writings needs to be read in this light. As for his account of their personal relationship, it may be significant that although Smith had a few "cronies" of the old school, according to the *Republican*, there had "for years" been "few intimates" for

him in Pittsfield and he "was really well known in man to man way by few."
One recalls what Melville himself had written in *John Marr* about another aging
man whose "growing sense of his environment threw him more and more upon
retrospective musings."[8]

The author of the biographical sketch of Melville is further characterized in
these relevant paragraphs from the *Republican*'s vignette of Smith:

> He was well read—he knew the best in literature. His tastes were, unfor-
> tunately, beyond possibility of satisfaction. He would have surrounded him-
> self with choice books, he would have done less fragmentary writing and
> essayed more comprehensive works. But he could not. However, his accom-
> plishments in book writing were not limited to those already mentioned, for
> he wrote, besides his large two-volume history of Pittsfield, three other his-
> tories of Pittsfield, also "The Genesis of Paper Making," "A Memoir of the
> First Zenas Crane," "A Memoir of Gov. G. N. Briggs," "An Account of the
> Pittsfield Soldiers' Monument," "A History of Free Education in Pittsfield,"
> and "Pontoosuc Lake".
>
> His peculiarities were many, as those who have talked with him on religion
> and social questions know. And he had many "hobbies," none of them, how-
> ever, more than "harmless." He had a warm place in his heart for the poor
> and unfortunate, and in recent years made by certain quiet influencing many
> a "stir" over what seemed to him wrongs and injustices to the poor—and to
> the Catholics especially. He believed in making the usefulness of the Athen-
> aeum and House of Mercy broader, and though perhaps radical, undoubtedly
> did much to make them more truly public institutions than they might have
> been. In his death those of the present day lose their chief medium of con-
> nection with the best spirit of the earlier days in Berkshire.

Smith's biographical sketch of Melville, written for the *Evening Journal* of
Pittsfield, began appearing in the issue of Tuesday, 27 October 1891, and continued through nine instalments until 25 January 1892. An accompanying
editorial, obviously by Smith himself, acknowledged characteristically that the
story of Melville's career had "occupied much more space than was anticipated
when it was commenced; expanding with new sources of information until it
covers much more than Mr. Melville's Berkshire life, making it well nigh his
complete biography." Smith had presumably begun with a regionally oriented
treatment of Melville in mind, like that of Holmes in the book he was to publish in 1895: *The Poet Among the Hills: Oliver Wendell Holmes in Berkshire,*
a volume in which Smith included additional material on Melville (see Appendix D below). The "new sources of information" he mentions were probably
the articles by Arthur Stedman which had appeared while the biographical
sketch was being written: certainly Smith's disquisitions about Melville's
removal from Pittsfield and the seclusion of his later years in New York were
prompted by his reactions to these issues as they had been raised by the New
York press. Smith shared with Melville's widow his hope of eventually

rewriting and enlarging the biographical sketch into "a small book similar to his 'Poet of the Hills,' " as she later observed,[9] but his own failing health and his death on 29 October 1896 prevented him from doing so. They had talked about the project in Pittsfield late in September of 1892, as Mrs. Melville reported at the time in a letter to Arthur Stedman. When she had asked Stedman to send Smith copies of the 1892 edition of *Typee,* she identified him as "the writer of these memorial articles" that she had evidently loaned to Stedman previously, and described Smith as "the most prominent literary man in Pittsfield."[10] Smith was to get in touch with Stedman, as Melville's literary executor, to request formal authorization for a Life of Melville or possibly to discuss a publisher for it. "With regard to a biography," she advised Stedman,

> I would simply tell him what you have written me—and let him go on with the plan if he wishes to—He spoke to me about it and I approved, if he would submit the proof to me to correct errors which must necessarily creep in to any such record—(as in his Pittsfield articles for the Journal)[.] He is quite advanced in years and much broken physically, though he does not admit it—and I fear the undertaking will be too much for him (always seeming to have some literary work in hand)—but let him take his own way—as he is so desirous to do it—[11]

After Smith had died in 1896 with his enlarged Life of Melville still unwritten, Mrs. Melville decided to collect and reprint his unrevised "Pittsfield articles." During the summer of 1897, while she was again in Pittsfield, she made arrangements to have them published in a thirty-one page pamphlet. Her own copy, now in the Melville Collection of the Harvard College Library, is dated in her hand "Sept. 4th 1897"; on the following day, while still in Pittsfield, she wrote to Catherine Ganesevoort Lansing, Melville's Albany cousin:

> I send you with this a pamphlet in which I have collected & had printed the memorial articles that Mr Smith wrote for the "Evening Journal" here, soon after Herman's death—they were scattered in poor type through many numbers of the paper where they would never be read and I thought they ought to be rescued from oblivion for the family and a few near friends, if only for Mr Smith's sake. . . . He was Herman's ardent admirer and most faithful friend for these many long years, and I value him for that and regret to lose him from the Pittsfield circle alas now so sadly diminished. . . .[12]

What she did not explain, however, is that she had been editing the newspaper text, not only to correct the "errors" she had mentioned to Stedman but also with the evident intention of softening Smith's more personal observations about her late husband and his family. Some of the differences between the original version and the pamphlet are of relatively little consequence, but others are of considerable interest: notably the omission of one entire instalment—that of 16 December 1891—dealing with the christening of Broadhall, Melville's own residence at Arrowhead, his "general method of literary work," and his personal and literary relations with Hawthorne.

Whether dropping this material was intentional or whether Mrs. Melville simply overlooked or mislaid the entire instalment is impossible to say. Clearly her hand was at work in other instances, however, such as her correcting Smith's account of the marriage of John C. Hoadley to Melville's sister Catherine and especially her deletion of material such as the following:

Smith's reference to Melville's "maiden aunt," p. 122 below

His mention of Broadhall as "a boarding house" kept by Robert Melvill and his sisters, p. 129

A sentence on the circumstances of Melville's removal from Pittsfield to New York, pp. 134-135

A discussion of Melville's supposed dissatisfaction with the Pittsfield village schools, pp. 135-136

A paragraph on the death of Lemuel Shaw and Mrs. Melville's subsequent inheritance of "a moderate fortune, which enabled the purchase" of a residence in New York City, p. 136

Part of a sentence on the wearing of mourning by the Melvilles, p. 137

A remark on the respective illnesses of Melville and Charles Sumner, p. 140

Smith's allusion to and lengthy quotation from Shakespeare's *Troilus and Cressida,* pp. 143-144

An unfavorable criticism of "the irrelevant rhapsodies which mar many of Mr. Melville's later works, and Pierre most of all," together with an extended comment on his use of personal experience for literary material, p. 146.

A full collation of the 1897 pamphlet with the newspaper text of 1891 is reported in Appendix E below, which also records minor emendations of the 1891 version as it is reprinted in the present volume.

Modern scholarship has gone further than Mrs. Melville in identifying the factual errors not only in Smith's biographical sketch but also in his other writings that deal with Melville. Apart from its misstatements the sketch, as Willard Thorp has remarked, still has value "as a friendly contemporary view" of Melville, though "disappointingly vague at points where precision would be useful."[13] Reticence, lack of information, or sheer failure of understanding may all be involved. How well the two men knew each other over the years, or even where and how often they met, is difficult to say, in spite of Smith's claims of familiarity; Mrs. Melville, in acknowledging his admiration for her husband, said nothing about Melville's reciprocal feelings for Smith. Clearly there were ranges of Melville's mind that extended beyond Smith's ability to follow or even to appreciate, though they had enough in common to bring them together companionably on Berkshire excursions, at Sarah Morewood's fancy-dress parties, or even in a discussion of Melville's European critics. Both had a reputation in

Pittsfield for outspoken and controversial views: anti-slavery sentiments in Smith's case, religious opinions in Melville's. Smith, though "sweetly tempered and courteous," in the words of a later Pittsfield historian, Edward Boltman, "could be excited to surprising wrath by that which he judged to be bigotry or injustice." Melville too could be aroused to anger: "Falsehood was abhorrent to his nature," as Smith justly wrote of him, "and if that involved hatred or hypocrisy, why that was the worse for the hypocrite." Melville, he said, was "eminently a self-contained man; but he was also a dear lover of and close communicant with nature, whether he found it in men, or in seas, mountains, woods and field"—a comment equally applicable to Smith himself. Indeed, the biographical sketch, in one way or another, tells as much about Smith as about Melville, particularly his frank distaste for what he called "the irrelevant philosophy or the mysticism" of Melville's later works. Otherwise, it amply confirms what Boltman has said of Smith's whole career: "in what he wrote there was never harshness, and he was by mental habit a searcher for the best in humankind."[14]

TITUS MUNSON COAN (1836–1921)

Arthur Stedman's anonymous article in the New York *Tribune* on "Herman Melville's Funeral"—J. E. A. Smith called it "by far the most correct and intelligent account which we have seen in any New York paper"—mentions Dr. Titus Munson Coan as among those present at the services and quotes his comments at the time on *Typee*. "Dr. Coan has enjoyed the friendship and confidence of Mr. Melville during most of the latter's residence in this city," Stedman added in his later article in the New York *World* headed " 'Marquesan' Melville," explaining there that Coan had first met Melville "while a student at Williams College over thirty years ago." During his student days Coan, a native of the Hawaiian Islands, had been reading Melville's books "with rapture," and in the spring of 1859 had set off for Pittsfield with a fellow student, John Thomas Gulick, to pay a call on Melville at Arrowhead, which they reached on the morning of 20 April. Coan was twenty-three at the time; Gulick was four years older. In a letter to his mother following the visit, "fortunately preserved by her," Coan described the "full tide of talk—or rather of monologue" in which they engaged Melville: "In vain I sought to hear of Typee and those Paradise islands, but he preferred to pour forth his philosophy and his theories of life. The shade of Aristotle arose like a cold mist between myself and Fayaway." To the young student Melville had "the air of one who has suffered from opposition, both literary and social. With his liberal views he is apparently considered by the good people of Pittsfield as little better than a cannibal or a 'beachcomber.' "

In the journal of Coan's friend Gulick, also an Hawaiian-American, is an account of the visit to Melville which corroborates and supplements Coan's letter. Melville, according to Gulick, "was evidently a disappointed man" in 1859, "soured by criticism and disgusted with the civilized world and with Christendom in general and in particular. The ancient dignity of Homeric times afforded the only state of humanity . . . to which he could turn with any complacency. What little there was of meaning in the religions of the present day had come down from Plato. All our philosophy and all our art and poetry was either derived or imitated from the ancient Greeks."[15] Thus the heritage of Plato and what Coan called "the shade of Aristotle" dominated Melville's conversation with his younger visitors. "We have quite enough of Greek philosophy at Williams College," Coan wrote to his mother, "and I confess I was disappointed in this trend of the talk." Coan's first impression of what Stedman called "our author's fondness for philosophical discussion" proved to be a lasting one. As J. E. A. Smith long remembered Melville's sociability during his first years in Pittsfield and especially his delight in Berkshire scenery and excursions, so Coan, who met an older Melville, continued to emphasize his supposedly inveterate philosophizing. "He seems to put away the objective side of life and to shut himself up as a cloistered thinker and poet," Coan wrote in 1859. During Coan's last years, when Raymond Weaver talked with him about Melville, he "repeatedly used to recount, with a sigh at his frustration, how he made persistent attempts to inveigle Melville into Polynesian reminiscences, always to be rebuffed by Melville's invariable rejoinder: 'That reminds me of the eighth book of Plato's *Republic.*' This was a signal for silence and leave-taking."[16]

If Melville preferred to talk philosophy with Coan and Gulick in 1859 rather than recalling his years in the South Seas, one reason may have been Coan's heritage as the son of a missionary, which Melville, in Weaver's words, "seems never to have quite forgiven him." Coan was born in Hilo, Hawaiian Islands, on 27 September 1836; his missionary parents were both of New England ancestry. After studying "at Punahou School, the royal school, and the Oahu college in Honolulu," according to an encyclopedia's account of his career, he sailed for the United States on a New Bedford whaler around Cape Horn, entered Yale College, and later transferred to Williams. After completing his course there in 1859 (the year of his visit to Melville), he studied medicine until 1861 at the New York College of Physicians and Surgeons, spent two years in Bellevue Hospital and the army hospitals of New York, and in 1863 became assistant surgeon in Admiral Farragut's West Gulf naval squadron.

He took part in the battle of Mobile Bay, and in other naval combats in the civil war, and in 1865 he was attached to the flagship Brooklyn, but resigned his position in the navy at the close of that year, and began the practice of medicine in the city of New York, where he has since resided. His first literary work to attract notice appeared in the "Galaxy," to which he contributed many essays on social and literary topics. He has written prose and verse for all the leading American magazines. Dr. Coan has devoted considerable time to visiting Europe and the health resorts of America, studying and describing their advantages and their mineral waters. He directs a bureau of revision, having as its object the reading of authors' manuscripts and the unbiased criticism and skilled revision of their work. His efforts in this direction have won success and the approval of the most eminent literary men of the day.[17]

Apart from Coan's magazine writing, he was the author of *Ounces of Prevention*, a collection of essays on hygiene (1885), editor of *Topics of the Times*, 6 volumes (1883), and a co-editor, with James Grant Wilson, of *Personal Recollections of the War of the Rebellion* (1891); in later years he contributed articles to various dictionaries and encyclopedias. From 1871 until 1874 he was in charge of the literary department of the New York *Independent*. Coan and his wife (who were living on East Fifty-Fourth Street in 1890) were not neighbors of the Melvilles, although Coan's office was somewhat closer to their residence: his New York Bureau of Revision, established in 1880, was located at 20 West Fourteenth Street until 1892, when it was moved to Fifth Avenue. The sociable Coan was active in the Yale Alumni Association of New York, the Century Club, and the Authors Club, and he knew other writers who had some acquaintance with Melville, such as Richard Henry Stoddard and E. C. Stedman. Stedman told Coan in 1889 that he proposed to include some of Coan's writing in his *Library of American Literature*, and in the summer of 1891, at Coan's request, furnished him with a one-paragraph commendation of the New York Bureau of Revision.[18] As Coan's voluminous correspondence reveals, he was particularly noted for what has been described as his negative attitude toward religion—an interesting orientation for the son of missionaries. Melville's strictures on the missionary enterprise in *Typee* and *Omoo* obviously did not offend Coan as a young man; religious questions may have been among the topics that he and Melville discussed during their later years in New York.

Other than philosophy, religion, and the Pacific Islands, Coan and Melville as world travelers would certainly have found common interests in their respective voyages around Cape Horn and the life of a whale-ship—Melville's own Yale College and Harvard. If they talked about events of the Civil War there is no record, although Coan later regaled Weaver with an obviously apocryphal story he had heard from "some old admiral" about Melville's supposed activities after hostilities had broken out: when feelings were running high against England because of her sympathy with the Southern cause, Melville allegedly went sailing on the Hudson aboard a schooner waving the British flag. Melville's daughter Mrs. Henry B. Thomas, on being questioned about this report, which she had never previously heard, dismissed it as having "absolutely *no* truth."[19] More significant is the possibility of literary discussions between the two men during the years 1865 to 1891 when both were living in New York. During "most" of this period, according to Stedman, Coan had Melville's "friendship and confidence." These were the years of Melville's *Battle-Pieces* (1866), *Clarel* (1876), and the later poetry, and ultimately of *Billy Budd*; Coan was writing for the *Galaxy* (published from 1866 to 1878) and other magazines of the day and establishing himself as an editor and literary advisor. In his article on Melville in the Boston *Literary World* of 19 December 1891, Coan asserted that he "repeatedly" visited Melville in New York "and had the most interesting talks with him," but he mentioned no dates and there appears to be no surviving correspondence between them. Other visitors such as Oliver Hillard and Peter Toft had little success in getting Melville to talk about his own writings; one suspects that Coan too was obliged to listen, as he had in 1859, to whatever topics Melville preferred to discuss out of his "stores of reading" and "reaches of philosophy"—Coan's phrases in the *Literary World*. "My books," Melville told him, "will speak for themselves."

In dealing with Melville's works Coan justly claimed "some authority" because of his own background. "I have spent years at sea," he wrote, "and I cannot overpraise the wonderful vigor and beauty" of *White-Jacket* and *Moby-Dick*. But *Typee*, in Coan's eyes, was Melville's "masterpiece": the book as he saw it was "the outcome of an opportunity that will never be repeated. Melville was the first and only man ever made captive in a valley full of Polynesian cannibals, who had the genius to describe the situation, and who got away alive to write his book." According to Arthur Stedman, Coan had made this same remark at Melville's funeral, following it with a comment unrepeatable in a Boston publication: " 'Typee' will be read when most of the Concord group are forgotten." Coan sent a copy of Stedman's article in the *Tribune* to his sister on 10 October 1891, obviously retaining another copy for reference in preparing his own essay on Melville. Within the limits of his space he proposed to indicate there "how directly" Melville's writings "flowed from real experience, like water from a spring." Thus

> *Typee* and *Omoo*, mistaken by the public for fiction, were, on the contrary, the most vivid truth expressed in the most telling and poetic manner. My father, the Rev. Titus Coan, went over Melville's ground in 1867, and while he has criticised the topography of *Typee* as being somewhat exaggerated in the mountain distances, a very natural mistake, he told me that the descriptions were admirably true and the characterizations faultless in the main.[20]

The works after *Moby-Dick* Coan thought "less powerful"; *Pierre* especially "roused a storm of critical opposition." *Clarel* excepted, all of Melville's books "were published almost as soon as written"; the "germ" of *Clarel* "had been unfolding for many years," Melville's visit to the Holy Land having provided much of its "material and imagery." As for the later poetry, Coan was able to say with gratification that copies of *John Marr* and *Timoleon,* each printed "in an edition of twenty-five copies only," lay before him as he wrote. There is no reference to the unpublished verse or to *Billy Budd,* and certainly no suggestion that Coan had in any way advised Melville professionally as either medical man or literary critic.[21]

Coan's observations, including his statement that he possessed the two privately printed volumes,[22] not only indicate his general knowledge of the Melville canon and his own preferences within it but also support to some degree his implied claims of intimacy with their author. Did he also speak with "some authority" in that portion of his *Literary World* article that constitutes another brief Life of Melville? Again the answer must be qualified. According to Coan himself, his biographical data are "now for the first time fully given," but in reality his article offers little information not already to be found either in the earlier biographical dictionaries or the more recent articles published by Arthur Stedman. Coan lacked the knowledge needed to correct long-standing errors about the dates of Melville's first two voyages and the length of his stay in the Marquesas. He is more precise about such dates as those of Melville's appointment to and resignation from the New York Custom House, which he may have verified by consulting Mrs. Melville;[23] indeed the idea of writing about Melville for a Boston publication may even have been her suggestion. His own letter of 1859 had already been quoted by Stedman; all Coan could really add was brief mention of later conversations in New York and endorsement of *Typee, Omoo, White-Jacket,* and *Moby-Dick* as "autobiographical books."

Coan's article in the *Literary World* ends with an appeal for information about "the 'Toby' of *Typee,* Mr. Richard T. Greene"; an answer to his request came eight months later from Arthur Stedman, who wrote on 16 October 1892 to inform him of Greene's recent death in Chicago, on 26 August. Stedman had received a note from Mrs. Melville of 8 October inviting him to call and look at a letter and photographs sent her by Greene's son Herman; to Dr. Coan he reported that "Toby's" cousin in New York, "John Green Kelley, of No. 650 8th Avenue, learned of his death through *me.*" Kelley, he explained,

was married in the house of his uncle, Toby's father. Toby, like Melville, was confined to his bed for a year before his death.

All this interesting & varied information, & much more, you can verify by calling on Mrs. Melville at No. 105 East 18th Street. She has asked me to say that she will be glad to tell you what she knows & show you various photographs of Toby & his son, which she showed to me when I called. Perhaps you might make an interesting article about it. There is no further chance of my writing any thing more about Melville.[24]

Stedman's letter, which suggests incidentally that he was in closer touch with Mrs. Melville than was Coan, is of further interest for several reasons: its statement that Melville as well as Toby Greene "was confined to his bed for a year before his death," its declaration that Stedman himself had no intention of writing again on Melville beyond his Introduction to *Typee* in the edition of 1892, and its suggestion that Coan himself "might make an interesting article" about Toby and his family. Apparently Coan did not respond to this prompting, even with the assurance that there would be no competition from Stedman himself. If Coan again wrote on Melville, the most likely attribution is an unsigned biographical article in Volume IV of the *National Cyclopaedia of American Biography*, published in New York in 1893 by James T. White & Company; he is listed among the contributors to this volume. The article in question, less than a column in length, repeats the then-standard information about Melville's career but gives the erroneous date of 1848 for the publication of both *Mardi* and *Redburn*; a drawing made from the 1885 Rockwood photograph and a facsimile signature accompany it (IV, 59).

To the store of factual information about Herman Melville's career Dr. Coan brought relatively little that was new, but to discussion of Melville the man, in his own day and later, he added one significant element. By allowing Arthur Stedman to publish an extract from his letter of 1859 describing Melville's addiction to philosophy, and by reemphasizing the point when he included a portion of the same letter in his own article on Melville in the *Literary World*, Coan helped to fix the persistent image of his friend as a man who by 1859 had already sacrificed his art for his philosophizing—an idea recurrent since the early 1850's. Arthur Stedman, who knew Melville for a much shorter time than Coan and perhaps less intimately, followed Coan's lead in his " 'Marquesan' Melville," which ends with this pronouncement on Melville's later years: "like Coleridge, he buried his wand in a grave of philosophical speculations and conjured no more, save in a few brief 'Ariel flights' of song." Raymond Weaver, who used Stedman's articles and who interviewed Coan himself while writing his *Herman Melville*, was to go even further: "in the middle of his life," Melville "turned his back upon the world, and in his recoil from life absorbed himself in metaphysics."[25] But was philosophy—or religion—still the standard subject when Coan "repeatedly" visited Melville in New York? Whatever Coan may have told Stedman, his own article does not actually say this, and on the testimony of his statement to Weaver one might well draw a wholly negative inference, since Melville apparently had used his allusions to Plato only as a well-understood "signal for silence and leave-taking." If Titus Munson Coan had not gone to Pittsfield in 1859, or if his letter describing Melville's conversation at Arrowhead had not been preserved and published, the biographers of 1891 and 1921 might not have written so sweepingly about the whole tenor of Melville's last years. To say this is not to deny Melville's abiding interest in philosophy—we know from independent evidence that he was reading Schopenhauer in 1891—but simply to place their statements in perspective by recognizing the influence of Dr. Coan, whose first impression of Melville colored his view of the man for over sixty years.[26]

ARTHUR GRIFFIN STEDMAN (1859-1908)

Among Melville's principal biographers of the 1890's, the youngest, Arthur Stedman, first met Melville in 1888 when Stedman was twenty-nine and Melville sixty-nine, continued to visit him for something less than four years in New York, and served as his literary executor after Melville's death, when his widow needed the advice and assistance of a professional literary man. He was born in New York in 1859—the year of Titus Munson Coan's pilgrimage to Arrowhead. A graduate of Yale like his father, Stedman took his degree in 1881 and became his father's secretary during the following winter, going with him to Europe in the spring of 1882. For a time after his return he was on the staff of a Connecticut newspaper, the *Windham County Transcript*, but later returned to New York and continued in journalistic and literary work there, except for a period in London (1901-1905), until his death in 1908. Stedman never married. The first of his writings to attract attention, a sketch of Constance Fenimore Woolson written for the *Book Buyer* in 1889, was widely copied. Besides preparing the "Short Biographies" of the authors included in the Stedman-Hutchinson *Library of American Literature*, printed in the concluding volume of that anthology (1890), he also contributed biographical articles to the *Review of Reviews* and *Appleton's Annual Cyclopaedia;* all three publications were to carry his notices of Melville. In 1891, the year of Melville's death, Stedman received the degree of Master of Arts from Yale for his studies in literary biography.[27] For the Fiction, Fact, and Fancy Series that he edited for Charles L. Webster & Co., Mark Twain's firm and publishers of the *Library of American Literature*, he prepared a number of volumes, including *Merry Tales* by Mark Twain, *Selected Poems* by Walt Whitman, and *Autobiographia: The Story of a Life*, a collection of Whitman's prose. Like his father, Stedman knew Whitman as well as Melville, having visited him in Camden while preparing the two books of selections, and after the poet's death in 1892 he wrote the article on Whitman for *Appleton's Annual Cyclopaedia* as he wrote that on Melville the year before. The elder Stedman had discussed Whitman with Melville in 1888 (*Log*, II, 805-806); it seems probable that Whitman was also a topic of conversation after Arthur Stedman too began visiting at 104 East Twenty-Sixth Street during that same year.

Beyond mentioning his first interview with Melville, in his Introduction to *Typee* (1892), Arthur Stedman had virtually nothing to say in his various published articles about the personal relationship between them, which he described only as having grown into "a friendly family acquaintance"; the first visit, it will be recalled, was for the purpose of securing Melville's portrait for the *Library of American Literature*. Like others who knew the older Melville, he too emphasized "his unwillingness to speak of himself, his adventures, or his writings in conversation." Both Melville's own reticence and Stedman's circumspection have led Melville's later biographers to speculate about the nature of their association. "What was the staple of Stedman's conversation is not known," Raymond Weaver remarked in 1921.

> But despite the fact that Melville was to him a crabbed and darkly shadowed hieroglyph, he clung to Melville with a personal loyalty at once humorous and pathetic. Melville to him was the "man who lived with the cannibals," and merited canonisation because of this intimacy with unholy flesh. . . . The friendship between Petrarch and Boccaccio is hardly less humorous than the relationship between Melville and Stedman; and surely Melville has suffered more, in death, if not in life, from the perils of friendship than did Petrarch: more even than did Baudelaire from the damaging admiration of Gautier. When one's enemy writes a book, one's reputation is less likely to be jeopardised by literary animosity than it is by the best superlatives of self-appointed custodians of one's good name. . . . Critical biographers have contrived a method to hand themselves down to posterity through the gods of literature, as did the Roman emperors through the gods of Olympus—by taking the heads off their statues, and clapping on their own instead. Criticism is a perennial decapitation.[28]

Taking Weaver's remarks about Stedman as gratuitous, Laura Stedman Gould, co-author of the standard *Life and Letters of Edmund Clarence Stedman* (1910), was moved at some time in the 1920's to draft a ten-page manuscript that not only champions her uncle against Weaver but also defends her grandfather against the old charges of neglecting Melville and being ignorant of his true genius—the counts brought against him by implication during the 1880's by the visiting Scotsman Robert Buchanan. Mrs. Gould's manuscript, "Concerning Herman Melville and the Stedmans,"[29] begins with a reference to Melville that she had come across in her grandfather's correspondence (a comment already noticed here): his assertion that Melville, as one of New York's "strongest geniuses, & most impressive *personalities*," ought to be an honorary member of the Authors Club (*Log*, II, 823). This remark of 1890, Mrs. Gould felt, "refutes the ⟨challenge⟩ sweeping statement that all the critics were oblivious of his genius, and indifferent to this neglect" (p. 1). Her draft essay then continues as follows:

> To ⟨an h⟩ biog[rapher] . with ↑penetrating↓ historical acumen, it should be highly improbable that E.C.S., who was notorious for his ⟨prodigal⟩ missionary zeal, his prodigal and unselfish advocacy ↑reckless of his own

⟨literary [?]⟩ work ↓ of the cause of even very minor writers, should have failed to be aware of Melville's claim for attention, should have failed to try to drag him forth from his self-imposed and coddled seclusion and at least on one /notable/signal/noteworthy/ occasion he did not fail, for as Prof. [Frank Jewett] Mather ⟨rightly⟩ pointed out some years ago

—and at this place in the draft (p. 2) Mrs. Gould indicated her intention of introducing a quotation, undoubtedly Mather's assertion in an article of 1919 that shortly before Melville's death the elder Stedman, "the magnanimous poet-critic," had "managed a complimentary dinner for him and with difficulty got him to attend it" (*Log,* II, 831).

After a generous reference to her grandfather's friend R. H. Stoddard, who was "also aware of Melville's genius" but respected his "stern preference for being let alone," Mrs. Gould then came to her principal subject, her uncle's "keen discernment and wholehearted loyalty" as demonstrated by his friendship with Melville and his service both to Melville and later to his widow. Arthur Stedman, she affirmed, "was a member of his father's household" when the friendship began; he was in his father's confidence, was familiar with his opinions, and was directly associated with his literary enterprises—specifically, the *Library of American Literature.* It was while this anthology was in preparation, as she correctly remembered, that

Arthur successfully penetrated Melville's seclusion, the first password being his father's ⟨and his⟩ determination that ⟨he should⟩ Melville should be adequately[?] represented in this series. The friendship between the older and younger men grew fast, and made [many?] a↑n↓ ⟨night wa⟩ evening was passed in yarns over their tobacco. This friendship was enthusiastically encouraged by E. C. S., who long had considered *Moby Dick* especially an American classic, its tale often on his lips, and the recommendation by all odds to read it at once to nearly every young writer who sought his counsel. Whereas Melville ↑certainly↓ seems to have spurned any advances from such older leaders ↑perhaps classed as a whole with the old hurt↓ he was less unwilling to contend with Arthur recently from college, eager with youthful admiration, and ↑so↓ sufficiently removed from the generation which had ⟨grieved⟩ hurt him so grievously. . . . Moreover Arthur had the /infectious/contagious/appeal of being somewhat sad himself. He was ever too poignantly ⟨awed⟩ ↑dazzled↓ by his father's brilliant light /to trust/to perceive/his own. And the melancholy ↑strain↓ in each undoubtedly ⟨held⟩ fostered sympathy. Be the bond what it was, it was strong, and Arthur gave unstinted devotion to Melville in his lifetime, and proved it still more by aiding his widow in her ⟨[?]⟩ problems and by helping her with her husband's literary effects. (pp. 3-5)

In another of her unpublished manuscripts Mrs. Gould further described her uncle as being "deaf, sensitive, often fancying himself sought because of his father"—and this feeling, she added, was indeed "sometimes true." Recurring here to his relations with Melville, she commented further on Stedman's pleasure in Melville's reciprocal response.

> He no doubt delighted in the fact that here was one friend who wanted him
> entirely for himself, and who aslso [also] admirably understood Arthur's own
> moods of depression, his dislike of crowds, his innate desire for solitude.
> And Melville was his very own, whom he did not have to share. For Arthur's
> more scintillating father had an inescapable way of attracting all comers to
> himself. I rather think it tickled Arthur, and was of immense satisfaction,
> that even his father did not have the entree to Melville's affections that he
> himself had. . . . For Arthur was modest, easily abashed; but he was sought,
> and with his own charm of scholarship, and with the advantages that surround-
> ed him, it lay in his power to offer a friendship that b[e] side the stimulating
> quality that ⟨ [?] ⟩ the admiration of a younger man can give, had its advant-
> ages for Melville, who ⟨ however great he w[a] s ⟩ despite his greatness had
> walled himself in from the friendships that would have made his days less
> solitary. . . .

The younger Stedman "used to like to smoke with Melville, and reminisce,"
she continued—without mentioning any specific topics of their reminiscence.
In addition to his "invaluable aid" to Melville's widow, "Arthur was undoubtedly able to do as much for M[elville]. and was in quite as distinguished a position
as that of some of his latter-day discoverers"—Mrs. Gould presumably meant
Weaver in particular. "And the greater credit goes to those who champion when
the cause is less popular."[30]
Even if one makes allowance for Mrs. Gould's natural partiality toward her
uncle and grandfather, her comments have an obvious value, not merely as a
counterbalance to Weaver's denigration of Arthur Stedman but as a character-
ization of the man by one who knew him directly, as Weaver apparently did
not. Mrs. Gould reflects the family sensitivity to Buchanan's earlier remarks
about her grandfather, already expressed with feeling by her uncle in the
articles he had published following Melville's death. What she says of E. C.
Stedman's regard for Melville and for *Moby-Dick* is striking: he "seemed never
to let an opportunity slip to feature Melville in his conversation (indeed he was
a household name)," though "he as regularly referred to him as *Arthur's friend.*"
If his son "had not been there" to write about Melville after his death, she
maintained, "E.C.S. would not have failed" to pay written tribute; but "E.C.S.'s
sensitive honor" forbade his trespassing "upon literary ground which he felt
preempted by another"—especially if that person was his own son (pp. 6-7).
In a letter to Mrs. Melville written in February of 1892 Stedman had acknowledged "the confidence which you have placed in my son—whose warm
feelings toward you . . . are very evident to us," and spoken of his own
"positive affection and reverence for your gifted husband—a man of noble
genius, a most original and independent man, if there ever was one."[31] Stedman's

sentiments as he expressed them to Mrs. Melville are in keeping with Mrs.
Gould's recollections. As for the younger Stedman, given his niece's sympathetic interpretation of his personality as she recalled it at least eighteen years
after his death, her comments again have the ring of truth—though it may certainly be questioned whether Arthur Stedman in later life, as she most probably
remembered him, was still the Arthur Stedman of twenty years earlier who had
smoked and talked with Herman Melville. Mrs. Gould's interpretation of Melville's side of the friendship, necessarily colored by what she had heard from
her grandfather and uncle, may of course be over-generous. One speculative
point that she might well have introduced turns on the repeated suggestion that
Melville's isolation in New York was related to the death of a son—Malcolm in
1867 or Stanwix in 1886; the one was ten years older than Arthur Stedman,
the other eight. As Melville, by Stedman's own account, took pleasure in the
visits of his grandchildren during these last years, so too must he have enjoyed
the company of a younger man, a writer, whom he perhaps regarded as surro-
gate for his own lost sons.

   What Mrs. Gould says about her uncle's assistance to Melville's widow is more
than supported by the record—especially the grateful letters he received over
the years from Mrs. Melville, which had come into his niece's possession after
his death and which are still preserved among the Stedman papers. Immediately
following Melville's funeral, Arthur Stedman had begun a systematic campaign
to revive and enhance his dead friend's nearly forgotten literary reputation,
using his professional knowledge of the literary marketplace and enlisting both
his own literary associates and Melville's English correspondents in furthering
his program. The intention was two-fold: to bring Melville's name repeatedly
before the public through discussion in newspapers and periodicals; to continue
sparking that discussion by the reissue of major works that could be sent out
for review. Whether these ideas originated with Stedman himself or with Mrs.
Melville is not clear, but certainly he had her full concurrence in what he set
out to do, as their correspondence clearly attests. By November of 1891, when
the American campaign was already well advanced, Mrs. Melville's receipt of a
letter from Henry S. Salt disclosed that similar plans were in the making in
England: Salt requested information about Melville that could be used in an
introduction to a new edition of his works, which an English publisher wished
to reissue in the Camelot Series. Replying for Mrs. Melville on 17 November,
Stedman endeavored to acknowledge Salt's expression of sympathy for her
loss, to provide the information requested, and at the same time, while encouraging the English project, to forestall possible competition between the
English and American editions of Melville.

   Stedman's long letter to Salt, a key document for its revelation of these plans
and his own role in them, deserves generous quotation.[32] It begins by saying
that when Mrs. Melville had received Salt's letter on the previous day and read

his request for information about her husband, she

> sent for me at once (I having had charge of his ⟨publishing⟩ ↑literary↓ affairs since his death). I visited her this afternoon, and it seemed best that I should write you a line at once in her place, in order to catch tomorrow's steamer.
>
> Mrs. Melville desires me to say in the first place that you do not seem like a stranger to her. She enjoyed, with her husband, your former correspondence with the latter, and she feels grateful to you for all you have done for her husband's reputation (in articles, etc.) and for what you propose to do. She asks me to thank you most sincerely for your kind expression of sympathy.
>
> By the *next* steamer . . . I shall send you three or four recent articles on Melville which I trust will furnish you with the information you desire. Since Mr. Melville's death I have written & published *five* ↑(5)↓ articles on him, of which I shall send you three. You are at liberty to use any of the material, provided you do not follow my text too closely!

Stedman mentions elsewhere in the letter that he had already written W. Clark Russell, providing him with "some ten articles ↑on Melville↓ (my own & others)" and "suggesting that he write an article himself for an English periodical." Russell had replied without committing himself, saying only that "the notices in ⟨England⟩ ↑English↓ papers were very meagre & few"; though Stedman was as yet unaware of it, Russell was in fact preparing an essay, though not for an English publication. (His article, "A Claim for American Literature," appearing in the *North American Review*, 154 [February 1892], 138–149, credits "an admirable account" of Melville "by Mr. Arthur Stedman" as its source of biographical information.) In America, Stedman was pleased to inform Salt, the recent articles on Melville have been "long & numerous." In whatever Salt himself might write for an English audience there should be one departure from his earlier article on Melville in the *Scottish Art Review*, which had alluded to Robert Buchanan's old charges that Melville had been neglected—Stedman was of course thinking of the implied slur at his father.

> I hope you will do away with Buchanan's misstatement as to Melville's neglect by brother writers here. As in Whitman's case it is a LIE! You will see what I have said on this subject in my sketches.

As Stedman explained—confidentially, he noted—to Salt, the United States Book Company of New York had already engaged to issue, "after New Year's," four volumes by Melville: " 'Typee,' 'Omoo,' 'The Whale,' & 'White-Jacket' (Melville's best books) "; as it turned out, the first of the books would not appear until September of 1892. Meanwhile, Stedman had "written & published" his own five articles as a contribution to the hoped-for revival of Melville's fame, beginning with "Herman Melville's Funeral" in the New York *Tribune* on 1 October 1891 and continuing with " 'Marquesan' Melville" in the New

York *World* on 11 October and "Melville of Marquesas" in the November number of *Review of Reviews;* the third piece, as Stedman's letter remarks, contains an allusion to Salt's earlier article on Melville. These are presumably the three essays that Stedman forwarded to Salt; the other two items of the five were probably reprints in the *Critic*, which had republished all of "Herman Melville's Funeral" and most of " 'Marquesan' Melville." What articles besides his own he may have sent to Clark Russell is not known, but one of them was surely the long general review of Melville's life and works that the Stedmans' friend Stoddard had published in the New York *Mail and Express* on 8 October; it too was excerpted in the *Critic*, which had evidently been enlisted in the campaign. Dr. Coan's article for the Boston *Literary World*, which appeared in the following month, may well have been written at Stedman's prompting, but J. E. A. Smith's biographical sketch, which began appearing on 27 October, certainly needed no active encouragement from either Stedman or Mrs. Melville.

During the early months of 1892, in addition to other editorial responsibilities for Webster's Fiction, Fact, and Fancy Series, Stedman was preparing the four Melville volumes for their American publication. In the text of *Typee* he made numerous editorial revisions, describing some of them in his Introduction as being "by written direction of the author" although the memorandum he was referring to is actually in Mrs. Melville's hand. With the consent of Melville's family, he explained, he had shortened "the long and cumbrous sub-title" of *Typee*, and assisted by Dr. Coan, with his knowledge of Pacific languages, he had "harmonised" the spelling of foreign words in *Typee* and *Omoo*.[33] Meanwhile, drawing on his earlier articles for material and making significant revisions and additions, he had also prepared his article on Melville for *Appleton's Annual Cyclopædia* and submitted a proof of it to Mrs. Melville, who on 18 March acknowledged its receipt, praised it as "admirably comprehensive and well done," and requested one correction of a date.[34] This article in turn became the basis for the biographical section of Stedman's Introduction to *Typee*, which is dated "June, 1892." On 4 May he had written again to Salt about Salt's article on Melville in the current *Eclectic Magazine* (evidently placed there by Stedman), saying that "we may congratulate ourselves" on its publication: such an essay should "be very helpful" to the forthcoming volumes. Stedman confessed himself to be "very much driven" by the pressure of recent events related to the new edition of Melville.

As I wrote you, the plates of "Typee" were one-half completed when the printing house where they were made was destroyed by fire. I supplied copy for the resetting sometime ago, and I now have received word that the plates are completed and [John W.] Lovell [president of the United States Book Company] is waiting for my Introduction. I have returned him word immediately that he can have my Introduction when I have passed upon the proofs of "Typee" which it was formerly agreed I should see. I have seen no such proofs at all. Mr. Lovell wrote me personally that my view of the matter was just, and that he would obtain the proofs and have them sent to me. That was four days ago and I have not yet received them. The edition of Melville's works is advertised to the extent of half a page in this month's "Century Magazine"; and in the same number you will see the two pages of Melville's poems selected from "Timoleon", his last little book, with an introductory note by myself.

The May number of the *Century*, as Stedman indicated, carried five "Poems by Herman Melville"—"Art," "Monody," "The Night-March," "The Weaver," and "Lamia's Song" (XLIV, 104–105); the introductory note has Stedman's by-line. As for *Omoo*, planned to appear with *Typee*, the printers had already received a copy, he told Salt, "and I suppose they are working on it."[35]

The cumulative delays in production were annoying and embarrassing to Mrs. Melville, who had expected the books to be available by the time of her summer visit to Pittsfield. "You can imagine how it would be," she wrote Stedman from there on 17 August, "among my husband's old townsmen who are so proud of him," since the books had already been advertised in the *Century*. The difficulties of seeing the books through the press—a familiar problem during her husband's lifetime—had left Stedman "prostrated," as he had told her; "you ought not to have so much mental strain," she replied, "but I well know how it is."[36] Both *Typee* and *Omoo* finally appeared in September, their sale being so great during the first week that the publishers immediately ordered a second printing; *White-Jacket* and *Moby-Dick* followed later in the fall.[37] The fullest notice of the new edition, that in the Philadelphia *Evening Bulletin*, was reprinted in the November *Literary News* (XII, 338). Its author had less to say of Melville's writing than of his "chosen obscurity" during his last years in New York, where he "was known to Mr. E. C. Stedman and his family and a few others, but he could never be tempted from his retirement into the active literary groups." The publishers of this new edition, the reviewer continued,

have entrusted the editorial care of the work to Mr. Arthur Stedman. Mr. Stedman's familiarity with the bibliography of older American authors is very well known, and was most judiciously exercised in his co-editorial position upon the *Library of American Literature*. He has now undertaken a labor of love, beside one requiring all the skill at his command, and in his introduction to this first volume of the series, he has shown a wide familiarity with his subject, excellent literary judgment and a regard for Melville's memory which must necessarily have grown out of intercourse with a character at once so reserved and so nobly endowed. Mr. Stedman's introduction is a model of condensation. He omits no essential point in his author's long life, yet gives the record in the brief space of a score of pages.

"It is good to think that we are once more to have a complete edition of this author's best books," the friendly review concluded, "and that the work has been entrusted to such sympathetic hands." This comment was probably among the various notices that Stedman collected and sent to Mrs. Melville, who was understandably "pleased . . . that they are all so favorable," as she replied.[38]

Meanwhile, arrangements for G. P. Putnam's Sons to issue the same four titles in England had also been delayed because the London house of John Murray claimed continuing English rights to *Typee* and *Omoo* under terms of its original publishing agreements of 1846 and 1847. On 21 October 1892 the United States Book Company asked Stedman for a report on Murray's claims; he replied on the 24th with a well-informed account of Melville's dealings with his London publishers, noting that he had "not consulted Mrs. Melville in this matter. . . . As I have examined Mr. Melville's papers very thoroughly since his death, I really know more about these matters than she does."[39] The publisher had also mentioned the possibility of adding a fifth title to its selection of Melville's works, *Israel Potter;* Stedman agreed to "investigate," and on 21 December expressed his willingness to "do whatever the . . . firm asks of me, and gladly. I suppose its issue will depend in a measure on the success of the other books."[40] Both Stedman and Mrs. Melville had been dissatisfied with the original agreement presented to her by the United States Book Company; on 12 December, when a revised contract was finally drawn up that they agreed was suitable, she signed it.[41] On 27 January 1893, following a careful re-reading of *Typee*, she wrote Stedman about possible corrections in case of a "second edition" of the new text: "a few very slight amendments and one important addition—the dedication to my father which I am very sorry was omitted."[42] An unexpected development foreclosed this possibility, however, when the United States Book Company was placed in receivership, mismanagement by its officers being blamed for its inability to meet the demands of creditors.

This new turn of events brought a prompt response from Stedman. On 31 January, the day after the receivership was announced, he secured for Mrs. Melville's records a memorandum assuring her "that her interest and the books of Mr Melville will in no way suffer by the alteration in the U. S. Book Co.'s affairs." He had also requested the receiver to "see that the plates run no risk of unworthy disposal or destruction." As Stedman conjectured to Mrs. Melville, "the whole row-de-dow" had been "got up to oust Mr. Lovell," the president of the firm; for "a complete history of the case" he referred her to a story in the morning *World.*[43] The newspaper had quoted an unnamed "Wall street broker" as saying that "Over a year ago the corporation was absolutely free from debt, . . . the biggest and best publishing-house in the world, on a

S.L.CLEMENS.

FRED.J.HALL.

Charles L. Webster & Co., Publishers,

Personal Memoirs of Gen't U.S. Grant,
Personal Memoirs of Gen't P.H. Sheridan,
Personal Memoirs of Gen't W.T. Sherman,
Library of American Literature,
Great War Library.

Mark Twain's Works,
Miscellaneous Publications.

67 Fifth Avenue,
NEAR 14 TH ST.

CABLE ADDRESS
"PUBLISHERS"

New York Jan. 31ˢᵗ 1893

My dear Mr. Melville,

I stepped into the Book Co. this morning, & got this memorandum.

I have told Mr. Hurd that we would like to have him see that the plates run no risk of unworthy disposal or destruction.

I think the whole row-dedow has been got up to oust Mr. Lovell, if you will pardon the homely expression.

Ever sincerely,
Arthur Stedman

See this morning's "World" for a complete history of the case.

The one known surviving letter from Arthur Stedman to Elizabeth Shaw Melville, 31 January 1893 (Melville Collection, Harvard College Library, by permission of the Harvard College Library).

sound financial basis"; now all was lost. Having read the newspaper account, which is long and detailed, Mrs. Melville concluded that *Typee* and "all the books" might well be "in great peril."

> It would be hard indeed if after all your labor, the plates should fall into un-worthy hands, or be destroyed—I could hardly be reconciled to that, for the desire of my heart has been to see my husband's books resurrected, as it were, to call forth as they have begun to do, the recognition which their birthright might reasonably claim—I do not know what I can do about it now but feel that I can rely on your continued interest to keep an eye on the plates and advise me should any action on my part be necessary to avert so dire a calamity as their destruction— . . . I shall carefully preserve the memorandum you enclosed—[44]

Despite Mrs. Melville's uneasiness about their possible destruction, the plates of the four volumes of the 1892 edition proved to be remarkably durable, for after they finally passed into the hands of the Publishers Plate Renting Company in 1900 they were repeatedly used by "a long succession of publishers," as the Northwestern-Newberry editors remark.[45] But the difficulties of the moment caused an interruption of Mrs. Melville's royalty payments and—more important to her—seemed to have ended the campaign to keep Melville's name before the American public. The London edition of these same four volumes, which appeared later in 1892, drew favorable notices from the English press, but at home a major financial crisis was impending that brought a stock market crash in June, the failure of hundreds of banks, and the closing of thousands of other businesses. Among the bankruptcies, in April of 1894, was the publishing firm with which Arthur Stedman had been associated, Charles L. Webster & Co.—weighed down, it is said, by such unprofitable ventures as the Stedman-Hutchinson *Library of American Literature.*[46] In 1894-95 Arthur Stedman was the New York correspondent of the fortnightly *Dial,* published in Chicago, and during this period there were few visits or even exchanges of letters with Mrs. Melville. She preferred "our new edition" of *Typee* and *Omoo* to the English printing, she told Stedman in January of 1894; in the following June, when thanking him for "the copies of your letter in 'The Dial' that you kindly sent me some time ago," she wrote that

> I did not think the whole year would pass without seeing you here, but I can understand—as perhaps few can so well, the absorption of a busy literary man. . . . I need not again express the pleasure it gives me to see or hear from you, but absent or silent you believe, I hope, that I am always your grateful friend.[47]

Stedman was consulted in 1896 when the receivers of the United States Book Company proposed issuing "high class paper editions" of the four titles, which according to Mrs. Melville "had a very good sale."[48] Her only surviving letter to him between 1894 and her death in 1906 was in reply to his request for use of selections from Melville's poetry in E. C. Stedman's *An American Anthology* (1900); in consenting she sent "kind regards" to the elder Stedman and "grateful remembrance" to his son.[49] This may have been their final communication.

From October of 1901 until September of 1905 the younger Stedman was in London, representing the Book Lovers' Library and writing letters on literary matters for American newspapers. He returned to New York following the death of his mother there, but apparently did not resume his visits with Mrs. Melville prior to her death in 1906. There were other deaths within his own family; his brother died in 1906 and his father in January of 1908; one of Arthur Stedman's few compositions in verse, a memorial ode, was published in the New York *Tribune* after his father's death. Arthur Stedman himself died in New York on 16 September 1908, having been ill for some time with Bright's disease. That his last years were unhappy ones is strongly suggested by his letter of 28 February 1906 to Salt, who had written him from England to bring up an old subject: a possible Life of Melville.

> It seems odd that I should have passed four years of my life in London and you should not have heard of it, nor *I* have been sufficiently free from worry over the problem of living to reach beyond London for "outlanders" like you. Perhaps I should have got to work looking up provincial friends, if I had not found those in London to whom I had been helpful all those years, so cold & discouraging during my starving period by the Thames.
>
> It was not until the beginning of last year that I began to be a little easier financially, & I was just about to take a holiday in July, conscious of the ownership of a little flat-full of furniture and of £20 in the P[ost].O[ffice]., when my Mother died, & left me a little legacy, poor soul, thus setting me free (she could not touch it before).
>
> So you see why you did not hear from me.
>
> —If I meditated a life of Melville, it passed out of my mind long ago. I do not know whether his widow is still living. As I look back, it seems to me that there would be little to tell outside of his books. After they petered out, he made his life a merely mechanical affair, you remember, & shut himself away from all events and associations. I don't believe a life would be worth while—though, if the English, or American, Men of Letters editors made me an offer for such a work, I should consider it (on a cash basis).
>
> Glad to have heard from you. Glad, too, I didn't trouble you over there. "I dare say" you are not in a position to distribute patronage, & that would have been a probable reason for my communicating with you while in London—but, as I say, there was "nothing doing" in that line where I might really have expected it.[50]

The idea of a Life of Melville was again presented to Stedman later in 1906. Some six months after his letter to Salt, his father received a request from Frank Jewett Mather, Jr., then associated with the New York *Evening Post* but later a distinguished professor of art and archaeology at Princeton. Referring to the recent death of Mrs. Melville, Mather explained that he had "made several efforts to meet her, using the introduction you kindly gave, but always missed her"; could Stedman now, before the dispersal or destruction of her memorials of her husband, write their daughter Elizabeth "asking what biographical materials are extant, suggesting, if you see fit, that letters should be given to a public library or otherwise preserved?" The elder Stedman responded on 28 September —the anniversary of Melville's death—with the requested letter to Miss Melville, enclosing what Mather had written and explaining that he would ask Mather

> to confer with my son, Arthur Stedman, who edited and wrote the preface to an edition of your Father's principal romances. Doubtless you will soon hear from either my son or Mr. Mather upon the subject. . . . I fully share Mr. Mather's estimate of your Father's genius and of the great importance of preserving everything that is related to it. . . .[51]

Mather himself subsequently talked directly with Miss Melville about her father and arranged to have at least two of Melville's English correspondents, Salt and James Billson, send her copies of the letters they had received from him.[52] Mather also had recourse to published appeals for other materials to be sent to Miss Melville, leading the firm of G. P. Putnam's Sons, which had brought out the London edition of *Typee, Omoo, White-Jacket* and *Moby-Dick,* to write her on the assumption that she herself had a Life of her father in mind.[53] What her reply may have been is not known. To Mather she had promised the use of all her papers for his projected Life "except Melville's letters to his wife," according to Mather's later account, and with "high hopes" he wrote to Houghton, Mifflin and Company in Boston, "the American publisher whose list is heaviest with our classics," proposing "a modest biography in one volume." In late November of 1906 he received a reply signed by Ferris Greenslet, who was then beginning his career as a Houghton Mifflin editor, reporting that "the proper authorities" in the firm "do not feel very sanguine over the possibility of making a publishing success of the life of Melville, interesting as is his personality and admirable as is his work." Consequently, they were declining both Mather's projected book and a similar proposal from another unnamed writer, on the ground that "the interest of the American reading public in Melville is scarcely sufficient to warrant them in undertaking a biography."[54] Discouraged by this response, Mather abandoned his project; whether he had applied to the Putnam firm, or even knew of its overture to Miss Melville, he did not say. Thus in 1906 Arthur Stedman, with but two more years to live, had no real interest in writing again on Melville. Mather's hopes had been dashed, and the first full-length Life was still fifteen years in the future.

If Mather consulted with Arthur Stedman before seeing Miss Melville, as the elder Stedman had suggested, there is no known record of their conversation. But in any discussion of a possible biography of her father, Stedman would have assured Mather that there would be no competitor in the field as far as he himself was concerned: "If I meditated a life of Melville," in the words of his letter to Salt, "it passed out of my mind long ago"—by October of 1892, presumably, for it was then that he told Dr. Coan there was "no further chance" of his "writing any thing more about Melville." Would he also have warned Mather that in his judgment a full-scale Life would not be "worth while"—except "on a cash basis," of course, should some publishing house happen to propose it—because there was so "little to tell" about Melville "outside of his books"? To the present-day student, contemplating the five-foot shelf of book-length studies, biographical and otherwise, that has accumulated since Weaver's biography of 1921, the question seems not merely ironic but downright ridiculous. But the issue was real enough in 1906, as Mather's own inquiries to publishers of the day were soon to make plain: there would be no outlet for a Life of Melville even if he wrote one. Melville himself, with another kind of book, had faced the same problem with publishers of an earlier period: "What I feel most moved to write," as he complained to Hawthorne at the time of *Moby-Dick*, "that is banned,—it will not pay" (*Letters*, p. 128). Had Arthur Stedman, like Mather, once been "moved" to write a book-length Life? Had he made similar overtures within the publishing world of which he was a part, late in 1891 or early in 1892, and received a negative reply? If he indeed "meditated" such a project but never took it to a publisher, were there other considerations to discourage him from carrying it to completion? Of his possible dealings with a publisher no evidence has come to light, but his own attitude toward a biography is a subject that admits further discussion.

Of the three biographers of the nineties whose work is examined here, Stedman was clearly the best equipped for such a further "labor of love"—as the Philadelphia reviewer had called his work on the Melville edition of 1892—had he wanted to undertake it. He was still a young man, though with considerable experience and recognized ability as a literary biographer; he had known Melville himself, become his literary executor with access to his papers, and maintained the confidence of his widow. All of these considerations were highly favorable. But perhaps Stedman's interest had simply run its course, once the four volumes comprising the new edition were finally published after many delays. Since negotiations for their appearance had begun, within the month following Melville's death, he had invested more than a year of protracted work, first writing his own series of biographical essays while soliciting additional notices from others, then laboring over the texts of *Typee* and its successors, and meanwhile struggling continually with the publisher, whether about a suitable agreement for Mrs. Melville to sign or over missing proofs needed to complete his own part of the project. There were other pressures and frustrations during the year 1892. Walt Whitman died on 26 March just as Stedman's new volume of selections from Whitman's prose was also nearing publication;

the times were becoming harder as the year progressed, and the prospects of the troubled Webster company were increasingly uncertain. And still another factor must be recognized: Stedman's conviction that Melville's life story was to be found virtually complete in his own writings would have proved inhibiting, possibly altogether fatal, to any intention of producing a biography longer than his essentially journalistic essays of 1891 or even his Introduction to the 1892 *Typee.* Such a conviction, made explicit in his letter to Salt in 1906, is already visible between the lines of the earlier biographical sketches.

Sharing to some degree the long-standing assumption that Melville began as an autobiographical writer and should have remained one, Stedman thus felt little call to seek out possible new information through which to test the veracity of *Typee, Omoo, Redburn,* and *White-Jacket* as supposedly authentic reports of their author's own experience. While writing " 'Marquesan' Melville" and "Melville of Marquesas" in October of 1891, he had the use of photographs from Mrs. Melville's collection and access to her file of Melville's agreements with publishers, as illustrations accompanying the articles and allusions within them attest; this was just at the time when the new edition was being contracted for and questions of copyright needed to be settled—especially when there were plans for exporting unbound sheets to London for a concurrent English edition. Additional information came from Mrs. Melville, along with possible suggestions and criticisms, through conversation when he visited her residence and possibly through written notes similar to the biographical portions of her personal memoranda. Specific examples of such information are certain dates appearing in the articles which were not widely known outside the family, the amount of salary Melville had received when he once taught school as a young man, the acknowledgment that Henry A. Smythe had secured his appointment as Inspector of Customs, and the like. Otherwise, Stedman at the outset depended either on his previous research—for example, a minor error in dating is carried over from his biographical sketch in the *Library of American Literature*—or consulted standard reference works. The 1852 edition of *The Men of the Time* was among Melville's own books; familiar phrasing turns up in the narrative section of Stedman's articles, recognizable to close readers of the Duyckincks' *Cyclopædia* and J. E. A. Smith's 1879 *Taghconic.*

As a biographer, Stedman thus summed up the record as it was known in the nineties rather than challenging its limitations and what are now recognized as its outright errors—notably the dating of Melville's first voyage and the supposed length of his sojourn among the Typees. As a critic, Stedman similarly reflected the taste of his age as represented by more celebrated men such as his father and Richard Henry Stoddard; like them, he set more store by Melville's writings than did many American critics of the day, but in his articles he nevertheless resorted to citations from other writers about Melville's achievement and stature rather than advancing new judgments of his own. Besides introducing the comments of contemporaries such as Stoddard and the British writers—Buchanan, Russell, and Salt—Stedman also went back to the older criticism, which he found by no means uncongenial. Fortified by Dr. Coan's emphasis on Melville's philosophical interests, he repeated the old charges that metaphysical speculation had been Melville's downfall in the 1850's. Fitz-James O'Brien's admonition to Melville to change his ways, published in *Putnam's Monthly* in 1853, is mentioned in "Melville of Marquesas"; Stedman had probably read it in the Melville or Stedman files of the magazine. His other references to early reviews of Melville's books, particularly those in foreign periodicals like *Blackwood's*, were probably garnered from an intermediate source, most likely Allibone's *Critical Dictionary*. Here again there is little evidence to suggest that Stedman was breaking new ground. Like the Duyckincks among the older writers and even Salt in the nineties, he was inclined to prefer *Typee* to *Moby-Dick*, despite Russell's published encomiums of *Moby-Dick* and his own father's enthusiasm for it. He also liked certain of the short stories, but wrote of *Mardi* and especially of *Pierre* as regrettable mistakes that were harmful to the progress of Melville's career; *Israel Potter* and *The Confidence-Man*, he thought, "do not seem to require criticism." Encouraged by Stoddard and possibly by his father, Stedman had come to appreciate Melville's shorter poetry but apparently not *Clarel*, which he does not discuss and may not even have read. He mentions the privately printed *John Marr* and *Timoleon* but takes no cognizance of other literary work done in Melville's last years that was left unpublished at the time of his death. His most recent compositions, according to "Melville of Marquesas," had been written chiefly "for his own amusement." Stedman presumably meant such verse as "his last little poem, the touching 'Return of the Sire de Nesle' " —the concluding piece of *Timoleon;* in later essays he again referred to this poem as Melville's last. (Here Stedman may have been making an inference from its position in the *Timoleon* volume: in presenting him with a copy, Mrs. Melville referred to it as containing Melville's "last lines": see the inscription as reproduced below.) That Melville might in fact have written still later verse, or prose, Stedman nowhere suggests. Unless he was simply unaware of the body of late manuscripts, it seems strange that he did not mention or quote other verse—from "Weeds and Wildings" in particular—in any of his essays. And in view of his expressed conviction that new publications are the key to sustaining public interest in an author, it is strange too that as Melville's literary executor he did not prepare *Billy Budd* for publication, either in one of the magazines like *Harper's* or the *Century* or as a separate volume, since Melville himself would presumably have wanted to see it in print, with *John Marr* and *Timoleon*, if he had lived. Did Stedman ever examine the *Billy Budd* manuscript? If he did, was he baffled by Melville's cabalistic hand—which Mrs. Melville could of course have helped him to interpret if both were so inclined? Or did Stedman, with his penchant for Melville's

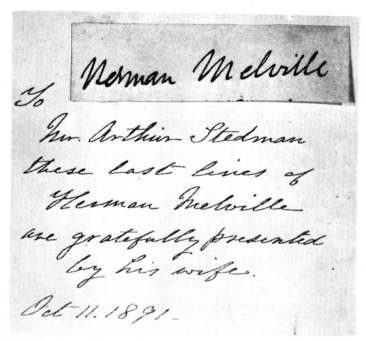

Mrs. Melville's inscription to Arthur Stedman in a presentation copy of Melville's *Timoleon* (1891). The cutting inscribed "Herman Melville" is from an addressed envelope; the full inscription would have read "Mrs. Herman Melville". The volume is now in the Yale Collection of American Literature, Beinecke Rare Book and Manuscript Library, Yale University. (By permission of the Yale University Library.)

autobiographical writings, simply pass it over as a piece of minor historical fiction, more suitable for Clark Russell than for Melville, or too "rugged and mystical" for *Typee*-lovers to enjoy? We shall probably never know.

After 1893, Stedman seems to have drifted away from Mrs. Melville, thus lessening the possibility of his working with the late manuscripts had there been any consideration of preparing some of them for publication. No letters from Stedman to Mrs. Melville later than that year survive; what she wrote to him continued to express her warm regard without making further claims upon him. As Stedman grew older, he apparently changed somewhat from the young admirer who had smoked with Melville and the professional literary man who had then worked with his widow in a gallant attempt to resurrect Melville's forgotten books and restore his fame. By 1906, as he pictured himself to Salt, he had become poor in purse, in health, and in spirit. If Mrs. Gould, who must have remembered him most clearly from these later years, was generous in estimating her uncle, Raymond Weaver was surely too harsh; Arthur Stedman was never the monster he is made out to be in Weaver's account. On the evidence of his own handling of both the man and the works, the full-length Life of Melville that he may once have meditated should probably not be regarded as a major loss to Melville studies; Stedman was a man of his time, and the time was not right either to produce or to accept a major work of revaluation. What was most immediately needed in the nineties was a new edition of Melville's principal works that would bring them again before the public and keep them in print and available. Despite the ill luck that befell the edition of 1892 at the outset, this is exactly what Stedman provided. As the Northwestern-Newberry editors of Melville have recently pointed out, noting the many later reprintings from its plates, "perhaps more people have read *Typee* in this edition than any other."[55] If they have read Stedman's Introduction as well, what they have found in it is a summation of more than forty years of published discussion of Melville. Among the biographical sketches, beginning with that of *The Men of the Time* in 1852, it stands as the best short Life written in the nineteenth century.

"THE BELATED FUNERAL FLOWER"

In the first of Stedman's articles after Melville's death, the account of his funeral published in the New York *Tribune,* occurs one of the few glimpses of Melville himself to appear anywhere in the younger man's essays. "He was always a great reader," Stedman wrote,

> and was much interested in collecting engravings of the old masters, having a large library and a fine assortment of prints, those of Claude's paintings being his favorite.
> His tall, stalwart figure, until recently, could be seen almost daily tramping through the Fort George district or Central Park, his roving inclination leading him to obtain as much out-door life as possible. His evenings were spent at home with his books, his pictures and his family, and usually with them alone.

In his second article, " 'Marquesan' Melville," Stedman added these words:

> A few friends felt at liberty to visit the recluse and were kindly welcomed, but he himself sought no one. His favorite companions were his grandchildren, with whom he delighted to pass his time, and his devoted wife, who was a constant assistant and adviser in his work. . . .

What Stedman says at the outset in these passages has been independently confirmed through studies of Melville's reading and his collection of books, engravings, and prints, many of which survive. From the manuscripts of his last years, with their clear indication that Mrs. Melville had been acting as her husband's amanuensis and perhaps at times as his friendly critic, we know too that Stedman had reason to call her Melville's "assistant and adviser." Finally we have the words of two of the four grandchildren about Melville himself, with his "brave and striking figure as he walked erect, head thrown back, cane in hand, inconspicuously dressed in a dark blue suit and a soft black felt hat," bound for Madison Square with Frances or to Central Park, "the Mecca" of most of his pilgrimages with Eleanor. "I am sure he took great comfort and pleasure in his grandchildren," Frances Thomas Osborne has affirmed, "and he showed a side of his nature to us that no one else knew he possessed."

Both the granddaughters have written vividly of their recollections of the house on Twenty-Sixth Street and those who lived in it; both mention a number of the same household objects and family customs. Frances, the younger, was fearful of the statues and paintings, though she liked to play among the books. She "never felt the least bit afraid" of Melville himself, however, despite his reputation among the family for "moods and occasional uncertain tempers." Her elder sister recalled that at long intervals "his interest in his grandchildren led him to cross the river and take the suburban train to East Orange, where we lived. . . . When he had had enough . . . he would suddenly rise and take the next train back to Hoboken." As she remembered, or perhaps was told, "he felt his grandchildren would turn against him as they grew older. He used to forebode as much." Eleanor was between nine and ten when "this quite special grandfather" died. During the next year, 1892, her grandmother sold the Twenty-Sixth Street house, and with her unmarried daughter Elizabeth— "Aunt Bessie" to the girls—moved into the Florence at 105 East Eighteenth Street. The Florence, as Eleanor Melville Thomas Metcalf recalled it sixty years later, was

an old-fashioned, high-studded apartment house with a spacious, darkly wooded, black-marble-pillared, crimson-carpeted dining room, where excellent meals were served to them at their own table by a faithful "Joe." Elizabeth and her crippled daughter were relieved of all further household worries and cares.

Elizabeth's main care now was for her husband's fame, but her intimate interest in all family concerns continued undiminished. Her grandchildren's memory of her is warm. She was humbly proud of their imagined gifts and attributes. And her son-in-law gave her the devotion of his own warm, sympathetic nature. When her trials were over, no one could hint that her life would be easier (and therefore happier). Indeed, one of her in-laws tried to; but an almost fierce pride that she had been Herman's wife silenced the imprudent tongue. A pride in his work and fame, which she had always cherished, grew further from this personal loyalty, and was the beginning of her inducting me into the service of him she had served so faithfully.[56]

Mrs. Metcalf's book of 1953, *Herman Melville: Cycle and Epicycle,* gathers many family letters, including those of her grandmother, which present Melville as revealed "by his contemporaries in his personal relations" (p. x)—an aspect virtually undisclosed in the carefully circumscribed writings of Stedman and Smith. Mrs. Melville's letters in particular, like those of Evert Duyckinck in the 1850's, show more of Melville than what either she or Duyckinck set down for the record—in her case, not in print but in private memoranda written for her own use and that of her family. Her jottings, entered in a well-worn "Pocket Diary," contain much miscellaneous information having nothing to do with Melville himself though serving to bring out much of her own sense of family and of family continuity. Thus she records in the first of the surviving entries—106 pages have been torn out and other entries erased—the numbers assigned by the photographer to two portraits of her daughter and the serial numbers of two of her bank books. Next in sequence, if not in time, comes this paragraph on the volumes Stedman had edited:

> A new edition of Typee, Omoo, Moby Dick, & White Jacket having been published in 1892—by Mr. Arthur Stedman—I received in royalties from the U[nited]. S[tates]. Book Co. and afterwards from the Am[erican]. Pub-[lishers]. Corporation both of whom failed $243.40—owing me $158.13 which was never paid. Then a new edition was published in 1900 from the rented plates—by Dana Estes & Co Boston—from which on a 5 p[e]r c[en]t royalty I have received $63.47—

(Following this entry, dated 1 February 1902, is the added notation "see later accounts".) What Mrs. Melville recorded in subsequent pages includes, as Raymond Weaver said, "a brief history of Arrowhead, . . . an inventory of legacies, and notes of furniture, plate, pictures, a blue quilted petticoat and an Empire gown. There is also, in two versions, the briefest biography of her dead husband."[57]

The first of what Weaver distinguishes, somewhat inaccurately, as the "two versions" of a biography tells about Melville's career only as Mrs. Melville herself had observed it after he had come back from the South Seas; her running comments make it the more interesting narrative of the pair. The little "Pocket Diary" was published in, or for, the year 1866; this first biographical account seems to have been copied into it from preexistent notes originally dated "May 1861". It opens with Melville's return from the Pacific in 1844; it must originally have run through the *Meteor* voyage of 1860, though as the account now stands it also includes references to his two attacks of erysipelas in later life. Mrs. Melville's remarks on the various events she chronicles emphasize two elements: the hard work her husband had put into his books and the deterioration of his health during the 1850's and after. In the thirteen years between 1844 and 1857, as she correctly notes, "he had written 10 books besides much miscellaneous writing." Her association of the poor health with the hard work of writing is obvious in her incidental observations, brief though they are, as she runs over the titles—especially *Mardi, Moby-Dick,* and *Pierre:*

Herman Melville
        May 1861 (1891)
Herman came home
from sea fall of 1844 —
Published Typee spring
of 1846 — We were married
Aug 4. 1847 — Winters of
'47 & '48 he worked very
hard at his books — sat
in a room without
fire — wrapped up —
wrote Mardi — publish
ed 1849 — Summer of
49 we remained in
New York — he wrote
"Redburn" & "White Jacket"
Same fall went to
England & published the
above — Staid 11 weeks

Elizabeth Shaw Melville, Memoranda, p. ⟦204⟧
Mrs. Melville's biographical account of her husband as of May 1861
(Photograph courtesy of the Berkshire Athenaeum)

Winters of '47 & '48 he worked very hard at his books—sat in a room without fire—wrapped up—wrote Mardi. . . .

Wrote White Whale or Moby Dick under unfavorable circumstances—would sit at his desk all day not eating any thing till four or five o clock. . . . Wrote "Pierre" published 1852—

We all felt anxious about the strain on his health in Spring of 1853. . . .

In Fall of 1856 he went to Europe . . . [;] came home . . . in 1857 . . . with much improved health. . . .

In Feb 1855 he had his first attack of severe rheumatism in his back—so that he was helpless—and in the following June an attack of Sciatica. . . . A severe attack of what he called crick in the back laid him up . . . in March 1858—and he never regained his former vigor & strength—

Mrs. Melville's second version of her husband's career, which lacks the cryptic but suggestive observations included in the first, follows after an intervening sequence of eleven blank pages. This version is a factual recital of dates and events running from Melville's birth in 1819 to his death in 1891. Internal evidence suggests that she probably compiled it with the aid of one or more of the various nineteenth-century biographical sketches available to her. The occurrence here of much-used phrasing going back as far as the article on Melville in the 1852 edition of *The Men of the Time* indicates that she may even have consulted her husband's copy of that work for its record of his earlier years. For his later career, in case her own memory needed refreshing, she possibly went to *Chambers's Encyclopædia,* which she had mentioned in the earlier account because of its misstatements about Melville's *Meteor* voyage of 1860. That some reference work or works lay before her is not the only inference to be drawn from analysis of this second account, however, since a further point to be noted is that the very same phrases, the same erroneous dates, and still other elements in common also turn up in the second of Arthur Stedman's newspaper articles on her husband, " 'Marquesan' Melville." Like the similarities between the handling of Melville's early life in *The Men of the Time* and the Duyckincks' later *Cyclopædia,* the parallels cannot be altogether coincidental. Again the juxtaposed passages tell their own story:

Mrs. Melville's memoranda	*Stedman's " 'Marquesan' Melville"*
Born in New York Aug 1. 1819	Herman was born in New York City on Aug. 1, 1819. . . .
Attended the Albany Classical School in 1835—His teacher Dr Chas. E. West is still living in Brooklyn N. Y. ↑ (1895) ↓	Melville passed most of his boyhood and youth at and near Albany. Dr. Charles E. West, now of Brooklyn, was his teacher at the Albany classical school in 1835, and well remembers the boy's love of English composition.
Made his first voyage before the mast in 1837*—in a New York merchantman bound for Liverpool & returned after a short cruise.	Two years later,* after teaching school at Greenbush, N. Y., and at Pittsfield, Mass., he was seized with the roving spirit. With the consent of his family, he shipped as a sailor in a
(See "Redburn")	

Herman Melville

Born in New York Aug 1. 1819
Attended the Albany Classical
School in 1835 – His teacher
Dr Chas. E. West is still living
in Brooklyn N.Y. (1875)
    Made his first voyage
before the mast in 1837 – in
a New York merchantman
bound for Liverpool & returned
after a short cruise
            (See "Redburn")
                previous
Spent the summer of 1836
on his Uncle Thomas Melville's
farm in Pittsfield. Mass.
Taught school at intervals
in Pittsfield and in Greenbush
(now East Albany) N.Y. –

Elizabeth Shaw Melville, Memoranda, p. ⟦223⟧
Mrs. Melville's second biographical account of her husband
(Photograph courtesy of the Berkshire Athenaeum)

Spent the ↑previous↓ summer of (183⟨8⟩6* on his Uncle Thomas Melville's farm in Pittsfield—Mass. Taught school at intervals in Pittsfield and in Greenbush (now East A[l] bany) N.Y—

Shipped again "before the mast" in the whaler "Acushnet" Jan 1st* —1841—

Left the ship, being oppressed with hard fare and harsh usage, in the summer of 1842 with a companion Richard T. Greene (Toby) at the bay of Nukuheva in the Marquesas Islands.

New York vessel for Liverpool, made a brief visit to London, and returned in the same capacity. "Redburn: His First Voyage," published in 1849, is partly founded on the experiences of this trip.

Four years afterwards* he again shipped before the mast, this time in a Pacific whaler. On Jan. 1,* 1841, the Acushnet sailed from New Bedford harbor, bound for the sperm fishery, and Mr. Melville began the voyage which was responsible for his chief romances. . . .

The Acushnet had cruised for eighteen months when it reached the island of Nukuheva, in the Marquesas group. To that island in the Summer of 1842 (being wearied with harsh fare and hard treatment) the young sailor escaped from the whaler with a single companion, familiarly known as "Toby."

Common to these parallel accounts, in addition to the phrases and dates that both Mrs. Melville and Stedman could have picked up from earlier biographical sketches, is just what the briefer Lives do *not* mention: they do not report Melville's attendance at the Albany Classical School or name Dr. West; they refer to a New Bedford whaler but not the *Acushnet;* they make no allusion to Melville's period of schoolteaching (which had been pointed to, however, in Smith's 1879 *Taghconic*). Although Stedman's successors, beginning with Raymond Weaver, have been aware of his general indebtedness to Mrs. Melville, they have missed the specific information she thus provided for him. One reason is that their attention, like Weaver's, has been focused on Stedman's later Introduction to *Typee*[58] rather than its various antecedents: Smith's biographical sketches, Stedman's own journalistic articles that Smith too had drawn on, and the partial source for " 'Marquesan' Melville" in Mrs. Melville's store of facts that were not widely known outside the family. It should now be clear that at the time when Stedman was writing that article he either had access directly to Mrs. Melville's memoranda or else had learned of their phrasing in some more precise way than through ordinary conversation; perhaps she read aloud to him parts of the Pocket Diary or, more probably, furnished him with a written extract from it. That Dr. Coan benefited in a similar way while writing about Melville for the Boston *Literary World* is an additional possibility.[59]

How one assesses the influence of Elizabeth Shaw Melville on the essays of

Stedman and Coan, and more importantly, how one interprets her role in her husband's career, depends both on personal impressions of Mrs. Melville's character and personality and on intuitions about the nature of the Melvilles' marriage relationship. That she earned the warm regard of her granddaughters is evident. Among the biographers, Stedman, like Smith, does not probe at all into the inner life of the family; both are content with conventional remarks about Melville's wife and granddaughters, though with never a word about the generation of sons and daughters between them. In a later day, Raymond Weaver, uninhibited by the restraints of the nineties, flatly blamed Elizabeth Melville for the "crisis" in her husband's life between 1851 and 1856. His Introduction to an edition of Melville's journal of 1856-57, where he quotes the whole of Mrs. Melville's first account of her husband, describes the Pocket Diary as

> a peculiarly intimate affair—the jottings of an old lady who has outlived her husband and her generation, and whose years have been crowded with tragic memories she was unable to understand and which she wished to efface. . . .

Her story of her husband, a "gaunt digest . . . crowded with 'facts,'"

> reveals more about Mrs. Melville than of the subject it purports to treat. It is of Melville's achievements, and the handicap of his bodily ills. He had been a busy man, and he came to be a sick one. Such is Mrs. Melville's *apologia* for her husband. And the limitations of her piety and imagination that narrowed her vision to this, were, I believe, among the prime instigating causes to provoke in Melville the emotional crisis which she was pitiably unable to understand.[60]

Though Eleanor Metcalf, "inducted" as she was by her grandmother "into the service of him she had served so faithfully," obviously saw her as Melville's wife in a perspective different from Weaver's, his less charitable view of Elizabeth Melville's role in their marriage still has its active proponents. In terms of the present study, however, the point to be emphasized is not the validity or invalidity of either Mrs. Metcalf's or Weaver's contentions about Mrs. Melville;[61] what is relevant here is the changing climates of opinion within which Melville's own life and works have been interpreted over the years. Weaver, writing in the 1920's and 1930's, offered a psycho-sexual explanation of Melville's personal problems; Mrs. Melville, like her contemporary J. E. A. Smith, stressed her husband's physical ailments while Arthur Stedman, with Dr. Coan and many another nineteenth-century reader, bewailed the shade of Aristotle that seemed to rise coldly between themselves and Fayaway. "Each age," as Emerson shrewdly said, "must write its own books; or rather, each generation for the next succeeding. The books of an older period will not fit this." The statement aptly applies to the successive Lives of Melville from 1852 to 1892; it is just as pertinent to the newer conceptions of literary biography that came into fashion during the present century. As Frank Jewett Mather remarked when reviewing the third full-length Life to appear in the 1920's, Lewis Mumford's *Herman Melville,*

> no man of my generation could have written so ardent and subtle a biography of Herman Melville as Mr. Mumford has produced. Whatever our conviction of Melville's greatness, such devotees as Arthur Stedman, Professor Archibald Mac Me[c] han, and myself could not but be muffled by the fact that all our weighty literary acquaintance assumed our task was to praise "Typee" and, beyond that, merely to apologize for its author. These things ought not to inhibit, but they do.[62]

There is no indication that Mrs. Melville in her time looked forward to a full-scale Life of her husband other than Smith's projected expansion of his serialized biographical sketch. The surviving memoranda certainly do not suggest that she was assembling material for anything more ambitious than the articles written in New York by Stedman and Coan. What did engage her immediate interest and active support was the new edition of Melville's principal works; "the desire of my heart," she told Stedman in 1893, was "to see my husband's books resurrected." Since Melville himself, by Stedman's testimony in his article for *Appleton's Annual Cyclopædia,* had "avoided every action on his own part and on the part of his family that might tend to keep his name and writings before the public," the question arises of whether the new edition was in violation of his express wishes or whether the restrictions placed on "his family" applied only during his own lifetime. Of the four titles selected for republication in 1892, three—*Omoo, White-Jacket,* and *Moby-Dick*—had gone out of print by 1887.[63] As for *Typee,* the undated directive in Mrs. Melville's hand that she turned over to Stedman—it is headed "Memoranda for re-issue of 'Typee' (made by Mr Melville)"—is tangible evidence that as her husband's "assistant and adviser" she had discussed with him a new and revised edition of at least that particular work. The matter had arisen late in 1889, when H. S. Salt wrote Melville from England about a "proposition to reprint 'Typee' " in the Camelot Series published by Walter Scott of London. Melville was ill at the time, but on 12 January 1890, when he felt well enough to reply, he addressed both Salt and John Murray expressing his interest but acknowledging Murray's rights in the book under provisions of the original agreement of 1846 for its publication in England. Murray withheld his approval, thus preventing Salt and Scott from going ahead with their new edition during Melville's lifetime—the term of the agreement (*Letters,* pp. 292-295). Meanwhile, however, the possibility of "re-issuing" *Typee* was evidently taken seriously enough for Melville either to draft or ask his wife to draft the revisions covered in the "Memoranda."[64] Whether he also discussed with her the desirability of a new American edition, either of *Typee* alone or *Typee* in association with other works already out of print in this country, can only be conjectured.

Certainly Mrs. Melville did not wait long after her husband's death to author-
ize the new selected edition. Under terms of Melville's will (dated 11 June
1888) she had been named sole executrix of his property; since the will makes
no specific reference to copyrighted books or other literary materials, any in-
structions concerning their disposition must have been separately communicated
to her, probably not in writing. It is therefore impossible to say what wishes
Melville may have expressed about his out-of-print works or unpublished manuscripts, or to know whether he and his wife had discussed the qualifications of
young Arthur Stedman as a professional literary man and prospective editor,
if not as potential biographer. That Mrs. Melville had lost no time in turning
to Stedman for assistance during or after Melville's last illness is clear from
Stedman's letter to Salt written on 17 November 1891, which explains not
only that he had been in charge of Melville's "literary affairs"—originally
written "publishing affairs"—since his death, but that he had also begun the
campaign to bring Melville's name again before the public by writing and publishing five articles about him and above all by arranging for the new American
edition of his selected works. In each of these activities Stedman was clearly
proceeding with Mrs. Melville's approval and tangible support. We know that
she had provided information and illustrations for Stedman's first articles on
Melville and had also turned over the publishing agreements, which he had examined "very thoroughly," as he told the United States Book Company, thus
becoming more familiar with their provisions than was Mrs. Melville herself.
The decisions about what to include in the new edition were probably worked
out jointly by Mrs. Melville and Stedman but laid before the publisher by
Stedman as her agent.

As Stedman explained to Salt, the edition would comprise Melville's four
"best books"; in "Melville of Marquesas"—the article which has most to say
about Melville's own publishing arrangements—he had already set forth the
rationale for their selection:

> Melville's most artistic work is to be found in "Typee," the first blossom
> of his youthful genius. This idyl, which set all the world to talking, undoubt-
> edly will hold a permanent position in American literature, and most people
> will wish to read its sequel, "Omoo." . . . As for "Moby Dick" and "White
> Jacket," they should be read wherever men go down to the sea in ships, and
> until the spirit of adventure, so strong in the English-speaking race, abandons
> its sway over the hearts of human beings.

A year later, when the publisher—or was it Mrs. Melville?—raised the possibility
of adding a fifth title to the edition if sales of the original volumes should be
encouraging enough, Stedman agreed to "investigate" *Israel Potter*, though his
printed comments on the book indicate that it had never been one of his favor-
ites. A more likely candidate in his eyes might well have been *The Piazza Tales,*
which he felt had been undervalued because of its publication "in an unattractive

form." Like Smith in *Taghconic* (1879), Stedman mentions "The Piazza" in relation to Melville's surroundings at Arrowhead, but his favorite tales from the volume were obviously "The Bell-Tower," the one piece of Melville's prose to be selected for *A Library of American Literature,* and "Benito Cereno," both of which he described as "powerful." Stedman's articles also name two other stories: "I and My Chimney," to which Smith had called attention in *Taghconic* as "a humorous and spicy essay," and "Cock-A-Doodle-Doo!," which the editor of *Harper's Magazine*, Henry M. Alden, had praised to Stedman as "about the best short story he ever read." These references to five of the stories may suggest that a collection of Melville's shorter prose was under consideration as well. Mrs. Melville had ready a file of all her husband's magazine fiction; in addition, she listed—possibly for Stedman's editorial use—their titles and place of first publication.[65] Beyond these pieces, as she knew though perhaps Stedman did not, was also the unpublished manuscript of *Billy Budd, Sailor.* But if a fifth volume—*Israel Potter*, the shorter fiction, or whatever— was actually under consideration by Stedman and Mrs. Melville, the publisher's bankruptcy shortly after the third and fourth titles of the new edition were released put an end to any idea of thus enlarging its scope.

In the light of Stedman's special relations with Mrs. Melville, what he had to say in print about the Melville canon and the changing course of Melville's reputation over the years deserves closer attention than it has so far been given. Mather spoke of him as "muffled" by the expectations of his professional contemporaries; to what degree was he also inhibited—or conversely, was he prompted—by Mrs. Melville, given his position as her literary advisor and spokesman? To ask the question is of course to raise the finally insoluble issue of whether his published essays reflect his own opinions, Mrs. Melville's, or a consensus of both. Whatever their ultimate views of Melville himself may have been, Stedman's approach to Melville's writings clearly had a good deal in common with hers. His Introduction to *Typee* and to the new edition offers a further explanation of the place of these "four most important books" in the Melville canon as a whole. Three of them, he asserts, "are directly autobiographical, and 'Moby Dick' is partially so; while the less important 'Redburn' is between the two classes in this respect." Here Stedman is following the division of Melville's work into "classes"—autobiographical writings and creative romances—that had been standard among commentators from the Duyckincks to H. S. Salt; he is also echoing the refrain running through the earlier paragraphs of Mrs. Melville's second résumé of her husband's career: "See 'Redburn' "; "See 'Typee' "; "See 'Omoo' "; "See 'White Jacket' ". In classifying most of Melville's other long prose works as "unsuccessful efforts at creative romance," Stedman was evidently thinking in particular of *Mardi* and the disastrous *Pierre.* In his article on Melville for *Appleton's Annual Cyclopaedia,* which Mrs. Melville was given in proof and which in effect she approved before its publication, Stedman singles out *Typee* and *White-Jacket* as Melville's "most consistent" books; *Moby-Dick* "is perhaps the most graphic and truthful description of whaling life ever written, although it contains some of the objectionable characteristics of 'Mardi.' " If *Mardi* was "objectionable," whether by reason of its matter or of its manner, *Pierre* was even more so, and both *Israel Potter* and *The Confidence-Man* further "detracted" from Melville's reputation.

Melville's attainment of fame with his earlier books and his loss of it with *Pierre* and its successors is a particular concern in Stedman's "Melville of Marquesas." "Melville's success as a writer," Stedman declares here,

> was undoubtedly continuous and constantly increasing up to the publication of "Moby Dick" in 1851. . . . With "Moby Dick" he was to reach the topmost notch of his fame. "Pierre, or the Ambiguities" (1852) was the signal for an outburst of protest against "metaphysical and morbid meditations" which already had made themselves apparent in "Mardi" and "Moby Dick."

Meanwhile, Melville's publishers, the Harpers, had the "sagacity" to give him a less favorable contract for *Pierre,* as Stedman explains in another section of this same essay headed "A Disastrous Year." In this section he also introduces a matter that Mrs. Melville stresses in her memoranda: her husband's hard work at his books as the cause of injury to his health; not even Smith, in his reminiscences of Melville's Pittsfield years, had assumed such a cause-and-effect relationship. "The year 1853," Stedman declares,

> was one of ill omen to Melville. He had removed to Pittsfield in 1850 in the flush of his youthful fame, and while "shaping out the gigantic conception of his 'White Whale,' " as Hawthorne expressed it. The book came out and he enjoyed to the full the enhanced reputation it brought him, although six years of the most engrossing literary work had somewhat injured his constitution. He did not, however, take warning from "Mardi," but allowed himself to plunge more deeply into the sea of philosophy and fantasy. "Pierre" appeared, and after it a long series of hostile criticisms ending with a severe, though impartial, article by Fitz-James O'Brien in *Putnam's Monthly.*

Criticisms such as O'Brien's may well have touched Melville himself, along with responses within the family to *Pierre* and its reception, during the "disastrous year." Though Stedman of course does not say so here, we know now that at this same time the Melvilles, Shaws, and Gansevoorts were trying in every way they knew to get Melville away from his desk, out of Pittsfield, and into some occupation other than writing. Family correspondence of the fifties says little about any of his particular works, but there was a tendency to agree with the professional critics of the day that in his more recent books he had left his "proper sphere"—straightforward narrative—for "crude theory

& speculation" and "metaphysical disquisitions" (*Log*, II, 584-585, 574). Along with the narrator of "I and My Chimney" (1856), Melville might well have exclaimed that his family, "like all the rest of the world, cares not a fig for my philosophical jabber."[66] It is his absorption in "philosophy and fantasy" that Stedman too came to specify as the primary cause of Melville's declining reputation after 1851. He began assembling the evidence in " 'Marquesan' Melville" and "Melville of Marquesas," both written when he was working closely with Mrs. Melville in planning the new edition. In these articles he touches on Melville's philosophical discussions with Hawthorne that began in 1850, the monologue on Greek philosophy delivered to Coan in 1859, and the contemporary protests against the "metaphysical and morbid meditations" of *Pierre*—the phrase is Fitz-James O'Brien's. In the same vein, the later biographical essay in *Appleton's Annual Cyclopædia* states flatly that Melville had been "led by his inclination for philosophical speculation to commit grave literary errors, which destroyed his popularity with the reading public." (This is the article that Mrs. Melville read in proof and found both "comprehensive and well done.") Elsewhere in the *Cyclopædia* essay Stedman again cites Hawthorne on Melville's fondness for philosophical discussion, but he does not take up Smith's earlier suggestion that this supposedly harmful trait was something Melville had been led into by Hawthorne's bad influence; instead, he affirms that Melville had habitually "indulged" in philosophical studies since the time of his "early manhood"—a point Stedman may have inferred from *Mardi* or perhaps learned from talking with Mrs. Melville. This habit grew as Melville "advanced in years," Stedman continues, "until his conversation with friends became chiefly a philosophical monologue." Here, though no names are mentioned, Stedman may have been thinking specifically of Coan's experience at Pittsfield; in the Introduction to *Typee* he modified this sentence to read: "This habit increased as he advanced in years, if possible." Indeed, philosophy as Melville's supposed "ruling passion" is virtually the theme of the Introduction, in which Stedman declares that "Mr. Melville's absorption in philosophical studies was quite as responsible as the failure of his later books for his cessation from literary productiveness."

How much Stedman knew at first hand about Melville's philosophizing, apart from his reading of Schopenhauer during his last illness, and how much he derived from Hawthorne and Coan, from critics like Fitz-James O'Brien, and from Mrs. Melville herself is difficult to estimate. Though there is of course no reason to deny Melville's long-standing interest in philosophy, one suspects that "philosophy and fantasy" had tended to become code words, among nineteenth-century critics and the Melville family alike, for all the otherwise undefined tendencies in *Mardi* and its successors that made them different from *Typee* and *Omoo*. What Stedman came to say, or was possibly prompted to say on this much-belabored subject has been picked up and repeated by later biographers even though it goes beyond the testimony of others who knew Melville in his late years, such as Toft, Hillard, Stedman's own father, or even Coan, though Weaver chose to read Coan's recollections of Melville in 1859 as typifying his way of talking to the end. Stedman may well have done likewise, if his own experience in listening to Melville tended to confirm Coan's early impression. But not all of Melville's acquaintances would have called his conversation a "monologue" or regarded it as particularly "philosophical." Another writer—anonymous—who knew Melville in his old age remembered not only "his gray figure, gray hair and coloring, and piercing gray eyes" but even more strongly his manner of speaking: "Though a man of moods, he had a peculiarly winning and interesting personality, suggesting Laurence Oliphant in his gentle deference to an opponent's conventional opinion while he expressed the wildest and most emancipated ideas of his own."[67]   To his friends as in his books Melville continued to display that persistent quality of mind that Hawthorne had long since characterized as his "freedom of view." It had sometimes shocked the more conventional Evert Duyckinck: "To one of your habits of thought," Melville had written, "I confess that in my last [letter], I seemed, but only *seemed* irreverent" (*Letters*, p. 79). It had later disturbed John Morewood and other "good citizens of Pittsfield" who knew Melville himself; it certainly troubled a proportion of his readers—the evangelical partisans who disliked his comments on the missionary enterprise or those readers of *Mardi* and *Pierre* who wanted adventure instead of allegory and narrative instead of metaphysics. The freedom, the "seeming" irreverence, were his to the last, whatever the terminology of those who recognized and reported it—readers, friends, or members of the family.

That Elizabeth Melville herself would have said publicly what Stedman wrote and printed about her husband's "grave literary errors" may be doubted; that Stedman published such things repeatedly without her challenge or amendment is a matter of record. The *Cyclopaedia* article she not only accepted but praised, and even on rereading the Introduction to *Typee* she could find nothing to change but a few minor errors in names and titles—certainly no deletions such as the passages she omitted from Smith's biographical sketch when preparing the 1897 pamphlet. What she did object to in publications other than Smith's and Stedman's is worth noting here: she tried unsuccessfully to have certain words removed from her husband's letters to Hawthorne as they were printed in Rose Hawthorne Lathrop's *Memories of Hawthorne* (1897); she was "so incensed" by the "atrocious portrait" of Melville in Julian Hawthorne's *Hawthorne and His Circle* (1904) that she wrote "asking him to withdraw it from future editions, or let me furnish him with a good one to replace it."[68] Would she have remembered how Melville and his Pierre had refused to be "oblivionated" by a daguerreotype (*Letters*, p. 121)? Probably not, since Melville himself had relaxed his old rule in permitting his portrait to appear in the

Library of American Literature and even earlier in *Appleton's Cyclopædia of American Biography*. Whatever her private thoughts may have been about his life and work, she was a jealous conservator of her husband's fame, quick to respond when she sensed an injury or saw an opportunity to enhance the positive appreciation of his achievement. The 1892 edition, published with Stedman's indispensable help, was her primary effort; it was unfortunate for them and for their goals that the edition seemed headed for oblivion, along with its publisher, within the first six months after its first volume had appeared.

In addition to her reprinting of Smith's biographical sketch in 1897, "for the family and a few near friends," there are two or three further examples of Mrs. Melville's realization of every new opportunity to keep her husband's name and fame before a larger audience. In 1895 she provided a previously unpublished portrait of Melville for use in the *Century Magazine* (see Plate I). In the Springfield, Massachusetts, *Sunday Republican* of 1 July 1900 is an article on Hawthorne and Melville by one of her Pittsfield friends, Harriette M. Plunkett, illustrated with portraits of the two authors and consisting in part of long extracts from Melville's "Hawthorne and His Mosses," which Mrs. Plunkett credited not only with creating "a profound sensation among discriminating readers" of the Duyckincks' *Literary World* but also with leading to a phenomenal increase in sales of *Mosses from an Old Manse*. At Mrs. Plunkett's request Mrs. Melville had previously agreed to furnish that "precious document," her own copy of the essay, should a file of the *Literary World* be unobtainable in Pittsfield.[69] A year later, when an anonymous "admirer of Herman Melville" wrote to the New York *Times* requesting information on Melville's various books, Mrs. Melville responded, making annotations on a list of titles that the paper subsequently published. *Battle-Pieces* was then still in print, as noted in the list; *Clarel*, she explained, had been "withdrawn from circulation by Mr. Melville on finding that it commanded but a very limited sale, being in strong contrast to his previous popular works," and *John Marr* and *Timoleon* had been printed for private circulation only. Otherwise, she remarked,

> I suppose that all of the later books are now out of print, but the principal sea stories—"Typee," "Omoo," "Moby Dick," and "White Jacket"—which have always been in demand, were reissued with new plates and with a memorial introduction by Mr. Arthur Stedman, under his able auspices, in 1892, and are now in the hands of Dana Estes & Co., Boston.[70]

Except for one later reference among her memoranda to the Boston printing, this is Mrs. Melville's last allusion to Stedman's editorial work. In 1906 she was dead, leaving her husband's papers in the hands of her invalid daughter Elizabeth; as we know, the daughter was willing enough to let Mather make use of everything for his projected biography except Melville's letters to her mother. Two years later Miss Melville too was dead; the papers passed in turn to her sister Frances (Mrs. Henry B. Thomas), to Eleanor Melville Thomas

Metcalf, and to the collections at Harvard and the Berkshire Athenaeum. It was Mrs. Metcalf who encouraged Raymond Weaver, Henry A. Murray, and other pioneering twentieth-century scholars interested in a Life of Melville; Mrs. Thomas entertained written inquiries submitted through her, but would go no further. After finding a reference to herself in John Freeman's *Herman Melville* (1926), she wrote to her daughter: "I absolutely refused to be interviewed by *any one* on the subject of H.M. I don't know him in the new light."[71]

As Mrs. Thomas's letter suggests, it was to yet another generation that Melville was obliged to look for "the eventual reinstatement of his reputation" mentioned in Stedman's Introduction to *Typee*: "Mr. Melville would have been more than mortal," in Stedman's words, "if he had been indifferent to his loss of popularity. Yet he seemed contented to preserve an entirely independent attitude, and to trust to the verdict of the future." Until that verdict should be returned, he would figuratively keep the open independence of his sea, like Bulkington in Chapter 23 of *Moby-Dick*, in preference to the false safety of the leeward land: "in the port is safety, comfort, hearthstone, supper, warm blankets, friends, all that's kind to our mortalities," yet for the storm-tossed ship, "the port, the land, is that ship's direct jeopardy; she must fly all hospitality," for "her only friend" is really "her bitterest foe." Such land-based friends as the Stedmans were confident that "had Melville been willing to join freely in the literary movements of New York," as Arthur Stedman put it in " 'Marquesan' Melville," "his name would have remained before the public and a larger sale of his works would have been insured." This is almost to imply that the virtue of "Hawthorne and His Mosses" was that it increased the sales figures of *Mosses from an Old Manse*. The Authors Club and the Century were not for him,[72] however kindly the suggestions were made or the invitations tendered. What Melville thought of the kind of "fame" that could be promoted by meeting and cultivating literary journalists is the burden of one of his letters to James Billson in England, that of 20 December 1885. It "must have occurred" to Billson, as it had to Melville himself, "that the further our civilization advances upon its present lines so much the cheaper sort of thing does 'fame' become, especially of the literary sort" (*Letters*, p. 281).

The sentiment is familiar: "All Fame is patronage," Melville had written to Hawthorne over thirty years earlier. "Let me be infamous." Over the years he had thrown away the Biographico-Solicito Circulars from the compilers of dictionaries and encyclopedias, evidently little concerned with the accuracy or even the inclusion or omission of a biographical sketch of "H.M. author of 'Peedee' 'Hullabaloo' & 'Pog-Dog.' " But beneath the carefully maintained reserve of the last years one detects a difference. It is visible in the letters to his various English correspondents, in the newly made photograph that accompanied the very letter to Billson that expressed his sentiments on fame, and in the portraits that began turning up in encyclopedias and anthologies; his willingness to consider a new edition of *Typee*—when the initiative came from beyond himself and his family—is still another indication. But the clearest evidence of Melville's private thinking is in the writing of his last years, most of it known only to himself and to his wife—the "Winnefred" to whom he dedicated the never-to-be-finished volume of "Weeds and Wildings." In the language of the late poetry, true fame must grow organically; it cannot be mechanically induced, though its natural flowering may "for decades" be delayed "owing to something retarding in the environment or soil." So Melville declared, with a glance at his own age and fame, in his prose headnote to "The American Aloe on Exhibition." Any reputation is evanescent at best, during a man's lifetime or after, he wrote in "Thy Aim, Thy Aim?"

> if, living, you kindle a flame,
> Your guerdon will be but a flower,
> Only a flower,
> The flower of repute,
> A flower cut down in an hour.
>
> But repute, if this be too tame,
> And, dying, you truly ennoble a name—
>
> Again but a flower!
> Only a flower,
> A funeral flower,
> A blossom of Dis from Proserpine's bower—
> The belated funeral flower of fame.[73]

In reading Schopenhauer during 1891 Melville came across and checked a remark by Tacitus that he may well have applied to himself: "The lust of fame is the last that a wise man shakes off." And the familiar lines from *Lycidas* must have run through his mind—

> Fame is the spur that the clear spirit doth raise
> (That last infirmity of noble mind)

—as he wrote the Nelson chapters of *Billy Budd* and essayed his portrait of Captain Vere: "The spirit that 'spite its philosophic austerity may yet have indulged in the most secret of all passions, ambition, never attained to the fulness of fame."[74] Thus even "the belated funeral flower" was denied to Vere, as it seemed beyond the reach of another austere philosopher who in years gone by had awakened to find himself a celebrity as "the author of *Typee*." To Melville and probably to his wife as well, the most secret of all passions was never entirely hidden; Arthur Stedman seems to have suspected it, though without ever entirely understanding its operations during Melville's last years. "With lessening fame his desire for retirement increased, until a generation of writers for the press grew up to whom the announcement of his death was the revelation of his previous existence." So runs the conclusion of Stedman's article in *Appleton's Annual Cyclopaedia.*

And so Melville maintained his distance, and with it his independence. Away from the city, back in Pittsfield in 1885 or in upstate New York a year or so later, he felt more freedom and less constraint: in Glens Falls during the summer of 1886 or 1887 the young Ferris Greenslet overheard him in a barbershop spinning a tall and ribald story about his exploits in *Typee*[75] —the very subject he refused to discuss with his callers in Twenty-Sixth Street. With the grandchildren too, who also heard "wild tales of cannibals and tropic isles," he was equally relaxed; "Little did I then know," wrote Eleanor Metcalf in later years, "that he was reliving his own past." Here Melville showed "a side of his nature" that others little suspected—or if they did, considered it out of place in a formal biographical essay. As for the biographers of the nineties, what Weaver said of Mrs. Melville's memoranda is true of their Lives of Melville: these writings too reveal more of their authors than of the subject they purport to treat. Something Julian Hawthorne once wrote about his father's friends—Melville included—is relevant to Melville's own acquaintances and even his family: "Seeing his congenial aspect towards their little round of habits and beliefs, they would leap to the conclusion that he was no more and no less than one of themselves; whereas they formed but a tiny arc in the great circle of his comprehension."[76] This is not an exaggerated observation; it applies to any man or woman of genius or even talent in dealing with other citizens of the world. "Ever the instinct of affection revives the hope of union with our mates," wrote Emerson in "Friendship," "and ever the returning sense of insulation recalls us from the chase."

While reading Schopenhauer during his last months of life Melville paused over and marked another passage in *The Wisdom of Life* that must have struck him as a comment on his own relations with his time:

> the more a man belongs to posterity, in other words, to humanity in general, the more of an alien he is to his contemporaries; since his work is not meant for them as such, but only for them in so far as they form part of mankind at large; there is none of that familiar local colour about his productions which would appeal to them; and so what he does, fails of recognition because it is strange. People are more likely to appreciate the man who serves the circumstances of his own brief hour, or the temper of the moment,—belonging to it, and living and dying with it. (*Log*, II, 832-833)

How to present as a man of their time this once-famous writer who had become a hermit, a recluse, in short an alien to his contemporaries—this was the problem confronting the biographers of the nineties that is unsolved in any of the early Lives of Melville. Their choices were either to apologize for the man who refused to remain "the author of *Typee*," to fly in the face of prevailing taste, or somehow to transcend both alternatives, as only biographers of a later generation and sensibility were finally able to do. That Melville belonged ultimately to posterity rather than among his fin de siècle contemporaries is a commonplace of twentieth-century criticism, but this is a conviction not generally accepted until the labors of Arthur Stedman and Elizabeth Melville were long since over and done. An essential preliminary was the "resurrection" of Melville's forgotten books: first the four titles of the much-reprinted American edition of 1892 and the corresponding edition in England, and later the Constable volumes of the 1920's that included even *Mardi* and *Pierre* as well as *The Confidence-Man*, the poetry, and the unknown *Billy Budd*. When successive generations of twentieth-century critics and scholars looked with new eyes at these books and their author they saw what was denied the vision of the first biographers. Their findings have justified Melville's own quiet confidence in the verdict of the future and his wife's unwavering faith in his work and fame.

PLATE I   83

Herman Melville

Left: circa 1845-1847, as painted by Asa Weston Twitchell (1820-1904); courtesy of the Berkshire Athenaeum. *Right:* in 1861, as drawn by Francis Day for the *Century Illustrated Monthly Magazine,* 50 (August 1895), 563; courtesy of the Memorial Library, University of Wisconsin-Madison. The drawing was made from a photograph by Rodney Dewey of Pittsfield that Mrs. Melville provided; see p. 172 below.

Allan Melville

From a photograph in the Gansevoort-Lansing Collection, The New York Public Library, Astor, Lenox and Tilden Foundations.

Evert A. Duyckinck   J. E. A. Smith

George L. Duyckinck   Titus Munson Coan

Evert Duyckinck: from an undated photograph in the Prints Division, The New York Public Library, Astor, Lenox and Tilden Foundations. George Duyckinck: from a drawing in the *National Cyclopaedia of American Biography* (1909), X, 502; courtesy of the State Historical Society of Wisconsin. J. E. A. Smith: from an undated photograph in the Berkshire Athenaeum. Titus Munson Coan: as photographed while a student at Williams College in 1859, the year in which he met Melville; courtesy of The New-York Historical Society, New York City.

PLATE III   85

J. E. A. Smith

Edmund Clarence Stedman

Titus Munson Coan

Arthur Stedman

J. E. A. Smith: from the frontispiece to a posthumous edition of his *Taghconic: The Romance and Beauty of the Berkshire Hills,* by Godfrey Greylock (Pittsfield: Eagle Printing and Binding Company, 1908). Titus Munson Coan: as photographed circa 1887; courtesy of The New-York Historical Society, New York City. Edmund Clarence Stedman: from a photograph circa 1892 in the Stedman Collection, Columbia University Libraries. Arthur Stedman: from an undated photograph by Pach, 841 Broadway, New York City, in the Stedman Collection, Columbia University Libraries.

Herman Melville   Elizabeth Shaw Melville
As photographed in October 1885 by Rockwood, Union Square, New York City

Frances C. (left), Katherine G., and Eleanor M. Thomas,
with "Luck"
As photographed by Brady, Orange, New Jersey, circa 1891

Herman and Elizabeth Melville: from photographs in the Gansevoort-Lansing Collection, The New York Public Library, Astor, Lenox and Tilden Foundations. Frances, Katherine, and Eleanor Thomas: from a photograph endorsed "About 1891" in the hand of Elizabeth Shaw Melville; courtesy of David M. Metcalf, her great-grandson.

PART II

The Documents

From Four Contemporary
Reference Works, 1852–1890

THE MEN OF THE TIME (New York, 1852)

From *The Men of the Time or Sketches of Living Notables* (New York: Redfield, 1852), pp. 350–351. Reprinted in the New York *Literary World*, 11 (14 August 1852), 100.

MELVILLE, HERMAN, the author of "Typee," and other works, was born in the city of New York, August 1, 1819. His father was an importing merchant, and a son of Thomas Melville one of the "Boston tea-party, of 1773." When about eighteen years of age, he made a voyage from New York to Liverpool, before the mast, visited London, and returned home in the same capacity. In after-years, the experience of this voyage suggested the author's "Redburn." About a year after his return home, he shipped on board a whaling-vessel, bound on a cruise to the Pacific, to engage in the sperm-whale fishery. Having been out about eighteen months, the vessel arrived at the port of Nukaheva, one of the Marquesa islands, in the summer of 1842. The captain had been harsh and tyrannical to the crew; and, preferring to risk his fortunes among the natives, than to endure another voyage on board, Mr. Melville determined to leave the vessel. In a few days the starboard watch, to which he belonged, was sent ashore on liberty, and he availed himself of the opportunity thus offered to put his design in execution. Accompanied by a fellow-sailor, he separated from his companions, intending to escape into a neighboring valley, occupied by a tribe of friendly natives. But, mistaking their course, after three days' wandering, the fugitives found themselves in the Typee valley, occupied by a warlike race, taking their name from that of the valley. Here Mr. Melville was detained in a sort of indulgent captivity for about four months. His companion shortly disappeared, and was supposed to have been murdered by the natives. He had long given up all hopes of ever being restored to his friends, when his rescue was effected by a boat's crew from a Sydney whaler. Shipping on board this vessel for the cruise,[1] he arrived at Tahiti the day the

French seized the Society islands. Here he went ashore. Several months passed in the Society and Sandwich islands afforded Mr. Melville opportunities for observing the effect produced by the missionary enterprise and foreign intercourse upon the native population. For some months he resided at Honolulu in the Sandwich islands. The frigate United States, lying at that port, offered the safest and quickest passage home, and Mr. Melville shipped aboard as "ordinary seaman," and arrived at Boston in October, 1844, after a homeward cruise of thirteen months. He thus added to his knowledge of the merchant and whaling service a complete acquaintance with the inner life on board a man-of-war. With this voyage home ended Mr. Melville's sailor-life. In 1847, he married the daughter of Chief-Justice Shaw, of Boston. Until 1850, he resided in New York, removing in the summer of that year to a farm in the neighborhood of Pittsfield, Massachusetts, where he now resides. Mr. Melville has published already (1852) six works. The first entitled "Typee, or a Peep at Polynesian Life, during a Residence of Four Months in a Valley of the Marquesas," was published by Murray, in London, early in 1846. It immediately appeared in the United States, and was soon translated into some of the European languages. It met with marked success, and the writer suddenly acquired a substantial reputation. "Omoo, or Adventures in the South Seas," appeared in 1847, and was also published by Murray. In 1849, "Mardi, and a Voyage thither," and "Redburn, or the Adventures of the Son of a Gentleman," were published; in 1850, "Whitejacket, or the World in a Man-of-War;" and in 1851, "Moby-Dick, or the Whale."

CYCLOPAEDIA OF AMERICAN LITERATURE (1855)

From Evert A. Duyckinck and George L. Duyckinck, *Cyclopædia of American Literature; Embracing Personal and Critical Notices of Authors, and Selections from their Writings. From the Earliest Period to the Present Day; with Portraits, Autographs, and Other Illustrations,* 2 vols. (New York: Charles Scribner, 1855), II, 672–676. The article is illustrated with Melville's autograph and an engraving by W. Roberts captioned "Melville's Residence." Footnote numbers in the present text replace the reference symbols originally used; the footnotes themselves are from the original printing. Three manuscript leaves of the article, comprising the opening paragraphs, are reproduced in Appendix A below, following discussion of their inscription.

The *Supplement to Cyclopædia of American Literature* (New York: Charles Scribner and Company, 1866), edited by Evert Duyckinck, has no entry on Melville. When a revision of the original *Cyclopaedia* was undertaken in the 1870's by M. Laird Simons, Melville was evidently given the opportunity to specify possible additions or corrections concerning his life and works. Replying on 8 September 1873 concerning "the Article in question," he declared: "I dont remember anything in it which it would be worth your while to be at the trouble of adding to or omitting or amending" (*Letters,* p. 241).

The revised *Cyclopædia,* "edited to date" by Simons, 2 vols. (Philadelphia: William Rutter & Co., 1877), II, 636-639, reprints the article on Melville as it stood in 1855 except for the following changes: (1) the first two footnotes, documenting the discussion of Melville's ancestry, are omitted and the corresponding reference marks in the text are deleted, with no justification of type in the lines affected; (2) the two paragraphs immediately preceding the concluding extract from *Redburn* (pp. 94-95 of the present text) are shortened by fourteen lines of type (so as to end with "intermediate territory."), omitting both "flanked by . . . upon his writings." and also the corresponding one-line footnote (no. 7 in the present text); (3) a new paragraph, as designated by a double asterisk, replaces the latter material, reading as follows:

> ** *The Piazza Tales,* republished from Putnam's Magazine, appeared in 1856; and it was followed the next year by *The Confidence Man: His Masquerade.* In 1860 Mr. Melville made another whaling voyage around the world. He subsequently settled in New York city, and is now inspector in the Custom House. In 1865 he wrote *The Refugee,* a tale of the Revolution which sketched the daring deeds of Paul Jones in the *Bon Homme Richard.* A year later he printed *Battle Pieces and Aspects of the War,* a series of disconnected verses, suggested by the varying incidents of the struggle for the Union.

Simons' added paragraph includes two errors: Melville did not make "another whaling voyage around the world" in 1860 (see p. 17 above) nor did he write a book called *The Refugee.* When T. B. Peterson and Brothers of Philadelphia, who had bought the copyright and plates of *Israel Potter* from Putnam, reprinted it under that "unwarrantably altered" title without Melville's authorization, he responded with a letter of remonstrance to the firm and a disavowal printed in the New York *World*: see *Letters,* p. 287 and note; p. 304; Richard Colles Johnson, "An Attempt at a Union List of Editions of Melville," *Book Collector,* 19 (Autumn 1970), 335.

HERMAN MELVILLE was born in the city of New York, August 1, 1819. On his father's side he is of Scotch extraction, and is descended in the fourth degree from Thomas Melville, a clergyman of the Scotch Kirk, who, from the year 1718 and for almost half a century, was minister of Scoonie parish, Leven, Fifeshire.[1] The minister of Scoonie had two sons—John Melville, who became a member of his majesty's council in Grenada, and Allan Melville, who came to America in 1748, and settled in Boston as a merchant. Dying young, the latter left an only son, Thomas Melville, our author's grandfather, who was born in Boston, and, as appears by the probate records on the appointment of his guardian in 1761, inherited a handsome fortune from his father. He was graduated at Princeton College, New Jersey in 1769, and in 1772 visited his relatives in Scotland. During this visit he was presented with the freedom of the city of St. Andrews and of Renfrew. He returned to Boston in 1773, where he became a merchant, and in December of that year was one of the Boston Tea Party. He took an active part in the Revolutionary war, and, as major in Craft's regiment of Massachusetts artillery, was in the actions in Rhode Island in 1776. Commissioned by Washington in 1789 as naval officer of the port of Boston, he was continued by all the presidents down to Jackson's time in 1829.[2] To the time of his death Major Melville continued to wear the antiquated three-cornered hat, and from this habit was familiarly known in Boston as the last of the cocked-hats. There is still preserved a small parcel of the veritable tea in the attack upon which he took an active part. Being found in his shoes on re-turning from the vessel it was sealed up in a vial, although it was intended that not a particle should escape destruction! The vial and contents are now in pos-session of Chief-Justice Shaw of Massachusetts.

Our author's father, Allan Melville, was an importing merchant in New York, and made frequent visits to Europe in connexion with his business. He was a well educated and polished man, and spoke French like a native.

On his mother's side Mr. Melville is the grandson of General Peter Gansevoort of Albany, New York, the "hero of Fort Stanwix," having successfully defend-ed that fort in 1777 against a large force of British and Indians, commanded by General St. Leger.

Herman Melville

The boyhood of Herman Melville was passed at Albany and Lansingburgh, New York, and in the country, at Berkshire, Massachusetts. He had early shown a taste for literature and composition.

In his eighteenth year he shipped as a sailor in a New York vessel for Liver-pool, made a hurried visit to London when he arrived in port, and returned home "before the mast." His next adventure was embarking, Jan. 1, 1841,* on a whaling vessel for the Pacific for the sperm fishery. After eighteen months of the cruise, the vessel, in the summer of 1842, put into the Marquesas, at Nu-kuheva. Melville, who was weary of the service, took the opportunity to aban-don the ship, and with a fellow sailor hid himself in the forest, with the inten-tion of resorting to a neighboring peaceful tribe of the natives. They mistook their course, and after three days' wandering, in which they had traversed one of the formidable mountain ridges of the island, found themselves in the bar-barous Typee valley. Here Melville was detained "in an indulgent captivity" for four months. He was separated from his companion, and began to despair of a return to civilization, when he was rescued one day on the shore by a boat's crew of a Sidney whaler. He shipped on board this vessel, and was land-ed at Tahiti the day when the French took possession of the Society Islands, establishing their "Protectorate" at the cannon's mouth. From Tahiti, Melville passed to the Sandwich Islands, spent a few months in observation of the people and the country, and in the autumn of 1843 shipped at Honolulu as "ordinary seaman" on board the frigate United States, then on its return voyage, which was safely accomplished, stopping at Callao, and reaching Boston in October, 1844. This voyaging in the merchant, whaling, and naval service rounded Melville's triple experience of nautical life. It was not long after that he made his appearance as an author. His first book, *Typee*, a narrative of his Marquesas adventure, was published in 1846, simultaneously by Murray in London[3] and Wiley and Putnam in New York. The spirit and vigorous fancy of the style, and the freshness and novelty of the incidents, were at once appreciated. There was, too, at the time, that undefined sentiment of the approaching practical importance of the Pacific in the public mind, which was admirably calculated for the reception of this glowing, picturesque narrative. It was received everywhere with enthusiasm, and made a reputation for its author in a day. The London Times reviewed it with a full pen, and even the staid Gentleman's Magazine was loud in its praises.

Mr. Melville followed up this success the next year with *Omoo, a Narrative of Adventures in the South Seas,* which takes up the story with the escape from the Typees, and gives a humorous account of the adventures of the author and some of his ship companions in Tahiti. For pleasant, easy narrative, it is the most natural and agreeable of his books. In his next book, in 1849—*Mardi, and a Voyage Thither*—the author ventured out of the range of personal observation and matter-of-fact description to which he had kept more closely than was generally supposed,[4] and projected a philosophical romance, in which human nature and European civilization were to be typified under the aspects of the poetical mythological notions and romantic customs and traditions of the aggregate races of Polynesia. In the first half of the book there are some of the author's best descriptions, wrought up with fanciful associations from the quaint philosophic and other reading in the volumes of Sir Thomas Browne, and such worthies, upon whose pages, after his long sea fast from books and literature, the author had thrown himself with eager avidity. In the latter portions, embarrassed by his spiritual allegories, he wanders without chart or compass in the wildest regions of doubt and scepticism. Though, as a work of fiction, lacking clearness, and maimed as a book of thought and speculation by its want of sobriety, it has many delicate traits and fine bursts of fancy and invention. Critics could find many beauties in Mardi which the novel-reading public who long for amusement have not the time or philosophy to discover. Mr. Melville, who throughout his literary career has had the good sense never to argue with the public, whatever opportunities he might afford them for the exercise of their disputative faculties, lost no time in recovering his position by a return to the agreeable narrative which had first gained him his laurels. In the same year he published *Redburn; his First Voyage, being the Sailor-boy*

Confessions and Reminiscences of the Son of a Gentleman, in the Merchant Service. In the simplicity of the young sailor, of which the pleasant adventure of leaving the forecastle one day and paying his respects to the captain in the cabin, is an instance, this book is a witty reproduction of natural incidents. The lurid London episode, in the melo-dramatic style, is not so fortunate. Another course of Melville's nautical career, the United States naval service, furnished the subject of the next book—*White Jacket, or the World in a Man-of-war,* published in 1850. It is a vivid daguerreotype of the whole life of the ship. The description is everywhere elevated from commonplace and familiarity by the poetical associations which run through it. There is many a good word spoken in this book, as in the author's other writings, for the honor and welfare of Poor Jack. Punishment by flogging is unsparingly condemned.

In 1851 *Moby-Dick, or the Whale,* appeared, the most dramatic and imaginative of Melville's books. In the character of Captain Ahab and his contest with the whale, he has opposed the metaphysical energy of despair to the physical sublime of the ocean. In this encounter the whale becomes a representative of moral evil in the world. In the purely descriptive passages, the details of the fishery, and the natural history of the animal, are narrated with constant brilliancy of illustration from the fertile mind of the author.[5]

Pierre, or the Ambiguities, was published in 1852. Its conception and execution were both literary mistakes. The author was off the track of his true genius. The passion which he sought to evolve was morbid or unreal, in the worst school of the mixed French and German melodramatic.

Since the publication of this volume, Mr. Melville has written chiefly for the magazines of Harper and Putnam. In the former, a sketch, entitled *Cock-a-doodle doo!* is one of the most lively and animated productions of his pen; in the latter, his *Bartleby the Scrivener,* a quaint, fanciful portrait, and his reproduction, with various inventions and additions, of the adventures of *Israel Potter,*[6] an actual character of the Revolution, have met with deserved success.

Mr. Melville having been married in 1847 to a daughter of Chief Justice Shaw of Boston, resided for a while at New York, when he took up his residence in Berkshire, on a finely situated farm, adjacent to the old Melville House, in which some members of the family formerly lived; where, in the immediate vicinity of the residence of the poet Holmes, he overlooks the town of Pittsfield and the intermediate territory, flanked by the Taconic range, to the huge height of Saddleback.

> Gray-lock, cloud girdled, from his purple throne,
>   A voice of welcome sends,
> And from green sunny fields, a warbling tone
>   The Housatonic blends.[7]

Melville's Residence

In the fields and in his study, looking out upon the mountains, and in the hearty society of his family and friends, he finds congenial nourishment for his faculties, without looking much to cities, or troubling himself with the exactions of artificial life. In this comparative retirement will be found the secret of much of the speculative character engrafted upon his writings.

[An extract from *Redburn* follows: Chapter 14, "He Contemplates Making a Social Call on the Captain in His Cabin"]

APPLETON'S CYCLOPAEDIA OF AMERICAN BIOGRAPHY (1888)

From *Appleton's Cyclopædia of American Biography,* edited by James Grant Wilson and John Fiske, 6 vols. (New York: D. Appleton and Company, 1887–1889), IV (1888), 293–294. The accompanying illustration is reproduced here (enlarged) with permission of the State Historical Society of Wisconsin from its holding of the *Cyclopædia.*

MELVILLE, Herman, author, b. in New York city, 1 Aug., 1819. His grandfather, Maj. Thomas Melvill (1751–1832), was a member of the Boston tea-party,

served in the Revolution, and is supposed to have been the last American that
adhered through life to the cocked hat. His maternal grandfather was Peter
Gansevoort (*q.v.*). His father, Allan, was a merchant, who travelled widely and
cultivated literary tastes. Herman shipped as a sailor before the mast in 1837*
for a voyage to Liverpool. Four years later he sailed round Cape Horn in the
"Dolly" for a whaling cruise in the south Pacific. But the treatment of the captain was so harsh, and the state of affairs on board was so bad in every respect,
that Melville and a companion resolved to leave the ship. While she lay in the
harbor of Nukahiva, in the Marquesas islands, in the summer of 1842, they
made their escape. The island, about twenty miles long by ten miles broad, is
mountainous in the centre, the highest peak rising nearly 4,000 feet, with al-
ternate ridges and valleys radiating to the sea. One of these valleys is inhabited
by the Typees, a war-like tribe of cannibals, and the next by the Happars, a
friendly tribe. Com. David Porter (*q.v.*), while refitting his ships here in 1813-
'14, had taken part with the Happars in a war against the Typees, which he described in his published journal. Melville and his companion, with great labor
and many narrow escapes, climbed the mountains, intending to descend into
the Happar valley, but lost their way and finally found themselves among the

Typees. While still uncertain where they were, they were surrounded by a group of savage chiefs, one of whom sternly demanded whether they were friendly to Happar or to Typee. "I paused for a second," writes Melville, "and I know not by what impulse it was that I answered 'Typee.' The piece of dusky statuary nodded in approval, and then murmured 'Mortarkee?' [good?] 'Mortarkee,' said I, without further hesitation—'Typee mortarkee.' The dark figures around us leaped to their feet, clapped their hands in transport, and shouted again and again the talismanic syllables, the utterance of which appeared to have settled everything."[1] Melville was held in captivity for four months, treated in most respects as an honored guest, but constantly watched to prevent his escape. His companion soon got away, and at length Melville himself was rescued. An Australian whaler, short of men, visited the harbor of Nukahiva, where the captain learned that there was an American sailor in the Typee valley, and accepted the offer of a native to obtain him. The native made his way to Melville, and guided him to the beach, where a boat from the whaler was in waiting, and Melville was taken off after a bloody fight. He spent two years more in the Pacific, and on his return home published "Typee: a Peep at Polynesian Life during a Four Months' Residence in a Valley of the Marquesas" (New York and London, 1846). This work, in which the story of his romantic captivity is told with remarkable vividness, had an immediate success and rapidly passed through several editions. It was dedicated to Chief-Justice Lemuel Shaw, of Massachusetts, whose daugher Mr. Melville afterward married. He removed to Pittsfield, Mass., in 1850, but subsequently returned to New York and was appointed to a place in the custom-house. His remaining works are "Omoo, a Narrative of Adventures in the South Seas" (1847); "Mardi, and a Voyage Thither," a philosophical romance (1848*); "Redburn," a novel (1848*); "White-Jacket, or the World in a Man-of-War" (1850); "Moby Dick, or the White Whale" (1851); "Pierre, or the Ambiguities" (1852); "Israel Potter, his Fifty Years of Exile" (1855); "The Piazza Tales" (1856); "The Confidence Man" (1857); "Battle-Pieces, and Aspects of the War," a volume of poems (1866); and "Clarel, a Pilgrimage in the Holy Land," a poem (2 vols., 1876).

A LIBRARY OF AMERICAN LITERATURE (1890)

From Arthur Stedman, "Short Biographies of American Authors Represented in 'A Library of American Literature,'" in *A Library of American Literature from the Earliest Settlement to the Present Time,* compiled and edited by Edmund Clarence Stedman and Ellen Mackay Hutchinson, 11 vols. (New York: Charles L. Webster & Co., 1888–1890), XI (1890), 554. Reprinted after Melville's death in the *Critic,* n.s. 16 (3 October 1891), 175.

MELVILLE, Herman, b. New York, N. Y., 1 Aug. 1819. Grandson of a member of the Boston "tea-party." At eighteen went to sea as a common sailor, landed at Liverpool, saw London, and shipped again for home. In 1841 joined a whaler for the sperm-fishery in the Pacific. After eighteen months' cruising the ship put into the Marquesas islands, whereupon Melville ran away, on account of the captain's severity, and with a shipmate lost his way in a forest on the island of Nukuhiva, where the Typee cannibals lived. Was captured by them, his mate escaping, and kept for four months in virtual but friendly captivity. On the arrival of an Australian ship a fight took place; he was rescued and joined the crew. After two more years afloat came home, and published "Typee" (1840*) in New York and London simultaneously. It proved to be a success, and was succeeded by "Omoo" (1847), a continuation of his adventures, and a novel, "Redburn" (1848*). In 1849 issued a philosophical romance, "Mardi, and a Voyage Thither," followed by "White Jacket, or the World in a Man of War" (1850), "Moby Dick" (1851), "Pierre, or the Ambiguities" (1852), "Israel Potter, his Fifty Years of Exile" (1855), "The Piazza Tales" (1856), "The Confidence Man" (1857), "Battle-Pieces, and Aspects of the War," poems (1866), and "Clarel, a Pilgrimage in the Holy Land," poem (1876). Mr. Melville voyaged around the world in 1860, and on his return held for some time a position in the custom-house of New York, in which city he afterward led a retired life.

Retrospective Essays, 1891–1892

ARTHUR STEDMAN, "HERMAN MELVILLE'S FUNERAL"

Published anonymously in the New York *Daily Tribune,* Thursday,
1 October 1891, p. 14. Reprinted in the *Critic,* n.s. 16 (10 October 1891), 190;
quoted in part in *Current Literature: A Magazine of Record and Review,* 8 (November 1891), 339-340.

The funeral of the late Herman Melville was held at the family residence in Twenty-eighth-st. yesterday afternoon, the Rev. Theodore C. Williams, of All Souls' Church, delivering a short address. Among the relatives and friends present, beside the widow and daughter [s] of the deceased were Mrs. Thomas Melville, widow of the late governor of the Sailors' Snug Harbor; the Misses Melville, daughters of the late Allan Melville; Samuel Shaw, of Boston; W. B. Morewood, George Brewster, Mrs. Griggs, Miss Lathers, Dr. Titus Munson Coan, Arthur Stedman and George Dillaway.[1]

The death of Herman Melville, although following a lingering illness, has come as a surprise to even his few acquaintances in the city, for their opportunities of seeing him have been extremely limited in number. Much has been written, particularly in English journals, concerning the alleged neglect and disregard of Mr. Melville by contemporary authors in this country, but it is a well-known fact here that his seclusion has been a matter of personal choice.[2]

This writer gained an international reputation at an earlier date than James Russell Lowell, although born in the same year, 1819. His practical abandonment of literary work some twenty-five years ago, however, has allowed general interest in his books to die out.

Mr. Melville came of patrician blood on both sides of his family, his fraternal and maternal grandfathers figuring prominently in the Revolution, being respectively of Scottish, New-England and Dutch descent. As in Richard Henry Dana's case, Melville's first literary success was a narrative of his own experience while a common sailor before the mast and in new countries: but unlike Dana, he continued work in the same field, and with credit. In regard to "Typee," Dr. Coan was heard to remark at the service yesterday that his father, the Rev. Titus Coan, of the Hawaiian Islands, had personally visited the Marquesas group, found the Typee Valley, and verified in every detail the romantic descriptions of the gentle but man-devouring islanders.[3] Dr. Coan further said: "Herman Melville was the first man who shared the life of a cannibal community in the South Seas—who had the consummate literary skill to describe it—and who got away alive to write his book. 'Typee' will be read when most of the Concord group are forgotten."

However this may be, Mr. Melville always has been an interesting figure to New-York literary circles. So far from being forgotten, he was among the very first to be invited to join the Authors' Club at its founding in 1882.[4] His declination of this offer, as well as his general refusal to enter into social life, are said to have been chiefly due to natural disposition, and partly to the very adverse critical reception afforded his novel, "Pierre, or the Ambiguities," published in 1852. He was always a great reader, and was much interested in collecting engravings of the old masters, having a large library and a fine assortment of prints, those of Claude's paintings being his favorite.

His tall, stalwart figure, until recently, could be seen almost daily tramping through the Fort George district or Central Park, his roving inclination leading him to obtain as much out-door life as possible. His evenings were spent at home with his books, his pictures and his family, and usually with them alone.

While at Pittsfield, Mass., from 1850 to 1862, he became the intimate friend of Hawthorne, who lived for a while near by at Lenox, and they often exchanged visits. It was at this place that most of Melville's writing was done. The place in the New-York Custom House was given up about 1881.*

At the beginning of failing health, some three years ago,[5] Mr. Melville wrote and privately circulated a little story entitled "John Marr." It was dedicated to Clark Russell, who was a cordial admirer and correspondent. Last spring, after his final illness set in, he collected and had printed his miscellaneous shorter poems under the title "Timoleon, etc." This volume is dedicated to "My countryman, Elihu Vedder." Both little books are limited to twenty-five copies. Mr. Melville's later style became somewhat rugged and mystical. His best-known poem was "Sheridan at Cedar Creek," thought by most literary experts to be superior to "Twenty Miles Away," though lacking a popular refrain.

The following poem is from "Timoleon":

L'ENVOI.

The Return of the Sire de Nesle.

A. D. 16—.

My towers at last! These rovings end,
Their thirst is slaked in larger dearth;

The yearning infinite recoils,
　　For terrible is earth.

Kaf thrusts his snouted crags through fog ;
Araxes swells beyond his span,
　　And knowledge poured by pilgrimage
　　Overflows the banks of man.

But thou, my stay, thy lasting love,
One lonely good, let this but be!
Weary to view the wide world's swarm,
　　But blest to fold but thee.[6]

ARTHUR STEDMAN, "MARQUESAN' MELVILLE"

Published over Stedman's signature in the New York *World*, Sunday, 11 October 1891, p. 26; partially reprinted in the *Critic*, n.s. 16 (24 October 1891), 222-223. The present text corrects eleven minor typographical errors in the newspaper version of the essay.[1] Mrs. Melville provided the original drawing and photographs on which the illustrations accompanying the newspaper article were based. The *World*'s four-bank headline and the illustrations are reproduced here with permission of the State Historical Society of Wisconsin from its file of the *World*.

" MARQUESAN " MELVILLE.

A South Sea Prospero Who Lived and Died in New York.

THE ISLAND NYMPHS OF NUKUHEVA'S HAPPY VALLEY.

Story of the Romantic Life of Herman
Melville, Who Died a Few Days Ago
— His Remarkable Adventures on
One of the Marquesas Islands Among
the Cannibals—His Story of "Typee"
and Its Popularity in England —
Robert Buchanan's Tribute to the
Story-Writer—W. Clark Russell Sends
His Praises—If a Man Will Bury Him-
self in Life the Busy World Will Al-
low Him to Do So.

Herman Melville—1885

As I gazed, a few days ago on the dead face of Herman Melville there came irresistibly to my mind those eloquent lines of Robert Buchanan's, a true inspiration, though conveying a grievous error:

> * * * Melville, sea-compelling man,
> Before whose wand Leviathan
> Rose hoary white upon the Deep,
> With awful sounds that stirred its sleep,
> Melville, whose magic drew Typee,
> Radiant as Venus, from the sea,
> Sits all forgotten or ignored,
> While haberdashers are adored!
>   Indifferent to the art of dress,
> Pictured the glorious South Sea maid
>   Almost in mother nakedness—
> Without a hat, or boot, or stocking,
> A want of dress to most so shocking,
> With just one chemisette to dress her
> She *lives*—and still shall live, God bless her,
> Long as the sea rolls deep and blue,
>   While Heaven repeats the thunder of it,
> Long as the White Whale ploughs it through,
> The shape my sea-magician drew
>   Shall still endure, or I'm no prophet!

These are the most poetical lines of a pasquinade printed in the London *Academy* for 1885. In a foot note is added:

> I sought everywhere for this Triton, who is still living somewhere in New York. No one seemed to know anything of the one great writer fit to stand shoulder to shoulder with Whitman on that continent.[2]

Mr. Buchanan apparently "sought everywhere" except in the one place where all of Mr. Melville's contemporaries made their search when they had occasion to visit him—the City Directory. Now Mr. Buchanan was among the advance guard of a band of British voyagers whose fad it has been to make expeditions of "discovery" to this country, in search of neglected great men and—the American circulating medium.

Meeting with cold comfort in Boston Town, and, I fear, in Gotham also, he sought the friendly shelter of Bohemian Camden, and poured out his feelings in the poem referred to, which was dedicated to Camden's "latter Socrates." Even now, after several corrections, this old story of neglect and forgetfulness of Mr. Melville by his brother writers is again repeated.

Parentage, Birth and Education

On his father's side, Mr. Melville was the grandson of Major Thomas Melville, a member of the Boston "tea-party" and an officer in the Revolution. Maj. Melville was the last man in Boston to wear a cocked hat and knee breeches, and in this way became the subject of Dr. Holmes's poem, "The Last Leaf." He was known for many years as "the last of the cocked hats," and died in 1832.[3] His son Allan was an importing merchant of this city, a man of much culture and one who had travelled widely. He died while Herman was still a youth. On his mother's side the latter was descended from Gen. Peter Gansevoort, also of the Revolution, and known as the "hero of Fort Stanwix."

Herman was born in New York City on Aug. 1, 1819. If 1809 is to be called the "poets' year," then 1819 should be called the "Belles-lettres" year, for of our American writers, James Russell Lowell, Walt Whitman, Thomas W. Parsons, E. P. Whipple, Julia Ward Howe, W. W. Story, Dr. J. G. Holland and Herman Melville were born within this twelvemonth.

Major Thomas Melville

Melville passed most of his boyhood and youth at and near Albany. Dr. Charles E. West, now of Brooklyn, was his teacher at the Albany classical school in 1835, and well remembers the boy's love of English composition.[4]

Two years later,* after teaching school at Greenbush, N. Y., and at Pittsfield, Mass., he was seized with the roving spirit. With the consent of his family, he shipped as a sailor in a New York vessel for Liverpool, made a brief visit to London, and returned in the same capacity. "Redburn: His First Voyage," published in 1849, is partly founded on the experiences of this trip.[5]

Four years afterwards* he again shipped before the mast, this time in a Pacific whaler. On Jan. 1,* 1841, the Acuschnet sailed from New Bedford harbor, bound for the sperm fishery, and Mr. Melville began the voyage which was responsible for his chief romances. In regard to its results he said in "Moby Dick": "If I shall ever deserve any real repute in that small but high hushed world which I might not be unreasonably ambitious of; if hereafter I shall do anything that, on the whole, a man might rather have done than to have left undone, * * * then here I prospectively ascribe all the honor and the glory to whaling; for a whale-ship was my Yale College and my Harvard."

The Acushnet had cruised for eighteen months when it reached the island of Nukuheva, in the Marquesas group. To that island in the Summer of 1842 (being wearied with harsh fare and hard treatment) the young sailor escaped from the whaler with a single companion, familiarly known as "Toby." How they entered the hostile Typee valley by mistake, how "Toby" mysteriously disappeared to meet Melville in America after the publication of "Typee," how Melville himself escaped, and all his experiences in the "happy valley" are duly recorded in the book itself. I venture to quote at some length what are probably the most artistic passages. . . .[6]

South Sea Experiences

Melville was rescued by the captain of an Australian whaler which had put into the Bay of Nukuheva short of hands and he shipped as one of her sailors, although in a weak condition from illness caused by a prolonged diet on the islanders' food. He reached Tahiti, in the Society Islands, on the day that the French Protectorate was established there and thence sailed to the Hawaiian Islands, remaining at both places long enough to become acquainted with them. At Honolulu he joined the crew of the American frigate United States, then on its return voyage, and after a sojourn at one of the Peruvian ports reached Boston in the Autumn of 1844, where he was discharged.

The following months were passed at Lansingburg in the writing of his first book, "Typee." About the time it was finished an old friendship between his father's family and that of the late Chief-Justice Lemuel Shaw was renewed, and this led to his engagement with Justice Shaw's daughter. Their marriage followed on Aug. 4, 1847, at Boston, Mass. Mr. and Mrs. Melville resided in New York City until 1850, when they purchased a farmhouse at Pittsfield, Mass.

The house was so situated as to command an uninterrupted view of Greylock Mountain and the adjacent hills. Here he remained for thirteen years, occupied with his writing and managing his farm. An article in *Putnam's Monthly* entitled "I and My Chimney," and the introduction to the "Piazza Tales," give faithful pictures of his place, Arrow Head, and its surroundings.[7] In a letter to Nathaniel Hawthorne, given in "Nathaniel Hawthorne and His Wife," his daily life is set forth. The letter is dated June 1,* 1851:

Melville's Chimney Corner at Pittsfield

"Since you have been here I have been building some shanties of houses
(connected with the old one) and likewise some shanties of chapters and essays. I have been ploughing and sowing and raising and printing and praying,
and now begin to come out upon a less bristling time and to enjoy the calm
prospect of things from a fair piazza at the north of the old farmhouse here.
Not entirely yet, though, am I without something to be urgent with. The
'Whale' is only half through the press; for, wearied with the long delays of
the printers and disgusted with the heat and dust of the Babylonish brick-kiln
of New York, I came back to the country to feel the grass and end the book,
reclining on it, if I may."[8]

Nathaniel Hawthorne

Mr. Hawthorne, who was then living in the "red cottage" at Lenox, had
passed a week at Arrow Head with his daughter Una the previous Spring. It is
recorded that the friends "spent most of the time in the barn, bathing in the
early Spring sunshine, which streamed through the open doors, and talking
philosophy."[9]

A passage in Hawthorne's "Wonder-Book" is interesting as describing the
number of literary neighbors in Berkshire.

"For my part I wish I had Pegasus here at this moment," said the student.
"I would mount him forthwith and gallop about the country within a circumference of a few miles, making literary calls on my brother authors. Dr.
Dewey would be within my reach, at the foot of the Taconic. In Stockbridge, yonder, is Mr. James [G. P. R. James], conspicuous to all the world
on his mountain-pile of history and romance. Longfellow, I believe, is not
yet at the Oxbow, else the winged horse would neigh at him. But here in

Lenox I should find our most truthful novelist, who has made the scenery and life of Berkshire all her own. On the hither side of Pittsfield sits Herman Melville, shaping out the gigantic conception of his 'White Whale,' while the gigantic shadow of Greylock looms upon him from his study window. Another bound of my flying steed would bring me to the door of Holmes, whom I mentioned last, because Pegasus would certainly unseat me the next minute and claim the poet as his rider."[10]

These two romancers—one of the land, the other of the sea—seem to have found a complement each in the other, drawing them closely together. Mr. Hawthorne, when United States Consul at Liverpool, at one time acted as Mr. Melville's agent with English publishers.[11]

While at Pittsfield he was induced to enter the lecture field. From 1857 to 1860 he filled many engagements in the Lyceums, chiefly speaking of his adventures in the South Seas. He lectured in cities as widely apart as Montreal, Chicago, Baltimore and San Francisco, visiting the last-named place in 1860 by the Isthmus route, for the benefit of his health. It is said that several of the American writers who were at that time popular in the lecture field, Mr. Curtis among them, helped to start him in his first course by referring to him in their own lectures before country audiences.[12]

Besides his voyage to San Francisco he had, in 1849 and 1856, visited England and the Continent, partly to superintend the publication of the English editions of his works and partly for recreation.

Dr. Coan's Glimpse of Melville

A pronounced feature of Melville's character was his marked unwillingness to speak of himself, his adventures or his writings in conversation. He was, however, able to overcome this reluctance on the lecture platform. Our author's fondness for philosophical discussion is interestingly described in a letter from Dr. Titus Munson Coan to his mother, written while a student at Williams College over thirty years ago and fortunately preserved by her. Dr. Coan has enjoyed the friendship and confidence of Mr. Melville during most of the latter's residence in this city. His letter reads:

"I have made my first literary pilgrimage—a call upon Herman Melville, the renowned author of 'Typee,' &c. He lives in a spacious farm-house about two miles from Pittsfield, a weary walk through the dust. But it was well repaid. I introduced myself as a Hawaiian-American and soon found myself in full tide of talk—or rather of monologue. But he would not repeat the experiences of which I had been reading with rapture in his books. In vain I sought to hear of Typee and those Paradise islands, but he preferred to pour forth his philosophy and his theories of life. The shade of Aristotle arose like a cold mist between myself and Fayaway. We have quite enough of Greek philosophy at Williams College, and I confess I was disappointed in this trend of the talk. But what a talk it was! Melville is transformed from a Marquesan to a gypsy student, the gypsy element still remaining strong in him. And this contradiction gives him the air of one who has suffered from opposition, both literary and social. With his liberal views he is apparently considered by the good people of Pittsfield as little better than a cannibal or a 'beach-comber.' His attitude seemed to me something like that of an Ishmael; but perhaps I judged hastily. I managed to draw him out very freely on everything but the Marquesas Islands, and when I left him he was in full tide of discourse on all things sacred and profane. But he seems to put away the objective side of life and to shut himself up in this cold North as a cloistered thinker."

T. M. C.[13]

It is an interesting fact that the Rev. Titus Coan, of the Hawaiian Islands, Dr. Coan's father, personally visited the Marquesas group, found the Typee Valley and verified in all respects the statements made in "Typee."[14]

The chief event of the residence in Pittsfield was the completion and publication of "Moby Dick, or the White Whale," in 1851. How many young men have been drawn to sea by this book is a question of interest. Meeting with Mr. Charles Henry Webb ("John Paul") the day after Mr. Melville's death, I asked him if he were not familiar with that author's writings. He replied that "Moby Dick" was responsible for his three years of life before the mast when a lad, and added that while "gamming" on board another vessel he had once fallen in with a member of the boat's crew which rescued Melville from his friendly imprisonment among the Typees.[15]

An Instant Success

It was late in the year 1845 that Melville completed the manuscript of "Typee." At nearly the same time his brother, Gansevoort Melville, sailed for England, as secretary of legation to Minister McLane, taking the manuscript with him. It was offered to John Murray, who at once accepted it, buying the book outright for England for a moderate sum. The condition of the English copyright law was such at that time that this ownership and copyright only lapsed with Mr. Melville's death. The same plan was followed a year later with "Omoo." Efforts have been made by other publishers to arrange for popular English editions of these works, but unsuccessfully.[16]

If I am not mistaken the house of Murray did not publish fiction in 1846. At any rate they wished to include both volumes in their "Colonial and Home Library," so the title "Typee" was omitted and that book was published in England as "Melville's Marquesas Islands."

In America Wiley & Putnam, whose London agent had contracted to publish the work, brought it out simultaneously with the English edition. It was issued in two parts, in March and April, 1846. More favorable terms were obtained from Bentley for Mr. Melville's later works, so long as it was possible to secure copyright in England.[17]

"Typee" was an instant success. Columns of praise and abuse were devoted to it, the latter on account of some serious reflections on missionary methods. The same thing happened in the case of "Omoo," although Mr. Melville asserted his lack of prejudice. It is a curious fact that both works proved of the greatest value to outgoing missionaries on account of the exact information contained in them with respect to the islanders.[18]

In the United States Harper & Brothers brought out "Omoo," and "Typee" was placed with them in 1849, somewhat shorn of the objectionable passages and containing the "Story of Toby." "Toby" was considered by many people a mythical personage, but his portrait is given herewith. His name was Richard T. Greene. The American firm mentioned have published all of Mr. Melville's works except three, not including the two privately-printed booklets. Copyright payments have been regularly made by them on all books sold, but I cannot find that any moneys have come from "oversea" since some time before the war.[19]

While at Pittsfield, besides his own family, Mr. Melville's mother and sisters resided with him. As his four children grew up he found it necessary to obtain for them better facilities for study than the village school afforded, and so, in the Autumn of 1863, the household was broken up and he removed with his wife and children to the New York house that was afterwards his home.[20] In December, 1866, he was appointed by Mr. H. A. Smyth, a former travelling companion in Europe, a district officer in the New York Custom-House.[21]

Letter from W. Clark Russell

During the later years of Mr. Melville's life he took great pleasure in a friendly correspondence with Mr. W. Clark Russell, the famous English novelist of

"Toby"
(From a daguerreotype in possession of Mrs. Melville)

the sea. Mr. Russell had taken many occasions to speak of Melville's sea-tales—his interest in them and his indebtedness to them. The latter felt impelled to write Mr. Russell in regard to one of his newly-published novels, and received in answer the following letter:

July 21, 1886.

My Dear Mr. Herman Melville: Your letter has given me a very great and similar pleasure. Your delightful books carry the imagination into a maritime period so remote that, often as you have been in my mind, I could never satisfy myself that you were still amongst the living. I am glad, indeed, to learn from Mr. Toft that you are still hale and hearty, and I do most heartily wish you many years yet of health and vigor.

Your books I have in the American edition. I Have "Typee," 'Omoo," "Redburn," and that noble piece "Moby Dick." These are all I have been able to obtain. There have been many editions of your works in this country, particularly the lovely South Sea sketches; but the editions are not equal to those of the American publishers. Your reputation here is very great. It is hard to meet a man whose opinion as a reader is worth having who does not speak of your works in such terms as he might hesitate to employ, with all his patriotism, towards many renowned English writers.

Dana is, indeed, great. There is nothing in literature more remarkable than the impression produced by Dana's portraiture of the homely inner life of a little brig's forecastle.

I beg that you will accept my thanks for the kindly spirit in which you have read my books. I wish it were in my power to cross the Atlantic, for you assuredly would be the first whom it would be my happiness to visit. * * * The condition of my right hand obliges me to dictate this to my son; but painful as it is to me to hold a pen I cannot suffer this letter to reach the hands of a man of so admirable genius as Herman Melville without begging him to believe me to be, with my own hand, his most respectful and hearty admirer,

W. Clark Russell.[22]

Final Days

It is generally admitted that had Melville been willing to join freely in the literary movements of New York, his name would have remained before the public and a larger sale of his works would have been insured. But more and more, as he grew older, he avoided every action on his part and on the part of his family that might look in this direction, even declining to assist in founding the Authors Club in 1881.[23]

It has been suggested that he might have accepted a magazine editorship, but I doubt it. He could not bear business details or routine work, and our *fin-de-siècle* magazine editors are nothing if not business men.[24] If they are philosophers their philosophy must be exerted patience over the delays of promised articles or in bearing their defeats by competitors. If they are poets their imaginations must be exercised in devising new features. The time has passed when even a Lowell can stroll about Boston and Cambridge with year-old manuscripts in his overcoat pockets.

A few friends felt at liberty to visit the recluse and were kindly welcomed, but he himself sought no one. His favorite companions were his grandchildren, with whom he delighted to pass his time, and his devoted wife, who was a constant assistant and adviser in his work, chiefly done of late for his own amusement. To her he addressed his last little poem, the touching "Return of the Sire de Nesle."[25] Otherwise he occupied himself with his fine collection of engravings and etchings, with books on philosophy and the fine arts, or with walks abroad, as long as they were possible.

With the completion of "Moby Dick" in 1851 his important literary work was practically ended. Twice more the enchanter waved his wand and the awful shapes of the skeleton figure-head and Bannadonna's domino arose in "Benito Cereno" and "The Bell Tower." Then, like Coleridge, he buried his wand in a grave of philosophical speculations and conjured no more, save in a few brief "Ariel flights" of song.

ARTHUR STEDMAN, "MELVILLE OF MARQUESAS"

Published as by Stedman in *The Review of Reviews* (New York), 4 (November 1891), 428-430. The present text corrects one minor typographical error.[1] The accompanying illustration is reproduced here by courtesy of the Newberry Library, Chicago, from its file of the periodical.

The last call has sounded of late for so many of our most noted generation of authors, that the death of Herman Melville came as a surprise to the public at large, chiefly because it revealed the fact that such a man had lived so long. This, also, in the case of a writer whose works forty years ago were as much a matter of comment as are the books of Rudyard Kipling to-day. When "Omoo" appeared in 1847, *Blackwood's Magazine* saw fit to say: "The volume was laid before us and we suddenly found ourselves in the entertaining society of Marquesan Melville, the phœnix of modern voyagers, sprung, it would seem, from the mingled ashes of Captain Cook and Robin Crusoe."[2] This was the final pæan of a chorus of praise that already had lasted a year in the case of Melville's first book, "Typee."

To the local literary colony, however, the residence of Mr. Melville in New York was a well-known fact; and his reserved manner of life was also known and respected. At different times efforts were made to draw him from his seclusion, but they could not continue indefinitely.[3] Doubtless many of our younger writers for the press had never heard of him. The meagre notices of his death would indicate as much. The reasons for this and the details of his life and work offer a tempting field for discussion.

The Late Herman Melville

Life and Adventures

The son of a New York merchant, and born in that city on August 1, 1819, he was compelled by his father's early death to seek his own fortune. It is more than probable that the publication of Dana's "Two Years Before the Mast," in 1840, influenced him to follow the sea as a vocation, and to ship for Liverpool as cabin boy the following year.[4] Returning, he devoted some time to school-teaching. His records show that he received for this work a salary of "six dollars a quarter and board." The most eventful period of his life began on January 1,* 1841, when he sailed from New Bedford, Mass., in the whaler Acushnet, bound for the Pacific sperm-fishery. After a four months' residence among the Nukuheva cannibals, and various experiences in the Society and Hawaiian groups, as related in "Typee" and "Omoo," he joined the crew of the frigate United States, and arrived at Boston, Mass., in the autumn of 1844. Thereafter he was to travel only in the conventional way.

His life in New York and at Pittsfield, Mass., followed. He lived in Pittsfield, where he enjoyed a close acquaintance with Hawthorne, from 1850 to 1863. The remaining years were passed in the metropolis. From 1866 to 1885 he performed the duties of a district officer of the New York custom house, preferring them to indoor clerical work. It was in connection with this position that he first met Richard Henry Stoddard, the poet, from whom some interesting reminiscences of the dead romancer may be expected.[5]

Melville's success as a writer was undoubtedly continuous and constantly increasing up to the publication of "Moby Dick" in 1851. "Redburn" and "Mardi" appeared in 1848–49,[6] the former founded on his experiences during the voyage to Liverpool, the latter a combination of the real and the fantastical which received adverse criticism in some quarters. "White-Jacket" (1850), based on his life aboard a man-of-war, is one of his two most consistent books, the other being "Typee." With "Moby Dick" he was to reach the topmost notch of his fame. "Pierre, or the Ambiguities" (1852), was the signal for an outburst of protest against "metaphysical and morbid meditations" which already had made themselves apparent in "Mardi" and "Moby Dick."[7] Some of the short stories in "Piazza Tales" (1856), one in *Harper's Monthly* entitled "Cock-a-Doodle-Doo," which Henry M. Alden, the editor of that magazine, considers about the best short story he ever read,[8] and a few notable poems comprise the remainder of Melville's important literary product. "Israel Potter" (1855) and "The Confidence Man" (1857) do not seem to require criticism.[9]

This author's power in describing and investing with romance experiences and scenes actually participated in and witnessed by himself, and his failure of success as an inventor of characters and situations, were early pointed out by his critics. More recently H. A. Salt has drawn the same distinction very carefully in an illuminating article contributed to the *Scottish Art Review*.[10] He divides Melville's books into those which are chiefly autobiographical and those which may be considered as fantasies. Of the former are "Typee," "Omoo," "Redburn," and "White-Jacket." Of the latter are "Mardi," "Pierre," and "Moby Dick." But "Moby Dick, or the White Whale," containing, as it does, so large a proportion of truthful description of the whaler's life, stands rather in a class by itself. The earlier critics agree with Clark Russell in placing it at the very head of Melville's books.[11] No more striking contrast of the latter's different methods of work can be found than that afforded between the chapter entitled "Stubb Kills a Whale," and the lurid closing chapter.

An editorial writer of the New York *Times* has been the first to draw a comparison between the pioneer in South Sea romance and Robert Louis Stevenson, considerably to Mr. Stevenson's disadvantage.[12] Although his sketches have grown less mortally dull of late, the Scottish author's hope of success appears to lie chiefly in the direction where Melville failed—the creations of his own fertile brain. Then, too, a seeker after romance in the Pacific must adopt (it would almost seem) the method of Melville himself, or of Pierre Loti, or of Lafcadio Hearn.[13]

Melville's most artistic work is to be found in "Typee," the first blossom of his youthful genius. This idyl, which set all the world to talking, undoubtedly will hold a permanent position in American literature, and most people will wish to read its sequel, "Omoo." The character of "Fayaway" and, no less, William S. Mayo's "Kaloolah,"[14] the enchanting dreams of many a youthful heart, will retain their charm; and this in spite of endless variations by modern explorers in the same domain. A faint type of both characters may be found in the Surinam "Yarico" of Captain John Gabriel Stedman, whose "Narrative of a Five Years' Expedition" appeared in 1796.[15] As for "Moby Dick" and "White-Jacket," they should be read wherever men go down to the sea in ships, and until the spirit of adventure, so strong in the English-speaking race, abandons its sway over the hearts of human beings. "Typee" and "Omoo" have been from the first of much value to outgoing missionaries for the information contained in them concerning the Pacific islanders.[16] A reference to "Typee" as "Melville's Marquesan Islands," under which title the book first appeared in England, was given in the *Popular Science Monthly* as recently as two weeks before the author's death, and shows the ethnological value of the work.[17]

Melville's Poetry

The events of the Civil War gave a strong lyrical movement to Melville's pen, which had rested for nearly ten years when the volume of "Battle-Pieces and Aspects of the War" appeared in 1866. Most of these poems originated, according to the author, "in an impulse imparted by the fall of Richmond,"[18] but they have as subjects all the chief incidents of the struggle. The best of them are "The Stone Fleet," "In the Prison Pen," "The College Colonel," "The March to the Sea," "Running the Batteries," and "Sheridan at Cedar Creek." Some of these had a wide circulation in the press, and were preserved in various anthologies. Mr. Stoddard has called "Sheridan" the "second best cavalry poem in the English language, the first being Browning's 'How They Brought the Good News from Ghent to Aix.'" There are in this poem lines as lofty in sentiment and expression as Bryant, or the author of "Lines on a Bust of Dante," or Mr. Stoddard himself could have written.[19] In the two privately printed volumes, "John Marr and Other Sailors" (1888) and "Timoleon" (1891), are several fine lyrics, the best of them being his last poem, "The Return of the Sire de Nesle." "Clarel, a Poem and Pilgrimate in the Holy Land" (1876), is a long mystical poem requiring, as some one had said, a dictionary, a cyclopaedia, and a copy of the Bible for its elucidation.[20]

A Disastrous Year

The year 1853 was one of ill omen to Melville. He had removed to Pittsfield in 1850 in the flush of his youthful fame, and while "shaping out the gigantic conception of his 'White Whale,'" as Hawthorne expressed it.[21] The book came out and he enjoyed to the full the enhanced reputation it brought him, although six years of the most engrossing literary work had somewhat injured his constitution. He did not, however, take warning from "Mardi," but allowed himself to plunge more deeply into the sea of philosophy and fantasy. "Pierre" appeared, and after it a long series of hostile criticisms ending with a severe, though impartial, article by Fitz-James O'Brien in *Putnam's Monthly.*[22] Close upon this came the great Harper fire, which destroyed the whole stock of his books, published for the most part on the half profit plan, and kept them out of print at a most important time. The plates were not injured, but in the case of all the works the printing and binding of new editions had to be done over again.

I do not know a better example of the sagacity with which the literary departments of our great publishing houses were managed, even a generation ago, than is presented by Melville's case. This sagacity is indeed necessary to their large incomes. With the exception of "Typee," which was purchased from another house, the American firm brought out all the works up to "Pierre" on a half profit system; but for "Pierre" they offered a much more conventional arrangement, and for his other books, except "Battle Pieces," Melville had to seek new publishers. It must be remembered, in connection with their action, that Melville was at the zenith of his reputation in 1852. The wisdom of the firm's attitude was abundantly proved.[23]

In the case of one of these later books Melville suffered the "authors' complaint" of having the plates bought in and a new edition issued without authority or compensation. Mr. Whitman also has gone through a similar experience. The novel feature of the Melville affair is that the volume was issued as a new book with a different title. Both gentlemen made use of the law to redress their grievances.[24] Mr. Melville's brother Allan was a New York lawyer, and up to his death in 1872 managed the former's affairs with ability, the author taking little interest in business details except scrupulously to pay all debts.[25]

The pirating of American books in England reached its worst form about 1851, and "Moby Dick" (brought out by Bentley in that year, as "The Whale," in three handsome volumes) was the last of Melville's works to be made a feature of by English publishers. Probably this was a good thing for his reputation in that country. Meanwhile the English rights in "Typee" and "Omoo" had been bought outright by a London publisher for small sums, and were held by him until Melville's death, so that soon all income from "oversea" was ended.[26]

Self-elected Retirement

It will be seen, then, that his reputation suffered much from his writing him-self down. This was the chief of the adverse influences already mentioned. Other factors were his growing inclination for a secluded life, and a marked avoidance of any action on his part toward keeping himself before the public. These were heavy obstacles for any publisher; but I fancy that if Melville had been a Boston author, even these would not have proved insurmountable.[22] Our New York firms do not thoroughly understand the gentle art of nourishing reputations.

In England Clark Russell has for many years, in most gracious ways, kept Melville's name constantly before the public. I have referred, in another sketch, to Robert Buchanan's famous expedition in New York, when he "sought everywhere for this Triton"—except in the City Directory—and to the same writer's *Academy* statement that Melville

> "Sits all forgotten or ignored,
> While haberdashers are adored."

Although to those in whose homes the romances of Melville and the chantings of Whitman have been household words with three generations—although, to such, the melodramatic prancings of latter-day enthusiasts are somewhat tedi-ous,[28] yet there was reason as well as rhyme in Mr. Buchanan's pasquinade.

Even now we may well forego at intervals the works of our brilliant deniers of romance and iconoclasts of genius—to follow through storm and stress the hardy Nimrods of the deep—or to float in aboriginal canoes over island lakes, wafted by breezes which swell the outspread draperies of olive-hued and brown-haired damsels of the Southern Seas.

THE RETURN OF THE SIRE DE NESLE

A.D. 16—.

[Herman Melville's last poem.]

My towers at last! These rovings end,
Their thirst is slaked in larger dearth;
The yearning infinite recoils,
    For terrible is earth.

Kaf thrusts his snouted crags through fog;
Araxes swells beyond his span,
And knowledge poured by pilgrimage
    Overflows the banks of man.

But thou, my stay, thy lasting love,
One lonely good, let this but be!
Weary to view the wide world's swarm,
    But blest to fold but thee.

TITUS MUNSON COAN, "HERMAN MELVILLE"

Published over Coan's signature in the Boston *Literary World*, 22 (19 December 1891), 492–493.

Considered as a seed-time of eminent names, the year 1819 was one of remarkable fertility. Keeping to England and the United States alone, in that year were born Herman Melville, John Ruskin, J. R. Lowell, Walt Whitman, Charles Kingsley, W. W. Story, T. W. Parsons, C. A. Dana, E. P. Whipple, J. G. Holland, H. P. Gray, Thomas Ball, Cyrus Field, Julia Ward Howe, and Queen Victoria.[1]

Of these names, which will endure the longer as author or artist? It seems to me that Melville's *Typee* has an intrinsic charm, born of concurring genius and circumstance, that make it surer of immortality than any other work by any other name on our list—not even excepting Queen Victoria's *Journal in the Highlands*.[2] But re-incarnation is not as yet, and who shall know the future dealings of fate with these various fames?

But I am anticipating. Let me give a brief outline of the events of Melville's life, and indicate—within these limits I can do no more—how directly his writings flowed from real experience, like water from a spring. Melville was born August 1, 1819, the third in a family of eight children, in New York City—the last place that one looks for a poet to be born in. Eminent men generally, according to popular statistics, are born in the country;[3] they nourish their genius there, and come to town to win their fame. If this theory has any truth, it is simply due to the fact that more people are born in the country, anyway, than in the town; a circumstance that does not occur to the popular statisticians.

In 1835 young Melville attended the "Albany Classical School;" his teacher, Dr. Charles E. West, still lives in Brooklyn, and makes an occasional appearance at the Saturday evenings of the Century Club. He speaks of his pupil as having been distinguished in English composition and weak in mathematics.[4]

In 1837,* when Melville was eighteen, he made his first voyage before the mast in a New York merchantman bound for Liverpool, returning after a short cruise. The record of this first voyage will be found in *Redburn,* which, however, was not his first but his fourth book, having been published in 1849. For three years young Melville had had enough of the sea. He spent the summer of 1838* working on his uncle's farm in Pittsfield, Mass., and at intervals he taught school, both there and in Greenbush, now East Albany, New York. This sea-going and this school-teaching were undertaken in the pluckiest spirit for self-support, his father being then in straitened circumstances. But the seeds of adventure and unrest were also in his nature; and he shipped again before the mast in the whaler "Acushnet," sailing from New Bedford, January 1,* 1841. This was the voyage that gave him his opportunity. In the summer of 1842, as detailed in the true history, *Typee,* he left his ship at the Bay of Nukuheva, in the Marquesas Islands, escaping to the Typee Valley. There he received from the natives the kindest treatment, and lived deliciously all the summer long; while, on the other hand, he was in constant fear of being sacrificed at any moment to their cannibal proclivities. He spent four months in this anxious paradise; finally he escaped from the valley to an Australian whaler, where he resumed the life of the forecastle. It would be curious to know whether any of the rough sailors with whom he herded during these tossing years recognized the presence of his gifts in their shipmate; in all probability they did not.

The Australian whaler touched at some of the smaller islands, and anchored at Tahiti on the day of its occupation by the French. These were stirring times in that peaceful group, and the young poet, as he sets forth in *Omoo,* was confined for alleged mutinous conduct, with others of his companions, but was honorably discharged. From Tahiti he made his way to Honolulu, where he spent four months. He has left some record of that time in the very biting comments upon political and missionary affairs, that may be found in the appendix to the English edition of *Typee;* an appendix, by the way, that is discreetly suppressed in the American edition. To get a passage homeward he shipped for the fourth time before the mast, this time upon the United States frigate "United States," then (I think) commanded by Captain James Armstrong,[5] and thus added the experience of man-of-war service to that of life on a New York merchantman and on American and English whaling-ships.[6] He spent more than a year upon the frigate, and was discharged in Boston in the fall of 1844. He then returned to his mother's home in Lansingburgh, and began the literary work for which he had such varied, ample, and profoundly interesting material. *Typee* was written during the winter of 1845–46, and published in London and New York in 1846. Its success was immediate and great. The entire English reading-world knew Melville's name, if not the book itself; it was the talk of the public and of the coteries. *Omoo,* which followed shortly after, was very well received, but not so widely read. August 4, 1847, he married the daughter of Chief-Justice Shaw of Massachusetts, removed to New York, and lived there until 1850. Meanwhile he published *Mardi,* a South Sea romance, prefacing a note to the effect that, as *Typee* and *Omoo* had been received as romance instead of reality, he would now enter the field of avowed fiction. In the same year, 1849, was published *Redburn,* the record, as already noted, of his first voyage before the mast.

In 1850 Melville went to Pittsfield, Mass., and lived there thirteen years, returning to New York again in October, 1863; and here he spent the remainder of his life, with the exception of two brief visits to Europe and a voyage to California. Leaving New York, October 8, 1849, he went to London to arrange for the publication of his works, returning about the first of February, 1850. He now addressed himself to writing *White Jacket,* a most vivid record of his man-of-war experience; it was published in 1850.[7] *Moby Dick,* the story of the great White Whale, appeared in 1851; the novel, *Pierre, or The Ambiguities,* in 1852; *Israel Potter* and *The Confidence Man,* in 1855,* and the *Piazza Tales* in 1856. All of Melville's works, except *Clarel,* were published almost as soon as written.

During these years Melville applied himself so closely to literary work that his health became impaired, and he made another visit to England, sailing October 11, and returning in May, 1857. During this time he visited his old friend, Nathaniel Hawthorne, at Southport; went up the Mediterranean, saw Constantinople and the Holy Land, and returned with new material for future work; but from this time he published little for some years. During the winters 1857 to 1860, however, he gave lectures in different cities, touching a large range of subjects: "The South Seas," "Travel," "Statues in Rome," among others. In 1860 he made a voyage to San Francisco *via* Cape Horn, sailing from Boston May 30, with his brother, Thomas Melville, who commanded the "Meteor," a fast-sailing clipper in the China trade, and returning in mid-November. In 1866 his poems, *Battle Pieces,* were published; and on the fifth of December of that year he was appointed collector of customs in the New-York Custom House by Henry A. Smyth, an office which he held for nineteen years and resigned the first of January, 1886. In the interim, 1876, his *Clarel* appeared, a work of which the germ had been unfolding for many years; his visit to the Holy Land gave much of the material and imagery in it. His latest books were privately printed. A copy of *John Marr and Other Sailors,* and one of his *Timoleon,* lie before me; each of these volumes of poetry appeared in an edition of twenty-five copies only. With these closed the exterior record of a life of extreme contrasts—years of the most restless activity, followed by a most unusual seclusion.

These data, now for the first time fully given, will help us to characterize Melville's life and literary work. *Typee* and *Omoo,* mistaken by the public for fiction, were, on the contrary, the most vivid truth expressed in the most telling and poetic manner. My father, the Rev. Titus Coan, went over Melville's ground in 1867, and while he has criticised the topography of *Typee* as being somewhat exaggerated in the mountain distances, a very natural mistake, he told me that the descriptions were admirably true and the characterizations faultless in the main. The book is a masterpiece, the outcome of an opportunity that will never be repeated. Melville was the first and only man ever made captive in a valley full of Polynesian cannibals, who had the genius to describe the situation, and who got away alive to write his book.[8]

His later works, equally good in their way—*White Jacket* and *Moby Dick*—had a different though equal misappreciation. They dealt with a life so alien to that of the average reader that they failed adequately to interest him; but they are life and truth itself. On this matter I may speak with some authority, for I have spent years at sea, and I cannot overpraise the wonderful vigor and beauty of these descriptions. The later works were less powerful, and *Pierre* roused a storm of critical opposition. Yet these misunderstandings and attacks were not the main cause of his withdrawal from society. The cause was intrinsic; his extremely proud and sensitive nature and his studious habits led to the seclusion of his later years. My acquaintance with Melville began in 1859, when I had a most interesting conversation with him at his home in Pittsfield, and wrote of him as follows:

> In vain I sought to hear of "Typee" and those paradise islands; he preferred to pour forth instead his philosophy and his theories of life. The shade of Aristotle arose like a cold mist between myself and Fayaway. . . . He seems to put away the objective side of life, and to shut himself up as a cloistered thinker and poet.[9]

This seclusion endured to the end. He never denied himself to his friends; but he sought no one. I visited him repeatedly in New York, and had the most interesting talks with him. What stores of reading, what reaches of philosophy, were his! He took the attitude of absolute independence toward the world. He said, "My books will speak for themselves, and all the better if I avoid the rattling egotism by which so many win a certain vogue for a certain time." He missed immediate success; he won the distinction of a hermit. It may appear, in the end, that he was right. No other autobiographical books in our literature suggest more vividly than *Typee, Omoo, White Jacket,* and *Moby Dick,* the title of Goethe, "Truth and Beauty from my own life." *Typee,* at least, is one of those books that the world cannot let die.

In conclusion: does any one know whether the "Toby" of *Typee,* Mr. Richard T. Greene, is living? He has disappeared from ken a second time, as heretofore he disappeared from "Tommo" in Typee Valley; has he gone where a second quest would be useless? If not, and if this meets the eye of any friend of his, will he send me word?[10]

20 W. 14th St., New York.

JOSEPH EDWARD ADAMS SMITH, "HERMAN MELVILLE"

Published anonymously in nine issues of the Pittsfield, Massachusetts, *Evening Journal* between October of 1891 and January of 1892. The nine instalments, each headed "HERMAN MELVILLE." but with variant subtitles ("A Great Pittsfield Author—Brief Biographical Sketch [*or* Sketches]"), appeared in the issues of Tuesday, 27 October (p. 4), Thursday, 29 October (p. 4), Saturday, 21 November (p. 4), Wednesday, 16 December (p. 2), Saturday, 19 December (p. 6), Thursday, 24 December (p. 4), Tuesday, 12 January (p. 6), Saturday,

16 January (p. 4), and Monday, 25 January (p. 4). In addition, the issue of 25 January 1892 carried an editorial, "Herman Melville and Pittsfield" (p. 4), taking note of the completion of the series. This editorial, presumably by Smith himself, as its second paragraph suggests, is also reprinted here.

During the summer of 1897 Melville's widow arranged for the reprinting— with some alterations and deletions—of all but one of the instalments (that of 16 December) in a 31-page pamphlet, without imprint. The cover and title page read "BIOGRAPHICAL SKETCH / OF HERMAN MELVILLE. / 1891." On p. 1 is the following heading, immediately preceding the text: "HERMAN MELVILLE / WRITTEN FOR THE EVENING JOURNAL, PITTSFIELD, MASS., / BY J. E. A SMITH, 1891." The pamphlet retains the newspaper subheadings and concludes with the editorial of 25 January 1892, captioned: "EDITORIAL IN EVENING JOURNAL. / HERMAN MELVILLE AND PITTSFIELD." Although the compositor of the pamphlet may be responsible for some of the minor differences between its text and that of the *Evening Journal,* it is evident from the character of the more significant alterations and deletions that Mrs. Melville herself had been editing the newspaper text, not only for the sake of factual accuracy where Smith had been in error but also with the obvious intention of softening certain of his personal observations about Melville and the Melville family.

The text printed here is based on the *Evening Journal* version of 1891–1892— never before reprinted in its entirety. A few minor omissions of individual letters or marks of punctuation have been silently supplied when evidently due only to missing or broken type, but occasional corrections of actual printing errors in both substantives and accidentals have been recorded in Appendix E below, which also gives a detailed report of differences between the newspaper text and the later pamphlet—including two handwritten corrections that Mrs. Melville made in her copy of the pamphlet (now in the Melville Collection of the Harvard College Library).

[1]

The later years of Herman Melville afford a striking illustration of the truth that however distinguished a man may be at one period of his life in literature, politics or otherwise, and although the world may in some cases keep his works in memory, his personality is sure to be forgotten by the busy, bustling crowd unless he constantly reminds them of it by new efforts and new achievements; and especially if at the same time he withdraws from the show which we call "society." An article on Mr. Melville's death in the New York Times of October 2d shows into what forgetfulness he had fallen in the great metropolis, where in the rush of life's tide one wave washes away the traces of that which precedes it. After remarking that, "There has died and been buried in this city, during the current week, at an advanced age, a man who is so little known, even by name, to the generation now in the vigor of life that only one newspaper contained an obituary account of him, and that of only three or four lines," the Times proceeds thus:

Forty years ago the appearance of a new book by Herman Melville was esteemed a literary event, not only throughout his own country, but so far as the English speaking race extended. To the ponderous and quarterly British reviews of that time, the author of "Typee" was about the most interesting of literary Americans, and men who made few exceptions to the British rule of not reading an American book not only made Melville one of them, but paid him the further compliment of discussing him as an unquestionable literary force. Yet when a visiting British writer a few years ago inquired at a gathering in New York of distinctively literary Americans what had become of Herman Melville, not only was there not one among them who was able to tell him, but there was scarcely one among them who had ever heard of the man concerning whom he inquired, albeit that man was then living within a half mile of the place of the conversation.[1]

This story is not very creditable to the "distinctively literary Americans of New York;" and we will venture to guess that one George William Curtis, who has a sort of distinctly, if not distinctively, American literary reputation, was not one of this gathering.[2]

The Tribune, which gives by far the most correct and intelligent account which we have seen in any New York paper, says:

"The death of Herman Melville, although following a lingering illness, has come as a surprise to even his few acquaintances in the city, for their opportunities of seeing him have been extremely limited in number. Much has been written, particularly in English journals, concerning the alleged neglect and disregard of Mr. Melville by contemporary authors in this country, but it is a well known fact here that his seclusion has been a matter of personal choice. * * * Mr. Melville always has been an interesting figure to New York literary circles. So far from being forgotten, he was among the very first to be invited to join the Authors' club at its founding in 1882." * * * "His tall, stalwart figure, until recently, could be seen almost daily tramping through the Fort George district or Central Park, his roving inclination leading him to obtain as much out-door life as possible. His evenings were spent at home with his books, his pictures and his family, and usually with them alone."[3]

This is all true. But it is also true that for the most part—not entirely—Mr. Melville has for many years past, withdrawn, not only from literary effort, but from the enjoyment of the fame which he had already abundantly earned, in general society; even that of a literary character. This was not due to the slightest failure of his mental powers, or any exhaustion of the resources of his genius; nor do we believe it was caused by the severe criticism which some of his later works received; at least not this alone. But of this we shall speak later in the biographical sketch of his life and especially that part of it which connects his name and fame with those of Pittsfield, which we now propose to give.

Biographical Sketch

Mr. Melville came of very honorable descent which he could trace on the paternal side to Scotch New England immigration and on the maternal side to Dutch emigration to New York—both in the days when some of the best blood of Europe was being transferred to America. Both of Mr. Melville's grandfathers are of historic note in the Revolution; and both were on the right side; which was rather exceptional in "patrician" families, as the Tribune very correctly says Mr. Melville's ancestors were.[4] His grandfather, Major Thomas Melville, was a leader in the famous party which made tea of the water in Boston Harbor, Dec. 16, 1773, a measure which frightened even Revolutionary Pittsfield into a vote of censure. Major Melville was an extreme conservative; but in this emergency, he considered what was to be conserved was the constitutional—British constitutional—rights of his country, and not Parliamentary tyranny; and he deemed it right to do something even in contravention of law and order in behalf of those rights. He was conservative even in his dress and in his love for old Boston, wearing in its streets as long as he walked them, the same costume of cocked hat and knee-breeches in which he went to the town meeting in Faneuil hall which led to the famous tea party; when

> "Not a better man was found
> By the crier in his round
>   Through the town" * * *
> "When he had a Roman nose
> And his cheek was like a rose
>   In the snow."

Thus he became the original of Dr. Holmes' "Last Leaf."[5]

His daughter, Herman's maiden aunt, had similar peculiarities and retained the ancestral home near High street in Boston until within about the last 40 years, although the families who had been her early neighbors—and whose carriages were still sometimes seen at her door—had long before yielded their elegant mansions to a rude, and generally foreign, tenantry. The present writer had occasion to call upon her there about the year 1850, and found a house, in furniture, interior construction, and carpentry almost precisely what it must have been 50 years before, with a mistress very much like what we may imagine her mother to have been. She was very fond of her handsome nephew, whom we had then never seen, and was proud of the fame which he had suddenly won by the publication of his stories of South Sea adventures; but she did not quite approve all of them, and had a mischievous idea that it would be a good thing to relieve the exuberant praises he was receiving wherever the English language was read, by a little good natured teasing as to one portion at least of the story.[6]

[ii]

Herman Melville's father, Allan, [observe that the spelling of the name is Scotch] was a merchant at first in Boston and afterwards in New York, holding a high social as well as business position in both cities. He married Miss Catherine, daughter of Gen. Peter Gansevoort, an officer of great merit in the Revolution, who was born at Albany in 1749, and died in 1812.[7] He was major in the 2d New York regiment in the 1775 invasion of Canada, which had an intense interest for Pittsfield, where it originated. In the summer of 1777, when Burgoyne's semi-barbarous invading army was slowly advancing down Lake Champlain and the Hudson, he was colonel in command of Fort Stanwix [afterwards re-named Fort Schuyler].

This fort stood in what is now the center of the city of Rome, New York. It was not safe for Burgoyne to leave it flanking his rear; nor could he spare a force from his main army sufficient to reduce it as he passed. But General St. Leger was at the time crossing the country from Oswego, to reinforce Burgoyne with a body of 1500 men, of whom about 700 were Indians, and, as a pleasant incident on his march, undertook the capture of Fort Stanwix, which he besieged August 3, demanding its surrender, vaunting the superiority of his force and enlarging upon the ferocity of his savage allies if provoked by resistance. Gansevoort replied simply that he would defend the fort to the last extremity. The importance at this time of protecting the inhabitants of the surrounding region against the ravages of the Indians, and, above all, of preventing a junction of St. Leger with Burgoyne cannot be over estimated. Col. Gansevoort with his small garrison of 500 men, could only aid in this by holding the fort.

But the gallant Gen. Herkimer, who commanded the militia of Tryon county, gathered what he could of his men and gave notice to Gansevoort that he intended at a specified time to cut his way through to the fort. Gansevoort determined to favor this design by a vigorous sortie and detailed over 200 men under Lieut. Col. Willett for that purpose. Unfortunately St. Leger, having obtained knowledge of the movement, drew Herkimer, as he advanced, into ambuscade in which he was killed and his force disastrously defeated, with the loss of over 400 men, killed or taken prisoners. The loss would have been still greater, had not Willett made the proposed sortie, checked the pursuit, driven the enemy to their camp and, falling upon them there driven some into the woods and others into the river, returning to the fort without the loss of a single man. St. Leger, however, continued to invest the fort, and Gansevoort as obstinately to defend it, until the great object of holding it—the prevention of a junction of St. Leger with Burgoyne— was attained. In the meantime Gen. Schuyler, recognizing the gravity of the situation, had reluctantly weakened his own force by sending Gen. Arnold, with three regiments, to the succor of the invaded region; but too late to do more than increase the panic-flight of St. Leger's men, which was caused by a report of the victory at Bennington as the total rout of Burgoyne's army, with a rumor that Arnold was advancing upon them with an overwhelming force. Col. Gansevoort's persistent defence of his post had, however, already served its grand purpose. It had prevented the junction of St. Leger with Burgoyne, which, if it had been effected, might have left the battle of Bennington unfought and changed the whole course of the subsequent campaign. Washington keenly and warmly recognized this and congress passed a vote of thanks to Col. Gansevoort. He did other brilliant service in the war, and after it closed was successively commissioner of Indian affairs and for fortifying. In 1771 he was made brigadier-general in the New York militia, and in 1809, when the war of 1812 was approaching, he was appointed to the same rank in the United States army. He was sheriff of Albany county from 1790 to 1792, and regent of the University of New York from 1808 until his death.

Of his two sons, Hon. Peter Gansevoort, who was born in Albany in 1789, was long one of the most prominent and honored citizens of that city. The elder son, Gen. Herman Gansevoort, from whom our author received his name, resided at Gansevoort, a village in the town of Northumberland, Saratoga county, N. Y. The brothers built what is now the hotel known as the Stanwix hotel in 1832-33. It stands on the site of the birthplace of the Revolutionary General Gansevoort and was named for the scene of his most important service. It was not built originally for hotel purposes; but we are sure the name made the house a favorite resort for Herman Melville when in Albany, although he was generally the guest of his uncle, General Peter Gansevoort in the earlier days of the hotel or before.[8]

Both the Gansevoorts and the Melvilles were ardent and efficient supporters of the government in the war of 1812.

Descended from such an ancestry as we have described, Herman Melville was born in New York city August 1, 1819. The writer knows little of his boyhood or school education until his 16th year; but he knows this, that he was a happy, lively boy, and that he received that home training which is better than all that can be taught to boys of that age in school. In despite of all later influences it made him for all his later life an inbred gentleman in manners, in thought and in soul. No influence, before the mast or elsewhere, could change that. Of course a man must be a prig and a bore if he does not vary his manner and his conversation to suit the company which he is in, and Mr. Melville had the happiest faculty for doing that; but in all that is essential he was the same in a lady's parlor, in his own hospitable home, on the summit of Greylock, wading barefooted through the rushing stream under the North Adams natural bridge, and we have no doubt, when with

Hawthorne and the Duyckincks he sought shelter from a summer shower in a hollow of Monument mountain.[9]

It is to be presumed from the character and position of Mr. Melville's family that, previous to his 16th year he had the best school education which could be had, at least in New York city.

In 1835 Professor Charles E. West, a Pittsfield man, whose after career as a leader in the education of young women is familiar to the readers of the JOURNAL as well as to all students of educational history, was president of the Albany classical institute for boys, and Herman Melville became one of his pupils. Professor West now remembers him as a favorite pupil, not distinguished in mathematics, but very much so in the writing of "themes" or "compositions," and fond of doing it, while the great majority of pupils dreaded it as a task, and would shirk it when they could. He was so strict in truthfulness that when Professor West read "Typee" for the first time he was shocked that he should send out "such a pack of lies," and was greatly relieved when an "ancient mariner" familiar with the Typee valley, assured him that they were not lies but veritable facts.[10] Mr. Melville's uncle, Hon. Peter Gansevoort, was one of the trustees of the institute, and we have reason to believe that he made his home with him.[11]

It is quite probable that Herman "ran over" to Pittsfield occasionally while at school in Albany; but, so far as we know, his acquaintance with the town began in 1836.* His uncle, Major Thomas Melville, had long been one of its most prominent citizens.[12] After an eventful residence of 21 years in France, he returned shortly before the opening of the war of 1812, and was soon sent to Pittsfield with the rank of major in the United States army, as commissary and superintendent of army supplies, deputy United States marshal, and commissioner in charge of the prisoners of war at the Cantonment. After the war he purchased what is now called the Broadhall [Morewood] place, in which he succeeded Elkanah Watson, the founder and first president of the Berkshire Agricultural society. He also succeeded him in that presidency and was at one time pronounced by high authority "the best farmer in Berkshire county." He took the first premium at the first ploughing match at the Berkshire cattle show; and the iron plow with which he did it is now in the cabinet of the Berkshire Athenaeum. His nephew, Herman, wrote the sketch of a portion of his life which is printed in the history of Pittsfield.[13] He could have written a history of his whole life which would have made as interesting a volume as ever came from his pen.

In that sketch, which also affords a specimen of his ordinary style as a writer, Mr. Melville gives a fair account of his own first life in Pittsfield; save that, as this was a memoir of his uncle's life and treats only incidentally of his own, he leaves us one incident to supply. We quote from the history:

In 1836* circumstances made me for the greater portion of a year an inmate of my uncle's family, and an active assistant upon the farm. He was then gray headed, but not wrinkled; of a pleasing complexion; but little, if any, bowed in figure; and preserving evident traces of the prepossessing good looks of his youth. His manners were mild and kindly, with a faded brocade of old French breeding, which—contrasted with his surroundings at the time—impressed me as not a little interesting, nor wholly without a touch of pathos.

He never used the scythe, but I frequently raked with him in the hay field. At the end of the swath he would at times pause in the sun, and taking out his smooth worn box of satin-wood, gracefully help himself to a pinch of snuff, while leaning on his rake; quite naturally; and yet with a look, which—as I recall it—presents him in the shadowy aspect of a courtier of Louis XVI, reduced as a refugee, to humble employment in a region far from the gilded Versailles.

        *   *   *   *   *

By the late October fire, on the great hearth of the capacious kitchen of the old farm mansion, I remember to have seen him frequently sitting just before early bed time, gazing into the embers, while his face plainly expressed to a sympathetic observer that his heart—thawed to the core under the influence of the genial flame—carried him far away over the ocean to the gay boulevards.

Suddenly, under the accumulation of reminiscences, his eye would glisten and become humid. With a start he would check himself in his reverie and give an ultimate sigh; as much as to say, "Ah, well! " and end with an aromatic pinch of snuff. It was the French graft upon the New England stock which produced this autumnal apple; perhaps the mellower for the frost.

*   *   *   *   *[14]

The incident which we have to add is this: Besides his labors with his uncle in the hay-field, he was for one term teacher of the common school in the "Sykes district," under Washington mountain, of which he had some racy memories—one of them of a rebellion in which some of the bigger boys undertook to "lick" him—with what result, those who remember his physique and character can well imagine.[15]

Another instance of the interest of the Melville family in Pittsfield is this: Before the "commonwealth" began to contribute to the support of the Berkshire Agricultural society it was necessary to depend upon private contributions and in 1813, Allan Melville, the father of Herman, obtained $138 for it from friends in Boston, and $50 from T. Storm, a friend in New York; and in 1814, Major Melville obtained $125 from friends in Boston. These sums may seem small now, but then they were large enough to be of great service, in nursing, if not preserving the life of, the infant society.[16]

[iii][17]

As a boy in the great seaport of New York, Herman Melville had become fascinated with a seaman's life, which had a far more romantic aspect in those days of wide spread American commerce under sail than that which it now has, with steam navigation to ports which are generally almost as well known as the great streets of New York, and better known to the world than some sections of the city. Doubtless Mr. Melville's family—not foreseeing, as no one could, what finally came of it,—wished him to adopt some other career than that of the sea—still it was not as a scape-grace or runaway, that he followed his early inclination. Immediately upon his return from his visit to his uncle in Pittsfield he therefore made a voyage, before the mast, from New York to Liverpool and back. He liked his marine experience on this voyage so well that on the 1st* of January, 1841, he shipped on a whaling voyage to the Pacific. In July of the next year his ship touched at Nukaheva, one of the Marquesas islands. There, with a companion, who, like himself, was tired of close quarters and a tyranically cruel captain, he left the ship "without waiting for the usual formality of a discharge." [18]

This would seem to landsmen much like jumping from the frying-pan into the fire; for they fell, as they were almost sure to do, into the hands of a warlike and savage, if not cannibal race, who kept him prisoner for four months in the Typee valley. Savage as they were and cruel as they may have been, they nevertheless treated Melville kindly, but with a determination to keep him with them. After four months of strange adventures, which, perilous as they were, afterwards proved more precious to him than the finding of hidden treasure, he was rescued by the crew of a Sydney whaler. He then spent some months in studying life, as it was then formed and was forming in the Sandwich and Society islands, under new and peculiar conditions and institutions. He was a wandering sailor, chance-cast upon these islands, but he was also qualified by education and genius to make this study. His report of it in Omoo and Mardi was sharply—not to say venomously—criticised. [19] But all who knew Herman Melville well knew well also that whatever he wrote he believed that he wrote truthfully. Falsehood was abhorrent to his nature; and if that involved hatred or hypocrisy, why that was the worse for the hypocrite. Mr. Melville wrote many words as he believed truthfully to his pecuniary injury; never one which he believed to be false. And this is proved by the fact that while sensitively religious critics were crying out against his comments upon missionary methods in the Sandwich islands, the missionaries themselves were more wisely using his books to aid them in their studies of the people to whom they were sent. [20] We might cite here the old proverb of learning from your enemy, but Mr. Melville was never an enemy to any genuine good work.

From the Sandwich islands he shipped on the Frigate United States, in which he reached Boston in October, 1844.

> "Oh, home returned, what joy to tell
> Of all the dangers that befell,
> The sailor boy at sea." [21]

It was eight years* since he became a sailor boy and in that interval he had opportunity to observe closely the commercial, whaling and national marine service of the country,[22] as well as the moral and intellectual condition of the several barbarous or semi-civilized tribes with whom he came in contact.

He was now 25 years old and, with little disposition to return to the sea, was considering what pursuit in life he should choose. He was not without friends. His family, although not wealthy, held a much more than merely respectable position in the world. They had lost nothing essential of what they had inherited from provincial and revolutionary days; and far back of those days from their Scotch and Dutch ancestry, whose story, if we had space to tell it, would be of great interest to any student of general history. Herman's elder brother, Gansevoort, was already well established in the law and had won a good and creditable position in politics. His younger brother, Allan, was beginning a successful legal career. But the law was hardly an attractive profession for Herman. One could not well see to what profession he was adapted. A chance word decided it.

The family had given their interesting wanderer a warm welcome home: and, one day, one of them, or one of their intimate friends, said to him: "Why don't you put in book form that story of your South Sea adventures which we all enjoy so much?" He at once accepted the suggestion and soon published "Typee: a Peep at Polynesian Life During Four Months Residence in a Valley of the Marquesas." Arthur Stedman, who seems to be well informed on this point, writing in the New York World says that the manuscript of Typee was finished late in 1845.[23] The author's brother, Gansevoort, was then about starting for London as secretary of the American Legation at the British court —in which position he died—and he took with him this manuscript which he offered to the great London publishing house of Murray—the same which in its earlier days published the works of Sir Walter Scott, Lord Byron and Thomas Moore. John Murray, who was the head of the house in 1846, bought, without hesitation, the Melville manuscript so far as the right of publication in England was concerned; and also that of "Omoo" which soon followed. Both works were published in 1846, in two parts in Murray's "Colonial and Home Library," under the title of "Melville's Marquesas Islands."[24] His later works were purchased in England for higher prices by Bentley. By an agreement made in England Typee and Omoo were brought out in New York by Wiley and Putnam simultaneously with their appearance in London. Afterwards the Harpers became Mr. Melville's American publishers.

The applause with which Typee and Omoo were received on both sides the Atlantic may well be called phenomenal, especially that in England where it was then hard for American genius to obtain recognition. We ought to add that when such recognition was obtained—as in the case of Bryant, Washington Irving and Catherine Sedgwick—it was like the proof of thrice refined gold. We have already alluded to the sudden popularity of Typee and Omoo, but we must fortify our statement by quotations from the most anti-American of all British reviews and newspapers. Blackwood, the most hostile of all towards anything that was American, and generally speaking the most unfair, said this of Omoo: "Musing the other day over our matutinal hyson, the volume itself was laid before us and we found ourself in the society of Marquesan Melville, the Phœnix of modern voyagers—springing, it would seem, from the mingled ashes of Captain Cook and Robinson Crusoe."

Writing of Typee, the "John Bull" said: "Since the joyous moment when we first read Robinson Crusoe and believed it, we have not met so bewitching a book as this narrative of Herman Melville's."

The London Times said, "that Mr. Melville will favor us with his further adventures in the South seas we have no doubt whatever. We shall expect them with impatience, and receive them with pleasure. He is a companion after our own hearts. His voice is pleasant, and we are sure that if we could see his face it would be a pleasant one," and the Times never came nearer to telling the exact truth than it did in this paragraph.[25]

Typee was dedicated to Chief Justice Lemuel Shaw of Massachusetts; not because he was chief justice, but because he had long been a most warm and valued friend of the author's family. Perhaps another reason may be suggested by the fact that on August 4, 1847, Mr. Melville married Judge Shaw's only daughter, Elizabeth; but, without disputing this, the other reason is also true. Judge Shaw's friendship for the Melville family was of long standing, and the regard which he manifested for its young representative on his return from his long wanderings was such that it might well be remembered by him.

In 1849*—or perhaps a year earlier—our memory may fail us as to the exact date—Mr. Melville's mind naturally turned to his uncle's old homestead in Pittsfield. Major Melville was dead and the grand old mansion had descended to his son, Robert, and his sisters. Robert kept it as a boarding house; and it was a great favorite with summer visitors of the highest class. Henry W. Longfellow and ex-President John Tyler had been among its recent guests. To this house, so full of memories, Herman Melville brought his young wife and child in 1849.* Perhaps we do wrong in calling it a boarding house. At least it was no resort for chance-comers, but a home for such guests as we have named, and who had no reason to shrink from companionship with their host and his sisters. We think that, besides Herman Melville and his wife, the only guests of the house in 1849,* were J. R. Morewood, his wife and friends.[26] A close intimacy was thus formed between the two congenial families, which extending to that of Mr. Melville's brother, Allan, and his relative by marriage, Col. Richard Lathers —and being cemented by inter-marriages—has continued unbroken to this day.[27]

[iv][28]

In October, 1850, Mr. Morewood bought the old Van Shaack-Watson-Melville mansion and it soon became his private residence. Some little time after this it was christened "Broadhall" in this wise. One evening in a merry party of men and women more or less distinguished, it was proposed to give it a name; each person present having the privilege of putting one in a basket; the first drawn out to be forever fixed upon the venerable historic mansion. Mr. Melville wrote on his slip the word Broadhall and that came first to the deft hand which was appointed to be the minister of fate. We have a very strong suspicion that the deft hand was guided by a deft brain, and that so happy a drawing was not so entirely a matter of chance as it purported to be. However that may be, no appeal was taken; and the story is one of the many pleasant incidents which preserve Herman Melville's memory in Pittsfield as adjuncts to his memory as a great author.[29]

In anticipation of the sale of Broadhall, Mr. Melville on the 14th of September, 1850, bought of Dr. John M. Brewster, Sr., the farm adjoining the Broadhall estate in the rear, but which as to its buildings faces easterly on the middle road to Lenox, and so near to that town that it renders access to it easy. On the farm was, and is, a large quaint old house, built in the early days of the settlement of the town, by Capt. David Bush. Mr. Melville named the place Arrowhead, from some Indian relics which were turned up in his first plowing of its soil. When white men first began to plow in that vicinity and in that of Dr. Holmes' villas, which included "The Canoe Meadows," relics of the aboriginal owners were found more abundantly than in any other part of the township. What has become of them? Mr. Melville renovated the old house and made it and the splendid landscapes which it commands famous by his "Piazza Tales" and others.[30] The villas of Dr. Oliver Wendell Holmes were a few rods north on the same street, and there was a very friendly intercourse between the two authors, although not so intimate as that between Melville and Hawthorne. But when at one time Mr. Melville was seriously ill, Dr. Holmes visited him with fraternal tenderness, incidentally of course giving him his best medical advice, without—that also of course—intruding upon the province of the local practitioner.[31]

During Mr. Melville's residence at Arrowhead his friend, Col. Lathers, was induced by it to buy a large estate on the opposite side of the street and build "Abby Lodge," in honor of his wife—the home taking the name of its mistress. For several years Mr. Melville's mother and four sisters were members of his family. The circle of friends and relatives with which he was surrounded at this time—including occasional visitors from abroad, was most congenial and delightful to him.

Although he sometimes wrote in the open air on the piazza to which he has given fame, and under the inspiration of the superb scenery spread out before him, his general method of literary work was to shut himself up in his library, having his luncheon, if needed, placed at the door in order to avoid interruption. Often he submitted his manuscript to one of his sisters for revision. Probably it came from her hand somewhat toned down from what he left it in the heat of composition; but not essentially changed.[32] This solitary labor continued until he was wearied, when he would emerge from his "den," join in family or social intercourse, indulge in light reading—which was not so very light; as it included much less of what we commonly call "light literature" than it did of profound reviews, abstruse philosophy in prose or verse, and the like—visit or entertain his friends or otherwise enjoy himself: But no more formal serious work for him until the next morning, although, consciously or unconsciously, his mind was always gathering material for it. And, yet again, this daily routine of life was not tediously continuous, it was often varied by excursions with a friend—or more often with a party of friends, in which the ladies of his own family, those of his friend, Morewood, and their visitors from abroad were sure to be included—to Berkshire localities, interesting either for their beauty, their marked peculiarities or their story, of these he knew many, and was constantly finding more, he was almost extravagantly fond of these excursions. We might say without much exaggeration that they were the great joy of his Berkshire days. Full of jovial life and enthusiasm, he was a most delightful companion, or rather leader, in them; one whose like is rarely found. He invested every scene with new charms, as he dilated upon its beautiful or otherwise interesting features; or rather, it would be more correct to say as he sparkled with spirited and graphic allusions to them. He was not much given to dilation on such occasions; but it was much to be with him when he lightly threw off thoughts suggested by the locality or the incidents of the day, although he seemed as unconscious of any effort as of his breathing or of the beating of his heart. It was as involuntary.[33] He was not of that class who when "going into society" are compelled to "prepare themselves for conversation"—"cram for it" as they say in college. But consciously or unconsciously, there was never the slightest ill nature in his wit; there was not a particle in his whole composition.

Nathaniel Hawthorne came to the little red cottage at the north end of Stockbridge Bowl—about six miles from Arrowhead—in the early summer of 1850 and remained until late in November, 1851. The two authors, both then in the first flush of their early fame, held opinions and had habits of life in common, to a degree which is surprising when we remember how unpremeditated was their coming together in Berkshire and how little opportunity either had previously to influence the other, even through their books, of which each had published only two or three. Hawthorne was the elder both in age and authorship. Years before he had published the "Twice-told Tales" whose great merit was recognized by the most competent critics in England; but which at home brought him little fame and less pecuniary profit—the more shame to the taste of his country-men in their native literature. It was only with the appearance of "The Scarlet Letter," at about the same time with that of Typee that Hawthorne sprang into fame and fortune—or rather, to tell the truth, while the fame came with the Scarlet Letter, the fortune came only with his appointment as consul at Liverpool by his friend and classmate, President Pierce, whose life he had written in the campaign which resulted in his election in 1852; a work forgotten now as an insignificant incident in a petty presidential campaign. It brought him more money in 12 months than the Scarlet Letter, the House of the Seven Gables and the Twice-told Tales did in as many years; although it is but fair to say that the president's ardent personal friendship for the author might have given him the appointment had he not written the memoir, which in its inception was a work of love; and not for any hope of pecuniary reward. This all came later; when the authors met in Berkshire in 1850 Melville was in the more comfortable circumstances of the two. Admired and sought for as the Scarlet Letter instantly became with the highest class of readers, it required some general knowledge of early Massachusetts history to comprehend and some little mental effort to enjoy it, neither of which is to be looked for in the mass of novel devourers. Typee, on the other hand, appealed to all classes of readers. The learned critic enjoyed it as well over his vesper wines as his "matutinal hyson."[34] It was read alike in the most luxurious and the humblest homes, at hours of leisure in workshops and manufactories; but probably most eagerly of all, on shipboard and on the wharves of seaports. *O, si sic omnes.*

[v]

It was under these circumstances that Melville and Hawthorne became Berkshire neighbors. There was nothing in the circumstances which we have stated to create jealousy between the two great authors, but much to create a community of feeling, and lay the foundation for a strong friendship, as it did. Still, both were of a shy temperament; shrinking from the notoriety which unavoidably attached itself to their fame. They were altogether too sensitive to a suspicion that any acquaintance which they might form was due to it. We might call them bashful, if that did not imply some awkwardness of manner, which neither had, except when some forward admirer approached them with coarse flattery. We ought perhaps to make an exception in Hawthorne's case; for when gazed upon too intently by honestly admiring, although beautiful eyes, he was, to say the least, not at his ease. Melville had seen too much of the world to be abashed in that way. This peculiarity of temperament, for a short time, kept apart those who were even nearer neighbors in their hearts than in their homes; and this, although Melville had published in the New York Literary World a most appreciative article upon Hawthorne as an author. This thin coat of sensitiveness was broken through by a characteristic incident. Hawthorne, like Melville, although not to the same degree, was fond of Berkshire excursions.

In one of them, in which one or both of the brothers Duyckinck of the Literary World joined, they were driven by a sudden summer shower under the shelter of a rock shelf on the west side of Bryant's Monument mountain, thoroughly wet. Thus baptized, they were brought into close communion, and—to change the metaphor—with the Literary World editors as a solvent, the restraint which had been irksome to both was dissipated. We have recently heard that Dr. Oliver W. Holmes was one of the party, but must be permitted to doubt it.[35] Hawthorne and Melville at once became friends in head and heart, with a close intimacy which extended to their families; their wives at least as "home bodies," which both eminently were, being of congenial characters. A biographer records that when Mr. Melville was seen approaching the Hawthorne home by the Stockbridge Bowl, the children welcomed him with a joyous shout, "Here comes Omoo!" Another biographer says that in the spring of 1851, Mr. Hawthorne with his daughter, Una, passed a week at Arrowhead and a letter writer says that the friends spent most of their time bathing in the early spring sunshine which streamed through the open doors—and talking philosophy. This was only one of many such philosophical seances.[36] Of course communion like this between two men of extraordinary mental powers, and of kindred thought and feelings amid the most pleasant surroundings, far away from any disturbing influences, must have been delightful to them. It is to be feared, however, that the philosophy which was talked, while it could well color Hawthorne's weird tales, where it had a place, had a very disastrous effect upon those of Melville, where it had none. The literary fields of the two writers were as wide apart as they well could be; and we are compelled to think that their excessive intimacy was a misfortune to the one whose charm lay in the simplicity, vigor and naturalness with which he related his observations of men and nature and his expression of the common sense, but keen and often eloquent, thoughts which they had excited in him.

While pursuing the life we have attempted to describe, Mr. Melville wrote at Arrowhead almost if not quite all his works after Omoo, Typee and Mardi. The first and most powerful of these was "Moby Dick," which simultaneously with its appearance in New York was brought out by the Bentleys in London under the title of "The Whale," in a large and luxuriously splendid edition, in which form it ought to be in the Athenæum library. At Arrowhead he also wrote that strange vagary "Pierre, or the Ambiguities," and also the "Piazza Tales," romances to which he gave this name because they were mainly written on a broad piazza built by the author on the north end of the house, which commands a bold and striking view of Greylock and the intervening heights and vales.[37] "My Chimney and I," a quaintly humorous essay of which the cumbersome old chimney—overbearing tyrant of the house—is the hero, was also written here, as well as "October Mountain," a sketch of mingled philosophy and word-painted landscape, which found its inspiration in the mossy and brilliant autumnal tints presented by a prominent and thickly wooded spur of the Hoosac mountains, as seen from Arrowhead on a fine day after the early frosts.[38]

It was, if we remember rightly, in 1853 that he was invited to become a contributor to Putnam's Magazine, then the best periodical of its class—or of any class in America—and one of the best in the world. It rivalled Blackwood in its tales and in what for lack of a better name we must call depictures of life, sometimes satirical like the Potiphar Papers;[39] but often also, in the tales, full either directly or incidentally of New England folk-lore. Some of the best of these came from the pen of Herman Melville and are mentioned above. He also wrote for the same magazine the extended serials, Benito Cereno and Israel Potter. Almost all his later works have a touch of Berkshire in them. Thus in "Moby Dick" he incorporates in three or four lines of his portrait of "Captain Ahab" a graphic picture of the old elm of Pittsfield park.[40]

The story of Israel Potter was founded upon a narrative of real adventure, written by its own hero and published at Providence in 1824; but Mr. Melville varied it much and introduced a great deal of what he had seen and known in Berkshire. Potter was not the real name of the hero of the story and we suspect that it was suggested by that of "Potter's Mountain," which long before it was the popular resort which a new road has since made it, was much frequented by the author, who greatly enjoyed its wide expanse of view and delighted to lead excursion parties to it.[41]

"Cock-a-doodle-doo," a quaint piece of humor and thought, of which a neighbor's Shanghai rooster was the hero—is also a memento of Mr. Melville's life at Arrowhead; but it was one of several articles which he contributed to Harper's Magazine.

We shall have more to say, in another connection, with regard to Berkshire as a study for our author in composing his tales.

Between 1857 and 1861, a rage for lyceum lectures prevailed all over the northern and western states. In Pittsfield the old Burbank hall, now Mead's carriage repository, was filled at least once every week to its full capacity of over a thousand seats, with eager and intelligent listeners to the most brilliant orators in the country. (It would not be matter for regret if that fever should prevail again.) Some of the most noted authors, as well as orators, were induced to mount the platform, partly by the liberal pay which they received directly, and also for the increased sale which it gave their books. Among these was Herman Melville, who lectured in Burbank hall, and in New York, Philadelphia, Montreal, St. Louis, San Francisco, as well as intermediate cities and towns. He did not take very kindly to the lecture platform, but had large and well pleased audiences.[42]

In about the year 1861 came
                    Mr. Melville's Removal from Pittsfield,
the end of his literary labors, and his seclusion from general society; but we do

not believe that the three events had any more than a merely incidental connection with each other.[43]

Several causes combined to lead to his removal. His experience of farming at Arrowhead had proved costly, and, delightful as the place was in many respects, there were, besides its costliness, others which rendered it no longer a desirable place of residence for him throughout the year. His children were beginning to come of school age, and Arrowhead was more than two miles distant from the central village of the town and its schools; so that it was inconvenient, and indeed well nigh impossible for them to attend them. In March, 1863, he therefore sold the place to his brother, Allan, who until his death in 1872, occupied it as a summer residence as some of his heirs still do; so that it is still "Melville's Arrowhead" with all the charms bestowed by the great author upon it and the scenery which it commands.

Herman, however, did not leave the place until November; and then not for New York but for the square old fashioned house on South street in the rear of Backus block. We do not think that as yet he had determined to make New York his home. If he seriously contemplated it we believe that it was not with a view of forsaking literary work, but to get nearer to its commercial center, and at the same time to have access to libraries in which Pittsfield had then a sad deficiency which has since been supplied to a degree which, although it can only remotely compare with the great metropolitan institutions of that class, may well be prized by scholarly students and writers. The Athenaeum is now rich in the class of rare books which in 1864 Mr. Melville loved and was compelled to seek elsewhere, if he wished for more than could be found on his own shelves, or those of a few friends.

[vi]

Mr. Stedman states in the World that Mr. Melville's removal was caused by his dissatisfaction with the village schools.[44] It is true that he pronounced New York schools which came under his observation superior, not only to those of Pittsfield, but to those of Boston, which claimed to be the model city in that class of instruction. Still we must take Mr. Stedman's statement with some qualification. It is an unfortunate fact that—even since the establishment of the High school in 1850—the public schools of Pittsfield have not been uniformly good for any long time or in all grades at any one time. Sometimes the reason for this has, to close observers, been apparent enough. But, for the most part, the best efforts of the most conscientious and competent committeemen after the brightest early prospects of success, have been rendered ineffectual by developments which it was impossible to foresee. But in 1864 the Pittsfield school system consisted simply of the High and the common district schools and there was no grading beyond this; no Grammar schools such as we now have having then been instituted. The public schools of the town were clearly not such as to invite to it new residents or retain old ones who had children to educate. If Mr. Melville left Pittsfield on that account, his is not the only instance in which it lost or missed of getting valuable citizens by its delay in providing the best possible schools and libraries. As a mere matter of money among the best paying investments the town has ever made were the sums paid for improving its worth and attractions through these educational institutions. But, for all this, in 1864, the private—quasi-public—seminaries of Pittsfield were of such a character and so widely famed that they drew hither families of moderate means who desired to educate their children in the best schools and also in a healthful moral as well as natural atmosphere. We need only name Maplewood institute and Miss Wells' South street seminary for young women, and Rev. Charles E. Abbott's Springside school for lads. The tuition at any of these institutions would not have been burdensome to Mr. Melville, and we must look elsewhere than to a dissatisfaction with "the village schools" to account for his change of residence. We cannot but think that an accident which befell him at this time had something to do with his removal; and also with other changes in his life, which accompanied it. A few days after he removed from Arrowhead, he had occasion for some small articles he had left behind, and, with a friend, started in a rude wagon to procure them. He was driving at a moderate pace over a perfectly smooth and level road, when a sudden start of the horse threw both occupants from the wagon; probably on account of an imperfectly secured seat. Mr. Melville fell with his back in an elbow of the frozen road, and was very seriously injured. Being conveyed to his home by Col. George S. Willis, near whose farm on Williams street the accident happened, he suffered painfully for many weeks.[45] This prolonged agony and the confinement and interruption of work which it entailed, affected him strangely. He had before been on mountain excursions, a driver daring almost to the point of recklessness; but he always brought his ride to a safe conclusion, and his, sometimes terrorized, passengers to a safe landing place. After this accident he not only abandoned the rides of which he had been so fond; but for a time shrank from entering a carriage. It was long before the shock which his system had received was overcome; and it is doubtful whether it ever was completely. It must have had its effect in discouraging him from literary and social effort for several months. Two other circumstances favored his removal to New York. Chief Justice Shaw died in 1861 at the age of 80, leaving his daughter, Mrs. Melville, a moderate fortune, which enabled the purchase of the very pleasant and convenient house, 104 East 26th street. Furnished like the old home at Arrowhead, to suit the tastes of its occupants, with its rare and story telling engravings and with Mr. Melville's curious library which had been so gathered that he was its soul, 104 East 26th street became a very attractive and satisfying home for people like Mr. and Mrs. Melville.

The other circumstance which may have favored their removal to New York was this: In 1865* Collector Smyth of the custom house in that city, an old friend and traveling companion of Mr. Melville, gave him an appointment, not as clerk, which would have been intolerably irksome to him, but as inspector or appraiser, which brought him into pleasant contact with his old marine life; experience in which well fitted him for the place. We do not know that, previous to his leaving Pittsfield, he had received any intimation of Mr. Smyth's desire to make this appointment, but it is very likely that he did, and that it had some influence upon his friend's mind in deciding the question of his removal.[46] His absorption in the duties of his office and the occupation which it gave his mind must also have contributed to the permanence of his withdrawal from literature and society, by preventing the restlessness which would otherwise in time have drawn him back to his old relations with both. He was eminently a self-contained man; but he was also a dear lover of and close communicant with nature, whether he found it in men, or in seas, mountains, woods and fields. The peculiar character of his office must have furnished him with abundant opportunities to study human nature; and the superb variety of scenery and romantic localities in and around New York city and its harbor left him little to regret even of what he had given up in Berkshire. He had no lack of figures and back ground for stories as entrancing as he had ever given to the world, if he could but have written with his early simplicity and perspicuity; or if the world would have accepted his fine thoughts in the garb in which he saw fit to clothe them. He would not—perhaps could not—return to his old style.

> "Alas, no life, no love
> Resumes its morning.
> What is past, is past."[47]

And the critics—possibly also his account with his publishers—told him that books in his later style, although they might find readers, would not be received with anything like the old favor, but with snarling censure.[48] Mr. Melville was too proud a man to submit tamely to this, or to appear before prejudiced judges. This was in part, although not wholly, the cause of our losing so much of what his mature and vigorous intellect might have given us after 1864.

[vii]

There were several reasons for Mr. Melville's seclusion from society in New York, so far as there was any such seclusion. For a time ill health and the exhaustion which follows it robbed his spirits of some of their old elasticity, and then death followed death among their relations and dearest friends in such rapid succession that there was scarcely a year when the family could be said to be out of mourning,—sincere mourning, although custom did not in all cases require the wearing of its outward symbols.[49] Neither Mr. or Mrs. Melville were what are technically called "society people;" but neither did they affect any contempt or disrelish for society in the class where birth and other circumstances had placed them. In Berkshire Mr. Melville frankly and cordially enjoyed the companionship of his personal friends, learned or unlearned, fashionable or unfashionable, as occasion offered, whether they were residents or visitors from abroad. Of course—"sarcumstanced as he was," as one of his North Woods admirers expressed it, the number of these personal friends was limited and he met some under very different conditions than he did others; but his manner to all was alike frank and friendly. In Pittsfield he did not exclude himself from the entertainments of the local social circle in which his family moved, nor was he ever neglectful of any of the reasonable observances required by its etiquette. He rather seemed to have modelled himself as a "gentleman of the old school" upon the pattern of his Boston-born and Parisian bred uncle, the democratic aristocrat Major Thomas Melville. In short as a resident of Pittsfield, he was a hospitable and courteous host; a pleasant and true friend; a gentleman of graceful and dignified manner, and as the head of a family as solicitous for the pleasure and as regardful of the wishes of its other members as for his own—or more so. But neither he or Mrs. Melville ever coveted prominence in fashionable society anywhere, and there was no reason why they should seek for it in its mad New York whirl; or enter into that whirl at all. There were on the contrary—as we have endeavored to explain—circumstances which disinclined them even for such social pleasures as had been dear to them in Berkshire, and in the social and intellectual metropolitan circles, into which they would naturally have entered; and which were ready to welcome them with open arms and warm hearts. Habit made this seclusion permanent to a certain extent, and the name of Melville vanished from the not absolutely all-seeing view of the crowd of metropolitan, literary and society newspaper itemizers; and therefore from the view of the great newspaper reading world. But notwithstanding all that has been said, we do not believe that in his New York home Herman Melville was ever morose or repulsive to old friends or to new ones who had any claim to his acquaintance, whether resident in New York or elsewhere. That would have required a change in his nature too strange to be believed; and we know well that no such change took place. His contribution to the history of Pittsfield was written subsequent to 1871, and it was furnished in his old kindly spirit, and with the same love for the town which he always manifested. All his intercourse regarding it was marked by his old frank, friendly and considerate manner—not one whit changed.[50]

With regard to the unavailing quest made for him by Englishmen lion hunting in New York city, of which mention has been made, we have only this to add. During the later years of his life Mr. Melville carried on an exceedingly pleasant correspondence with the great English sea novelist, W. Clark Russell, who was one of the most ardent and intelligent admirers of his work in the same field—or sea—of literature. And if their correspondence was thus pleasant, so their meeting would have been had Mr. Russell crossed the Atlantic. He would have met no difficulty in finding his friend; nor do we believe that any other Englishman of much reputation would. It depends a good deal sometimes upon who asks and who answers a question. Thus, after Mr. Melville had lived a couple of years in Pittsfield and of course was much spoken of, a seeker after knowledge asked of a local bookseller, "Who is this Herman Melville, that people are talking so much about?" "Why," was the truthful reply, "Why, he's the fellow that bought Dr. Brewster's farm. I guess he's a cousin of Bob's." The intelligent bibliopole did not know that he was the writer of the books, he was himself selling daily. If a visitor to Pittsfield had asked him where he could find the author of Typee and Omoo, he would probably have been as much at a loss as the "gathering of distinctively literary Americans" of New York were when inquired of by the lion-hunting Englishmen.[51]

His Last Visit to Pittsfield

was in 1885 when he was for some days a guest at the Homestead Inn—the Pomeroy homestead on East street, which was for a short time converted into a fashionable hotel. While there, he did not show even the changes which time commonly works on men in the number of years which elapsed between 1864 and 1885. He did not evince the slightest aversion to society, but appeared to enjoy the hearty welcome which it gave him; time having enhanced instead of diminishing the local pride in and regard for him. Perhaps his manner was a little more quiet than in the old time; but in general society it had always been quiet. It had eminently that repose which stamps the caste of Vere de Vere, although it covered no heartlessness, and savored nothing of arrogance. The Melvilles were never forgetful of the patrician character of their family,[52] while they never manifested their consciousness of it to the outer world, except by their scrupulous obedience to that grand law which is grandly condensed in the axiom, noblesse oblige, which imperatively demands of all who claim high rank that their acts should always be noble, never ignoble; proudly assuming that each individual recognizes what constitutes nobility of action. This is too often only an "assumption," but in the Gansevoort-Melville family it was a governing principle. To traverse a phase used by the representative of another old family, there "was no mean streak" in the Gansevoort-Melville blood.

In this last visit to Pittsfield Mr. Melville bore nothing of the appearance of a man disappointed in life, but rather had an air of perfect contentment, and his conversation had much of his old jovial, let-the-world-go-as-it-will spirit. It would be well nigh a climatic miracle, if a brief ride to Pittsfield and a few sniffs of Berkshire air should so restore to society and its enjoyment, a man who had just been the recluse and almost misanthrope pictured by some of the New York newspaper writers. If it could be proved true, our sanitarian city would rise even higher than it now is in the world's esteem, and dyspeptic patients would flock to it in crowds, from the world over. We know that it will perform wonders; but a wonder is not necessarily a miracle. Pittsfield with the aid of Lenox, performed wonders in curing Charles Sumner of his early dyspeptic troubles, but it required more weeks than it did hours to effect a cure in Melville's case, and moreover in that of Sumner the climate and the scenery were largely aided by an intermingling of rides, walks and talks with Fanny Kemble, then the queen of his thoughts; so that his cure, although wonderful, was no miracle.[53] In Mr. Melville's case, we suspect that the miracle may be easily disposed of, so far as any morbid connection is concerned, by the fact that there was little or nothing to be cured. Memories of glad days and dear friends that had become only memories must have crowded upon him; but if he dwelt upon them in a morbid spirit, he gave no sign of it. Even the natural and healthful emotions which these memories excited were not exhibited to the common eye; as all who knew him will readily believe; and they will as fully believe that they nevertheless existed in his breast, and were deeply felt there. He was not one to display to the common world what should be sacred to his own breast. Perhaps he erred in not always seeking sympathies, even where he could rightfully look for, and was certain to find, them. But of that we can only conjecture.

[viii]

Mr. Melville's recluse habits in New York have been sufficiently discussed and explained but something more must be said of his retirement from book making. This did not occur until more than two years after he left Pittsfield which goes to confirm our theory that he did not contemplate it at the time of his removal. His last work of much merit was published late in 1866. It was a volume of poems entitled "Battle Pieces" and was almost a chronicle in verse of the war for the Union. It shows that all through the war and in the year which followed its close he was in full and ardent sympathy with the best thought and feeling of the country. Neither in the poems or the prose comments which accompanied them was there the least trace of the irrelevant philosophy or the mysticism which marred most of his later works. Some of the poems show much poetic power; and if the book had been published as from a new author it would have been hailed as a success. In a very discriminating as well as appreciative review of Mr. Melville's life and works, the Springfield Republican says well that it is startling to read these lines, called "The Portent:"—

> Hanging from the beam
>   Slowly swaying (such the law)
> Gaunt the shadow on your green,
>   Shenandoah!

The cut is on the crown,
(Lo! John Brown,)
And the stabs shall heal no more.

Hidden in the cap
  In the anguish none can draw;
So your future veils its face,
  Shenandoah!
But the streaming beard is shown,
(Weird John Brown,)
The meteor of the war! [54]

The poem on General Bartlett, although not precisely historically accurate, is nevertheless so realistic that it brings back vivid memories of the departure of the 49th regiment from Pittsfield and its return. Mr. Melville uses poetic license with regard to Gen. Bartlett's two commands as colonel; but the poem is realistic, for all that, and we copy it, although it has been once printed in the JOURNAL.

The College Colonel.

He rides at their head;
  A crutch by his saddle just slants in view,
One slung arm is in splints, you see,
  Yet he guides his strong steed—how coldly, too!

He brings his regiment home—
  Not as they filed two years before,
But a remnant half-tattered, and battered and worn,
Like castaway sailors, who—stunned
  By the surf's loud roar,
  Their mates dragged back and seen no more,—
Again and again abreast the surge,
  And at last crawl, spent, to shore.

A still rigidity and pale,—
  An Indian aloofness lines his brow;
He has lived a thousand years
  Compressed in battle's pains and prayers,
Marches and watches slow.

There are welcoming shouts, and flags;
  Old men doff hat to the boy,
Wreaths from gay balconies fall at his feet,
  But to him—there comes alloy.

It is not that a leg is lost,
  It is not that an arm is maimed,
It is not that the fever has racked,—
  Self he has long disclaimed.

> But all through the Seven Days' fight
> And deep in the Wilderness grim,
> And in the field hospital tent,
> And Petersburg crater, and dim
> Lean brooding in Libby, there came—
> Ah heaven! —what truth to him.[55]

The volume of Battle Pieces was received by the press without harsh criticism; but also without the favor which it merited as its author must have well known and felt. The same was true of some other of his later works which had merit that would have been recognized by the critics and the public, had not the shadow of that unhappy Pierre come between them and the splendor of his early fame. We cannot deny that sensitiveness to this criticism had much to do with his retirement from literary work, although other circumstances which we have mentioned also contributed to it.[56] We have Mr. Melville's own authority for saying that he was sensitive to the criticism of foreign reviews; for once when reading one of them, he looked up to say, "Well, it is pleasant to read what those fellows over the water say about us!" And he was greatly amused when he found the critic, thinking that his name was altogether too fine for common use in America, concluded that it was a pseudonym. And, if he was sensitive to the praise of these reviews, so also he must have been to their censure.[57] And authors who have been accustomed to extreme laudation are most of all, impatient of even moderate censure, and that intermingled with praise, as most of the criticism of Mr. Melville was. We cite a single instance from the Dublin University Magazine, which is of the highest authority:

> Herman Melville is undoubtedly an original thinker, and he boldly and unreservedly expresses his opinion—often in a way which startles and enchains the interest of the reader. He possesses amazing powers of expression. He can be terse, copious, eloquent, brilliant, imaginative, poetical, sarcastical, pathetic at will. He is never stupid, never dull, but, alas, he is often mystical and unintelligible—not from any lack of ability to express himself, for his writing is pure, manly English, and a child can understand what he says, while the ablest critic cannot always tell what he means—such is Herman Melville; a man of whom America has reason to be proud, with all his faults, and, if he does not eventually rank as one of her giants in literature, it will not be owing to lack of innate genius, but to his own incorrigible perversion of rare and lofty gifts.[58]

Surely there was nothing in such criticism as this to check a man like Mr. Melville in midcareer, "as the soaring eagle falls death struck in his upward flight." Other circumstances, such as we have recited, must have contributed to his first neglect of literary work and ambition; and if after a time he wished to resume his flight, he must have recognized a difficulty which he did not care to encounter. It is more difficult to return to habits of life which have been for a time laid aside, than it was to acquire them in the first place. It is something we all shrink from. And again it is much easier for a new author to obtain popularity than for an old one who has lost prestige by long silence to recover it—supposing their works to be of equal merit. We do not know that Mr. Melville at any time desired to resume his place in literature; but, if he did, these obstacles met him.

There is a little Shakespearian wisdom on this point, which commends itself to all who live in the public eye and upon the public breath, whether they are soldiers, statesmen, politicians or authors. Poets may be an exception, as well as those whose works require long and quiet study before they ripen.

It is the wise Ulysses who speaks to his friend, the brave Achilles, who, during the siege of Troy had been unwisely "sulking in his tent," and who consequently, had just been purposely passed by with insolent neglect by his fellow officers who had kept the field.

> Time hath, my lord, a wallet at his back,
> Wherein he puts alms for oblivion,
> A great siz'd monster of ingratitudes:
> Those scraps are good deeds past; which are devoured
> As fast as they are made, forgot as soon
> As done: Perseverance, dear, my lord,
> Keeps honor bright: To have done, is to hang
> Quite out of fashion, like a rusty mail
> In monumental mockery. Take the instant way;
> For honor travels in a strait so narrow,
> Where one but goes abreast: keep then the path:
> For emulation hath a thousand sons,
> That one by one pursue: If you give way,
> Or hedge aside from the direct forthright,
> Like to an enter'd tide, they all rush by,
> And leave you hindmost;—
> Or, like a gallant horse fallen in first rank,
> Lie there for pavement to the abject rear,
> O'errun and trampled on: Then what they do in present,
> Though less than yours in past, must o'ertop yours;
> For time is like a fashionable host,
> That slightly shakes his parting guest by the hand;
> And with his arm out-stretch'd, as he would fly,
> Grasps in the comer; Welcome ever smiles,
> And farewell goes out sighing. O, let not virtue seek
> Remuneration for the thing it was;
> For beauty, wit,
> High birth, vigor of bone, desert in service,
> Love, friendship, charity are subject all
> To envious and calumniating time.

> One touch of nature makes the whole world kin,—
> That all, with one consent, praise new born gawds,
> Though they are made and moulded of things past;
> And give to dust, that is a little gilt,
> More land than gold o'er dusted.
> The present eye praises the present object;
> Then marvel not, thou great and complete man,
> That all the Greeks begin to worship Ajax;
> Since things in motion sooner catch the eye,
> Than what not stirs.   The cry went once on thee,
> And still it might; and yet it may again,
> If thou wouldst not entomb thyself alive,
> And case thy reputation in thy tent;
> Whose glorious deeds, but in these fields of late,
> Made emulous missions 'mongst the gods themselves,
> And drave great Mars to faction.[59]

But, whatever influence—be it what it may—the general criticism of his later works had upon Mr. Melville's withdrawal from literary work, those who attributed it to the unlimited censure of Pierre, show a strange forgetfulness of dates, for that work was published in 1852, and he continued to write with energy for 12 years afterwards. As for Pierre itself its condemnation was just; but Herman Melville was not the first great author who ever made a single lapse. Among the greatest there are writings to which oblivion would be the best charity. That charity should have been bestowed upon Pierre, and its memory not preserved to cloud judgment of the author's later works. That it was not done is an exceptional case in literary history. Yet there are keen and just thoughts scattered here and there through the book, and at least a score of pages of local interest which we of Berkshire could ill afford to lose. First comes the dedication to "King Greylock" in which the author in his own peculiar quaintness proclaims the devoted loyalty of himself and his fellow subjects to that great monarch of all he surveys; sitting in regal—or rather as Mr. Melville describes it in imperial—majesty upon a throne whose everlasting stability is so grandly in contrast with the tumble-down things which human monarchs mount and call eternal. We transcribe it.

To Greylock's Most Excellent Majesty.
    In old times authors were proud of the privilege of dedicating their works to Majesty. A right noble custom which we of Berkshire must revive, for whether we will or no, majesty is all around us; sitting as in a grand congress of Vienna of majestical hill tops, and eternally challenging our homage. But since the majestic mountain, Greylock, my own more immediate sovereign lord and king, hath now for innumerable ages been the one grand dedicatee of the earliest rays of all the Berkshire mornings, I know not how his imperial purple majesty (royal born: porphyro genitus) will receive the dedica-

tion of my own poor solitary ray. Nevertheless, forasmuch as I, dwelling with my loyal neighbors, the maples and the beeches, in the amphitheater over which his central majesty presides, have received his most bounteous and unstinted fertilizations, it is but meet that I here devoutly kneel, and render up my gratitude, whether thereto the most excellent purple majesty, Greylock, benignantly incline his hoary crown, or no.[60]

[ix]

Even better than this is the pen picture of our pet local monster and geological mystery

The Balanced Rock.

in Lanesboro on the edge of Pittsfield. The description in "Pierre" of this wonderful natural problem for the learned and of marvelling curiosity for all, is the best ever written; and for that reason we copy it.

Pierre plunged deep into the woods, and paused not for several miles; paused not till he came to a remarkable stone, or rather, smoothed mass of rock, huge as a barn, which wholly isolated horizontally, was yet sweepingly overarched by beechtrees and chestnuts.

It was shaped something like a lengthened egg, but flattened more; and, at the ends, pointed more; and yet not pointed, but irregularly wedge-shaped. Somewhere near the middle of its under side, there was a lateral ridge; and an obscure point of this ridge rested on a second lengthwise-sharpened rock, slightly protruding from the ground. Beside that one obscure and minute point of contact, the whole enormous and most ponderous mass touched not another object in the wide terraqueous world. It was a breathless thing to see. One broad haunched end hovered within an inch of the soil, all along to the point of teetering contact; but yet touched not the soil. Many feet from that—beneath one part of the opposite end, which was all seamed and half riven—the vacancy was considerably larger, so as to make it not only possible, but convenient to admit a crawling man; yet no mortal being had ever been known to have the intrepid heart to crawl there.

It might well have been the wonder of all the country round. But strange to tell, though hundreds of cottage hearthstones—where, of long winter evenings, both old men smoked their pipes and young men shelled their corn—surrounded it, at no very remote distance, yet had the youthful Pierre been the first known publishing discoverer of this stone, which he had thereupon fancifully christened the Memnon Stone. Possibly, the reason why this singular object had so long remained unblazoned to the world, was not so much because it had never before been lighted on—though indeed, both belted and topped by the dense deep luxuriance of the aboriginal forest, it lay like Captain Kidd's sunken hull in the gorge of the river Hudson's Highlands,—its crown being full eight fathoms under high foliage;—and besides this, the cottagers had no special motive for visiting its more immediate vicinity at all; their timber and fuel being obtained from more accessible woodlands—as because, even, if any of the simple people should have chanced to have beheld it, they, in their hoodwinked unappreciativeness, would not have accounted it any very marvelous sight, and therefore, would never have thought it worth their while to publish it abroad. So that in real truth, they might have seen it, and yet afterward have forgotten so inconsiderable a circumstance. In short, this wondrous Memnon Stone could be no Memnon Stone to them; nothing but a huge stumbling block deeply to be regretted as a vast prospective obstacle in the way of running a handy little cross road through that wild part of the Manor.   *   *   *   *   *

Not only might this stone well have been the wonder of the simple country round, but it might well have been its terror. Sometimes, wrought to a mystic mood by contemplating its ponderous inscrutableness, Pierre had called it the Terror Stone. Few could be bribed to climb its giddy height, and crawl out upon its more hovering end. It seemed as if the dropping of one seed from the beak of the smallest flying bird would topple the immense mass over, crashing against the trees.

It was a very familiar thing to Pierre; he had often climbed it, by placing long poles against it, and so creeping up to where it sloped in little crumbling stepping places; or by climbing high up the neighboring beeches and then lowering himself down upon the forehead-like summit by the elastic branches. But never had he been fearless enough—or rather fool-hardy enough, it may be, to crawl on the ground beneath the vacancy of the higher end; that spot first menaced by the Terror Stone should it ever really topple.[61]

As a picture this is perfect. It is as realistic as a photograph, with the addition of whatever interpretation a poetic artist could give it. But the story attached to it is purely imaginary, as is also what is said of the location and its surroundings. The portion whose omission is indicated by stars is only one of the irrelevant rhapsodies which mar many of Mr. Melville's later works; and Pierre most of all. Even in books where he was not avowedly his own hero, he often idealized himself in portions of the story of some of his characters; or it may be more correct to say that he often, and sometimes very closely, modelled incidents in his stories upon real ones in his own experience; very often in cases where he had been magna pars. Of course he did not incorporate these incidents literally and bodily into the story; and still less was his idealization of himself a portrait of what he was in his own eyes. Like other novelists, he adapted both to the exigences of the plot. Unfortunately, in Pierre, the exigences of the plot were—in the author's own estimation, "ambiguous." The book itself was simply a freak of genius, and should have been so regarded by the world. We catch here and there in it, glimpses of the family portraits,—there is one by the bye, in the Athenæum, which is valuable, but not as a work of art. There is also a shadowy vision of the author's maiden aunt.[62] But Greylock and Balance Rock are what chiefly interest Berkshire readers. In the case of the rock, aside from its photographic likeness the variations were wide;

Pierre, even in fiction, was not "the first known publishing discoverer of the stone," for it was early known to geologists like Professors Emmons and Dewey, and already had its place in story.[63] Nor was the surrounding population so indifferent to its wondrous character as the story would indicate. Lanesboro society at that time and for years before, was as refined and intelligent as that of any town or city in the commonwealth, and its members were fully alive to the beauties and wonders with which nature surrounded them; and, after the nearer Constitution hill and Pontoosuc lake, the first to which they invited their friends from abroad, was the Balance Rock—or as they called it "The Rolling Rock," probably because it would not roll. To reach it Pierre had no occasion to plunge madly or otherwise, through miles of original forest, for there had not been a forest within a mile of it for more than a century. The last relics of one were a few beeches, chestnuts and maples, whose bark was thickly inscribed with the names or initials of generations of visitors. Sorry we are to say it, but these too have mostly disappeared.

The true story of the Memnon naming is this: One charming summer day, Mr. Melville, passing with his accustomed party of merry ladies and gentlemen, over smooth roads, came to the rock, and there had their usual picnic. While the party were enjoying their woodland meal one of the ladies crept into that fearful recess under the rock into which no man dare venture. And soon there issued from its depths sweet and mysterious music. This cunning priestess had hidden there a magnificent music box whose delicious strains must still be remembered, by some in Pittsfield and New York. This mysterious music completed in Mr. Melville's mind the resemblance to the Egyptian Memnon suggested by the size and form of the rock. And voila—Pierre's Memnon![64]

Since the foregoing paragraphs were in type we have met a second excellent article upon Mr. Melville by Arthur Stedman, from which we quote his opinion and that of Richard Henry Stoddard—both of the highest authority—upon his poetical works. We accept generally whatever modification of our own statements is implied, but must insist that John Brown's weird "Portent" must be counted among the most inspired of Melville's poems:

> The events of the Civil war gave a strong lyrical movement to Melville's pen, which had rested for nearly 10 years when the volume of "Battle-Pieces and Aspects of the War" appeared in 1866. Most of these poems originated, according to the author, "In an impulse imparted by the fall of Richmond," but they have as subjects all the chief incidents of the struggle. The best of them are "The Stone Fleet," "In the Prison Pen," "The College Colonel," "The March to the Sea," "Running the Batteries," and "Sheridan at Cedar Creek." Some of these had a wide circulation in the press, and were preserved in various anthologies. Mr. Stoddard has called "Sheridan" the second best cavalry poem in the English language, the first being Browning's "How They Brought the Good News from Ghent to Aix." There are in this

poem lines as lofty in sentiment and expression as Bryant, or the author of "Lines on a Bust of Dante," or Mr. Stoddard himself could have written. In the two privately printed volumes, "John Marr and Other Sailors," (1888) and "Timoleon" (1891) are several fine lyrics, the best of them being his last poem, "The Return of the Sire de Nesle." "Clarel, a Poem and Pilgrimage in the Holy Land" (1876) is a long mystical poem requiring, as some one has said, a dictionary, a cyclopaedia, and a copy of the Bible for its elucidation.[65]

Herman Melville died at his home in New York, Sunday night, Sept. 27,[*] 1891, after a lingering and painful illness of several years, during which he manifested heroic fortitude, and patience, and also a considerate regard for those who attended him which commanded their admiration as well as their gratitude.[66] Of his immediate family only Mrs. Melville with her two daughters, Miss Melville, and Mrs. H. B. Thomas, outlives him with one of his sisters, the widow of John C. Hoadley. Mr. Hoadley was for years one of the most active and valuable citizens of Pittsfield, being a man of letters, of public spirit, and of high personal character as well as of great business ability. He had great faith in Pittsfield's future although with his senior partner in the firm of McKay and Hoadley in the Depot street Iron works, he was induced to leave it in the midst of a successful business career. He was one of the most influential promoters of the building of the Ashley water works and the present First Congregational church. His marriage did not take place until he had removed to Lawrence, and the Melville family to New York.[67] He signalized his alliance with the Gansevoort-Melville family by editing a memorial of Gen. Henry Sanford Gansevoort, a grandson of Gen. Gansevoort of the Revolution, and himself a man of fine character and ability, who was a most meritorious officer in the war for the union. This memorial forms a superb octavo volume of 330 octavo pages and is a fitting tribute to the gallant and patriotic officer whom it commemorates. Besides interesting biographies of Gen. H. S. Gansevoort and his ancestors, it is composed largely of Gen. Gansevoort's own letters, those of his brother officers and others who knew him well. In his letters there are pleasant allusions to his kinsman Melville, of which we transcribe one, written on shipboard in a tropic sea and relates to the flag which both loved as patriots, one as a soldier and the other as a sailor:

"I sit down and watch the roll of the waves,—

'With undulating, long-drawn flow,
As rolled Brazilian billows go
Voluminously o'er the line.'

"This is Herman Melville's description of the wavy folds of the star-spangled banner. It is good."[68]

We now bid farewell to Herman Melville by quoting his last poem, in which some may detect a home significance although the scene is laid far away.

The Return of the Sire de Nesle, A. D., 16—

My towers at last! These rovings end,
Their thirst is slaked in larger dearth;
The yearning infinite recoils,
        For terrible is earth.

Kaf thrusts his snouted crags through fog;
Araxes swells beyond his span,
And knowledge poured by pilgrimage
        Overflows the banks of man.

But thou, my stay, thy lasting love,
One lonely good, let this but be!
Weary to view the wide world's swarm,
        But blest to fold but thee.[69]

Herman Melville and Pittsfield

We to-day complete the story of the life of Herman Melville, as a great Pittsfield author and one whose world wide fame is a part of that of the town. It has occupied much more space than was anticipated when it was commenced; expanding with new sources of information until it covers much more than Mr. Melville's Berkshire life, making it well nigh his complete biography. We do not so much regret this, as Mr. Melville made himself intensely a Berkshire man, and it would have given him pleasure to know that his fame and works would give the county a higher place in the world's esteem than it would otherwise have had. We hope that in his life he recognized that this would be so. We trust that our Berkshire readers will so regard it.

One of the most eminent—the most eminent of living American literary editors and critics, in a letter to the writer concerning some earlier Berkshire authors, said: "You do well to clothe your magnificent scenery with the memory of them and their works. That is something in which no new found landscape can rival it: Persevere." We think that is true and the number of romantic regions which have had a long renown, both in scenery and associations, to rival the Berkshire hills and valleys, has but a brief catalogue. And all the Berkshire story has not yet been told. Holmes at least is yet to come. Berkshire is already famous as the home of genius and when its story is fully told it will be still more so.[70]

ARTHUR STEDMAN, "HERMAN MELVILLE" IN *APPLETON'S ANNUAL CYCLOPAEDIA* (1892)

Published anonymously in *Appleton's Annual Cyclopaedia and Register of Important Events of the year 1891*, n.s. XVI, whole series XXI (New York: D. Appleton and Company, 1892), 503–505. This biographical essay is a compound of materials originally appearing in Stedman's earlier articles on Melville: "Herman Melville's Funeral," " 'Marquesan' Melville," and "Melville of Marquesas." If its author resorted to scissors and paste, like his predecessors among the encyclopedia-writers, in preparing his copy, he also compressed and restated much of his already published phrasing while introducing a limited amount of new material—mostly observations of a critical nature. The article was in type by early March of 1892, when Stedman sent a set of galley proofs to Mrs. Melville (they are now in the Melville Collection of the Harvard College Library). As noted above, p. 53, she wrote to Stedman on 18 March 1892 complimenting him on the article. Her only requested change was the correction of a typographical error in the opening sentence, where the date of Melville's death was wrongly printed. The published version makes the change; the present text corrects a second minor error in printing.[1] The accompanying illustration (enlarged) is reproduced here with permission of the State Historical Society of Wisconsin; this is the same cut previously used in *Appleton's Cyclopaedia of American Biography*, IV (1888), 293, which had also printed Melville's signature in facsimile (p. 96 above).

MELVILLE, HERMAN, an American romancer, born in New York city, Aug. 1, 1819; died there, Sept. 28, 1891. His great-grandfather, Allan Melville, emigrated to America from Scotland in 1748, and established himself as a merchant in Boston. Allan's son, Major Thomas Melville, was a member of the Boston "tea party." He was the last person in that city to retain the old-fashioned cocked hat and knee breeches, and in this way became the original of Dr.

Holmes's poem, "The Last Leaf." His son Allan, father of Herman, was an importing merchant of New York, a gentleman of fine culture, and an extensive traveler. On his mother's side, Herman was descended from Gen. Peter Gansevoort, also of Revolutionary fame, and known as "the hero of Fort Stanwix." His father's early death compelled the lad, who had passed most of his boyhood at and near Albany, to seek his own fortune. His fondness for English composition was early noticed by his Albany instructor, Dr. Charles E. West, now of Brooklyn, N. Y.[2] It was doubtless the stories of travel told by his father and a seafaring uncle which originally influenced Melville to follow the sea as a vocation, and to ship for Liverpool as cabin boy in 1837.* Returning, he devoted some time to teaching at Lansingburg, N. Y., and Pittsfield, Mass., and received at one period, as his records show, a salary of "six dollars a quarter and board."[3] Not long afterward he was again seized with the roving spirit, induced this time, perhaps, by the reading of Dana's "Two Years before the Mast," which appeared in 1840. On Jan. 1,* 1841, the whaler "Acushnet" sailed from New Bedford, bound for the Pacific sperm-fishery, and Melville began the voyage that was responsible for his chief romance.[4] The "Acushnet" had cruised for eighteen months when it reached the island of Nukuheva, in the Marquesas group. To that island in the summer of 1842, being wearied with harsh fare and hard treatment, the young sailor escaped from the whaler, with a single companion, familiarly known as "Toby." The latter's real name was Richard T. Greene. The comrades entered the hostile Typee valley by mistake, but through a fortunate accident made friends with the gentle but man-devouring savages. Their sojourn in the "happy valley" is the basis of Melville's first book, "Typee," and it may justly be said that in romantic descriptions of the South Sea islanders, their surroundings, and their ways of life, this book has never been excelled. "Toby" mysteriously disappeared, to find Melville in New York some months after the appearance of the first edition of "Typee."[5] Melville himself remained for four months in the valley, and was finally rescued from his friendly captivity by an Australian whaler after a fight on the island's beach between two factions of the natives. From Nukuheva he sailed to the Society Islands in this vessel, and thence to the Hawaiian group, remaining long enough at both places to take observations of the countries and their people. At Honolulu he joined the crew of the frigate "United States," then on its return voyage, and, after a sojourn at one of the Peruvian ports, reached Boston in the autumn of 1844, where he was discharged. The following months were passed at Lansingburg, in the writing of his first book, "Typee." About the time it was finished an old friendship between his father's family and that of the late Chief-Justice Lemuel Shaw, of Massachusetts, was renewed, and this led to his engagement with Justice Shaw's daughter. Their marriage followed on Aug. 4, 1847, in Boston. Mr. and Mrs. Melville resided in New York city until 1850, when they purchased a farm-house at Pittsfield, Mass. The house was situated so as to command an uninterrupted view of Greylock Mountain and the adjoining hills, and was named Arrow Head, from the numerous Indian antiquities found in the neighborhood. Here he remained for thirteen years, occupied with his writing and with managing his farm. He had many literary neighbors in the surrounding towns, but was more intimate with Hawthorne than with any others during the latter's residence at the "red cottage" in Lenox.[6] While at Pittsfield he was induced to enter the lecture field, and from 1857 to 1860 he filled many engagements in lyceums, chiefly speaking of his adventures in the South Seas. He lectured in cities as widely apart as Montreal, Chicago, Baltimore, and San Francisco, visiting the last-named place in 1860, by the Isthmus route, for the benefit of his health. Besides this voyage, he journeyed to England and the Continent in 1849 and 1856, partly to superintend the publication of English editions of his works and partly for recreation.[7] At Pittsfield, besides his own family, Mr. Melville's mother and sisters were with him. As his children grew up, he found it necessary to obtain for them better facilities for study than the village school afforded; and so, in the autumn of 1863, the household was broken up and he removed with his wife and children to the New York house that was afterward his home, No. 104 East 26th Street. In December, 1866, he was appointed by H. A. Smyth, a former traveling companion in Europe, a district officer in the New York Custom House. This place he held until 1885, preferring it to indoor clerical work, and then resigned when the duties became too arduous for his failing strength.[8]

Melville from early manhood indulged deeply in philosophical studies. Hawthorne has described in the "English Note-Books" his fondness for discussing such matters. This habit grew as he advanced in years, until his conversation with friends became chiefly a philosophical monologue.[9] He was also much interested in all matters relating to the fine arts, and devoted most of his leisure hours to the two subjects. A notable collection of etchings and engravings from the old masters was gradually made by him, those from Claude's paintings being a specialty. After he retired from the Custom House, his tall, stalwart figure could be seen almost daily tramping through the Fort George district or Central Park, his roving inclination leading him to obtain as much out-door life as possible. His evenings were spent at home with his books, his pictures and his family, and usually with them alone; for, in spite of the melodramatic declarations of various English gentlemen, Melville's seclusion in his later years, and in fact throughout his life, was a matter of personal choice.[10] More and more, as he grew older, he avoided every action on his own part and on the part of his family that might tend to keep his name and writings before the public. A few friends felt at liberty to visit him; he himself sought no one. Various efforts were made by the New York literary colony to draw him from his retirement, but without success. It has been suggested that he might have accepted a magazine editorship, but this is doubtful, as he could not bear business details or routine work of any sort. His brother Allan was a New York lawyer, and, until his death in 1872, managed Melville's affairs with ability, particularly the literary accounts.[11] It was late in the year 1845 when Melville completed the manuscript of "Typee." At nearly the same time his brother, Gansevoort Melville, sailed for England as secretary of legation to Minister McLane, taking the manuscript with him. It was offered to John Murray, who at once accepted it, buying the book outright for England for a moderate sum. The same plan was followed a year later with "Omoo." The house of Murray wished to include both volumes in their "Colonial and Home Library," so the title "Typee" was omitted, and that book was first published in England as "Melville's Marquesas Islands." In the United States Wiley & Putnam, whose London agent had contracted for the work, brought it out simultaneously with the English edition in the spring of 1846. Both "Typee" and "Omoo" (1847) were immediate successes, and Melville gained an international reputation at an earlier date than James Russell Lowell, who was born the same year. Harper & Brothers issued "Omoo" in the United States and "Typee" was placed with them two years later.[12] This firm published all of Melville's works except four, not including two privately printed booklets. "Mardi, and a Voyage Thither" (1849) was severely criticised in some quarters for certain "metaphysical and morbid meditations." "Redburn, his First Voyage" (1849), more favorably received, was partly based on Melville's own experiences on his trip to Liverpool. "White Jacket, or the World in a Man-of-War" (1850) of course repeated much of his life on board the frigate "United States." "Typee" and "White Jacket" are the most consistent of his books. With "Moby Dick, or the White Whale" (1851) he reached the topmost notch of his fame. It is perhaps the most graphic and truthful description of whaling life ever written, although it contains some of the objectionable characteristics of "Mardi." "Pierre, or the Ambiguities" (1852) was the signal for an outburst of hostile criticism.[13] In the year following its publication the great Harper fire occurred, destroying the whole stock of Melville's books—although the plates were preserved—and keeping them out of print at a most unfortunate time. Thereafter Melville's star waned.[14] "Israel Potter" (1855) and "The Confidence Man" (1857) detracted from his reputation; and "The Piazza Tales" (1856), while containing the powerful stories of "Benito Cereno" and "The Bell-Tower," was published in an unattractive form.[15] "Battle-Pieces, and Aspects of the War" (1866) embraces some of the best lyrics inspired by the civil war, notably "Sheridan at Cedar Creek." "Clarel, a Poem and Pilgrimage to the Holy Land" (1876), is written in the author's most mystical style.[16] At the beginning of his physical decline he wrote and privately circulated a little story entitled "John Marr, and other Sailors" (1888), to which a few poems were appended. This volume was dedicated to W. Clark Russell, a genial correspondence with whom cheered Melville's last years. Mr. Russell considers Melville the first of "the poets of the deep," using the word "poet" in its general sense. A few months before his death Melville collected his remaining shorter poems in a similar book, "Timoleon, etc." (1891), which was dedicated to "My Countryman, Elihu Vedder."[17] The causes of the decline in popularity of Melville's writings may be found chiefly in his own career. Had he confined himself closely to an amplification of the interesting materials first discovered by himself, after the manner of a later California romancer, he might have gone on indefinitely producing works of more than common respectability.[18] But he was led by his inclination for philosophical speculation to commit grave literary errors, which destroyed his popularity with the reading public. Perhaps, also, having once recited the story of his adventures in a series of romances, he felt his inability to create new characters and situations in the same domain; and his subsequent efforts might be considered as vain seeking after new successes.[19] With lessening fame his desire for retirement increased, until a generation of writers for the press grew up to whom the announcement of his death was the revelation of his previous existence.

ARTHUR STEDMAN, INTRODUCTION TO THE 1892 EDITION OF *TYPEE*

Published in *Typee: A Real Romance of the South Seas,* by Herman Melville, with Biographical and Critical Introduction by Arthur Stedman (New York: United States Book Company, 1892), pp. xv-xxxvi. The essay was not written until some time after Stedman had completed his article on Melville for *Appleton's Annual Cyclopaedia,* which was in proof early in March of 1892; it was evidently ready for the printer before 4 May 1892, when he remarked in a letter to H. S. Salt that he was holding back the Introduction until the publisher furnished him with proofs of the text of *Typee* (see pp. 53-54 above). The date of "June, 1892." (p. xxxvi) very likely indicates that by or during that month Stedman had either released the Introduction for setting or else had approved the entire volume for printing, the Introduction included. The volume was published in mid-September of 1892.

In two copies of the 1892 *Typee* that are now in the Melville Collection of the Harvard College Library Mrs. Melville listed on the front flyleaf four "Errors corrected in next edition" (i.e., printing): three in Stedman's Introduction ("pp xvi-xx-xxiii") and one in the text, where John La Farge's drawing of Fayaway "should face page 196". In the Introduction itself she indicated the necessary corrections: on p. xvi.10, "Catherine" Gansevoort should be "Maria"; on p. xx.26-27, the "lovely and accomplished" daughter of Lemuel Shaw—herself—should be merely the "only" daughter; on p. xxiii.14, Thomas Melville should properly be called not the "superintendent" of Sailor's Snug Harbor but the "Governor". Moreover, in one of the copies (*AC85.M4977.846tm) but not the other (*AC85.M4977.846to) she lined out on p. xxi.10-11 an erroneous reference to "another" story supposedly by Melville "called 'October Mountain'" that Stedman had picked up from J. E. A. Smith's *Taghconic* (1879); nevertheless, this wording has remained unchanged in the many subsequent printings from these same plates. Unmarked in Mrs. Melville's copies but subsequently corrected was an error on p. xxii.22-23: "Jaconic" for "Taconic"— a Berkshire place-name evidently puzzling to New York printers; an earlier version of the passage in Stedman's "'Marquesan' Melville" had originally read "Teutonic". The present text corrects "Jaconic" to "Taconic" and makes one other minor correction,[1] but otherwise follows the first printing of 1892; the accompanying notes call attention to Mrs. Melville's markings in the passages concerned.

[[xv]] Of the trinity of American authors whose births made the year 1819 a notable one in our literary history,—Lowell, Whitman, and Melville,—it is interesting to observe that the two latter were both descended, on the fathers' and mothers' sides respectively, from families of British New England and Dutch New York extraction. Whitman and Van Velsor, Melville and Gansevoort, were the several combinations which produced these men; and it is easy to trace in the life and character of each author the qualities derived from his joint ancestry. Here, however, the resemblance ceases, for Whitman's forebears, while worthy country people of good descent, were not prominent in public or private life. Melville, on the other hand, was of distinctly patrician birth, his paternal and maternal grandfathers having been leading characters in the Revolutionary War; their descendants still maintaining a dignified social position.[2]

Allan Melville, great-grandfather of Herman Melville, removed from Scotland to America in 1748, and established himself as a merchant in Boston. His son, Major Thomas Melville, was a leader in the famous Boston "Tea Party" [[xvi]] of 1773, and afterwards became an officer in the Continental Army. He is reported to have been a Conservative in all matters except his opposition to unjust taxation, and he wore the old-fashioned cocked hat and knee-breeches until his death, in 1832, thus becoming the original of Doctor Holmes's poem, "The Last Leaf." Major Melville's son Allan, the father of Herman, was an importing merchant,—first in Boston, and later in New York. He was a man of much culture, and was an extensive traveller for his time. He married Catherine Gansevoort, daughter of General Peter Gansevoort, best known as "the hero of Fort Stanwix." This fort was situated on the present site of Rome, N.Y.; and there Gansevoort, with a small body of men, held in check reinforcements on their way to join Burgoyne, until the disastrous ending of the latter's campaign of 1777 was insured. The Gansevoorts, it should be said, were at that time and subsequently residents of Albany, N.Y.[3]

Herman Melville was born in New York on August 1, 1819, and received his early education in that city. There he imbibed his first love of adventure, listening, as he says in "Redburn," while his father "of winter evenings, by the well-remembered sea-coal fire in old Greenwich Street, used to tell my brother and me of the monstrous waves at sea, mountain high, of the masts bending like twigs, and all about Havre and Liverpool." The death of his father in reduced circumstances necessitated the removal of his mother and the family of eight brothers and sisters to the village of Lansingburg, on the Hudson River. There Herman remained until 1835, when he attended the Albany [[xvii]] Classical School for some months. Dr. Charles E. West, the well-known Brooklyn educator, was then in charge of the school, and remembers the lad's deftness in English composition, and his struggles with mathematics.[4]

The following year* was passed at Pittsfield, Mass., where he engaged in work on his uncle's farm, long known as the "Van Schaack place." This uncle was Thomas Melville, president of the Berkshire Agricultural Society, and a successful gentleman farmer.[5]

Herman's roving disposition, and a desire to support himself independently of family assistance, soon led him to ship as cabin boy in a New York vessel bound for Liverpool. He made the voyage, visited London, and returned in the same ship. "Redburn: His First Voyage," published in 1849, is partly founded on the experiences of this trip, which was undertaken with the full consent of his relatives, and which seems to have satisfied his nautical ambition for a time. As told in the book, Melville met with more than the usual hardships of a sailor-boy's first venture. It does not seem difficult in "Redburn" to separate the author's actual experiences from those invented by him, this being the case in some of his other writings.[6]

A good part of the succeeding three years,* from 1837 to 1840, was occupied with school-teaching. While so engaged at Greenbush, now East Albany, N.Y., he received the munificent salary of "six dollars a quarter and board." He taught for one term at Pittsfield, Mass., "boarding around" with the families of his pupils, in true American fashion, and easily suppressing, on one memorable occa- [[xviii]] sion, the efforts of his larger scholars to inaugurate a rebellion by physical force.[7]

I have a fancy that it was the reading of Richard Henry Dana's "Two Years Before the Mast" which revived the spirit of adventure in Melville's breast. That book was published in 1840, and was at once talked of everywhere. Melville must have read it at the time, mindful of his own experience as a sailor.[8] At any rate, he once more signed a ship's articles, and on January 1,* 1841, sailed from New Bedford harbour in the whaler Acushnet, bound for the Pacific Ocean and the sperm fishery. He has left very little direct information as to the events of this eighteen months' cruise, although his whaling romance, "Moby Dick; or, the Whale," probably gives many pictures of life on board the Acushnet. In the present volume he confines himself to a general account of the captain's bad treatment of the crew, and of his non-fulfilment of agreements. Under these considerations, Melville decided to abandon the vessel on reaching the

Marquesas Islands; and the narrative of "Typee" begins at this point. However, he always recognised the immense influence the voyage had had upon his career, and in regard to its results has said in "Moby Dick,"—

"If I shall ever deserve any real repute in that small but high hushed world which I might not be unreasonably ambitious of; if hereafter I shall do anything that on the whole a man might rather have done than to have left undone, . . . then here I prospectively ascribe all the honour and the glory to whaling; for a whale-ship was my Yale College and my Harvard."[9]

⟦xix⟧ The record, then, of Melville's escape from the Dolly, otherwise the Acushnet, the sojourn of his companion Toby and himself in the Typee Valley on the island of Nukuheva, Toby's mysterious disappearance, and Melville's own escape, is fully given in the succeeding pages; and rash indeed would he be who would enter into a descriptive contest with these inimitable pictures of aboriginal life in the "Happy Valley." So great an interest has always centred in the character of Toby, whose actual existence has been questioned, that I am glad to be able to declare him an authentic personage, by name Richard T. Greene. He was enabled to discover himself again to Mr. Melville through the publication of the present volume, and their acquaintance was renewed, lasting for quite a long period. I have seen his portrait,—a rare old daguerrotype,— and some of his letters to our author. One of his children was named for the latter, but Mr. Melville lost trace of him in recent years.[10]

With the author's rescue from what Dr. T. M. Coan has styled his "anxious paradise," "Typee" ends, and its sequel, "Omoo," begins. Here, again, it seems wisest to leave the remaining adventures in the South Seas to the reader's own discovery, simply stating that, after a sojourn at the Society Islands, Melville shipped for Honolulu. There he remained for four months, employed as a clerk. He joined the crew of the American frigate United States, which reached Boston, stopping on the way at one of the Peruvian ports, in October of 1844. Once more was a narrative of his experiences to be preserved in "White-Jacket; or, the World in a Man-of-War."[11]

⟦xx⟧ Thus, of Melville's four most important books, three, "Typee," "Omoo," and "White-Jacket," are directly autobiographical, and "Moby Dick" is partially so; while the less important "Redburn" is between the two classes in this respect. Melville's other prose works, as will be shown, were, with some exceptions, unsuccessful efforts at creative romance.[12]

Whether our author entered on his whaling adventures in the South Seas with a determination to make them available for literary purposes, may never be certainly known. There was no such elaborate announcement or advance preparation as in some later cases. I am inclined to believe that the literary prospect was an after-thought, and that this insured a freshness and enthusiasm of style not otherwise to be attained.[13] Returning to his mother's home at

Lansingburg, Melville soon began the writing of "Typee," which was completed by the autumn of 1845. Shortly after this his older brother, Gansevoort Melville, sailed for England as secretary of legation to Ambassador McLane, and the manuscript was intrusted to Gansevoort for submission to John Murray. Its immediate acceptance and publication followed in 1846. "Typee" was dedicated to Chief Justice Lemuel Shaw of Massachusetts, an old friendship between the author's family and that of Justice Shaw having been renewed about this time. Mr. Melville became engaged to Miss Elizabeth Shaw, the lovely and accomplished daughter of the Justice, and their marriage followed on August 4, 1847, at Boston.[14]

The wanderings of our nautical Othello were thus brought to a conclusion. Mr. and Mrs. Melville resided in New ⟦xxi⟧ York City until 1850, when they purchased a farmhouse at Pittsfield, their farm adjoining that formerly owned by Mr. Melville's uncle, which had been inherited by the latter's son. The new place was named "Arrow Head," from the numerous Indian antiquities found in the neighbourhood. The house was so situated as to command an uninterrupted view of Greylock Mountain and the adjacent hills. Here Melville remained for thirteen years, occupied with his writing, and managing his farm. An article in *Putnam's Monthly* entitled "I and My Chimney," another called "October Mountain," and the introduction to the "Piazza Tales," present faithful pictures of Arrow Head and its surroundings. In a letter to Nathaniel Hawthorne, given in "Nathaniel Hawthorne and His Wife," his daily life is set forth. The letter is dated June 1,* 1851.

> "Since you have been here I have been building some shanties of houses (connected with the old one), and likewise some shanties of chapters and essays. I have been ploughing and sowing and raising and printing and praying, and now begin to come out upon a less bristling time, and to enjoy the calm prospect of things from a fair piazza at the north of the old farmhouse here. Not entirely yet, though, am I without something to be urgent with. The 'Whale' is only half through the press; for, wearied with the long delays of the printers, and disgusted with the heat and dust of the Babylonish brick-kiln of New York, I came back to the country to feel the grass, and end the book reclining on it, if I may."[15]

Mr. Hawthorne, who was then living in the "red cottage" at Lenox, had passed a week at Arrow Head with his daughter Una the previous spring. It is recorded that the friends "spent most of the time in the barn, bathing in the early spring sunshine, which streamed through the ⟦xxii⟧ open doors, and talking philosophy."[16] According to Mr. J. E. A. Smith's volume on the Berkshire Hills, these gentlemen, both reserved in nature, though near neighbours and often in the same company, were inclined to be shy of each other, partly, perhaps, through the knowledge that Melville had written a very appreciative review of "Mosses from an Old Manse" for the New York *Literary World,* edited by their mutual friends, the Duyckincks. "But one day," writes Mr. Smith, "it chanced that when they were out on a picnic excursion, the two were compelled by a thundershower to take shelter in a narrow recess of the rocks of Monument Mountain. Two hours of this enforced intercourse settled the matter. They learned so much of each other's character, . . . that the most intimate friendship for the future was inevitable."[17] A passage in Hawthorne's "Wonder Book" is noteworthy as describing the number of literary neighbours in Berkshire:—

"For my part, I wish I had Pegasus here at this moment," said the student. "I would mount him forthwith, and gallop about the country within a circumference of a few miles, making literary calls on my brother authors. Dr. Dewey would be within my reach, at the foot of the Taconic. In Stockbridge, yonder, is Mr. James [G. P. R. James], conspicuous to all the world on his mountainpile of history and romance. Longfellow, I believe, is not yet at the Oxbow, else the winged horse would neigh at him. But here in Lenox I should find our most truthful novelist [Miss Sedgwick], who has made the scenery and life of Berkshire all her own. On the hither side of Pittsfield sits Herman Melville, shaping out the gigantic conception ⟦xxiii⟧ of his 'White Whale,' while the gigantic shadow of Greylock looms upon him from his study window. Another bound of my flying steed would bring me to the door of Holmes, whom I mention last, because Pegasus would certainly unseat me the next minute, and claim the poet as his rider."[18]

While at Pittsfield, Mr. Melville was induced to enter the lecture field. From 1857 to 1860 he filled many engagements in the lyceums, chiefly speaking of his adventures in the South Seas. He lectured in cities as widely apart as Montreal, Chicago, Baltimore, and San Francisco, sailing to the last-named place in 1860, by way of Cape Horn, on the Meteor, commanded by his younger brother, Captain Thomas Melville, afterward superintendent of the "Sailor's Snug Harbor" at Staten Island, N.Y. Besides his voyage to San Francisco, he had, in 1849 and 1856, visited England, the Continent, and the Holy Land, partly to superintend the publication of English editions of his works, and partly for recreation.[19]

A pronounced feature of Melville's character was his unwillingness to speak of himself, his adventures, or his writings in conversation. He was, however, able to overcome this reluctance on the lecture platform. Our author's tendency to philosophical discussion is strikingly set forth in a letter from Dr. Titus Munson Coan to the latter's mother, written while a student at Williams College over thirty years ago, and fortunately preserved by her. Dr. Coan enjoyed the friendship and confidence of Mr. Melville during most of his residence in New York. The letter reads:—

⟦xxiv⟧ "I have made my first literary pilgrimage,—a call upon Herman Melville, the renowned author of 'Typee,' etc. He lives in a spacious farmhouse about two miles from Pittsfield, a weary walk through the dust. But it was well repaid. I introduced myself as a Hawaiian-American, and soon found myself in full tide of talk, or rather of monologue. But he would not repeat the experiences of which I had been reading with rapture in his books. In vain I sought to hear of Typee and those paradise islands, but he preferred to pour forth his philosophy and his theories of life. The shade of Aristotle arose like a cold mist between myself and Fayaway. We have quite enough of deep philosophy at Williams College, and I confess I was disappointed in this trend of the talk. But what a talk it was! Melville is transformed from a Marquesan to a gypsy student, the gypsy element still remaining strong within him. And this contradiction gives him the air of one who has suffered from opposition, both literary and social. With his liberal views, he is apparently considered by the good people of Pittsfield as little better than a cannibal or a 'beach-comber.' His attitude seemed to me something like that of Ishmael; but perhaps I judged hastily. I managed to draw him out very freely on everything but the Marquesas Islands, and when I left him he was in full tide of discourse on all things sacred and profane. But he seems to put away the objective side of his life, and to shut himself up in this cold north as a cloistered thinker."[20]

I have been told by Dr. Coan that his father, the Rev. Titus Coan, of the Hawaiian Islands, personally visited the Marquesas group, found the Typee Valley, and verified in all respects the statements made in "Typee." It is known that Mr. Melville from early manhood indulged deeply in philosophical studies, and his fondness for discussing such matters is pointed out by Hawthorne also, in the "English Note Books." This habit increased as he advanced in years, if possible.[21]

The chief event of the residence in Pittsfield was the completion and publication of "Moby Dick; or, the Whale," ⟦xxv⟧ in 1851. How many young men have been drawn to sea by this book is a question of interest. Meeting with Mr. Charles Henry Webb ("John Paul") the day after Mr. Melville's death, I asked him if he were not familiar with that author's writings. He replied that "Moby Dick" was responsible for his three years of life before the mast when a lad, and added that while "gamming" on board another vessel he had once fallen in with a member of the boat's crew which rescued Melville from his friendly imprisonment among the Typees.[22]

While at Pittsfield, besides his own family, Mr. Melville's mother and sisters resided with him. As his four children grew up he found it necessary to obtain for them better facilities for study than the village school afforded; and so, in the autumn of 1863, the household was broken up, and he removed with his wife and children to the New York house that was afterwards his home. This house belonged to his brother Allan, and was exchanged for the estate at Pittsfield. In December, 1866, he was appointed by Mr. H. A. Smyth, a former travelling companion in Europe, a district officer in the New York Custom

House. He held the position until 1886, preferring it to in-door clerical work, and then resigned, the duties becoming too arduous for his failing strength.[23]

In addition to his philosophical studies, Mr. Melville was much interested in all matters relating to the fine arts, and devoted most of his leisure hours to the two subjects. A notable collection of etchings and engravings from the old masters was gradually made by him, those from Claude's paintings being a specialty.[24] After he retired from the [[xxvi]] Custom House, his tall, stalwart figure could be seen almost daily tramping through the Fort George district or Central Park, his roving inclination leading him to obtain as much out-door life as possible. His evenings were spent at home with his books, his pictures, and his family, and usually with them alone; for, in spite of the melodramatic declarations of various English gentlemen, Melville's seclusion in his latter years, and in fact throughout his life, was a matter of personal choice. More and more, as he grew older, he avoided every action on his part, and on the part of his family, that might tend to keep his name and writings before the public.[25] A few friends felt at liberty to visit the recluse, and were kindly welcomed, but he himself sought no one. His favorite companions were his grandchildren, with whom he delighted to pass his time, and his devoted wife, who was a constant assistant and adviser in his literary work, chiefly done at this period for his own amusement. To her he addressed his last little poem, the touching "Return of the Sire de Nesle." Various efforts were made by the New York literary colony to draw him from his retirement, but without success. It has been suggested that he might have accepted a magazine editorship, but this is doubtful, as he could not bear business details or routine work of any sort. His brother Allan was a New York lawyer, and until his death, in 1872, managed Melville's affairs with ability, particularly the literary accounts.[26]

During these later years he took great pleasure in a friendly correspondence with Mr. W. Clark Russell. Mr. Russell had taken many occasions to mention Melville's [[xxvii]] sea-tales, his interest in them, and his indebtedness to them. The latter felt impelled to write Mr. Russell in regard to one of his newly published novels, and received in answer the following letter:—

> July 21, 1886.
> My dear Mr. Melville,—Your letter has given me a very great and singular pleasure. Your delightful books carry the imagination into a maritime period so remote that, often as you have been in my mind, I could never satisfy myself that you were still amongst the living. I am glad, indeed, to learn from Mr. Toft that you are still hale and hearty, and I do most heartily wish you many years yet of health and vigour.
> Your books I have in the American edition. I have "Typee," "Omoo," "Redburn," and that noble piece "Moby Dick." These are all I have been able to obtain. There have been many editions of your works in this country, particularly the lovely South Sea sketches; but the editions are not equal

to those of the American publishers. Your reputation here is very great. It is hard to meet a man whose opinion as a reader is worth having who does not speak of your works in such terms as he might hesitate to employ, with all his patriotism, toward many renowned English writers.

Dana is, indeed, great. There is nothing in literature more remarkable than the impression produced by Dana's portraiture of the homely inner life of a little brig's forecastle.

I beg that you will accept my thanks for the kindly spirit in which you have read my books. I wish it were in my power to cross the Atlantic, for you assuredly would be the first whom it would be my happiness to visit.

The condition of my right hand obliges me to dictate this to my son; but painful as it is to me to hold a pen, I cannot suffer this letter to reach the hands of a man of so admirable genius as Herman Melville without begging him to believe me to be, with my own hand, his most respectful and hearty admirer,

W. Clark Russell.[27]

It should be noted here that Melville's increased reputation in England at the period of this letter was chiefly [[xxviii]] owing to a series of articles on his work written by Mr. Russell. I am sorry to say that few English papers made more than a passing reference to Melville's death. The American press discussed his life and work in numerous and lengthy reviews. At the same time, there always has been a steady sale of his books in England, and some of them never have been out of print in that country since the publication of "Typee." One result of this friendship between the two authors was the dedication of new volumes to each other in highly complimentary terms—Mr. Melville's "John Marr and Other Sailors," of which twenty-five copies only were printed, on the one hand, and Mr. Russell's "An Ocean Tragedy," on the other, of which many thousand have been printed, not to mention unnumbered pirated copies.[28]

Beside Hawthorne, Mr. Richard Henry Stoddard, of American writers, specially knew and appreciated Herman Melville. Mr. Stoddard was connected with the New York dock department at the time of Mr. Melville's appointment to a custom-house position, and they at once became acquainted. For a good many years, during the period in which our author remained in seclusion, much that appeared in print in America concerning Melville came from the pen of Mr. Stoddard.[29] Nevertheless, the sailor-author's presence in New York was well known to the literary guild. He was invited to join in all new movements, but as often felt obliged to excuse himself from doing so. The present writer lived for some time within a short distance of his house, but found no opportunity to meet him until it became necessary to obtain his portrait [[xxix]] for an anthology in course of publication. The interview was brief, and the interviewer could not help feeling, although treated with pleasant courtesy, that more important matters were in hand than the perpetuation of a romancer's countenance to future generations; but a friendly family acquaintance grew up from the incident, and will remain an abiding memory.[30]

Mr. Melville died at his home in New York City early on the morning of September 28, 1891. His serious illness had lasted a number of months, so that the end came as a release.[31] True to his ruling passion, philosophy had claimed him to the last, a set of Schopenhauer's works receiving his attention when able to study; but this was varied with readings in the "Mermaid Series" of old plays in which he took much pleasure. His library, in addition to numerous works on philosophy and the fine arts, was composed of standard books of all classes, including, of course, a proportion of nautical literature. Especially interesting are fifteen or twenty first editions of Hawthorne's books inscribed to Mr. and Mrs. Melville by the author and his wife.[32]

The immediate acceptance of "Typee" by John Murray was followed by an arrangement with the London agent of an American publisher, for its simultaneous publication in the United States. I understand that Murray did not then publish fiction. At any rate, the book was accepted by him on the assurance of Gansevoort Melville that it contained nothing not actually experienced by his brother. Murray brought it out early in 1846, in his "Colonial and [[xxx]] Home Library," as "A Narrative of a Four Months' Residence among the Natives of a Valley of the Marquesas Islands; or, a Peep at Polynesian Life," or, more briefly, "Melville's Marquesas Islands." It was issued in America with the author's own title, "Typee," and in the outward shape of a work of fiction. Mr. Melville found himself famous at once. Many discussions were carried on as to the genuineness of the author's name and the reality of the events portrayed, but English and American critics alike recognised the book's importance as a contribution to literature.[33]

Melville, in a letter to Hawthorne, speaks of himself as having "no development at all" until his twenty-fifth year, the time of his return from the Pacific;[34] but surely the process of development must have been well advanced to permit of so virile and artistic a creation as "Typee." While the narrative does not always run smoothly, yet the style for the most part is graceful and alluring, so that we pass from one scene of Pacific enchantment to another quite oblivious of the vast amount of descriptive detail which is being poured out upon us. It is the varying fortune of the hero which engrosses our attention. We follow his adventures with breathless interest, or luxuriate with him in the leafy bowers of the "Happy Valley," surrounded by joyous children of nature. When all is ended, we then for the first time realise that we know these people and their ways as if we too had dwelt among them.[35]

I do not believe that "Typee" will ever lose its position as a classic of American Literature. The pioneer in [[xxxi]] South Sea romance—for the mechanical descriptions of earlier voyagers are not worthy of comparison—this book has as yet met with no superior, even in French literature; nor has it met with a rival in any other language than the French. The character of "Fayaway," and, no less, William S. Mayo's "Kaloolah," the enchanting dreams of many a youthful heart, will retain their charm; and this in spite of endless variations by modern explorers in the same domain. A faint type of both characters may be found in the Surinam "Yarico" of Captain John Gabriel Stedman, whose "Narrative of a Five Years' Expedition" appeared in 1796.[36]

"Typee," as written, contained passages reflecting with considerable severity on the methods pursued by missionaries in the South Seas. The manuscript was printed in a complete form in England, and created much discussion on this account, Melville being accused of bitterness; but he asserted his lack of prejudice. The passages referred to were omitted in the first and all subsequent American editions. They have been restored in the present issue, which is complete save for a few paragraphs excluded by written direction of the author. I have, with the consent of his family, changed the long and cumbersome sub-title of the book, calling it a "Real-Romance of the South Seas," as best expressing its nature.[37]

The success of his first volume encouraged Melville to proceed in his work, and "Omoo," the sequel to "Typee," appeared in England and America in 1847. Here we leave, for the most part, the dreamy pictures of island life, and find ourselves sharing the extremely realistic discomforts ⟦xxxii⟧ of a Sydney whaler in the early forties. The rebellious crew's experiences in the Society Islands are quite as realistic as events on board ship and very entertaining, while the whimsical character, Dr. Long Ghost, next to Captain Ahab in "Moby Dick," is Melville's most striking delineation. The errors of the South Sea missions are pointed out with even more force than in "Typee," and it is a fact that both these books have ever since been of the greatest value to outgoing missionaries on account of the exact information contained in them with respect to the islanders.[38]

Melville's power in describing and investing with romance scenes and incidents witnessed and participated in by himself, and his frequent failure of success as an inventor of characters and situations, were early pointed out by his critics. More recently Mr. Henry S. Salt has drawn the same distinction very carefully in an excellent article contributed to the *Scottish Art Review.* In a prefatory note to "Mardi" (1849), Melville declares that, as his former books have been received as romance instead of reality, he will now try his hand at pure fiction. "Mardi" may be called a splendid failure. It must have been soon after the completion of "Omoo" that Melville began to study the writings of Sir Thomas Browne. Heretofore our author's style was rough in places, but marvellously simple and direct. "Mardi" is burdened with an over-rich diction, which Melville never entirely outgrew. The scene of this romance, which opens well, is laid in the South Seas, but everything soon becomes overdrawn and fantastical, and the thread of the story loses itself in a mystical allegory.[39]

⟦xxxiii⟧ "Redburn," already mentioned, succeeded "Mardi" in the same year, and was a partial return to the author's earlier style. In "White-Jacket; or, the World in a Man-of-War" (1850), Melville almost regained it. This book has no equal as a picture of life aboard a sailing man-of-war, the lights and shadows of naval existence being well contrasted.[40]

With "Moby Dick; or, the Whale" (1851), Melville reached the topmost notch of his fame. The book represents, to a certain extent, the conflict between the author's earlier and later methods of composition, but the "gigantic conception" of the "White Whale," as Hawthorne expressed it, permeates the whole work, and lifts it bodily into the highest domain of romance. "Moby Dick" contains an immense amount of information concerning the habits of the whale and the methods of its capture, but this is characteristically introduced in a way not to interfere with the narrative. The chapter entitled "Stubb Kills a Whale" ranks with the choicest examples of descriptive literature.[41]

"Moby Dick" appeared; and Melville enjoyed to the full the enhanced reputation it brought him. He did not, however, take warning from "Mardi," but allowed himself to plunge more deeply into the sea of philosophy and fantasy.

"Pierre; or, the Ambiguities" (1852) was published, and there ensued a long series of hostile criticisms, ending with a severe, though impartial, article by Fitz-James O'Brien in *Putnam's Monthly*. About the same time the whole stock of the author's books was destroyed by fire, keeping ⟦xxxiv⟧ them out of print at a critical moment; and public interest, which until then had been on the increase, gradually began to diminish.[42]

After this Mr. Melville contributed several short stories to *Putnam's Monthly* and *Harper's Magazine*. Those in the former periodical were collected in a volume as "Piazza Tales" (1856); and of these "Benito Cereno" and "The Bell Tower" are equal to his best previous efforts.

"Israel Potter: His Fifty Years of Exile" (1855), first printed as a serial in *Putnam's,* is an historical romance of the American Revolution, based on the hero's own account of his adventures, as given in a little volume picked up by Mr. Melville at a book-stall. The story is well told, but the book is hardly worthy of the author of "Typee." "The Confidence Man" (1857), his last serious effort in prose fiction, does not seem to require criticism.[43]

Mr. Melville's pen had rested for nearly ten years, when it was again taken up to celebrate the events of the Civil War. "Battle Pieces and Aspects of the War" appeared in 1866. Most of these poems originated, according to the author, "in an impulse imparted by the fall of Richmond;" but they have as subjects all the chief incidents of the struggle. The best of them are "The Stone Fleet," "In the Prison Pen," "The College Colonel," "The March to the Sea," "Running the Batteries," and "Sheridan at Cedar Creek." Some of these had a wide circulation in the press, and were preserved in various anthologies. "Clarel, a Poem and Pilgrimage in the Holy Land" (1876), is a long mystical poem requiring, as some one has said, a dictionary, a cyclopaedia, and a copy of the Bible for its elucidation. ⟦xxxv⟧ In the two privately printed volumes, the arrangement of which occupied Mr. Melville during his last illness, there are several fine lyrics. The titles of these books are, "John Marr and Other Sailors" (1888), and "Timoleon" (1891).[44]

There is no question that Mr. Melville's absorption in philosophical studies was quite as responsible as the failure of his later books for his cessation from literary productiveness. That he sometimes realised the situation will be seen by a passage in "Moby Dick": —

" 'Didn't I tell you so?' said Flask; 'yes, you'll soon see this right whale's head hoisted up opposite that parmacetti's.'

"In good time Flask's saying proved true. As before, the Pequod steeply leaned over towards the sperm whale's head, now, by the counterpoise of both heads, she regained her own keel, though sorely strained, you may well believe. So, when on one side you hoist in Locke's head, you go over that way; but now, on the other side, hoist in Kant's and you come back again; but in very poor plight. Thus, some minds forever keep trimming boat. Oh, ye foolish! throw all these thunderheads overboard, and then you will float right and light."[45]

Mr. Melville would have been more than mortal if he had been indifferent to his loss of popularity. Yet he seemed contented to preserve an entirely independent attitude, and to trust to the verdict of the future. The smallest amount of activity would have kept him before the public; but his reserve would not permit this. That ⟦xxxvi⟧ he had faith in the eventual reinstatement of his reputation cannot be doubted.[46]

In the editing of this reissue of "Melville's Works," I have been much indebted to the scholarly aid of Dr. Titus Munson Coan, whose familiarity with the languages of the Pacific has enabled me to harmonise the spelling of foreign words in "Typee" and "Omoo," though without changing the phonetic method of printing adopted by Mr. Melville.[47] Dr. Coan has also been most helpful with suggestions in other directions. Finally, the delicate fancy of Lafarge has supplemented the immortal pen-portrait of the Typee maiden with a speaking impersonation of her beauty.[48]

New York, June, 1892.

Family Reminiscences

ELIZABETH SHAW MELVILLE, MEMORANDA
(May 1861–February 1902)

    Mrs. Melville's memoranda about her husband, her family, and their possessions are written in a small notebook now in the Melville Room of the Berkshire Athenaeum at Pittsfield, Massachusetts, to which it was given by a granddaughter, the late Eleanor Melville Metcalf. Though generous excerpts from the notebook have appeared in previous Melville scholarship, the memoranda have not heretofore been published in their entirety. They are printed here with the kind permission of Mrs. Melville's surviving granddaughters, conveyed by Mrs. A. D. Osborne, her great-grandsons David M. Metcalf and Paul C. Metcalf, and the Berkshire Athenaeum.

    The notebook is bound in worn leather now appearing grayish-blue, probably faded from an original black. Set into its cover flap is a strap of approximately 3/4 inch; there may originally have been a tape passing under this strap for use in tying the book shut. The volume is without a publisher's imprint, its illuminated title page reading only "Pocket / Diary / 1866. / Published Annually / For the Trade." Its unnumbered pages, measuring approximately 3 by 4 3/4 inches, comprise a printed almanac followed by a section for diary entries. Each page of the latter section is ruled and dated, with a uniform scroll decoration in black ink at the top, leaving a space for handwritten entries measuring approximately 2 1/2 by 4 inches. Mrs. Melville's notations are miscellaneous memoranda rather than diary-entries for 1866 or any other single year. The earliest material in point of composition appears to be an account of her husband's career headed "May 1861" that must have been transcribed here from some other document; the latest date entered is 1 February 1902.

    For purposes of reference and tabulation I have assigned the numbers 1 through 365 to those pages of the diary following its half-title, with "1" designating the page for 1 January 1866, and "365" that for 31 December. (The printed dates themselves, it should be emphasized, have no bearing upon the dating or the sequence of Mrs. Melville's entries on surviving pages. On some

167

pages she lined out the printed date but on others she left it as printed.) At
least 63 leaves of the diary have been torn out, leaving occasional stubs; some
of these stubs bear fragmentary inscription in black ink, apparently by Mrs.
Melville, that is insufficient for determining the nature of the material thus
removed. The missing leaves carried 125 pages of the diary proper (Nos. 1–
106, 329–332, 351–365). Among the surviving pages Mrs. Melville left 189
blank; she inscribed 51, mostly in ink, but later erased her penciled inscription
on two of these; she also made a notation in pencil inside the back cover.

The present text prints all of Mrs. Melville's surviving inscription except the
unrecovered pencilling erased on pp. 139–140; the accompanying notes keyed
to the text print all additional inscription by "F[rances]. M[elville]. T[homas]."
and "E[leanor]. M[elville]. M[etcalf]." (her daughter and granddaughter, respectively). All inscription is in ink unless otherwise indicated. The assigned
page numbers are printed in double square brackets within the text: [[1]]–[[365]];
there is also indication, within square brackets at the point of occurrence, of
pages lacking or left blank. Paired arrows [↑ . . . ↓] enclose insertions made in
the manuscript; angle brackets [⟨ . . . ⟩] enclose deletions. Spelling and punctuation are unchanged, with two exceptions: paragraph indention has been nor-
malized throughout; missing punctuation has been supplied, within square
brackets, where it seemed necessary for clarity.

[[1]]–[[106]] [torn out]
[[107]]–[[108]] [blank]
[[109]]   Various Mem⁰.

Bessies photographs taken at Rockwoods ↑1884↓¹ 17 Union Sq: N.Y
Profile 141708
Full face 141718²

⟨Bessies Bank Books
Seaman's Bank for Savings 74 Wall st—New York
No 202116
Manhattan Savings Inst. 644 Broadway
No 98286 ⟩³

[[110]] [blank]
  [[111]] A new edition of Typee, Omoo, Moby Dick, & White Jacket having
been published in 1892—by Mr Arthur Stedman—I received in royalties from
the U[nited]. S[tates]. Book Co. and afterwards from the Am[erican].
Pub[lishers]. Corporation both of whom failed $243.40—owing me $158.13
which was never paid. Then a new edition was published in 1900 from the
rented plates—by Dana Estes & Co Boston—from which on a 5 p[e]r c[en]t
[[112]] royalty I have received $63.47—
                    Feb. 1— 1902

↑see later accounts↓[4]

[[113]]-[[138]] [blank]
[[139]]-[[140]] [erased pencil entries, unrecovered]
[[141]]-[[203]] [blank]
[[204]]   Herman Melville
                        May 1861 ↑(1891)↓[5]
Herman came home from sea fall of 1844–Published Typee spring of 1846.
We were married Aug 4, 1847–Winters of '47 & '48 he worked very hard at
his books–sat in a room without fire–wrapped up–wrote Mardi–published
1849–Summer of 49 we remained in New York–he wrote "Redburn" &
"White Jacket["]. Same fall went to England & published the above–Staid 11
weeks [[205]] took little satisfaction in it from mere homesickness and hurried
home–leaving attractive invitations to visit various distinguished people–one
from the Duke of Rutland to pass a week at Belvoir Castle–see his journal–
    We went to Pittsfield and boarded in the summer of 1850–Removed ↑to
Arrowhead↓ there in fall October 1850–
    Wrote White Whale or Moby Dick under [[206]] under [sic] unfavorable cir-
cumstances–would sit at his desk all day not eating any thing till four or five
o clock–then ride to the village after dark–Would be up early and out walking
before breakfast–sometimes splitting wood for exercise. Published White
Whale in 1851–Wrote "Pierre" published 1852–
    We all felt anxious about the strain on his health in Spring of 1853–
    In 1854-5-& 6 wrote [[207]] two books first published as serials in ["]Put-
nam's Monthly"–and afterwards in book form–these were Israel Potter and
the Encantadas–Also "Piazza Tales" some of which had previously appeared
in Magazines–
    In Fall of 1856 he went to Europe and travelled 6 or 7 months going to the
Holy Land[;] came home about the time the Confidence Man was published in
1857–and with [[[208]]-[[209]] blank] [[210]] much improved health. In 13
years he had written 10 books besides much miscellaneous writing–
    He lectured in many parts of the country during the winters of '58, '59 &
'60.
    In Feb 1855 he had his first attack of severe rheumatism in his back–so
that he was helpless–and in the following June an attack of Sciatica–Our
neighbor in Pittsfield Dr O. W. Holmes attended & prescribed for [[211]] him–
A severe attack of what he called crick in the back laid him up at his mothers
in Gansevoort in March 1858–and he never regained his former vigor &
strength–[6]

    Herman had two attacks of erysipelas–the last in April 1890–both of
which weakened him greatly–

It is erroneously stated in Chambers' Encyclopedia that "in 1860 Herman M. left his farm and made a voyage round the world in a whaling vessel"[7]

⟦212⟧   ↑1851↓[8]
Mr Hawthorne came to Arrowhead in March (13th) with Una, and passed several days[9]

⟦213⟧-⟦222⟧ [blank]
⟦223⟧   Herman Melville[10]
Born in New York Aug 1. 1819   Attended the Albany Classical School in 1835—His teacher Dr Chas. E. West is still living in Brooklyn N.Y. ↑(1895)↓[11]
Made his first voyage before the mast in 1837*—in a New York merchantman bound for Liverpool & returned after a short cruise
                              (See "Redburn")
Spent the ↑previous↓ summer of 183⟨8⟩6* on his Uncle Thomas Melville's farm in Pittsfield—Mass. Taught school at intervals in Pittsfield and in Greenbush (now East A[l] bany) N. Y—
⟦224⟧ Shipped again "before the mast" in the whaler "Acushnet" Jan 1st*—1841—
Left the ship, being oppressed with hard fare and harsh usage, in the summer of 1842 with a companion Richard T. Greene (Toby) at the bay of Nukuheva in the Marquesas Islands. He made his way to the Typee valley and was there detained in captivity by the natives four months—was then rescued by an Australian whaler
                              (See "Typee")
After touching at various islands he ⟦225⟧ landed at Tahiti on the day of its occupation by the French—was there arrested with other shipmates on the whaler for alleged mutinous conduct but was honorably discharged—spent some time in visiting the neighboring islands and made his way to Honolulu where he spent four months—
                              (See "Omoo")
From Honolulu as a means of returning home he shipped again before the mast in the United States ⟦226⟧ Frigate (United States) and was discharged in Boston in the Fall of 1844—
                              (See "White Jacket")

Returned to his mother's home in Lansingburgh, N.Y. and there wrote "Typee" which was published in London and New York in Spring of 1846—his brother Gansevoort Melville then being Sec. of Legation at the court of St James—London—

Was married Aug 4. 1847 lived in New York till 1850 when he removed to

[[227]] Pittsfield Mass—Returned to New York in Oct. 1863—On Oct 8 1849 he went to London to arrange for the publication of his works there (in the sailing packet ship Southampton, Capt Griswold)—Made brief visits to France and Germany and sailed for home in the "Independence" (Capt R. T. Fletcher) arriving in New York about 1st Feb. 1850—

In Oct. 1856 his health being impaired by too close application he again sailed for London—taking manuscript books with him for [[228]] publication there—He went up the Mediterranean to Constantinople and the Holy Land—For much of his observation & reflection on that interesting quarter see his Poem of "Clarel"

Sailed for home in the steamer "City of Manchester" May 6, 1857—

In May 1860 he made a voyage to San Francisco sailing from Boston on the 30th with his brother Thomas Melville who commanded the "Meteor" a fast sailing Clipper in the China trade—[[229]] and returning in November he being the only passenger—He reached San Francisco Oct 12th—Returned in the "Cortez" Oct 20th to Panama—Crossed the Isthmus & sailed for New York in the "North Star"—(This voyage to San Francisco has been incorrectly given in many of the papers &c of the day)[12]

During the winters of 1857 to 1860 he gave lectures in different American Cities & towns embracing a large range—

[[230]] He was appointed Inspector of Customs in New York Dec 5—1866—Resigned office Jan 1. 1886—

He died Sept. 28th ↑1891↓ after two years of failing health—induced partly by severe attacks of erysipilas—terminating finally in enlargement of the heart—[13]

<Nov. 1897>[14] His last Custom house office was at Simonson's Lumber yard—foot of 79th st on East River

[[231]]-[[232]] [blank]

[[233]] Mr James Billson of Leicester England—friend of James Thomson poet—sent Herman "Vane's story" a poem by Mr Thomson Oct. 1884 Also, "The City of Dreadful Night," by the same author Jan. 1885.[15]

In Liverpool "Daily Post" Mr Billson wrote an article on Thomson & sent it to Herman Feb. 18, 1885—[16]

Mr Billson sent Thomson's "Essays & Phantasies" and "Satires & Profanities"—[17]

In letter of Jan 31. 1885 Mr Billson writes of Mr. [J.W.] [[234]] Barrs—a friend of Mr H. S. Salt who wrote notice in the Scottish Art Review[18]

"Mr Barrs one of your readers desires to forward you "A Voice from the <Hill"> ↑Nile" &c↓ by James Thomson. Mr Barrs had Thomson for a visitor, and Mr Barr[s] also figured in the poem "Belvoir"—Mr Barrs sister was the subject of the poem "The Sleeper" in the above named volume["] —sent Feb 15th 1886—At same date Mr Billson sent a "semi-manuscript" copy of a poem of "Omar Khayam["] translated by Fitzgerald—[19]

Dec 4. 1888 Mr Billson [235] sent Thomsons "Essay on Shelley" long out of print and very scarce—a copy at "Scribners["] was 7.00—[20]

Mr Salt sent his "Life of James Thomson" Feb. 2d 1890[21]

[236] [blank]

[237] Herman went to Virginia with Allan in April 1864[.] Visited various battle-fields & called on Gen. Grant[.] Henry Gansevoort then in the service—in camp at Vienna Virginia—[22]

---

[238][23] The Major Melvill house in Green St Boston was vacated by the family after their parents death—and torn down in 1833—

Major M. was fire-ward No 4—1779—[24]

Major M's watch—Le Roy No 174—1826—Another one by Stephen Twycross[?] London—No 1358—

One of them engraved "45" from a celebrated political article favoring independence in the North British Review [i.e., *The North Briton*] by John Wilkes—so numbered—

[239] Major M's portrait & that of his wife was painted by Francis Alexander—1826—

Bequeathed by their granddaughter Mrs. Downer to the Bostonian Society in 1901—The "bottle of Tea" was also sent to the Society by George Melvill—Galena—[25]

Herman's portrait taken from the Pittsfield ambro-type was sent to Mr [Richard Watson] Gilder for the Septr. no of the Century Magazine 1894 (& returned) See bound vol of Century for 1894.* Article on Literary Berkshire—[26]

[240]-[266] [blank]
[267][27]

Old piano found in Pittsfield after Allan [Melville] had given it away—from Arrowhead—Imported from London by Davis & Gibson New York 1801— Given to Maria Gansevoort in Albany by her father when she was 10 yrs old— ↑I had picture frame made from the wreck↓

Old clock from Gansevoort [New York] made by Devereux Bowly London—[28]

Old Kitchen at Arrowhead 175237—photo by Rockwood

⟦268⟧-⟦269⟧ [blank] [29]
⟦270⟧[30] Dr Holmes large pine tree on his place at Pittsfield was photographed by Clifton Johnson—Boston

⟦271⟧-⟦307⟧ [blank]
⟦308⟧ Sir Robert Strange the celebrated engraver was born in the Orkneys, July 14. 1721—Married Isabella Lumasdon 1747—Died 1792—See the Scollay Family Tree—[31]

⟦309⟧-⟦312⟧ [blank]
⟦313⟧[32] <Vases from Miss Magee to Bessie. One "Copenhagen" the other "Cypriote" from the collection discovered in Cyprus by Gen. Di Cesnola Director of the Art Museum in New York>[33]

Grandmother Shaws old worked chair covers bought May 4"—1774[34]

Little mahogany bureau belonged to my grandmother Shaw, when she was ten years old. I have given it to Bessie. [35]

⟦314⟧[36] <Marks on some of my silver
Old tea spoons D. H. Eagle B. Indian[37] O. B. O.
M. tea spoons D.L very small
Scollay spoons. J. Coburn—T. Marsh A. C. F.
J.W. Forbes—anchor—star—head. C
N. Francis C
C. Q. spoons M. P. Lion-Head. C
Silver tumblers—Loring>[38]

⟦315⟧ <Minnie Hoadley's pewter plates from Gansevoort marked P. M C.
Trademark an oval shield with a lamb hanging and S on top>[39]

<Dark blue & gilt cups & saucers from Aunt Lucretia "Coblits" ↑ "Willow pat[tern]. "Wedgwood["] mark out of line also subdivisions of a circle or the whole O—or OO↓>[40]

Staffordshire mark on china E. W. S—or E. Wood & Sons
Lowestoft—with pink roses—Tudor Arms surmounted by a crown[41]

⟦316⟧-⟦319⟧ [blank]

⟦320⟧ <In 1777. Mather Byles a Tory in the Revolutionary War was Born in Boston in 1706—graduated at Harvard in 1725—Was ordained first pastor of Hollis St church in 1773–In 1777 he was tried and sentenced to be banished and sent with his family to England, but it was not enforced and he was permitted to remain under guard in his own house cor. of Nassau & Tremont sts— He died there in 1788 ⟦321⟧ leaving two daughters who grew to advanced age there, stanch Loyalists to the end

His shaving mug that I have with the head of Queen Charlotte was given to my grandfather Knapp by one of them after his ↑(Mather Byles)↓ death—>[42]

⟦322⟧ The blue quilted petticoat was bequeathed by Dorothy Wharton (my mothers' great-aunt) to her namesake, my aunt D. W. Dow—her daughters, <also> having no descendants, have given it to me, hoping that [it] will go down to future generations

The "Empire" gown was my mothers' who died in 1822—

E. S. M

⟦323⟧ "Broadhall" Pittsfield built by Henry Van Schaick in 1781. Elkanah Watson bought it in 1807. Major Thos. Melvill Sen. bought it in 1816—his son Thos. lived there but moved to Galena Ill. in 1837–Mr & Mrs Rowland Morewood bought it in 1851

"Arrowhead" Pittsfield built before 1800 by David Bush & kept as an inn— Herman Melville bought it in Oct. 1850—and named it—He named also a spur of the Hoosac Range on the S. E. October Mt. from its brilliant display ⟦324⟧ of foliage in that month—Lived there till Oct. 1863 when he <bought> ↑moved into↓ a house in New York—104 East 26th st <from his> bought from his brother Allan giving ↑7,750↓[43] and the Arrowhead estate valued at $3000 and assuming a mortage of 2000 to Mrs. Thurston which was afterwards paid off by Dr [George] Hayward's legacy to me of $3000 in May 1864—about $1000 <from> Aunt Priscilla's ↑legacy↓ was spent in repairs—

We lived there till April 1892—when this house was sold ⟦325⟧ for 16,250— immediate payment i[n] cash—Left the house <May 2d> ↑Apr 28↓[44] 1892— 40.00 <bonus>[45] from Mr Hutchinson for earlier removal—↑Moved into the Florence Apt. House June 7th 1892↓[46]

⟦326⟧ Herman paid 134.00 for his share of expenses in the A[l]bany Cemetery—
        ↑April 1890↓[47]

Uncle Peter Gansevoort gave him $500 in 1872—the same to Tom [Thomas Melville]—Also gave Herman $1000 to enable him to publish Clarel in 1876—[48]

◇

Herman's portrait was painted by J. O. Eaton in the summer of 1870—Mr Hoadley ordered it for a present for Herman's mother—She left it to her daughter Catherine G. Hoadley who gave it to me—E. S. M.[49]

[[327]] [blank]
  [[328]] Lemuel Shaw [Jr.] died in Boston May 6th 1884—↑Funeral 9th Dr Rufus Ellis officiated—↓[50]
Thomas Melville died March 5th 1884
Fanny Melville died July [9] 1885—Brookline
Helen M. Griggs died in Brookline [14 December 1888]
Augusta Melville died in New Brighton Staten Island April 4—1876[51]

[[329]]-[[332]] [torn out]
[[333]]-[[335]] [blank]
  [[336]] Two ivory miniatures
            (Veil) Caroline Knapp
                (Mrs Dr Geo. Hayward)
            Martha Knapp
                (Mrs. Philip Marett)
Linen fire bag—marked "No 1 J. Knapp 1788" Josiah Knapp[52]

  [[337]] <The "Dana snuff-box["] was given to my Uncle John Knapp by the heirs of Judge Francis Dana with autograph letter, signed by all—>
  <The watch set with pearls belonged to Mrs. Craigie—who was Elizabeth Shaw my fathers cousin—she left it in her will to Mother who gave it to me—>[53]

  [[338]] Statuette given to my ↑uncle↓ John Knapp by Washington Allston <by> his friend and classmate—in 1805—graduated at Harvard in my fathers class 1800—[54]

◇

The celebrated statue of "Ariadne sleeping" formerly called Cleopatra from the asp on the arm was in the Vatican at Rome—and celebrated under that name by Castiglione in a Latin poem written in honor of its discovery—Murray's Handbook of Central Italy— Brauns Handbook adds [[339]] that she has just been left by the perfidious Theseus on the desolate Isle of Naxos—The serpent was a sacred symbol of betrothal in common use as the wedding ring of the modern[55]

◇

<Inscription on Longhi's engraving of Napoleon—Translation from Horace
"Alone by valor thou hast secured Italian liberties—by virtue thou hast
given glory to the laws thou hast reformed">[56]

⟦340⟧   "Whale Pictures"
                            by
Ambroise Louis Garnery—French painter—son of Jean Francois Garnery—
Painted marine subjects and battles—Battle of Naverino &c also published a
pictorial work on the Ports & Coasts of France—[57]

<The burial of Gustavus Adolphus was painted by Helquist—Swedish
artist—>[58]

⟦341⟧ Our portrait of Gen. Gansevoort is a copy from Stuarts by Joseph
Ames (1816-1872) son of Ezra Ames—a carriage painter—also president of the
Mechanics and Farmers Bank—Albany He also painted portrait of Herman's
mother about 1814—[59]

<Madam Recamier by Gerard—costume of Consulate—bare feet and neck
on a Roman chair in a niche beneath a pillared arch—Same by David represents
her leaning back on a rustic seat>[60]

⟦342⟧-⟦344⟧ [blank]
⟦345⟧ Mrs. Mary E. Root of Pittsfield—her father was James Bradford—
clergyman in Sheffield—her uncle Dr John Bradford who married Miss Lush—
He officiated at Mrs. Melvilles wedding in Albany Oct. 4—1814—and afterwards
baptised her children—

⟦346⟧ [blank]
⟦347⟧ Characters in "Tales of a Wayside Inn"—Longfellow
        Musician—Ole Bull
        Student—Henry Wales
        Young Sicilian—Luigi Monti
        Spanish Jew—Edrehei
        Theologian—Prof. Treadwell
        Poet—T. W. Parsons

Host of the Red Horse Tavern—Lyman Howe—

Present owner of the "Wayside Inn" Sudbury Mass April 1897—Edward R.
Lemon—He has an old jug 200 years old used by General Peter Gansevoort—
from his historic home in Saratoga Co—N. Y[61]

⟦348⟧ Distinguished men born in 1819
—From Dr Titus A [*i.e.,* M.] Coan who writes "I think Mr Melville's name
will be remembered as long as any on the list ["]:
Herman Melville
James Russell Lowell
Walt Whitman
John Ruskin
Thomas Ball
Queen Victoria
Charles Kingsley
W. W Story
T. W. Parsons
E. P. Whipple
C. A Dana
J. G. Holland
H. P. Gray
⟦349⟧ Cyrus ↑W↓ Field
Julia Ward Howe
↑Richard Storrs Willis↓[62]

⟦350⟧ <Boarding place at Princeton Mass—highly recommended by Miss
Whitwell—July 21. 1882.
Mr. Edwin Grimes—>[63]

Legacy from Aunt Lucy to Herman—$150—and to me—(E.S.M) $100—

Aunt Priscilla left $900. to Herman[64]

The "Gansevoort Jug" at the Wayside Inn was bought by the proprietor Mr
Lemon of a Mr Blake, a dealer in Albany[65]

⟦351⟧-⟦365⟧ [torn out]
[inside back cover] American Law Review Vol 2—p. 47 article about father
Little Brown Co[66]

ELEANOR MELVILLE THOMAS METCALF, RECOLLECTIONS (1921, 1953)

Mrs. Metcalf's recollections of her grandfather, previously printed in Raymond M. Weaver, *Herman Melville: Mariner and Mystic* (New York: George H.
Doran Company, 1921), pp. 377–380, and again in her own *Herman Melville:*

Cycle and Epicycle (Cambridge: Harvard University Press, 1953), pp. 282–283, are reprinted here with the kind permission of her sons, David M. Metcalf and Paul C. Metcalf, and with the concurrence of Sidney A. Burrell (for the estate of Raymond Weaver) and of Harvard University Press.

I was not yet ten years old when my grandfather died. To put aside all later impressions gathered from those who knew him longer and coloured by their personal reactions, all impressions made by subsequent reading of his books, results in a series of childish recollections, vivid homely scenes wherein he formed a palpable background for my own interested activities.

Setting forth on a bright spring afternoon for a trip to Central Park, the Mecca of most of our pilgrimages, he made a brave and striking figure as he walked erect, head thrown back, cane in hand, inconspicuously dressed in a dark blue suit and a soft black felt hat.[1] For myself, I skipped gaily beside him, anticipating the long jogging ride in the horse cars, the goats and shanty-topped granite of the upper reaches of our journey, the broad walks of the park, where the joy of all existence was best expressed by running down the hills, head back, skirts flying in the wind. He would follow more slowly and call "Look out, or the 'cop' may catch you!" I always thought he used funny words: "cop" was surely a jollier word than "policeman."

We never came in from a trip of this kind, nor indeed from any walk, but we stopped in the front hall under a coloured engraving of the Bay of Naples, its still blue dotted with tiny white sails. He would point to them with his cane and say, "See the little boats sailing hither and thither." "Hither and thither"— more funny words, thought I, at the same time a little awed by something far away in the tone of voice.

I remember mornings when even sugar on the oatmeal was not enough to tempt me to finish the last mouthful. It would be spring in the back yard too, and a tin cup full of little stones picked out of the garden meant a penny from my grandmother.[2] He would say in a warning whisper, "Jack Smoke will come down the chimney and take what you leave!" That was another matter. The oatmeal was laughingly finished and the yard gained. Across the back parlour and main hall upstairs ran a narrow iron-trimmed porch, furnished with Windsor and folding canvas chairs. There he would sit with a pipe and his most constant companion—his cane, and watch my busy activity below. Against the wall of the porch hung a match holder, more for ornament than utility, it seems. It was a gay red and blue china butterfly.[3] Invariably he looked to see if it had flown away since we were there last.

Once in a long while his interest in his grandchildren led him to cross the river and take the suburban train to East Orange, where we lived. He must have been an impressive figure, sitting silently on the piazza of our little house, while my sister and I pranced by with a neighbour's boy and his express wagon, filled with a satisfied sense of the strength and accomplishment of our years.

When he had had enough of such exhibitions, he would suddenly rise and take the next train back to Hoboken.

Chiefly do I think of him connected with different parts of the 26th Street house.

His own room was a place of mystery and awe to me; there I never ventured unless invited by him. It looked bleakly north. The great mahogany desk, heavily bearing up four shelves of dull gilt and leather books; the high dim book-case, topped by strange plaster heads that peered along the ceiling level, or bent down, searching blindly with sightless balls; the small black iron bed, covered with dark cretonne; the narrow iron grate; the wide table in the alcove, piled with papers I would not dream of touching—these made a room even more to be fled than the back parlour, by whose door I always ran to escape the following eyes of his portrait, which hung there in a half light. Yet lo, the paper-piled table also held a little bag of figs, and one of the pieces of sweet stickiness was for me. "Tittery-Eye" he called me,[4] and awe melted into glee, as I skipped away to my grandmother's room, which adjoined.

That was a very different place—sunny, comfortable and familiar, with a sewing machine and a *white* bed like other peoples'[.] In the corner stood a big arm chair, where he always sat when he left the recesses of his own dark privacy. I used to climb on his knee, while he told me wild tales of cannibals and tropic isles. Little did I then know that he was reliving his own past. We came nearest intimacy at these times, and part of the fun was to put my hands in his thick beard and squeeze it hard. It was no soft silken beard, but tight curled like the horse hair breaking out of old upholstered chairs, firm and wiry to the grasp, and squarely chopped.

Sad it is that he felt his grandchildren would turn against him as they grew older. He used to forebode as much. As it is, I have nothing but a remembrance of glorious fun, mixed with a childish awe, as of some one who knew far and strange things.

FRANCES CUTHBERT THOMAS OSBORNE, RECOLLECTIONS (1965)

Mrs. Osborne's recollections of her grandfather, previously printed as "Herman Melville through a Child's Eyes," *Bulletin of the New York Public Library,* 69 (December 1965), 655–660, are reprinted here with the kind permission of the author and the New York Public Library. In a footnote to the original printing Mrs. Osborne "expresses her appreciation to Mr Stuart C. Sherman . . . for assisting with the editing and publication of these reminiscences."

I have been asked by my family and by some of my interested friends, to record just as I have sometimes told them, the memories of my childhood visits to the home of my grandfather, Herman Melville.

I have never written for publication before. My early efforts at poetry at the age of eleven burned out in one poem entitled "The Snow." Mother subsequently sent it to Oliver Wendell Holmes, knowing that he would be interested in the literary attempts of a granddaughter of his old acquaintance, Herman Melville, when they were neighbors in Pittsfield. A highly prized letter from Dr Holmes to my mother is all that remains of this episode. The rest of my writings consist of letters to my children, giving them the good advice which is not often followed, and relating bits of home gossip so uninteresting that they are always destroyed upon reading.

The trips which I made to my Melville grandparents from my home in East Orange, New Jersey, in the suburbs of New York, began when I was about five years old. I was eight years old when my grandfather died in 1891. These visits left such an impression that, though fifty years or more have passed, I can still see very clearly the timid little girl clinging to her mother's skirts, making the big trip to the city and being left there often for several days or a week.

One thing which strikes me now as quite significant is that, although I was a shy and timid child, I never felt the least bit afraid of my Grandfather Melville. His looks were awe-inspiring; he was tall and imposing; and his amazing beard and deep voice alone might well have frightened me. Many visitors to that household had cause to fear him but to me he was always gentle and I was never the victim of his moods and occasional uncertain tempers. He never revealed to me any of the impatience, and even anger, which he was known to have visited on various people with whom he came in contact. I was too small to criticize him, too young to be impatient with, and too trusting to incur his anger.

My own father, when he first paid an evening call upon my mother, was dismayed to hear her father stride down the hall to the front parlor door and shout, "Young man, do you prefer oatmeal or mush for breakfast?" The question having the desired effect, the young man hastily bade the family goodnight, and mother wondered whether she would ever see him again.

Although grandpa was always a mysterious person to me, there was no mystery whatever about my grandmother and my Aunt Bessie (Herman's daughter Elizabeth Shaw Melville). My grandmother I loved dearly. She never tolerated black hair ribbons on her grandchildren. She had been in mourning so often for members of her family that whenever her grandchildren appeared in black she changed them to bright colors.[1] Aunt Bessie was always ready to amuse me and often met me at the door to unfasten my coat and untie my muslin cap strings when I came back from walks. Although she was badly crippled with arthritis she was a remarkable person with a wonderful mind. When I was older she often took me to the theatre and to a French church and instilled within me a love for French which has given me pleasure ever since.

I spent a great deal of time in grandmother's room cutting out paper dolls, painting, and listening to the stories my Aunt Bessie read aloud so well. I often wondered what grandpa could be doing for hours on end in his study. He slept in a large, double bed in the adjoining room connected by a little passageway. Sometimes I could hear him walking back and forth for a long time and I would think how much pleasanter it would be if he were walking in the park with me, a pastime which, except for one memorable occasion, was always most delightful. But the days when he paced up and down in his small study were not often the happiest ones for me, and surely not for him. He must have been walking off energy instead of turning to writing as a safety valve for smoldering fires. When he emerged he was usually quiet—too much so to be interesting to me.

Grandpa once had a severe nosebleed while I was visiting there. It was the first time I had ever seen one and it concerned me greatly. Grandma said it was nothing and that it would soon pass. It was probably caused by high blood pressure. Mr and Mrs Melville each suffered from erysipelas and at such times the children were not allowed to visit.

One walk in the park which stands out more clearly than any other, and which might have had a disastrous ending, took place on a lovely spring day.[2] Our home was one of a long row of houses on East 26th Street, each exactly alike except for the number on the door, or perhaps for the tawny color of the cat walking on the iron fence in front. I suppose different kinds of people did really come out of those houses at times, but even that seemed an impossibility for their sameness was such that one imagined each to contain a grandfather, grandmother and Aunt Bessie, just like mine.

On the spring day of which I speak the tulips were in bloom in Madison Square and the warm air coming in my grandfather's study window must have coaxed him out, for he thought a walk in the park would be refreshing. I joyfully ran for my cap and waited while Aunt Bessie tied the strings. It was wonderful what she was able to do with her hands, so crippled were they with an incurable form of arthritis. At last the crisp bow met with her satisfaction and I took my grandfather's hand ready for one of those walks which were always such a pleasure, for one never could tell what we might do or where we might go. Children in those days were not consulted as to what they would like to do best, and the uncertainty of grandfather's choice was one of the most interesting features of our expeditions.

I seem to remember him wearing dark glasses that day. He often did, as the bright sunshine was sometimes too much for his eyes. I never quite got used to the glasses, which were rectangular with the corners cut off, and which made him look so different I was always relieved when he took them off at home.

We crossed Fourth Avenue and went to the square. I have wondered since whether Madison Square Garden took its name from the fact that there really was a garden there. Grandpa, as his grandchildren called him, always carried a cane so that his right hand was occupied completely. His left hand held my small one tightly and gave me great confidence. His long stride required fast trotting for me to keep abreast of him. We walked along, I talking busily and he answering my question with great, long, interesting words which sounded pleasant but had no meaning whatever for me. Sometimes he pointed with his cane to this or that or stopped for some reason known only to him.

The tulips were gorgeous and we walked round and round the circle admiring them. Perhaps their beauty was overpowering, for grandpa let go of my hand and went to a nearby bench to rest. I continued to run around the circular garden. It had become a game by that time, and I had forgotten the tulips. So had grandpa. Perhaps by then he was off in some distant land, or on a rolling ship at sea with nothing to distract his thoughts. Wherever he was, there was no little granddaughter with him. She had ceased to exist. Tiring after a while of running continuously in a ring, I went to the bench on which I had last seen grandpa sitting. To my dismay he was gone, was nowhere in sight and had vanished just like the mysterious person I had always imagined him to be. There were a few men dozing behind newspapers, all strangers, not caring the least about me. I was really frightened.

Running as fast as I could, I reached Fourth Avenue, just by chance and not by cleverness, as my relatives later insisted. Dodging a few horses and wagons, I crossed the Avenue and took the first street which luckily was Twenty-sixth Street. Running along in a panic by that time, I looked dismayed at the long, interminable row of brick houses. There was nothing to tell me which was which, for I was too young to know my numbers. I think I should soon have collapsed from sheer fright had I not at that moment caught sight of grandpa coming hurriedly down the steps of a nearby house closely followed by Aunt Bessie. That is the only time in my life that I ever saw my aunt move quickly. She had met grandpa at the door, ready to untie the cap strings and relieve me of their starchy discomfort when, to her horror, she found him alone. Their relief must have been great when they saw me in my non-stop flight, for grandpa later confessed that he had no idea of where or when he had left me. It must have been wonderful to have had an imagination strong enough to carry him away so far that he could lose a grandchild in the big city and never know it. After that day, Aunt Bessie used always to ask where we were going when we started forth.

We took frequent trips to Central Park to see the animals. Experience made me cling tightly to his big hand, for to be lost amid lions and tigers would have been something too fearful to contemplate.

There were occasions when grandpa would order a swan boat to take us about the lake and we would experience the delicious sensation of gliding about on the water. If you didn't turn your head you did not see the man behind you working the pedals to propel the boat and you could pretend he wasn't there, just the beautiful swan drawing you along. At that time I did not know enough to think what must have been grandpa's thoughts on those trips across the lake. Long voyages in pursuit of the monstrous whale, on stormy seas in rugged ships—what an absurd contrast! Yet, I know now that he thoroughly enjoyed these excursions. Had he not, we surely would not have taken them.

Grandpa took great delight in the wax figures at the Eden Musée, the long since forgotten building on Fourteenth Street which housed the most remarkable people, people who appeared to be just like everyone else and yet in some indescribable way were not. I never knew just what the difference was until I was much older. There was a policeman in his smart uniform and large blue helmet; the newspaper boy, ragged, and yet so much cleaner than those I had seen in the streets; the old gentleman who sat on the freshly painted green bench looking at his trousers in dismay—these were all far more interesting to me than the historical groups or royal families displayed in all their grandeur inside glass cases within the museum. Once, and only once, did I go down into the chamber of horrors below. The sight of the beautiful pale lady in the arms of the hideous gorilla was so terrifying that I never could be persuaded to go downstairs again. I couldn't believe that she was not real, and I thought of her long afterward. Grandpa must have enjoyed my childish reactions, for we often visited the Eden Musée. I am sure he took great comfort and pleasure in his grandchildren, and he showed a side of his nature to us that no one else knew he possessed. My older sister, Eleanor, used to go to Twenty-sixth Street too sometimes, but, being older, she was more easily left at home when domestic upheavals necessitated sending away one of the little girls for safekeeping.

Grandpa had one delightful custom. Sometimes he would ask me to lend him five cents. It would always be when he knew I had that amount in my possession, having just been paid for picking stones from Grandma's little garden, a penny for every time I filled a certain small gill measure.[3] The first time grandpa asked me for a loan I gave up my nickel rather reluctantly for it had just been earned, but he returned it in the form of a dime. I had to have it explained that it was twice as much, for the dime looked so small and thin compared to my nickel. After that I was always ready to lend my money whenever he asked for it, for it always came back with interest.

If I had no fear of my grandfather, mysterious though he was, I had great fear of some of his possessions. He used to buy pictures, statuary, vases, or ornaments which pleased him, and one of these treasures was a more than life size bust of Antinous.[4] It stood on a tall white pedestal in the corner of the front parlor, draped with a long white net veil to keep the city dust from settling on the beautiful features and curly hair of the young Roman. I had to pass the parlor door every time I went to the basement dining room and many was the time I scurried fearfully past the door, glancing hastily in, to see if the still, white figure would raise its inclined head to discover who was going past in such a hurry. Once I tried going on tiptoe, but discarded that way as too slow a method, preferring the quick run which had the added advantage of breaking the ominous silence.

The oil paintings of the Whalers,[5] hanging on the stairway leading to my little room on the third story, was also something to contend with. I reached my bedroom at the head of the stairs after each trip, trying not to look back at those fearful creatures destroying boats in their jaws and plunging men into foaming seas in a most frightening manner.

On rare occasions I was allowed into grandpa's study—such a wonderful place! There was no wall space at all, just books, books, books. His huge desk had interesting things on it including a rolling ruler decorated with different varieties of green ferns, a large velvet pincushion mounted on an iron stand and a little black metal candlestick for sealing wax. I could play with anything on those days when I was invited into the study. Sometimes I piled books into houses on the floor. A set of Schopenhauer pleased me most—they were not too heavy to handle and of a nice palish blue color.[6] I was not concerned with the contents.

My games amused grandpa and when I had tired of them he would take me on his knee and let me pat his wonderful beard. He told me stories which I did not always understand. I enjoyed the sensation of sitting on the slippery leather chair in the safety of his lap. Once when I was alone, I stepped on the upturned foot-rest and the back sat up so suddenly that it alarmed me. But when grandpa was in it I discovered that it never behaved thus.

There were days when it was stormy and we could not go walking, so a dusty, chill back porch enclosed in shutters provided a place for a constitutional. Grandpa would walk back and forth, I trotting alongside in this uninteresting spot until I suppose enough energy had been worked off to warrant going inside again. One of the redeeming features of the piazza walks was the sight of a blue and red china butterfly.[7] I think it was intended to hold matches behind its wings and had come from "Arrowhead," the Pittsfield home in the Berkshires. It was high in one corner and, looking very life-like to me, I always hoped it would fly lower one day so that we could touch it. The other intriguing thing was the music of the Aeolian harp on the windowsill. The wind blowing through it must have reminded grandpa of the wind in the rigging at sea. In *White Jacket* he mentions an Aeolian harp as a cure for the blues.[8]

As I think back on those happy days spent with my grandparents, other memories come to me. I recall the sight of my grandfather going off on a voyage to Bermuda in a heavy coat and plush cap, with a bundle called a shawlstrap in one hand and the inevitable cane in the other.[9] I also recall vividly the blizzard of '88 with the tremendous snow and deep slush which made it impossible for me to return to the suburbs for a week. The storm had started the day before as rain when my father took me to Twenty-sixth Street. The next morning I remember sitting in the window with grandfather watching the police haul the horses out of the drifts. I complained of the funny food, including condensed milk, which I had for the first time.

These vivid recollections have given me much pleasure through the years, and it is my hope that they may be of some value to persons interested in the personal life of Herman Melville.

Reference Matter

Appendix A

"HERMAN MELVILLE" IN *CYCLOPAEDIA OF
AMERICAN LITERATURE* (1855):
The Surviving Manuscript Leaves

Preserved by Evert Duyckinck and now among the Melville papers in the Duyckinck Collection, Manuscripts and Archives Division, the New York Public Library, are three manuscript leaves comprising the three opening paragraphs of the article on Melville in the *Cyclopædia of American Literature* (1855), edited by Duyckinck and his brother George (reprinted on pp. 91-95 above). Geoffrey Stone, *Melville* (New York: Sheed & Ward, 1949), p. 45, note 3, in calling attention to this material, implies that the surviving manuscript is that of the entire article rather than of the opening paragraphs only. "Possibly Melville was his own first biographer," Stone speculates, taking the manuscript in question to be a fair copy with "corrections and additions in Melville's hand." William H. Gilman, *Melville's Early Life and "Redburn"* (New York: New York University Press, 1951), p. 350, note 54, though "doubtful if the handwriting is actually Melville's" as Stone had suggested, attempts no identification.

A study of the manuscript leaves themselves, which are reproduced below with permission of the New York Public Library (Astor, Lenox and Tilden Foundations), reveals the presence of at least four hands, none of which I take to be Herman Melville's:

1. The opening lines of the manuscript ("Herman Melville was [Leaf 1] . . . in the British Army." [Leaf 2]) are inscribed in a hand that I have been unable to identify.

2. The footnotes on Leaf 1 and Leaf 2 and the continuation of the text on Leaves 2 and 3 are inscribed in the hand of Melville's brother Allan. Comparison of the inscription with known examples of Allan Melville's writing—e.g., his signature (see Plate I)—has convinced me that the hand is his. Similarities

189

between his writing and that of Herman Melville account for Stone's error.

3. Several penciled changes, reflected in the printed text, are presumably editorial alterations made by one of the Duyckincks.

4. The name "Jennings," written in pencil in the upper left corner of Leaf 1, presumably designates a printer's "take."

The first leaf of the manuscript must have been inscribed at some time after 20 June 1855, the date of death of Dr. George Brewster referred to in the third sentence. On the remainder of the *Cyclopaedia* article, the manuscript of which apparently has not survived, see the discussion on pp. 10-13 above.

Herman Melville was born at 55 Courtlandt street in the City of New York August 1 1819. On his fathers side he is of Scotch extraction and is descended in the fourth degree from Thomas Melville a Presbyterian Clergyman of the Scotch Kirk who from the year 1718 and for almost half a century was minister of Scoonie Parish, Seven, Fifeshire #

Dr George Brewster Minister of Scoonie who died June 20th 1855, succeeded Revd David Swan who was the successor of our authors ancestor. It is worthy of remark that the united years of these three Clergyman in the same desk was one hundred and thirty six years.

The minister of Scoonie had two sons. John Melville who became a member of his majestys council in Grenada and Allan Melville who came to America in 1748 and settled in Boston as a Merchant, dying young he left an only son Thomas Melville our authors grand father who was born in Boston and as appears by the Probate records on the appointment of his guardian in 1761 inherited a handsome fortune from his father. He graduated at Princeton College New Jersey in 1769 and in 1772 visited his relatives in Scotland. During this visit he was presented with the freedom of the city of St Andrews and of Renfew. He returned to Boston in 1773 where he became a merchant and in December of that year was one of the Boston Tea Party. He took an active part in the Revolution war

article Scoonie - Sinclairs statistical account of Scotland Vol 5 p. 115 -

& obituary notice in Scotsman June 23 1855

[2]

in Was Major in Crafts Regiment of Mass. Artillery
was in the actions in Rhode Island in 1776. Commissioned by Washington in 1789 as [naval officer] of the
Port of Boston. he was continued by all the Presidents
down to 1829 [when Jackson] was elected. He was
the nearest surviving male relative of General
Robert Melville who was descended from a brother
of the minister of Scoonie the first and only Captain
General and Governor in chief of the Islands ceded to England by France in 1763 and at the
time of his death which occurred in 1809 was with
one exception the oldest General in the British
Army. In the genealogy of General Melville contained
in Douglass' Baronage of Scotland, (published in 1798) the Boston family
and John Melville Esq of Granada are stated to be
descended from the same Branch of the Melville
family as General Melville.) To the time of his
death Major Melville continued to wear the
antiquated three cornered hat and from this
habit was familiarly known in Boston as the
last of the cocked hats. There is still preserved
a small parcel of the veritable tea in the destruction of which he took an active part.
Being found in his shoes on returning home it was sealed up
in a vial, although it was intended that
not a particle should escape destruction.
The vial and contents are now in possession
of Chief Justice Shaw of Massachusetts &
Our authors father. Allan Melville was an

X County annual Register — Scotland 1809 + 10
Vol 1. part 6th — Also Monthly Magazine Vol 28 year 1809
p. 442 — and European Magazine Vol 56 p 234 —

[left margin: Major Melville / note]

3

inipating merchant in New York. and made frequent visits to Europe in connection with his business. He was a well educated and polished man and spoke French like a native. After the death of General Melville his father kinsman and on the occasion of one of his numerous trips to Europe he visited Scotland and was entertained by the Earl of Leven & Melville at Melville House Fifeshire. During this visit to Fifeshire he saw & conversed with an old resident who ~~remembered~~ had seen his ancestor the minister of Scoonie.

On his mothers side Mr Melville is the grandson of General Peter Gansevoort of Albany N. Y. known to those familiar with the stories of the American Revolution as the "Hero of Fort Stanwix" having successfully defended that fort in 1777 against a large force of British and Indians commanded by General St. Ledger. Stones Life of Brant the Indian contains a steel engraving from a portrait by Stuart of Mr Melville's maternal grandparent.

Appendix B

Passages on Melville in J. E. A. Smith's *Taghconic; or Letters and Legends about Our Summer Home,* by Godfrey Greylock (Boston: Redding and Company, 1852).

On the Pittsfield Elm, p. 13

. . . the question is asked anxiously, "Will the Old Elm survive this year, also?"

Yet even in its death it is fortunate; the long, white streak, where the scathing lightning passed adown its trunk, caught the eye of Herman Mellville, who interwove it with his strong-lined portrait of Captain Ahab. "Threading its way," he says, "out from among his grey hairs, and continuing right down one side his tawny, scorched face and neck, till it disappeared in his clothing, you saw a slender, rod-like mark, lividly whitish. It resembled that perpendicular seam sometimes made in the straight, lofty trunk of a great tree, when the upper lightning tearingly darts down it, and, without wrenching a single twig, peels and grooves out the bark, from top to bottom, ere running off into the soil,—leaving the tree still greenly alive, but branded." There you have a graphic picture of one of the most noticeable features of our Old Elm; and thus, in its death stroke it received a new life,—as the ancients fabled that they who died by the lightning's bolt, thereby became immortal.[1]

On "Herman Mellville," p. 16

Adjoining the estate of Dr. Holmes is that of HERMAN MELLVILLE, who has retired thus far from the sea, where nothing can remind him of the familiar sounds of Ocean, save the roar of the wind among the forest trees.

"Oh, home returned, what joy to tell
Of all the dangers that befell
The sailor boy at sea."[2]

These gentlemen come hither for quiet; let us leave them to it, hoping that they may find in the bracing mountain air inspiration for a hundred things as wise and witty as "Astrea," and as enchantingly truthful as "Typee."

On the Balanced Rock, pp. 42-43

We had a little intellectual amusement in deciphering the names of innumerable Julias and Carolines, Rosalinds, Janes, and "Roxany Augustys," inscribed by affectionate jack-knives, upon the bark of the surrounding trees. Some classic gentleman, dolefully destitute of a doxy, had inscribed among them the words, "MEMNON," and "PEUCINIA." I have since heard the story of the merry hour when "Memnon" was inscribed, by a hand which has written many a witty and clever volume. Indeed, indeed there must have been a deal of witchery in the cunning priestess who made that stern old rock breathe such mysterious and enchanting music, I wonder if ever there was anything ⟦43⟧ in that broken champagne bottle which lay at the foot of the rock.[3]

On Nathaniel Hawthorne, p. 211

To the other attractions of this lake, at the time of our visit, was added, that upon its banks then lived Nathaniel Hawthorne. It was no small thing to breathe for a while the same air with that marvellous genius. The mountain lake should record that brief acquaintance as its first honor. By the bye I am told Mr. Hawthorne honored the mountain and the lake with far more of his attention than he bestowed upon his neighbors. I believe Herman Mellville and G. P. R. James were among his friends; but for the most part he is said to have lived in great seclusion. One is not much surprised to learn that the creator of Hester Prynne and little Pearl, Zenobia, and the Pynchons, does not find his highest pleasure in the chit-chat of fashionable or even of literary coteries. Nor should it surprise us if a touch of melancholy, or even seeming moroseness, tinges his manner. The knowledge of the soul's anatomist is that which "by suffering entereth."[4]

Appendix C

Passages on Melville in J. E. A. Smith's *Taghconic, the Romance and Beauty of the Hills,* by Godfrey Greylock (Boston: Lee and Shepard; New York: Charles T. Dillingham; Pittsfield: S. E. Nichols, 1879).[1]

On the Pittsfield Elm, pp. 34-35

But, escaping all peril, to trees as to men, comes at last that which is not danger, but doom. And, as with man, so with the tree to whose mortality the sacred writers so often liken our own, the life which aspires the most loftily best chances to meet a noble death. It so happened with our Elm. A thunderbolt fell crashingly upon it, and darting straight ⟦35⟧ down its tall trunk, ploughed a wound of ghastly whiteness from stricken bough to seared root. The fiery fluid dried up the juices in its old veins, and the whole tree, although cared for with almost filial tenderness, began slowly to perish. But, even in its death it was fortunate. The long white streak pencilled by the scathing lightning in its smooth bark, caught the eye of Herman Melville, who, in his wonderful story of "The White Whale," thus interwove it in his strong-lined portrait of Captain Ahab:

"Threading its way out from among his grey hairs, and continuing straight down one side his tawney scorched face and neck until it disappeared in his clothing, you saw a slender, rod-like mark, lividly whitish. It resembled that perpendicular seam sometimes made in the straight, lofty trunk of a great tree, when the upper lightning tearingly darts down it, and without wrenching a single twig, peals and grooves out the bark, from top to bottom, ere, running off into the soil, leaving the tree still greenly alive, but branded."

There you have a graphic picture of the old Elm in its decay. And thus in its death-stroke, it found a new life: as the ancients fabled that they who were slain by Jove's thunderbolts thereby became immortal.[2]

196

On the Balanced Rock, p. 84

We had a little intellectual amusement in deciphering the names of innumerable Julias and Carolines, Rosalinds, Janes, and "Roxany Augustys," inscribed by affectionate jack-knives, upon the bark of the surrounding trees. Some classic gentlemen, dolefully destitute of a doxy, had enrolled among them the words, "MEMNON," and "PEUCINIA." I have since heard the story of the merry hour when "Memnon" was inscribed by a hand which has written many a witty and clever volume. Indeed, indeed there must have been a deal of witchery in the cunning priestess who made that stern old rock breathe such mysterious and enchanting music.

> "Can any mortal creature of earth's mould
> Breathe such divine enchanting ravishment?"

I should think not. Was it a wood-nymph then with her music box! Was there ever anything in that broken champagne bottle at the foot of the sphinx? And do wood-nymphs drink champagne? This grove is very questionable and full of marvels.[3]

On Melville and Arrowhead, pp. 198-199

A very few rods beyond the Wendell Farms, we come to Arrow-head, the fine estate formerly owned by Herman Melville. Mr. Melville is a grandson of that Major Thomas Melville, who, a few generations ago, was known to all Bostonians as the last genuine specimen of the gentleman of the old school left in the city, the last wearer of the costume of the Revolution, and the last survivor of the Harbor tea party. His son, of the same name and rank, was commandant of the military post at Pittsfield during the war of 1812, and, after the war, president of the Agricultural Society, and otherwise a leader of men in Berkshire, besides being a man of rare culture. With him, his nephew, Herman, was domiciliated for a time, while in his youth, he, played schoolmaster in a wild district—under the shadow of Rock Mountain, I think.[4]

⟦199⟧ It was probably the memory of this early experience which led Mr. Melville in 1850, in the first flush of his literary success, to retire to Pittsfield, and soon purchase a fine estate with a spacious old house; adjoining, in the rear, the farm of his early residence with his uncle. This quaint old mansion, he made the home of the most free-hearted hospitality; and also a house of many stories—writing in it Moby Dick and many other romances of the sea, and also "The Piazza Tales," which took their name from a piazza built by their author upon the north end of the house, and commanding a bold and striking view of Greylock and the intervening valley. "My chimney and I," a humorous and spicy essay, of which the cumbersome old chimney—overbearing tyrant of the home—is the hero, was also written here. And so, of course, was "October Mountain," a sketch of mingled philosophy and word-painting, which found its inspiration in the massy and brilliant tints presented by a prominent and thickly-wooded projection of Washington Mountain, as seen from the south-eastern windows at Arrow-Head, on a fine day after the early frosts. Mr. Melville was almost a zealot in his love of Berkshire scenery, and there was no more ardent and indefatigable excursionist among its hills and valleys.[5]

On Melville and Hawthorne, p. 318

One is not much surprised to learn that the creator of Hester Prynne, and Little Pearl, Zenobia and the Pynchons, did not find his highest pleasure in the chit-chat of fashionable circles, or even in literary coteries. Nor need it surprise us that a touch of melancholy, or even at times seeming moroseness, tinged his manner. The knowledge of the soul's anatomist is that which "by suffering entereth in."

But that Mr. Hawthorne's heart was warm and tender, I am well assured by more than one circumstance, which I do not know that I am at liberty to recall here. But there can be no wrong in mentioning the origin, as I have heard it, of the brotherly friendship which existed between him and Herman Melville. As the story was told to me, Mr. Hawthorne was aware that Melville was the author of a very appreciative review of the Scarlet Letter, which appeared in the Literary World, edited by their common friends, the Duyckincks; but this very knowledge, perhaps, kept two very sensitive men shy of each other, although thrown into company. But one day it chanced that when they were out on a pic-nic excursion, the two were compelled by a thunder-shower to take shelter in a narrow recess of the rocks of Monument Mountain. Two hours of this enforced intercourse settled the matter. They learned so much of each other's character, and found that they held so much of thought, feeling and opinion in common, that the most intimate friendship for the future was inevitable.[6]

Appendix D

A passage on Melville in J. E. A. Smith's *The Poet Among the Hills: Oliver Wendell Holmes in Berkshire* (Pittsfield: George Blatchford, 1895), pp. 27-33.[1]

But let us resume our purpose of citing a few examples of authors, besides Dr. Holmes, distinguished in the higher walks of literary com-⟦28⟧position and eloquent utterance, who have helped to invest Pittsfield with interest for the admirers of genius and the lovers of literature. Naturally the first which comes to mind is Dr. Holmes' nearest neighbor, of the guild of letters—Herman Melville. A gentle elevation on the west side of Holmes Road, a few rods south of its namesake's summer villa, is crowned by a spacious, old-fashioned gambrel-roofed mansion, rich in the memories of more than a century. Mr. Melville must have known it well in his youth, when he was in the family of his uncle, Major Thomas Melville, in the still more historic old mansion now known as Broadhall; and was master of a district school so located that his nearest way to it was through the farm attached to the gambrel-roofed house of Holmes Road. In 1848,* shortly after his marriage, and the brilliant success of his first books, "Omoo" and "Typee," he passed the summer in the same old broad-halled mansion,[2] which ⟦29⟧ was then a boarding-house, where, among other agreeable fellow-boarders, he found the poet Longfellow with his wife and children.[3] This summer at Broadhall reviving his acquaintance, with its neighbor, the old farm-house of Holmes Road, he bought it, and it was his well-loved home for many years. He named the place "Arrowhead;" having, in his first plowing of its fields, turned up one of "the pointed flints that left the fatal bow" of the Mohegan warrior or hunter. He found the mansion a spacious gambrel-roofed house of two stories; he made it a house of many stories; writing in it almost all his later works. Among these the most locally interesting, though far from the most widely known, is the "Piazza Tales;" so titled because its stories were built upon a piazza which he added to the north end of the house where it overlooks a noble landscape, extending through a picturesque vista of twenty miles, 〚30〛 to Greylock,—to Greylock, ever companionably present in Berkshire, whatever miles may intervene. A New England farm-house so venerable as that at Arrowhead could not fail of its huge old elephantine chimney; and Mr. Melville made it the hero of one of his most curious and characteristic sketches, "My Chimney and I." He regarded it as the overbearing tyrant of his home, as he, himself, very decidedly was not.

Mr. Melville was extravagantly fond of excursions among the Berkshire hills and valleys; a well-preserved relic of his early passion for far wider wanderings. His rambles were never solitary, and rarely with a single companion unless they involved more than one day's tramp on foot. He rather delighted to lead parties of kindred tastes; often including guests of note from abroad, and always some ladies of his own and intimately friendly families. In such fellowship he climbed to every alluring hill-top, and explored every picturesque corner and hidden nook that he could hear of, or find by seeking. Picnic revelers may be sure that whatever romantic camping-ground they choose in Berkshire, Herman Melville has been there before them, and that its echoes have rung with the laughter and the merry shouts of his rollicking followers. From many of these resorts he drew pictures for his tales; among others, from Bal-〚31〛ance Rock, Potter Mountain—a favorite with him—and the grand rounded summit—about two miles southwest from his residence and from that of Dr. Holmes—which he named October Mountain for the gorgeousness of its autumn tints.[4]

An incident of singular interest marked one of his excursions; and though it happened between Stockbridge and Great Barrington, it will bring us back to Holmes Road. We constantly need something to bring us back from the wanderings to which we are enticed by Berkshire's beauties.

In 1849, Nathaniel Hawthorne came to live awhile in the little red cottage, which he made famous, on the border of the Stockbridge Bowl[5]—the Sedgwick-Sigourney name for what the learned map-makers call Lake Mahekanituck—some seven miles south of Arrowhead. Melville had written for *The New York Literary World*, edited by his friends the brothers Duyckinck, a most appreciative and singularly sympathetic review of "The Scarlet Letter." This article was not only appreciative of, but appreciated by, Hawthorne. Yet when the two authors came to be neighbors, as neighborhood is reckoned in the country, there was at first a certain shyness in their intercourse; probably from the fear of each lest he should seem to the other to presume too much upon what he had 〚32〛 said and done. It was a sensitiveness natural to the pride of genius; but so shadowy and irksome a barrier could not long keep apart men so formed for fellowship. It was broken down during an excursion when the two were

driven by a sudden, severe, and prolonged summer shower to take refuge together in a narrow recess on the west side of Bryant's Monument Mountain.
There, undisturbed by the tumult of the elements, the two great original
thinkers and writers, neither of them "made altogether by the common pattern," learned to know each other; mind to mind and heart to heart. Thence-
forward their friendship was that of kindred though diverse intellects; and of
faith and feeling in which they were not diverse.[6]

The intercourse thus founded extended to the families of the two friends.
Hawthorne's biographer tells us that when Melville was approaching the cottage by the lake, a joyous shout went up: "Here comes Typee!" the pet name
they had given him. With Mr. Melville's free, hearty, and jovial, although
always high-bred and dignified, manner, this might have been expected; but
Mr. Hawthorne, also, could throw off his reserve for a roll and a frolic with
children; and he was as welcome at Arrowhead as Melville was at the lakeside.
It is not this chiefly, however, that brings us back to Holmes [[33]] Road. As
we learn from the same biographer, one who passed over it in 1849-50*—
might sometimes have enjoyed a rare spectacle. If it chanced to be in summer
or early autumn, the great barn-doors of the Arrowhead barn would have been
wide open, and if he cast a glance within he might have seen the two friends,
reclining on piles of fragrant new-mown hay, and basking in the genial inpouring rays of the sun, while they held high converse on the mysteries and
revelations of the world and those who people it.[7]

Appendix E

J. E. A. SMITH, "HERMAN MELVILLE":
The Newspaper Text and the 1897 Pamphlet

The following notes record (1) occasional corrections made in the present text of printing errors occurring in Smith's sketch of Melville as it was originally printed in 1891-1892 in the Pittsfield *Evening Journal* (here designated *EJ*); and (2) differences between the newspaper text and that of the pamphlet printed by direction of Mrs. Melville in 1897 (here designated *P*).

[i] Instalment of 27 October 1891

120.34 and new achievements   *P* and achievements   *120.35* withdraws *P* withdraw   *120.37* metropolis   *P* Metropolis   *120.40* known,   *P* known; *121.17* this gathering   *P* the gathering   *121.20* "The death   *P* The death *121.26* always has   *P* has always   *121.27* forgotten,   *P* forgotten   *121.35* had already   *P* had   *122.3* immigration   *P* immigration,   *122.10* Dec. *P* Dec   *122.21* town"   *P* town."   *122.25* Holmes'   *EJ* Holmes   *P* Holmes' *122.26-44* His . . . story.   *P* [*omitted*]   *122.26* Herman's   *EJ* Herman,s

[ii] Instalment of 29 October 1891

123.4 cities.   *P* cities   *123.5* Catherine   *P* Maria   *123.7* 2d   *P* second *123.7* regiment   *P* Regiment   *123.11* Schuyler].   *EJ* Schuyler]   *P* Schuyler]. *123.15* Oswego,   *P* Oswego   *123.16-17* and, as   *P* and as   *123.17* on his march   *P* on the march   *123.18* vaunting   *P* and vaunting   *123.24* aid in this by   *P* aid by   *123.26* Gen.   *P* General   *123.34* greater,   *P* greater *123.35* camp   *P* camp,   *123.36* there   *P* there,   *124.2* panic-flight   *P* panic flight   *124.3* rout   *EJ* route   *P* rout   *124.5* defence   *P* defense   *124.12* 1771   *EJ* 1871   *P* 1771   *124.12* brigadier-general   *P* brigadier general *124.20* Northumberland,   *P* Northumberland   *124.24* purposes;   *P* purposes,

124.31 city *P* city,   *125.16* familiar *P* who was familiar   *125.21* but,
P but   *125.26* marshal, *P* marshal   *125.33* show; *P* show,   *125.34*
Athenæum *EJ* Athenaeum *P* Athanæum   *126.3* gray headed *P* gray-
headed   *126.3* complexion; *P* complexion,   *126.18* observer *P* observer,
126.22 reverie *P* reverie,   *126.25-26* frost. * * * * * *P* frost. * * * * * *
126.28 hay-field *EJ* hay-/field *P* hay field   *126.31* result, *P* results,
126.34 "commonwealth" *EJ* "commonwealth *P* commonwealth   *126.40*
of, *P* of

[iii] Instalment of 21 November 1891

127.4 Doubtless *P* Doubtless,   *127.12* islands *P* Islands   *127.12* who,
P who   *127.25* chance-cast *P* chance cast   *127.26* and Mardi *P* [*deleted*
in ink in Mrs. Melville's copy]   *127.28* Melville *EJ* Mellville *P* Melville
127.34 missionaries themselves *P* missionaries   *127.41* befell, *P* befell
127.43 boy *P* boy,   *128.16* The *EJ* This *P* The   *128.16* home: *P*
home,   *128.17* friends, *P* friends   *128.19* suggestion *P* suggestion,
128.20 "Typee: *P* "Typee,   *128.22* World *P* World,   *128.23* brother,
Gansevoort, *EJ* brother, Gansevoort *P* brother Gansevoort,   *128.24* secretary of *P* secretary for   *128.26* house *EJ* oouse *P* house   *128.28*
Murray, *EJ* Murray *P* Murray,   *128.29* hesitation, *EJ* hesitation *P* hesi-
tation,   *128.30* "Omoo" *P* "Omoo,"   *128.32* Marquesas *EJ* Marquesan
P [*corrected in ink to* Marquesas *in Mrs. Melville's copy*]   *128.33* Bentley
EJ Bently *P* Bentley   *128.34* England *P* England,   *129.3* speaking
P speaking,   *129.5* ourself *EJ* our self *P* ourself   *129.12* South seas
P South Seas   *129.18* had long been *P* had been   *129.21* but, *P* but
129.25 1849 *P* 1850   *129.27* dead *P* dead,   *129.28* and his sisters.
Robert kept it as a boarding house; and it *P* and his brothers and sisters and
it   *129.31* 1849. *P* 1850.   *129.32-34* Perhaps . . . sisters. *P* [*omitted*]
129.35-36 in 1849, *P* in that year

[iv] Instalment of 16 December 1891,
omitted in the 1897 pamphlet

131.27-28 conversation"–"cram *EJ* conversation–"cram"   *131.31*
¶ Nathaniel *EJ* Nathaniel   *131.42* country-men *EJ* country–men
132.8 Twice-told *EJ* Twice told

[v] Instalment of 19 December 1891

132.25 jealousy between the *P* jealousy in the   *132.31* forward *EJ*
awkward *P* forward   *132.35* in that *P* that   *133.14* letter writer *P*
letter-writer   *133.15* time *P* time in the barn   *133.17* many such

P many   *133.17* communion   *P* communication   *133.18* powers, *P*
powers   *133.20* influences, *EJ* influences *P* influences,   *133.23* Melville, *EJ* Melville *P* Melville,   *133.24* wide apart *P* far apart   *133.27*
common sense *P* commonsense   *133.30* Omoo, Typee and *P* Typee,
Omoo, and   *133.35* vagary *P* vagary,   *133.38* intervening *EJ* inter-
viewing *P* intervening   *133.39* "My Chimney and I," *P* "I and My Chimney,"
133.40 chimney— *P* chimney,   *133.42* word-painted *P* word painted
134.9 folk-lore *P* folk lore   *134.12* all his *P* all of his   *134.13* Ahab"
P Ahab,"   *134.18* story *P* story,   *134.33* matter *P* a matter   *134.35*
platform, *P* platform   *134.36* directly, *P* directly   *134.37* New York,
P Boston, New York   *134.38* San Francisco *P* San-Francisco   *134.41-*
135.2 In . . . other. *P* [*omitted*]   *135.3* removal. *P* removal from Pittsfield.
135.4 and, *P* and   *135.11* 1872 *EJ* 18 *P* 1872   *135.13* upon it *P*
upon it,   *135.14* Herman, *P* Melville,   *135.14* November; *P* November,
135.15 old fashioned *P* old-fashioned   *135.21* metropolitan *P* Metroplitan
135.22 class, *EJ* class *P* class

[vi] Instalment of 24 December 1891

135.25-136.13 friends. ¶ Mr. Stedman . . . Mr. Melville, and we *P* friends,
and we [*omitting* Mr. Stedman . . . Mr. Melville,]   *136.7* 1864, the *EJ*
1864. The   *136.22* an elbow *P* a hollow   *136.27* excursions, *P* excursions   *136.28-29* and his, *P* and his   *136.30* fond; *P* fond,   *136.34-36*
months. Two . . . purchase of *P* months. On his removal to New York he
purchased   *136.38* its occupants *P* the occupants   *136.39* story telling
P story-telling   *136.40* 104 East 26th street *P* it   *136.41* people like
P such people as   *136.42* The other *P* One   *137.2* traveling *P* travelling
137.10-11 the permanence . . . withdrawal *P* his partial withdrawal   *137.16*
opportunities *EJ* oportunities *P* opportunities   *137.19* back ground *P*
background   *137.26* past, *P* past   *137.27* also his *P* his   *137.28* books
P his books   *137.28* readers *P* sympathetic readers   *137.29* with snarling
censure *P* rather with censure   *137.32* us after 1864. *P* us.

[vii] Instalment of 12 January 1892

137.39-40 mourning,—sincere . . . symbols. *P* mourning.   *138.1* technically
called *P* called   *138.7* limited *P* limited,   *138.13-14* Parisian bred *P*
Parisian-bred   *138.14* democratic *EJ* Democratic *P* democratic   *138.14*
short *P* short,   *138.18* ever coveted *P* coveted   *138.29* But *P* But,
138.41 sea novelist *P* sea-novelist   *138.42-139.1* his work in the same *P* his
same   *139.6* of course was *P* was   *139.9* "Why, he's *P* "Why he's
139.11 books, *P* books   *139.12-13* probably have been *EJ* probably been
P probably have been   *139.16* Inn— *P* Inn,   *139.19-20* which elapsed

between 1864 and 1885. *P* which had elapsed.   *139.20* society, *P* society
139.29 noblesse oblige *P noblesse oblige*   *139.31* proudly *P* grandly
139.38 old jovial *P* jovial   *139.38* let-the-world-go-as-it-will   *P* let-the-
world-go as-it-will   *140.1-2* dyspeptic patients *P* patients   *140.3-9*
Pittsfield . . . miracle. *P* [*omitted*]   *140.10* is concerned *P* was concerned
140.16 were *P* they were   *140.19* find, *P* find

[viii] Instalment of 16 January 1892

   140.23 explained *P* explained,   *140.24* more than two *P* several
140.27 Pieces" *P* Pieces,"   *140.32* most *P* some   *140.33* power; *P*
power,   *140.36* "The *P* the "The   *141.3* more. *EJ* more, *P* more.
141.44 Gen. *P* General   *141.16* JOURNAL *P* Journal   *141.24* remnant
P remnant,   *141.27* more,– *P* more–   *141.29* shore. *EJ* shore, *P*
shore.   *141.30* pale,– *P* pale–   *141.40* maimed *EJ* mained *P* maimed
141.41 the fever *P* fever   *142.4* crater, *P* crater   *142.7* without harsh
P with scant   *142.9* some other *P* some   *142.10* critics *EJ* cities *P*
critics   *142.10* public *EJ* pubilc *P* public   *142.16* looked up *EJ* looked,
up *P* looked up   *142.18* critic, *EJ* critic *P* critic,   *142.22* all, *P* all
142.28 sarcastical *P* sarcastic   *142.29* but, *P* but   *142.36* gifts. *EJ*
gifts." *P* gifts.   *143.1* than *EJ* then *P* than   *143.7-144.16* ¶ There . . .
faction. *P* [*omitted*]   *143.10* as those *EJ* of those   *144.31* surveys;
EJ surveys;" *P* surveys,   *144.36* In *P* "In   *145.6* no. *P* no."

[ix] Instalment of 25 January 1892

   145.8 than *EJ* that *P* than   *145.14* Pierre *EJ* "Pierre *P* "Pierre
145.15-16 mass of rock, huge as a barn, *P* huge mass of rock,   *145.18* It
P "It   *145.24* terraqueous *EJ* teraqueous *P* terraqueous   *145.31* It
P "It   *145.32* tell, *P* tell   *145.42* this, *P* this   *146.4* truth, *P* truth
146.8 cross road *P* cross-road   *146.9* * * * * * *P* * * * * * * *   *146.10*
Not *P* "Not   *146.12* had called *P* called   *146.17* It *P* "It   *146.23*
topple. *EJ* topple." *P* topple."   *146.25* poetic *P* poet   *146.27-37* The
portion . . . ambiguous." *P* [*omitted*]   *146.38* The book *P* ¶ The book
146.39 it, *P* it   *146.39* portraits,– *P* portraits–   *147.4* wondrous *EJ*
wonderous *P* wondrous   *147.10* Rock," *EJ* Rock; *P* Rock,"   *147.16*
day, *P* day   *147.18* rock, *P* rock   *147.22-23* remembered, *P* remembered   *147.25* voila *P voila*   *147.33* nearly 10 *P* some   *147.40-41*
second best *P* second-best   *147.41* cavalry *EJ* calvary *P* cavalry
147.41 Browning's *P* "Browning's   *148.3* Other *EJ* other *P* Other
148.5 Nesle." *P* Nesle,"   *148.6* (1876) *EJ* (18 6) *P* (1886),   *148.7*
cyclopaedia *P* cyclopedia   *148.9* Sunday night, Sept. 27 *P* Monday, Sept.
28   *148.10* painful illness of several years, *P* painful illness,   *148.11* also a

P a   *148.13* Mrs. Melville   *P* Mrs. Melville,   *148.14* Miss Melville,   *P* Miss Melville   *148.14* him   *P* him,   *148.16* letters,   *EJ* letters   *P* letters,   *148.22-23* His . . . York.   *P* [*omitted*]   *148.27-28* octavo pages   *P* pages   *148.30* Gansevoort's   *EJ* Gansevoort,   *P* Gansevoort's   *148.35-40* "I sit . . . is good."   *EJ* [*extract:*] "I sit down and watch the roll of the waves,—/As rolled Brazilian billows go/Voluminously o er the line./ ¶ [*text:*] This is Herman Melville's description of the wavy folds of the star spangled banner. It is good."   *P* [*extract:*] "I sit and watch the roll of the waves,—/As rolled Brazilian billows go/Voluminously o'er the line."/ ¶ [*text:*] This is Herman Melville's description . . . banner. It is good.   *148.42* some   *P* we

"Herman Melville and Pittsfield"

149.14 Herman . . . Pittsfield   *EJ* HERMAN MELVILLE AND PITTSFIELD. *P* EDITORIAL IN EVENING JOURNAL./HERMAN MELVILLE AND PITTS-FIELD.   *149.16* word wide   *P* world-wide   *149.20* intensely   *EJ* intensly   *P* intensely   *149.30* associations   *P* association   *149.33* genius   *P* genius,

Notes

As explained in the Preface, references throughout this book to *The Letters of Herman Melville*, *The Melville Log*, and individual volumes of Melville's works published in the Northwestern-Newberry Edition are by short title only: *Letters*, *Log*, and for example, *Typee* (1968). In the notes which follow, references to these frequently cited items are also in abbreviated form:

Allibone, S. Austin. *A Critical Dictionary of English Literature and British and American Authors. . . .* 3 vols. Philadelphia: J. B. Lippincott & Co., 1854–1871.

Duyckinck, Evert A. and George L. *Cyclopædia of American Literature. . . .* 2 vols. New York: Charles Scribner, 1855.

Family Correspondence of Herman Melville 1830–1904 in the Gansevoort-Lansing Collection. Edited by Victor Hugo Paltsits. New York: The New York Public Library, 1929.

Hawthorne, Julian. *Nathaniel Hawthorne and His Wife: A Biography.* 2 vols. Boston: James R. Osgood and Company, 1884.

Melville, Herman. *Collected Poems.* Edited by Howard P. Vincent. Chicago: Packard and Company (Hendricks House), 1947.

The Men of the Time or Sketches of Living Notables. New York: Redfield, 1852.

Metcalf, Eleanor Melville. *Herman Melville: Cycle and Epicycle.* Cambridge: Harvard University Press, 1953.

National Cyclopædia of American Biography. 47 vols. New York: James T. White & Company, 1892–1965.

Sealts, Merton M., Jr. *Melville's Reading: A Check-List of Books Owned and Borrowed.* Madison: University of Wisconsin Press, 1966.

Smith, Joseph Edward Adams. *The History of Pittsfield, (Berkshire County,) Massachusetts, from the Year 1800 to the Year 1876.* Springfield, Mass.: C. W. Bryan & Co., 1876.

———. *The Poet Among the Hills: Oliver Wendell Holmes in Berkshire.* Pittsfield, Mass.: George Blatchford, 1895.

———. *Taghconic; or Letters and Legends about our Summer Home.* By Godfrey Greylock. Boston: Redding and Company, 1852.

———. *Taghconic, the Romance and Beauty of the Hills.* By Godfrey Greylock.

Boston: Lee and Shepard; New York: Charles T. Dillingham; Pittsfield: S. E. Nichols, 1879.

Stedman, Edmund Clarence, and Ellen Mackay Hutchinson, editors. *A Library of American Literature.* 11 vols. New York: Charles L. Webster & Co., 1888-1890.

Tanselle, G. Thomas. "The Sales of Melville's Books." *Harvard Library Bulletin,* 17 (April 1969), 195-215.

Weaver, Raymond M. *Herman Melville: Mariner and Mystic.* New York: George H. Doran Company, 1921.

A MAN OF THE TIME

1. Perry Miller, *The Raven and the Whale: The War of Words and Wits in the Era of Poe and Melville* (New York: Harcourt, Brace and Company, 1956), pp. 306, 307; see also Heyward Ehrlich, " 'Diving and Ducking Moralities' . . . ," *Bulletin of the New York Public Library,* 70 (1966), 552-553.

2. Here, Miller remarks, "Evert Duyckinck picks up one corner of his judiciousness just enough to reveal a New Yorker's rancor" (*The Raven and the Whale,* p. 328).

3. William H. Gilman, *Melville's Early Life and "Redburn"* (New York: New York University Press, 1951), p. 178. In "Melville's Liverpool Trip," *Modern Language Notes,* 61 (December 1946), 543-547, Gilman first announced that 1839 rather than 1837 is the correct date of the voyage.

4. *Melville's Early Life and "Redburn,"* p. 347, note 5. Gilman goes on to suggest that the mistake "may have originated in the office of Richard Bentley," the London publisher of *Redburn,* "whose announcement *Works Published in 1849* stated that 'Melville sailed in 1837 as ship's boy from New York to Liverpool and back.' All subsequent accounts down to 1946 repeat the error. . . ." Although Melville's own handling of dates, like his spelling, was sometimes erratic, he correctly observed in his journal of 1849 that he was returning to England "after the lapse of ten years" (*Log,* I, 325). In *Omoo* (1847) he had recalled meeting in the South Seas—presumably in 1842—"a young man, whom, four years previous [*sic*], I had frequently met in a sailor boarding-house in Liverpool" (p. 6).

5. *Melville's Early Life and "Redburn,"* p. 193. Though the Duyckincks' *Cyclopaedia,* II, 672-673, has been cited as confirmation that Melville himself journeyed to London in 1839, Gilman points out here that the *Cyclopaedia's* reference to such a visit "was evidently borrowed from *The Men of the Time,*" which "may have taken it from *Redburn.*" Although Gilman was aware of the dependence of the *Cyclopaedia* upon *The Men of the Time,* he mistakenly cited the first London, 1852 edition of that work as well as Redfield's first New York edition of the same year (Gilman, p. 350, note 54); the first London edition to include an account of Melville was actually the revision of 1853.

6. See *Chambers's Encyclopaedia,* 10 vols. (London: W. & R. Chambers, 1868), VI, 397: in 1860 Melville "left his farm in Massachusetts and embarked

in a whaling vessel on a voyage round the world." One American edition of *Chambers's* (Philadelphia: Lippincott, 1875 and 1891) mentions no such voyage; another (New York: Collier, 1886) reads somewhat differently: "In 1860, he embarked in a whaling-vessel for a new tour round the world" (V, 321).

7. There is no indication in the *Cyclopaedia* itself of the authorship of individual articles. I have had no success in attempting to locate relevant information in surviving papers of either the Appleton firm, of Wilson, Stedman, or Stoddard, or of Melville himself. Wilson's file of newspaper clippings, now in the New York Public Library, includes no items indexed under Melville's name; his collection of signed photographs, willed to either the Metropolitan Museum of Art or the New York Genealogical and Biographical Society, was declined by both and subsequently dispersed. In my judgment the *Cyclopaedia* article with its exclusive emphasis on *Typee* was not written by Stoddard, who took a special interest in Melville's poetry and who wrote in 1888 that *Moby-Dick* "is probably his greatest work"; see my "Melville and Richard Henry Stoddard," *American Literature*, 43 (November 1971), 359-370. Another possible author of the sketch might be Melville's friend Titus Munson Coan, who in 1891 collaborated with Wilson in editing *Personal Recollections of the War of the Rebellion*, although his published comments on Melville, like Stoddard's, are also in a different vein.

8. Letter from E. C. Stedman to Charles Henry Webb, 10 November 1900, in Laura Stedman and George M. Gould, *Life and Letters of Edmund Clarence Stedman*, 2 vols. (New York, 1910), II, 274.

9. From an undated clipping mounted in a scrapbook kept by Mrs. Ellen Brittain of Pittsfield, now in the Berkshire Athenaeum. Alexander Young, whose interest in Melville has not been previously recognized, was a graduate in 1862 of the Harvard Law School, a practicing lawyer, and later associate editor of the Boston *Globe*. He wrote *A Concise History of the Netherlands* (Boston, 1884), became the regular Boston correspondent of the New York *Critic*, and also contributed to other New York publications: the *Independent*, *Christian Union*, *Century*, *Golden Age*, and *Harper's Weekly*; his column "Here in Boston" appeared regularly in the Boston *Post* before his death. See the obituary article in the Boston *Evening Transcript*, 19 March 1891, p. 2. The *Post* continued "Here in Boston" as written by another hand until October of 1891, when the column was dropped on the ground that its preoccupation with the past was out of keeping with new objectives of the paper.

10. Concerning the glass ship, see William H. Gilman, *Melville's Early Life and "Redburn,"* pp. 38-39, 177, 221, 226. On the vial of tea and its subsequent history, see Elizabeth Shaw Melville's memoranda, p. 172 above and note 25 on p. 247 below.

11. "Herman Melville," New York *Times*, 2 October 1891, p. 4: ". . . when a visiting British writer a few years ago inquired at a gathering in New-York of distinctly literary Americans what had become of HERMAN MELVILLE, not only was there not one among them who was able to tell him, but there was

scarcely one among them who had ever heard of the man concerning whom he inquired, albeit that man was then living within a half mile of the place of the conversation."

12. Boston *Post,* 19 November 1890, p. 4; for other passages of the article, see *Log,* II, 827.

13. In *Literary Shrines: The Haunts of Some Famous American Authors* (Philadelphia: J. B. Lippincott Company, 1897), pp. 190-192, Wolfe described Melville's "Arrow-Head" at Pittsfield and a visit there by Hawthorne and his daughter Una: "This visit . . . was the topic when, not so long agone, we last looked upon the living face of Melville in his city home." In a letter to the *New York Times Saturday Review,* 20 July 1901, p. 523, Wolfe mentioned a call on Melville's widow and her daughter at their apartment in New York, saying that "she was able to give me much valuable information concerning the authors contemporary with her gifted husband." (A clipping of this item is in the Melville Collection of the Harvard College Library.) Wolfe was then collecting material for his *Literary Haunts and Homes: American Authors* (Philadelphia: J. B. Lippincott Company, 1903), which mentions her "delightful apartments" (p. 76).

14. Hugh W. Hetherington has surveyed this material in two publications: "A Tribute to the Late Hiram Melville," *Modern Language Quarterly,* 16 (December 1955), 325-331, which takes its title from the caption given Hillard's letter to the New York *Times* of 6 October 1891; and more briefly in *Melville's Reviewers British and American 1846-1891* (Chapel Hill: University of North Carolina Press, 1961), pp. 284-291, where he is also concerned with Melville's general situation in New York during his last years. Hetherington emphasizes the persistent identification of Melville as "the author of *Typee*" and the "man who lived among the cannibals." The figures given above follow the tabulation in Hetherington's article, p. 325.

THE BIOGRAPHERS OF THE NINETIES

1. The account of Smith's career quoted here and below is incorporated in the obituary notice carried by the *Eagle* of 29 October 1896, the day of his death, from an earlier article "published in the Springfield Graphic in 1894"; I have silently corrected a few minor typographical omissions and errors. This and other articles which the Pittsfield and Springfield papers carried at the time of his death—also quoted below—are mounted in a scrapbook concerning Smith which was given to the Berkshire Athenaeum by his cousin Sarah Jane Smith Dresser in 1953. The scrapbook also includes the photograph of Smith as a young man reproduced in Plate II of the present volume.

2. In note 14 below, at the close of this section, is a listing by page of all quotations from Smith's own biographical sketch of Melville (1891-1892) that occur in the ensuing discussion. The quotations are listed in the order of their occurrence here and identified by terminal words; each item is followed by a page reference to the text of the sketch as printed on pp. 120-149 of this volume.

3. Luther Stearns Mansfield, "Glimpses of Herman Melville's Life in Pittsfield, 1850-1851: Some Unpublished Letters of Evert A. Duyckinck," *American Literature*, 9 (March 1937), 41.

4. Edward Boltman, *The History of Pittsfield, Mass.* (Pittsfield, 1916), p. 315, remarks of Smith that "from about the year 1850 until his death the columns of Pittsfield's newspapers were enriched by his labor and during most of that time he was constrained to derive a livelihood from newspaper employment."

5. Several items concerning Melville and "The Encantadas," then running in *Putnam's Monthly Magazine*, appeared on 24 February, 10 March, 7 April, and 4 May 1854 (*Log*, I, 484-487). In July and August of 1854 the *Eagle* also noticed *Israel Potter*, already said to be Melville's, and reprinted an item on capture of a whale reminiscent of Moby Dick (*Log*, I, 490-491).

6. Further information concerning Melville's projected removal to New York in 1857 has recently come to light. Patricia Barber, "Herman Melville's House in Brooklyn," *American Literature*, 45 (November 1973), 433-434, notes that on 3 July 1857 Allan Melville signed an agreement for his brother to purchase, for $4250, a house on St. Felix Street in Brooklyn. But after a visit from George Griggs of Boston, brother-in-law of the Melvilles, Allan Melville wrote to Lemuel Shaw on 11 August that "there might be reasons why Herman had better get released from the contract," and on that same day he persuaded the owner of the house to sign a release.

7. Boltman, *The History of Pittsfield*, p. 317.

8. *Collected Poems*, p. 164.

9. Letter to Catherine Gansevoort Lansing, 5 September 1897, in *Family Correspondence of Herman Melville*, p. 67.

10. Letter to Arthur Stedman, 23 August 1892 (Stedman Collection, Columbia University Libraries); on 17 August she had asked Stedman to return the "Pittsfield articles."

11. Letter to Arthur Stedman, 8 October 1892 (Stedman Collection, Columbia University Libraries).

12. *Family Correspondence of Herman Melville*, p. 67.

13. *Herman Melville: Representative Selections*, ed. Willard Thorp (New York: American Book Company, 1938), p. cxxxix.

14. Boltman, *The History of Pittsfield*, p. 317. Quotations in the foregoing discussion from Smith's biographical sketch of Melville are listed herewith by page in the order of their occurrence, with each passage identified by terminal words and followed by a page reference to the text of the sketch as printed on pp. 120-149 above. *31:* "very . . . them", p. 122. *32:* "the . . . naturalness", p. 133; "excessive . . . misfortune", p. 133; "philosophical seances", p. 133; "disastrous effect", p. 133; "to . . . lose", p. 144; "simply . . . world", p. 146. *33:* "touch . . . Berkshire", p. 134; "the . . . joy", p. 131; "often . . . experience", p. 146; "looked . . . pseudonym", p. 142. *34:* "sensitive . . . censure", p. 142; "in . . . towns", p. 134. *35:* "had . . . life", p. 136; "forsaking . . . work", p. 135; "intimation", p. 137; "moderate . . . Melville", p. 136. *36:* "written . . . changed", p. 138; "modelled . . . aristocrat", p. 138. *37:* "he

... quiet", p. 139; "his ... spirit", p. 139; "seclusion ... mourning", p. 137; "after ... gratitude", p. 148. *38:* "occupied ... biography", p. 149. *41:* "Falsehood ... hypocrite", p. 127; "eminently ... fields", p. 137; "irrelevant ... mysticism", p. 140.

15. Mentor L. Williams, "Two Hawaiian-Americans Visit Herman Melville," *New England Quarterly,* 23 (March 1950), 98.

16. Raymond M. Weaver, *Herman Melville,* p. 128.

17. *National Cyclopaedia of American Biography,* XI, 273.

18. Letter from Coan to Stedman, 8 June 1889 (copy); letter from Stedman to Coan, 18 July 1891, accompanied by a personal note. This correspondence is included in the Coan papers in the New-York Historical Society, which are also the source of other information in the present discussion. Among Coan's many correspondents, David Dudley Field, Julian Hawthorne, John La Farge, George Parsons Lathrop, and Arthur Stedman were also associated in some way with Melville.

19. Mrs. Thomas's notation on a letter from her daughter, Eleanor Melville Metcalf, 28 September [August?] 1919 (Melville Collection, Harvard College Library); Mrs. Metcalf, in Raymond Weaver's behalf, had submitted a number of questions about Melville to her mother.

20. See Titus Coan, *Life in Hawaii, an Autobiographical Sketch of Mission Life and Labors (1835-1881)* (New York, 1882), pp. 199-200; an extract is given in Leyda's *Log,* II, 781-782. The Library of Congress recently acquired the papers of the senior Coan.

21. Melville's personal physician in his last illness was Everett S. Warner, M.D., whose attendance began in July of 1891 (*Log,* II, 836). Coan was still in active practice as late as the summer of 1887, when he served at Albert Leffingwell's Dansville, N.Y., Sanatorium.

22. I have not located Coan's copies of *John Marr* and *Timoleon.* A print of the 1885 Rockwood photograph of Melville (see Plate IV) is among Coan's papers at the New-York Historical Society.

23. There is some correspondence in phrasing between Coan's article and Mrs. Melville's memoranda of her husband's career, which she may have drawn up in part for use of Stedman and Coan. See p. 70 above and note 62 on pp. 251-252 below.

24. Arthur Stedman, letter to Coan, 16 October 1892 (New-York Historical Society); elsewhere in the letter Stedman remarks that Greene " 'bore to the grave' the mark left by the Happar weapon in his attempted escape from the Typee valley." Mrs. Melville's note to Stedman of 8 October 1892 is in the Stedman Collection, Columbia University Libraries.

25. Weaver, *Herman Melville,* p. 350.

26. Quotations in the foregoing discussion from Coan's "Herman Melville" are listed herewith by page in the order of their occurrence, with each passage identified by terminal words and followed by a page reference to the text of the article as printed on pp. 116-119 above. *44:* "repeatedly ... him", p. 119; "stores ... philosophy", p. 119; "My ... themselves", p. 119; "some ... beauty", pp. 118-119; "masterpiece ... book", p. 118; "how ... spring",

p. 116; "*Typee* . . . main", p. 118; "less powerful . . . opposition", p. 119; "were . . . written", p. 118; "germ . . . imagery", p. 118. *45:* "in . . . only", p. 118; "now . . . given", p. 118; "autobiographical books", p. 119; "the 'Toby' . . . Greene", p. 119.

27. Information concerning Stedman's career comes from an obituary record kindly supplied by the Alumni Records Office, Yale University, and from his publications and surviving correspondence.

28. Raymond Weaver, *Herman Melville*, pp. 128-129.

29. This heretofore unpublished manuscript, drafted on letterhead of The Inn at Buck Hill Falls, Pennsylvania, is among Mrs. Gould's papers in the Stedman Collection of the Columbia University Libraries. It must have been written in 1926 or later, since there is an internal reference on p. 6 to John Freeman, *Herman Melville* (New York: The Macmillan Company, 1926), p. 185, which in Mrs. Gould's paraphrase "mentions that only a few but loving hands (Arthur's among them) paid written tribute to Melville at his death." Additional notes and clippings among her papers appear to suggest that she planned but never completed an essay on Melville himself. In the extracts from manuscript materials printed below, angle brackets (⟨ . . . ⟩) denote cancellations; paired arrows (↑ . . . ↓) denote insertions; slash marks (/ . . . / . . . /) separate two or more alternative words where Mrs. Gould did not indicate a final choice among them.

30. The paragraph is typed on a single loose sheet following a quotation from E. C. Stedman's correspondence: his remark about Melville's genius and personality that Mrs. Gould mentions at the beginning of her draft essay "Concerning Herman Melville and the Stedmans." This sheet is also among her papers in the Stedman Collection.

31. Eleanor Melville Metcalf, *Herman Melville*, p. 287.

32. This and other letters to Salt which are now in the Melville Collection of the Newberry Library were given by Salt to Willard Thorp in 1935; Salt's letters to Professor Thorp are also at the Newberry.

33. For a consideration of Stedman's textual editing, see the Northwestern-Newberry *Typee* (1968), pp. 312-314.

34. In the proof (Melville Collection, Harvard College Library), the date of Melville's death is given as "Sept. 2, 1891" rather than "28"; Mrs. Melville's letter of 18 March 1892 to Stedman (Stedman Collection, Columbia University Libraries) blames "a typographical oversight probably."

35. Arthur Stedman to Henry S. Salt, 4 May 1892 (Melville Collection, Newberry Library); like most of Stedman's business letters of 1892, it is written on letterhead of Charles L. Webster & Co.

36. Mrs. Melville to Arthur Stedman, 17 August 1892 (Stedman Collection, Columbia University Libraries).

37. United States Book Company to G. P. Putnam's Sons (of London), 22 September 1892 (Yale Collection of American Literature, Beinecke Rare Book and Manuscript Library, Yale University); Mrs. Melville to Arthur Stedman, 12 December 1892 (Stedman Collection, Columbia University Libraries).

38. Mrs. Melville to Arthur Stedman, 2 November 1892 (Stedman Collection, Columbia University Libraries).

39. Arthur Stedman to United States Book Company, 24 October 1892 (Yale Collection of American Literature, Beinecke Rare Book and Manuscript Library, Yale University). After writing this letter, Stedman evidently requested a further look at Melville's publishing correspondence: a letter from Mrs. Melville on 2 November tells him that "The Bentl[e]y letters are at hand for you at your own convenience. I shall be glad to collect my scattered papers together once more—as soon as I have little more leisure I shall set them out in better regular order" (Stedman Collection, Columbia University Libraries). Stedman's perusal of these materials is reflected in his subsequent articles.

40. Arthur Stedman to United States Book Company, 24 October 1892, and to "Mr. Putnam" of G. P. Putnam's Sons (London), 21 December 1892 (Yale Collection of American Literature, Beinecke Rare Book and Manuscript Library, Yale University).

41. Mrs. Melville's copy of the contract is now in the Melville Collection of the Harvard College Library. The contract, which makes no reference to Arthur Stedman or his editorial work, provides for payment to Mrs. Melville of "5 per cent. royalty on the retail price for the first 2,000 copies sold and paid for of each book and 10 per cent. royalty on the retail price for all copies of each book sold and paid for after the first 2,000, no royalty to be paid on books given away for editorial or advertising purposes." An account was to be rendered and royalty paid to her every six months.

42. Mrs. Melville to Arthur Stedman, 27 January 1893 (Stedman Collection, Columbia University Libraries). Her "Memoranda for re-issue of 'Typee' (made by Mr Melville)" had originally called for omitting the dedication, although this directive was later altered; see *Typee* (1968), p. 312. Mrs. Melville's copies of *Typee* (1892) with the desired corrections indicated are in the Melville Collection of the Harvard College Library; see pp. 154-155 above.

43. Memorandum signed by A. D. Hurd, 31 January 1893 (Melville Collection, Harvard College Library); Arthur Stedman to Mrs. Melville, 31 January 1893 (Melville Collection, Harvard College Library); see the lead article in the New York *World* of that date, pp. 1-2, captioned "LIKE HUMPTY DUMPTY The Big Novel-Cornering Trust Finds It Hard to Rise Again. . . ."

44. Mrs. Melville to Arthur Stedman, 1 February 1893 (Stedman Collection, Columbia University Libraries).

45. *Typee* (1968), p. 314.

46. Justin Kaplan, *Mr. Clemens and Mark Twain: A Biography* (New York: Simon & Schuster, 1966), p. 317.

47. Mrs. Melville to Arthur Stedman, 30 January, 7 June 1894 (Stedman Collection, Columbia University Libraries).

48. W. B. Hadley, for the receiver of the United States Book Company, to Mrs. Melville, 23 January 1896 (Melville Collection, Harvard College Library); Mrs. Melville to Catherine Gansevoort Lansing, 14 April 1897, in *Family Correspondence of Herman Melville*, p. 66. The books carried the imprint of the American Publishers Corporation. For a succinct report of various printings

from the 1892 plates during Mrs. Melville's lifetime, drawn from the publishers' accounts rendered to her, see G. Thomas Tanselle, "The Sales of Melville's Books," pp. 202-203. As Tanselle notes, 270 copies of each of the four titles were sold in sheets to G. P. Putnam's Sons in 1892 for issue in England, where in the fall of 1893 John Murray also brought out new impressions of his *Typee* and *Omoo*.

49. Mrs. Melville to Arthur Stedman, 30 November [1898? 1890?] (Stedman Collection, Columbia University Libraries).

50. Stedman to Henry S. Salt, 28 February 1906 (Melville Collection, Newberry Library); a postscript gives the inclusive dates of his stay in London.

51. Eleanor Melville Metcalf, *Herman Melville*, pp. 291-292, prints the full text of E. C. Stedman's letter and the copy of Mather's he had enclosed.

52. Elizabeth Melville's undated acknowledgment to Salt is in the Melville Collection of the Newberry Library; for Billson's response, in a letter to her of 20 November 1906, see Mrs. Metcalf, *Herman Melville*, p. 292.

53. On 10 December 1906; the letter (now in the Melville Collection, Harvard College Library), sent from the New York office of the firm, reads as follows: "We understand from literary announcements in the 'Athenaeum' and elsewhere, that you have in preparation a Memoir of the late Hermann Melville. We shall be interested in having an opportunity of considering this book for publication through our New York and London Houses, or in case arrangements may already have been made for the American edition, for publication in London alone." The notice in the *Athenæum* (London), No. 4126 (24 November 1906), 658, reads: "THE family of the late Herman Melville, author of 'Typee,' 'The Whale,' &c., are collecting materials for a memoir, and would be grateful if any persons having letters by him would send them to Miss Elizabeth Melville, 'The Florence,' Fourth Avenue and Eighteenth Street, New York. Such letters will be promptly copied and returned."

54. Frank Jewett Mather, Jr., review of Lewis Mumford, *Herman Melville*, *Saturday Review of Literature*, 5 (27 April 1929), 945; letter, Ferris Greenslet to Mather, 20 November 1906, in George Monteiro, "Mather's Melville Book," *Studies in Bibliography: Papers of the Bibliographical Society of the University of Virginia*, 25 (1972), 226-227. Mather's account does not mention other points covered in Greenslet's letter: (1) that if an English publisher should undertake Mather's proposed book, Houghton Mifflin would be interested in importing "a moderate edition of the work in sheets for sale in this country"; (2) that the *Atlantic Monthly* "might be able to use . . . one good critical and appreciative paper on Melville, or possibly two papers based upon fresh manuscript material"; and (3) that the firm's Department of Limited Editions would consider an anthology of Melville's unpublished poetry, though Greenslet was doubtful that the verse of "a not very popular author" would prove successful. Apparently Mather pursued none of these possibilities.

55. *Typee* (1968), p. 314.

56. Eleanor Melville Metcalf, *Herman Melville*, pp. 288-299.

57. Raymond Weaver, Introduction to Herman Melville, *Journal up the Straits: October 11, 1856-May 5, 1857* (New York: The Colophon, 1935), p. xv.

58. Raymond Weaver, *Herman Melville,* p. 113: "in the Commonplace Book of his wife" that period of Melville's life "between Liverpool and the South Seas is dismissed in a single sentence. . . . Arthur Stedman (who got his facts largely from Mrs. Melville), in his 'Biographical and Critical Introduction' to *Typee,* slightly enlarges upon" what she had written there about Melville's schoolteaching.

59. See Mrs. Melville's memoranda, p. 177 above; a similar passage in Coan's "Herman Melville," p. 116 above; and the notes accompanying each.

60. Weaver, Introduction to Melville's *Journal up the Straits,* pp. xiv, xvi.

61. Although a discussion of Mrs. Melville's memoranda is a necessary part of this study, I have no wish to speculate further about the larger issues of the family relationship. Amy Elizabeth Puett's recent doctoral dissertation, "Melville's Wife: A Study of Elizabeth Shaw Melville" (Northwestern University, 1969), "achieves a new perspective on the Melville marriage by examining it primarily from Elizabeth Melville's point of view"; I look forward to the publication of her findings.

62. Frank Jewett Mather, Jr., "Herman Melville," *Saturday Review of Literature,* 5 (27 April 1929), 945. Concerning Professor MacMechan, see p. 27 above.

63. G. Thomas Tanselle, "The Sales of Melville's Books," p. 202.

64. The manuscript of the "Memoranda" is now in the Stedman Collection of the Columbia University Libraries; for the text, see *Typee* (1968), p. 312. The Northwestern-Newberry editors write as though the memoranda had been prepared for Stedman's particular use; I take it that Mrs. Melville was transcribing Melville's earlier notes or her own, made when the Camelot *Typee* was under discussion.

65. Both the file and Mrs. Melville's list are now in the Melville Collection of the Harvard College Library.

66. What the narrator says is of course not "my family" but "my wife"; Mrs. Melville, obviously reading the story autobiographically and taking its narrator to be Melville, nevertheless refused to identify herself with the nagging "wife." On her copy of the story (the magazine text, not the "manuscript," as Weaver mistakenly said), she wrote defensively in the margin that "All this about his wife, applied to his mother—who was very vigorous and energetic about the farm, etc."; see *Billy Budd and Other Prose Pieces,* edited by Raymond Weaver, vol. XIII of the Standard edition of Melville's works, 16 vols. (London: Constable & Co., 1922-24), pp. 309, 287.

67. From the unsigned article on Melville in *A Library of the World's Best Literature,* ed. Charles Dudley Warner et al., 45 vols. (New York: The International Society, 1897), XXV, 9868. E. C. Stedman was offered the editorship of this project but declined because of his prior commitment to the *Library of American Literature.*

68. See (1) George Monteiro, "Elizabeth Shaw Melville as Censor," *Emerson Society Quarterly,* 62 (Winter 1971), 32-33; (2) Mrs. Melville to Catherine Gansevoort Lansing, 22 March 1904, *Family Correspondence of Herman Melville,* p. 72.

69. Mrs. Melville to Harriette M. Plunkett, 31 May 1900 (Berkshire Athenaeum). Mrs. Plunkett's article is headed "Unveiling of a Great Genius. Melville and Hawthorne"; Mrs. Melville's letter suggests that it was originally prepared as a reading. There is internal evidence of indebtedness to Stedman's Introduction to *Typee* (1892).

70. *New York Times Saturday Review,* 6 July 1901, p. 490; 5 October 1901, pp. 706-707.

71. Mrs. Henry B. Thomas to Eleanor Melville Metcalf, 17 May 1926 (Melville Collection, Harvard College Library).

72. As noted above, E. C. Stedman had been one of the founders of the Authors Club in 1882; a number of Arthur Stedman's letters are written on stationery of the Century Club (later the Century Association), and Dr. Coan's "Herman Melville" mentions seeing Dr. West there occasionally at its "Saturday evenings." According to a New York correspondent of the Boston *Literary World,* writing in the issue of 28 November 1885, p. 448, the Authors Club at that time was "composed chiefly of young literary men—men whose brows are yet uncrowned by victorious wreaths"; he regretted that "the Century which once represented all that was best and brightest in literature, art, law, music, and the drama, has become more and more every year a mere society club." In this same column, ironically, the correspondent reports having recently seen in a bookstore "an old gentleman with white hair" identified to him as Herman Melville, whose "romances of the South Sea" had once delighted him. "Had he possessed as much literary skill as wild imagination his works might have secured for him a permanent place in American literature."

73. See *Collected Poems,* pp. 278, 378.

74. *Billy Budd, Sailor,* ed. Harrison Hayford and Merton M. Sealts, Jr. (Chicago: University of Chicago Press, 1962), p. 129.

75. Letter from Ferris Greenslet to Willard Thorp, 22 November 1946 (Melville Collection, Newberry Library). Melville had driven up from Gansevoort in a buggy. "Clad in a blue double-breasted suit of a seagoing flavor, he was seventy-ish, with a lot of hair and beard well grizzled, a vigorous body, 'plump sphericity,' a well tanned countenance, a bright and roving eye, all making up a singularly vital and impressive personality. I remember no one that I have met in the fifty odd years since more vividly." Greenslet was eleven or twelve when he thus "saw Melville plain," as he put it. For another report of Melville recalling his own adventures, this time in New York City about 1865 at a reception given by Alice and Phoebe Cary, see *Log,* II, 676-677.

76. Julian Hawthorne, *Nathaniel Hawthorne and His Wife,* I, 89.

FROM FOUR CONTEMPORARY REFERENCE WORKS:
THE MEN OF THE TIME (New York, 1852)

1. In the words of an honest scholar, my senior, "The likelihood of Allan Melville being Redfield's informant," as suggested on p. 8 above, "may be increased by the use of the phrase 'for the cruise' in the sketch. The phrase was not picked up by later users of this material because it apparently had no

significance for them. But for Allan, a lawyer, it would imply that Melville left the ship legally in Papeete. Melville himself made no such claim at his trial, and the circumstances of his rescue from the Marquesas permitted little formality in signing aboard the *Lucy Ann.* But he apparently signed for the cruise or voyage on the *Charles and Henry,* and it is a matter of record that he did so on the *United States.*" See the Chronology below and, for further details, Leon Howard, *Herman Melville: A Biography* (Berkeley and Los Angeles: University of California Press, 1951), pp. 54 ff.

FROM FOUR CONTEMPORARY REFERENCE WORKS:
CYCLOPAEDIA OF AMERICAN LITERATURE (1855)

1. "Article Scoonie, Sinclair's Statistical Account of Scotland, vol. v. p. 115. Dr. George Brewster, minister of Scoonie, who died June 20, 1855, succeeded the Rev. David Swan, who was the successor of our author's ancestor. It is worthy of remark that the united years of these three clergymen, in the same desk, was one hundred and thirty-six years.—Obituary notice in Scotsman, June 23, 1855" [Duyckincks' note].

2. Major Thomas Melvill (1751-1832), was for forty years Collector of the Port of Boston, from 1789 to 1829. As the Duyckincks' note at this point explains, "Major Melville was the nearest surviving male relative of General Robert Melville, who was descended from a brother of the minister of Scoonie, the first and only Captain-General and Governor-in-chief of the Islands ceded to England by France in 1763, and at the time of his death, which occurred in 1809, was with one exception the oldest General in the British army.— County Annual Register, Scotland, 1809 and '10, vol. i. part 6. In the genealogy of General Melville, contained in Douglass's Baronage of Scotland, published in 1798, the Boston family are stated to be descended from the same branch of the Melville family as General Melville."

3. "It was brought to the notice of Mr. Murray in London by Mr. Gansevoort Melville, then Secretary of Legation to the Minister, Mr. Louis McLane. Mr. Gansevoort Melville was a political speaker of talent. He died suddenly in London of an attack of fever in May, 1846" [Duyckincks' note].

4. "Lt. [Henry A.] Wise, in his lively, dashing book of travels—An Inside View of Mexico and California, with Wanderings in Peru, Chili, and Polynesia—pays a compliment to Melville's fidelity: 'Apart from the innate beauty and charming tone of his narratives, the delineations of island life and scenery, from my own personal observation, are most correctly and faithfully drawn'" [Duyckincks' note].

5. "Just at the time of publication of this book its catastrophe, the attack of the ship by the whale, which had already good historic warrant in the fate of the Essex of Nantucket, was still further supported by the newspaper narrative of the Ann Alexander of New Bedford, in which the infuriated animal demonstrated a spirit of revenge almost human, in turning upon, pursuing, and destroying the vessel from which he had been attacked" [Duyckincks' note].

6. " 'The Life and Adventures of Israel R. Potter (a native of Cranston,

Rhode Island), who was a soldier in the American Revolution,' were published in a small volume at Providence, in 1824. The story in this book was written from the narrative of Potter, by Mr. Henry Trumbull, of Hartford, Ct." [Duyckincks' note].

7. "Ode for the Berkshire Jubilee, by Fanny Kemble Butler" [Duyckincks' note].

FROM FOUR CONTEMPORARY REFERENCE WORKS: *APPLETON'S CYCLOPAEDIA OF AMERICAN BIOGRAPHY* (1888)

1. Quoted, with minor omissions, from *Typee,* Ch. 10. See *Typee* (1968), p. 71.

RETROSPECTIVE ESSAYS, 1891-1892: STEDMAN, "HERMAN MELVILLE'S FUNERAL"

1. The obvious error in locating the family residence (uncorrected here) is presumably typographical rather than authorial, Stedman himself having been a visitor to and near neighbor of the Melvilles on East Twenty-Sixth Street; the misstatement appears again in the *Critic's* reprinting of his article. The probable error of "daughter" for "daughters" may be Stedman's; he presumably knew Elizabeth Melville, who lived at home, but perhaps had not met her married sister, Mrs. Henry B. Thomas, who was living in New Jersey. Which of Allan Melville's daughters attended the funeral is not known. Among the others present, in addition to Dr. Coan and Stedman himself, Samuel Shaw was Mrs. Melville's half-brother; William B. Morewood had married Allan Melville's daughter Maria Gansevoort; George Brewster had known Melville through the Gansevoorts and Lansings (p. 26 above); "Mrs. Griggs" is Stedman's error for "Mrs. [John C.] Hoadley"—i.e., Melville's sister Catherine rather than his sister Helen Melville Griggs, who had died in 1888; "Miss Lathers" was a daughter of Melville's friend Richard Lathers of New Rochelle and Pittsfield, who had married a sister of the first Mrs. Allan Melville; George Dillaway, who has not been otherwise associated with the Melvilles, was a lawyer with offices at 18 Wall Street and residence near the Melvilles, at 38 Union Square East. Note that Stedman's list is not offered as a complete one ("*Among* the relatives and friends . . .").

2. Stedman is alluding to the published observations of Robert Buchanan, some of which had implied neglect of Melville by Stedman's father; see pp. 23-24 above.

3. Concerning the senior Coan and his comments, see *Log,* II, 781-782, and p. 118 above.

4. On Melville's invitation to join the Authors Club, see pp. 25-26 above.

5. There are no references to the state of Melville's health during his late years in Stedman's subsequent essays, though in writing to Coan he later recalled that Melville "was confined to his bed for a year before his death" (p. 45 above). He may have been responding to the wishes of Mrs. Melville: note

her alteration of Smith's phrasing "painful illness of several years" (p. 148 above) to "painful illness" in the 1897 pamphlet.

6. The final poem in the privately printed *Timoleon* (1891).

RETROSPECTIVE ESSAYS, 1891-1892:
STEDMAN, " 'MARQUESAN' MELVILLE"

1. I have emended the newspaper text as follows: *104.4* Dick":] Dick:" *104.32* Aug.] Aug *105.23* Taconic] Teutonic *106.24* unwillingness] unwillingnets *106.28* Williams] William's *106.33* spacious] spacious, *109.5* July] July, *109.12* "Omoo,"] "Omoo;" *109.13* Dick."] Dick," *109.35* grew] grew.

2. "Socrates in Camden, With a Look Round (Written after first meeting the American Poet, Walt Whitman, at Camden, New Jersey.)," *Academy* (London), 15 August 1885, pp. 102-103. Melville, in acknowledging a copy of the poem sent him from England by James Billson, observed that Buchanan had "intuitively penetrated beneath the surface of certain matters here" (*Letters*, p. 278). Concerning Stedman's reactions to Buchanan's charges, see his comments in "Herman Melville's Funeral," p. 99 above, and the discussion on pp. 23-24, 25-26 above.

3. Stedman is drawing on what the Duyckincks had said of Major Melvill, pp. 91-92 above, adding that the Major was indeed the subject of "The Last Leaf" by Dr. Oliver Wendell Holmes. The sentences which follow, on Allan Melvill and on Herman Melville's boyhood, paraphrase the Duyckincks' *Cyclopaedia*.

4. The reference to Charles Edwin West (1809-1900) is Stedman's addition to the Duyckincks' account of Melville's youth, prompted by Mrs. Melville's knowledge that her husband had once studied with West at the Albany Classical School; see the parallel passages from this account and from Mrs. Melville's memoranda, pp. 68 and 70 above. West, born in Berkshire County, Massachusetts, and educated in Pittsfield and at Union College, founded the Albany Classical School in 1835; in later years he served as principal at three other institutions—the Rutgers Female Institute in New York City, 1838-1850, the Buffalo Female Academy, 1850-1860, and the Brooklyn Heights Seminary, 1860-1889—and finally retired at the age of eighty to write his autobiography. See Dr. Coan's further reference to West and Melville in his "Herman Melville," p. 116 above; a feature story on West in the *New York Times Magazine*, 5 December 1897, p. 12; an obituary article in the New York *Tribune*, 10 March 1900, p. 9; and a notice of West in the *National Cyclopaedia of American Biography*, VIII, 235, possibly written by Coan, who knew West and was a contributor to the *Cyclopaedia*. West was noted for his broad learning and also for his fine library. After Melville's death he was among the purchasers of books once belonging to his former student that a Brooklyn dealer, A. F. Farnell, had bought from Mrs. Melville, but neither the late Charles Olson nor I have been able to trace them. See my *Melville's Reading: A Check-List of Books Owned and Borrowed*, pp. 6-7.

5. In these three sentences, Stedman has added to the Duyckincks' account by mentioning Melville's schoolteaching and asserting that the Liverpool voyage was made with the consent of Melville's family—a point probably emphasized by Melville's widow. He does not question the "brief visit to London." See the parallel passages, pp. 68 and 70 above.

6. Stedman's résumé of Melville's Pacific voyage names his first whaler, the *Acushnet,* and adds to the factual information given in previous biographical sketches by quoting from *Moby-Dick,* Ch. 24, and more extensively from *Typee:* for the description of Fayaway in Ch. 11 and the account of canoeing with Fayaway and Kory-Kory in Ch. 18, see *Typee* (1968), pp. 85-86, 133-134.

7. In these three sentences, Stedman is drawing upon J. E. A. Smith, *Taghconic* (1879), p. 199; see Appendix C above.

8. Julian Hawthorne, *Nathaniel Hawthorne and His Wife,* I, 399; there and in *Letters,* pp. 132-133, the letter is dated 29 June 1851.

9. Hawthorne and his daughter Una visited Arrowhead for at most three days, beginning on 13 March 1851; Mrs. Melville also mentions this visit in her memoranda, p. 170 above. Melville's own recollections of the occasion are reported by Dr. Theodore F. Wolfe (see p. 26 above and note 13 on p. 210 above), who was possibly the source of the "recorded" words in Stedman's paragraph; no published source for them has been located.

10. Nathaniel Hawthorne, *A Wonder-Book for Girls and Boys* (Boston: Ticknor, Reed, and Fields, 1852), pp. 252-253.

11. In going over Melville's contracts with publishers, Stedman had observed that the agreement for the English edition of *The Confidence-Man* was signed on 20 March 1857 by Hawthorne, "U.S. Consul, on behalf of Herman Melville" (*Log,* II, 560).

12. Stedman is correct in associating Curtis with Melville's first lectures, as we now know from correspondence unavailable to him in 1891; he may have had the story from Mrs. Melville or even from Curtis himself. Melville lectured in Montreal, Chicago, and Baltimore, though not in San Francisco, as Stedman might have determined by consulting Melville's notebook of lecture engagements (reproduced in my *Melville as Lecturer,* Cambridge: Harvard University Press, 1957, following p. 188). The voyage to San Francisco in 1860 was via Cape Horn; only the return trip was "by the Isthmus route."

13. Coan himself was to publish a briefer extract from the letter in his "Herman Melville," p. 119 above. There are several differences in phrasing, particularly in the final sentence, between the wording of the present passage and that of Coan's article.

14. See "Herman Melville's Funeral," p. 100 above.

15. Charles Henry Webb (1834-1905), remembered today as the editor and publisher of Mark Twain's *The Celebrated Jumping Frog of Calaveras County and Other Sketches* in 1867, was known in his own period as a journalist and playwright. The sketch of Webb in the *National Cyclopaedia of American Biography,* X, 42, asserts as does Stedman that a reading of *Moby-Dick* late in 1851 was responsible for Webb's first going to sea.

16. Another reflection of Stedman's perusal of Melville's publishing correspondence; see *Log*, II, 820-821, for an exchange of letters between Melville and John Murray in 1890 and Stedman's own summary of the matter, made in 1892.

17. Richard Bentley, publisher of the English editions of *Mardi, Redburn, White-Jacket,* and *Moby-Dick,* was uneasy about accepting *Pierre* after it was determined that American authors could not hold copyright in England; he later declined to take the manuscript without having it revised in London. See his letters to Melville of 3 March and 5 May 1852—letters which Stedman must have read—as extracted in *Log*, II, 930-931.

18. Possibly suggested to Stedman by Dr. Coan, the son of missionaries.

19. Since Murray and Bentley made outright purchases from Melville of the works which they respectively published, they furnished no periodic statements of account like those rendered over the years by Melville's American publishers. See G. Thomas Tanselle, "The Sales of Melville's Books," pp. 196-199, for details of his transactions with English publishers.

20. "Do you know why he [Melville] left Pittsfield to go to New York?" This question was propounded to Melville's daughter Frances in a letter of 28 September [August?] 1919 by her own daughter Mrs. Metcalf (Melville Collection, Harvard College Library); Mrs. Thomas replied, in a marginal comment: "To send the children to school". See also Eleanor Melville Metcalf, *Herman Melville,* p. 201.

21. Melville had met Henry A. Smythe (1817-?), "merchant of N[ew].-Y[ork].," while en route to Basel, Switzerland, on 19 April 1857 (*Log,* II, 573). After Smythe's return from Europe he became successively a business man, a bank president, and in 1866 Collector of the Customs for the Port of New York. He submitted Melville's nomination as Inspector on 28 November 1866 and secured its prompt approval (*Log,* II, 683).

22. William Clark Russell (1844-1911), a prolific author of marine fiction, published lives of Dampier (1889), Nelson (1890), and Collingwood (1891) during years when Melville was working on *Billy Budd;* on their correspondence, see pp. 20-21 above. The artist Peter Toft, whose name occurs in Russell's letter, was a mutual friend.

23. Compare "Herman Melville's Funeral," p. 100 above.

24. Stedman is taking issue with a point advanced by Oliver G. Hillard in a letter to the New York *Times* published on 6 October 1891, p. 9: Melville, though "in no sense a man of business," according to Hillard, "would probably have accepted" a magazine editorship had he been offered it and would have "filled it well; but to seek and ask that or any other position would for him have been impossible." From Mrs. Melville, Stedman may well have heard an appraisal like that she had given Catherine Gansevoort Lansing in 1872, when Allan Melville's death meant the loss of his services as his brother's business agent: "because Herman from his studious habits and tastes" is "unfitted for practical matters, all the *financial* management falls upon me" (*Log,* II, 729).

25. The final poem in the privately printed *Timoleon* (1891), previously

quoted at the conclusion of "Herman Melville's Funeral" (pp. 100-101 above). The inscription by Mrs. Melville in the copy of *Timoleon* she gave Stedman is dated 11 October 1891—the date of publication of " 'Marquesan' Melville"; see p. 63 above.

RETROSPECTIVE ESSAYS, 1891-1892:
STEDMAN, "MELVILLE OF MARQUESAS"

1. I have emended as follows: *112.15* Ambiguities" (1852),] Ambiguities (1852),"

2. Quoted inexactly from a review in *Blackwood's Magazine,* 61 (1847), 754-767—probably by way of a secondary source such as S. Austin Allibone, *A Critical Dictionary of English Literature,* II, 1264.

3. As in his two previous articles, Stedman is thinking of his father's efforts to "draw" Melville into the Authors Club and other social activities.

4. Stedman's chronology here is confused: Melville's first voyage, to Liverpool, took place in 1839; he then read *Two Years Before the Mast* (1840), as he later told Dana himself (*Letters,* p. 106); in January of 1841 he sailed for the South Pacific.

5. Stedman may have written this sentence before Stoddard, a family friend, published his general review of Melville's life and works in the New York *Mail and Express,* 8 October 1891, p. 5; there are further comments on Melville in "My Life in the Custom-House," a chapter of Stoddard's *Recollections Personal and Literary,* ed. Ripley Hitchcock (1903).

6. Stedman had previously misdated *Redburn* (1849) in *A Library of American Literature;* see p. 98 above.

7. For the quoted phrase, see Fitz-James O'Brien, "Our Authors and Authorship: Melville and Curtis," *Putnam's Monthly Magazine,* 9 (April 1857), 390.

8. Henry Mills Alden (1836-1919) edited *Harper's New Monthly Magazine* from 1869 until his death; Melville's story had appeared in the magazine in December of 1853.

9. In 1892 Stedman would be asked to consider adding *Israel Potter* to the new edition of Melville's "best works" (p. 55 above).

10. Henry S. [not "A."] Salt, "Herman Melville," *Scottish Art Review,* 2 (November 1889), 186-190. On Stedman's correspondence with Salt, see pp. 51-53, 53-54, 58 above.

11. Russell's praise of *Moby-Dick* as Melville's "finest work" had been voiced in 1884 and reaffirmed in 1885; see p. 21 above.

12. "Herman Melville," New York *Times,* 2 October 1891, p. 4: Stevenson has recently been working in Melville's own "field," the South Pacific, the article concludes, but has not taken its "laureateship" from Melville. "In fact," his readers "abandon as quite unreadable what he has written from that quarter."

13. Julien Viaud (1850-1923), Pierre Loti, had by 1891 published such books as *Aziyadé* (1879), *Rarahu* (1880; later called *Le Mariage de Loti,* 1882), *Pêcheur d'Islande* (1886), *Madame Chrysanthème* (1887), and *Japoneries*

d'Automne (1889); Hearn (1850-1904) had recently published *Some Chinese Ghosts* (1887), *Chita* (1889), *Two Years in the French West Indies* (1890), and *Youma* (1890).

14. William Starbuck Mayo (1811-1895), *Kaloolah; or, Journeyings to the Djébel Kumri* (1849), is a romance concerning a Yankee's marriage to an African princess.

15. John Gabriel Stedman, *Narrative of a Five Years' Expedition Against the Revolted Negroes of Surinam, in Guiana, on the Wild Coast of South America from the Year 1772 to 1777 Elucidating the History of That Country and Describing Its Production, etc.*, first published in London in 1796. In the words of Rudolf van Lier in his Introduction to a recent edition (Amherst: University of Massachusetts Press, 1972), p. xi, "Stedman (1744-1797) was a member of a prominent Scots family with a history dating back to the sixteenth century. . . . The family name, originally Barton, was changed to Stedman when Charles Barton married the daughter of Charles Stedman and Janet Neilson of Leith, who owned considerable property." I have found no evidence of a family relationship between Arthur Stedman and John Gabriel Stedman.

16. See " 'Marquesan' Melville," p. 108 above.

17. A. B. Ellis, "On Polyandry," *Popular Science Monthly*, 39 (October 1891), 801-809, quotes on p. 802 from "Melville's Marquesas Islands, p. 213," the observation that in the Marquesas "no man has more than one wife, and no wife of mature years has less than two husbands—sometimes she has three, but such instances are not frequent." Ellis goes on to say that in these islands "the males considerably outnumber the females."

18. *Battle-Pieces and Aspects of the War* (New York: Harper & Brothers, 1866), p. v.

19. Stedman's allusions are to: (1) Richard Henry Stoddard, review of Melville's *John Marr and Other Sailors* (1888), New York *Mail and Express,* 20 November 1888, p. 3; and (2) Thomas William Parsons, "On a Bust of Dante"—lines highly praised by Stedman's father in his *Poets of America* (1885), p. 55.

20. As in " 'Marquesan' Melville," p. 110 above, Stedman again writes here of "The Return of the Sire de Nesle" as Melville's "last" poem.

21. In *A Wonder-Book,* quoted more extensively in " 'Marquesan' Melville," pp. 105-106 above.

22. Fitz-James O'Brien, "Our Young Authors—Melville," *Putnam's Monthly Magazine,* 1 (February 1853), 155-164.

23. Stedman the professional man of letters is speaking in these paragraphs. As the Harper fire of 10 December 1853 had kept Melville's books out of print "at a most important time," so the new edition of 1892 was intended to bring four of them back into print to restore his fame at a later "important time." Stedman writes correctly about the changed arrangements with the Harpers concerning *Pierre,* for which Melville was to receive not half profits but a royalty of 20 cents per copy beyond the first 1,190 sold; see *Pierre* (1971), p. 378. This information Stedman had of course learned from his study of Melville's publishing agreements.

24. The reference is to the re-issue of *Israel Potter* in 1865 as *The Refugee* (pp. 17, 91 above).

25. See " 'Marquesan' Melville," p. 109 above and note 24 on p. 222 above.

26. See " 'Marquesan' Melville," p. 108 above.

27. Stedman—or Mrs. Melville—may have recalled Alexander Young's remarks to this effect in the Boston *Post* of 19 November 1890; see p. 25 above.

28. Stedman's niece Laura Stedman Gould was to corroborate these remarks about Melville's standing within the Stedman household and to take issue similarly with later Melville "enthusiasts"; see p. 50 above.

RETROSPECTIVE ESSAYS, 1891-1892: COAN, "HERMAN MELVILLE"

1. In "Herman Melville's Funeral," p. 99 above, Stedman had previously observed that Lowell too was born in 1819. Coan's opening sentences, with their listing of eminent persons born in that year, parallel an entry among Mrs. Melville's memoranda, p. 177 above, which is accompanied by this notation: "From Dr Titus A [*i.e.,* M.] Coan who writes 'I think Mr Melville's name will be remembered as long as any on the list.' " Mrs. Melville may either be paraphrasing the present essay or—more probably—quoting an earlier letter or memorandum from Coan. His article, purporting to incorporate unspecified "data . . . for the first time fully given" (p. 118 above), may well include materials provided by Mrs. Melville and perhaps by Stedman. Coan's essay can properly be regarded as part of the campaign then current to revive Melville's fame and prepare the way for the impending reissue of four of his books. Mrs. Melville would certainly have cooperated in the preparation of an article for a Boston publication; placing something there may even have been her own idea, as suggested above (p. 45).

2. *Leaves from a Journal of our Life in the Highlands, 1848-61*, privately printed in 1867 and published in 1868; *More Leaves* followed in 1883.

3. "So with Pierre. It had been his choice fate to have been born and nurtured in the country . . ." (*Pierre*, 1971, p. 5).

4. Concerning Dr. West, see " 'Marquesan' Melville," p. 103 above, and Mrs. Melville's memoranda, p. 170 above.

5. Coan is correct: Armstrong was in command during Melville's homeward voyage until the *United States* reached Callao in early June of 1844, when he left the ship to assume command of the entire Pacific squadron. See Charles R. Anderson, *Melville in the South Seas* (New York: Columbia University Press, 1939), p. 357.

6. Here Coan is adapting phrases first used in the account of Melville in *The Men of the Time* (1852) which may have come to him either directly from that work or by way of some intermediate source; the wording was widely copied. See p. 90 above.

7. Coan is of course in error about the composition of *White-Jacket*, the already completed work for which Melville was seeking a publisher during his visit to London in 1849.

8. Coan is quoting his own words as Stedman had previously reported them in "Herman Melville's Funeral," p. 100 above, omitting an additional sentence evidently not suitable for a Boston publication: " 'Typee' will be read when most of the Concord group are forgotten."

9. Stedman had given a fuller extract of Coan's letter in " 'Marquesan' Melville," pp. 106-107 above; there are verbal differences in the two versions.

10. Greene was indeed "living" in 1891; he died in Chicago on 26 August 1892, as Arthur Stedman was later to inform Coan (p. 45 above).

RETROSPECTIVE ESSAYS, 1891-1892:
SMITH, "HERMAN MELVILLE"

1. New York *Times,* 2 October 1891, p. 4; Smith's quotation of this editorial called the attention of Raymond Weaver and other later biographers to its erroneous statement that "only one newspaper carried an obituary account of him." See Hugh W. Hetherington's survey of contemporary notices in newspapers and magazines: "A Tribute to the Late Hiram Melville," *Modern Language Quarterly,* 16 (December 1955), 325-331; and pp. 27-28 above. (Hetherington's title alludes to the heading given O. G. Hillard's letter concerning Melville in the *Times* of 6 October 1891, p. 9.) The "visiting British writer" mentioned in the editorial was Robert Buchanan.

2. Curtis (1824-1892) published travel books in the early 1850's that were compared with Melville's own. He became an editorial advisor to *Putnam's Magazine* and an associate of the firm of Dix & Edwards, which published *The Piazza Tales* and *The Confidence-Man;* as Stedman noted in " 'Marquesan' Melville," p. 106 above, he later helped Melville secure lecture engagements. No scholar has established any association between Melville and Curtis in later years, when Curtis edited *Harper's Weekly* (after 1863) and contributed the Editor's Easy Chair column to *Harper's Magazine.*

3. Smith is quoting "Herman Melville's Funeral" (see pp. 99-100 above) without knowledge of Stedman's authorship.

4. See "Herman Melville's Funeral," p. 99 above.

5. Oliver Wendell Holmes, "The Last Leaf" (1831), lines 10-12, 28-30; Smith quotes somewhat inexactly. "To Bostonians the death of Herman Melville should recall . . . the novelist's grandfather," wrote Charles E. L. Wingate in his "Boston Letter" to the *Critic* of 10 October 1891. Three weeks later Wingate added that he had asked Holmes himself whether Melville's grandfather was indeed "the original of the quaint old gentleman" in the poem. Holmes replied: "I remember Major Thomas Melville very well—in the early thirties, probably. He was one of the last, if not the last, of the three-cornered cocked-hat wearers, and like many others of his time and after it—my own father was one of them—wore knee-breeches. The figure of the sturdy old gentleman thumping round with his cane suggested my poem 'The Last Leaf.' " See *Critic,* n.s. 16, 184-185, 235.

6. Smith's reference is to Priscilla Melvill (1784-1862). Mrs. Melville omitted this entire paragraph from the 1897 pamphlet version of Smith's articles.

7. Allan Melvill (1782-1832) married not "Catherine" but Maria Gansevoort (1791-1872), daughter of Peter and Catherine Van Schaick Gansevoort of Albany; Mrs. Melville corrected the name in the 1897 pamphlet. Square brackets in the text both here ("[observe . . . Scotch]") and below are Smith's.

8. The hotel, Stanwix Hall, stood on North Market Street in Albany until 1932, when it was torn down to make way for a new post office building. It was originally built as a business block by Melville's Gansevoort uncles Peter (1789-1876) and Herman (1779-1862), converted into a hotel in 1844, and extensively remodeled in 1876. Although Smith refers to both brothers as "General," the title belonged in fact only to Herman, who served as a brigadier general of militia in 1821-1822. See Alice P. Kenney, *The Gansevoorts of Albany: Dutch Patricians in the Upper Hudson Valley* (Syracuse, N.Y.: Syracuse University Press, 1969), *passim*.

9. Smith's allusion is to the first meeting of Melville and Hawthorne on 5 August 1850 (*Log*, I, 383-385); for his other treatments of this same occasion, see *Taghconic* (1879), p. 318 (Appendix C above), and *The Poet Among the Hills* (1895), pp. 31-32 (Appendix D above).

10. Smith, who evidently knew West ("a Pittsfield man"), confirms and adds to what Stedman had reported in "'Marquesan' Melville," p. 103 above, concerning West's recollections of Melville. The "ancient mariner" who supposedly reassured West about *Typee* may have been Dr. Coan, who had been to sea and who knew West in New York (Coan, "Herman Melville," p. 116 above); Coan too reports West as saying that Melville when a student was "weak in mathematics." But if Coan is indeed the "ancient mariner," Smith has confused him with his father: it was Rev. Titus Coan and not his son who "went over Melville's ground in 1867" (p. 118 above).

11. Though a frequent visitor at Peter Gansevoort's residence in Clinton Square, Albany, Melville never "made his home with him," as Smith believed.

12. Although Melville had previously been taken to Pittsfield as a child, in 1823 (*Log*, I, 15), the first visit that he remembered in later years occurred in August of 1831 (*Log*, I, 48), when his parents, en route from Albany to Boston, stayed for two days with his father's brother, Major Thomas Melvill, Jr. (1776-1845). In the summers of 1832 and 1833 Melville returned to Pittsfield for short periods (*Log*, I, 54-55, 59), as Smith correctly surmised, and during most of 1834 he lived with Major Melvill as "an active assistant upon the farm" at a time when his uncle was suffering from lameness (*Log*, I, 63-64). Smith's date of "1836" comes from Melville's own account of his uncle, which is quoted below.

13. Major Melvill left Pittsfield in 1837 for Galena, Illinois, where he died in 1845; Melville's sketch of his later years appeared in part in Smith's own compilation, *The History of Pittsfield, 1800-1876*, where it is attributed only to an unnamed "relative" (p. 399). A manuscript copy of the complete text of the sketch, made by an unidentified hand, is now in the Gansevoort-Lansing Collection of the New York Public Library; it is headed "Sketch of Major Thomas Melville, Jr. by a Nephew."

14. *The History of Pittsfield, 1800-1876*, pp. 399-400.

15. In *Taghconic* (1879), p. 198, Smith had previously written that "in his youth" Melville "played school-master in a wild district" of Pittsfield, "under the shadow of Rock Mountain, I think," while "domiciliated" with his Uncle Thomas (Appendix C above); in *The Poet Among the Hills* (1895), p. 28, he remarked of the farm that became Arrowhead: "Mr. Melville must have known it well in his youth, when he was in the family of his uncle . . . and was master of a district school so located that his nearest way to it was through the farm attached to the gambrel-roofed house of Holmes Road" (Appendix D above). But when Melville was teaching in Pittsfield, beginning in the fall of 1837, he described himself in a letter to Peter Gansevoort as currently boarding not with Thomas Melvill but rather an unnamed "Yankee" living on a lonely mountain "a mile and a half from any other tenement whatever." The school, he wrote, was "situated in a remote & secluded part of the town about five miles from the village"; his "scholars" were "about thirty in number, of all ages, sizes, ranks, charaterrs [*sic*], & education" (*Letters*, p. 5), but if they were indeed rebellious he did not say so in the letter. Arthur Stedman's Introduction to *Typee* (1892), pp. xvii-xviii, correctly dates Melville's schoolteaching "from 1837 to 1840. . . . He taught for one term at Pittsfield, Mass., 'boarding around' with the families of his pupils, in true American fashion, and easily suppressing, on one memorable occasion, the efforts of his larger scholars to inaugurate a rebellion by physical force" (p. 156 above). Although Stedman's reference to the "rebellion" may be based on what Smith says here, there was in fact an independent contemporary report of some such occurrence: according to the Boston *Museum*, 31 January 1852, Melville "was driven out of school by two naughty boys" (*Log*, I, 445); see S. Foster Damon, "Why Ishmael Went to Sea," *American Literature*, 2 (November 1930), 281-283, for the suggestion that Melville's difficulties as a schoolmaster may have helped to send him to sea. During the winter of 1839-1840 Melville returned to teaching, at Greenbush, New York; and in the following May he again taught briefly, at Brunswick, New York.

16. This paragraph incorporates information that Smith had previously recorded in *The History of Pittsfield, 1800-1876*, p. 664, note.

17. The *Evening Journal* of 21 November 1891, in which this instalment appeared, also carried another Melville item on p. 8, headed "HERMAN MELVILLE. His Literary Career a Rare Instance so far as Fame is Concerned." The article, reprinted from *Town Topics*, 1 October 1891, had also been reprinted in the *Critic* for 10 October.

18. Like earlier biographers, Smith too makes 1837—or even late 1836—the year of Melville's Liverpool voyage by assuming that it "immediately" followed the visit to Thomas Melvill, Jr., that he had dated in 1836. For the last three sentences of this paragraph Smith was probably drawing upon S. Austin Allibone's *Critical Dictionary*, II, 1264, which he also used elsewhere in his sketch. Allibone states that Melville "in his 18th year made a voyage from New York to Liverpool, and back home, before the mast, and liked his marine experience sufficiently to embark on a whaling-vessel for the Pacific, Jan. 1,* 1841. About July of the next year, the vessel arrived at Nukaheva [*sic*], one of the Marquesas

Islands, and Melville, with a fellow-sailor, who like himself was tired of strait quarters and a tyrannical captain, embraced the opportunity of leaving the ship without waiting for the usual formality of a discharge." The verbal parallels in Smith's account are evident.

19. In Mrs. Melville's copy of the 1897 pamphlet the words "and Mardi" in this sentence have been lined out. Like Smith himself, she apparently accepted *Typee* as literally a "Narrative of a Four Months' Residence" in the Marquesas—the phrasing of the book's original printed title (note 24 below on this page)—although it has since been established that Melville lived with the Typees for only a single month: 9 July to 9 August 1842.

20. Smith's reference to the use of Melville's books by missionaries, obviously borrowed from " 'Marquesan' Melville," p. 108 above, may ultimately derive from Coan as a likely source of Stedman's remark there.

21. Smith first quoted these lines with reference to Melville in *Taghconic* (1852), p. 16 (Appendix B above); I have not identified their authorship.

22. The phrasing here, as in Coan's "Herman Melville," p. 117 above, derives ultimately from *The Men of the Time* (1852), p. 90 above: "He thus added to his knowledge of the merchant and whaling service a complete acquaintance with the inner life on board a man-of-war."

23. See " 'Marquesan' Melville," p. 107 above.

24. Murray published Melville's first book in 1846 as *Narrative of a Four Months' Residence among the Natives of a Valley of the Marquesas Islands; or, A Peep at Polynesian Life*, and the second in 1847 as *Omoo: A Narrative of Adventures in the South Seas; Being a Sequel to the "Residence in the Marquesas Islands."*

25. The article on Melville in Allibone's *Critical Dictionary*, II, 1264, which Smith had already drawn on above, p. 127, probably furnished him with all three of the passages quoted inexactly here. They derive respectively from reviews in *Blackwood's Edinburgh Magazine*, 51 (June 1847), 754; *John Bull*, 26 (7 March 1846), 156; and *The Times* of London, 24 September 1847, p. 7. Stedman had also quoted *Blackwood's* in "Melville of Marquesas," p. 110 above.

26. In his *History of Pittsfield, 1800-1876*, p. 7, Smith had written that "the large, square flat-roofed mansion, now the residence of J. R. Morewood, was built by Henry Van Schaack, in 1781, with extraordinary care and liberal expenditure; and was for many years much the best-built edifice in the town. The wooden walls were lined with brick, and the carpentry exhibits a perfection of skill which excites the admiration of modern workmen. . . . It is little changed except by the removal of the broad chimney and the old-fashioned balustrade which surrounded the roof." From 1807 to 1816, Smith continues, the house belonged to Elkanah Watson. "It was then purchased by Major Thomas Melville, who resided in it until 1837, and was succeeded by his son, Robert Melville. For some years previous to its purchase by Mr. Morewood, in 1851 [i.e., 1850], it was kept as a boarding-house, and numbered among its guests Henry W. Longfellow, Nathaniel Hawthorne, Herman Melville, and President John Tyler." In *The Poet Among the Hills* (1895), pp. 28-29, Smith

erroneously dated the Melvilles' summer at Broadhall in "1848,*" when the Longfellows were guests there (Appendix C above).

27. John Rowland Morewood (1821-1903) married Sarah Huyler (1824-1863); Allan Melville and Colonel Richard Lathers (1820-1903) married sisters; the Morewoods' oldest son, William, married Allan Melville's daughter Maria Gansevoort in 1874. Mrs. Melville's changes in this paragraph for the 1897 pamphlet included (1) the deletion of Smith's reference to the Robert Melvill residence as a "boarding-house" and (2) two corrections of "1849*" to "1850".

28. The 1897 pamphlet omits this entire instalment.

29. Mrs. Morewood's sister Mrs. Ellen Brittain (1814-1897) placed on p. 179 of her Berkshire scrapbook (now in the Berkshire Athenaeum) a clipping, headed "The Name of Broadhall," from an unidentified newspaper that tells much the same story, mentioning "a box" rather than "a basket" but similarly crediting Melville with proposing the name chosen. Smith also refers to the drawing in a note to *The Poet Among the Hills* (1895), pp. 28-29, where he inferentially dates the party as taking place about 1851 (Appendix D above). But the name had been applied to the mansion at least as early as 1850, when Cornelius Mathews, writing anonymously in the *Literary World*, 7 (24 August 1850), 145, on "Several Days in Berkshire," referred to his sojourn while there (with Evert Duyckinck, the Melvilles, and the Morewoods) "at a square, old Country House" standing "like a broad-brimmed patriarchal old gentleman in the very heart of the hills. . . . Old Broad-Hall is a glorious fellow," with "claims and enjoyments" including "ancient Family Portraits and a small bottle of tea (reserved by an ancestor of the house [Major Thomas Melvill]) from the dumpage in Boston Harbor." According to Sarah Morewood herself, in a letter to George Duyckinck, 21 November 1851, the christening had taken place at a recent party when "we agreed by way of amusement to write names for our cows and house—and to decide by drawing lots—I drew for the house Broadhall—for the three cows—Molly Polly & Dolly. Miss Kate Melville had the naming of the house—Herman Melville the cows" (*Log*, I, 434).

30. In *The History of Pittsfield, 1800-1876*, p. 7, Smith had first written of Arrowhead as "the broad-chimneyed, hospitable-looking old dwelling, built some years previous to 1800, by Captain David Bush, under whose rule, and that of his son, it was a famous inn. It faces upon Wendell street; and now, but slightly changed in its general outline, it is the summer home of the family of the late Allan Melville. The old place had the good fortune, in 1852,* to be purchased by Herman Melville, then in the freshness of his early fame. Mr. Melville named it Arrow-Head, from the Indian relics found on the estate, and made it a house of many stories; writing in it, besides Moby Dick, and other romances of the sea, the Piazza tales, which took their name from a piazza built by the author upon the north end of the house, which commands a bold and striking view of Greylock and the intervening valley." Three years later, in his *Taghconic* (1879), pp. 198-199, Smith expanded his account of "the fine estate formerly owned by Herman Melville" (Appendix E above). His last version of Melville's life at Arrowhead occurs in *The Poet Among the Hills* (1895), pp. 29-30 (Appendix D above).

31. Dr. Holmes attended Melville in June of 1855, according to Mrs. Melville's memoranda (p. 169 above).

32. For similar comments on Melville's habits of work during the years 1847-1851, see Mrs. Melville's letter to her stepmother, 23 December 1847 (*Log*, I, 266); Melville's letter to Evert Duyckinck, 13 December 1850 (*Letters*, p. 117); and Mrs. Melville's memoranda, p. 169 above. During the winter of 1851-1852, while Melville was at work on *Pierre*, Sarah Morewood wrote on 28 December 1851 to George Duyckinck that Melville was said to be "engaged in a new work as frequently not to leave his room till quite dark in the evening—when he for the first time during the whole day partakes of solid food—he must therefore write under a state of morbid excitement which will soon injure his health . . ." (*Log*, I, 441). In the book itself, *Pierre*, the hero writes until half-past four, when he is called so as not to strain his eyes in the twilight. "From eight o'clock in the morning till half-past four in the evening, Pierre sits there in his room;—eight hours and a half!" Then he goes out for a stroll in the city (*Pierre*, 1971, p. 303). Although Melville's schedule at Pittsfield must have varied during the summer when he had farm work, or when he was entertaining the frequent visitors to Arrowhead, it is clear from correspondence that the condition of his eyes ordinarily prevented him from reading or writing in the late afternoon or evening. Other members of the family served as Melville's copyists: Mrs. Melville for "Hawthorne and His Mosses," his sister Helen for *Pierre* (*Log*, I, 441), and his sister Augusta for *The Confidence-Man* (*Log*, II, 517). The surviving manuscripts of "Hawthorne and His Mosses" and "The Two Temples" (also copied by Helen Melville) show little evidence of revision at the fair-copy stage by any hand other than Melville's own.

33. In *Taghconic* (1879), p. 199, Smith had observed that Melville "was almost a zealot in his love of Berkshire scenery, and there was no more ardent and indefatigable excursionist among its hills and valleys" (Appendix C above). Smith's fullest treatment of this aspect of Melville's personality is in *The Poet Among the Hills* (1895), pp. 30-32 (Appendix D above).

34. Smith is echoing the reviewer for *Blackwood's Magazine* whom he had previously quoted (p. 129 above).

35. This is the second of Smith's three versions of the encounter on Monument Mountain, the others occurring in *Taghconic* (1879), p. 318 (Appendix C above), and *The Poet Among the Hills* (1895), pp. 31-32 (Appendix D above). It should be emphasized that Smith himself was not present on 5 August 1850 when Hawthorne and Melville first met, and that his second-hand information is not altogether accurate—e.g., the party that day included Evert Duyckinck but not his brother George, who did not visit Melville at Pittsfield until 1851; Dr. Holmes was in fact one of the group on the Mountain. Moreover, Melville had not reviewed *The Scarlet Letter*, as Smith erroneously declared in *Taghconic* (1879) and again in *The Poet Among the Hills*, nor had he yet published "Hawthorne and His Mosses," which appeared in the *Literary World* on 17 and 24 August. Smith's various misstatements about the occasion have been repeated by later writers on Melville and Hawthorne who assumed that his information was authoritative. An early

example is Theodore F. Wolfe, *Literary Shrines: The Haunts of Some Famous American Authors* (Philadelphia: J. B. Lippincott Company, 1897), p. 190, which cites "Godfrey Graylock" in naming "Melville's review of the 'Scarlet Letter'" as the supposed cause of the initial "coyness" between the two authors. See Willard Thorp, "Did Melville Review *The Scarlet Letter?*," *American Literature,* 14 (November 1942), 302-305.

36. These three sentences, with their references to two unnamed "biographers" and "a letter writer," are confusing if not confused, and therefore demand close attention. (1) Smith's first reference to a "biographer" may involve his free handling of what Julian Hawthorne had reported of Melville in *Nathaniel Hawthorne and His Wife.* "Herman Melville ('Omoo,' as they [the Hawthornes] called him, in allusion to one of his early romances) soon became familiar and welcome" at Lenox, according to Julian Hawthorne, who quotes a letter in which Mrs. Hawthorne had remarked, "This morning 'Mr. Omoo' arrived" (I, 377). With reference to the Hawthorne children, Julian Hawthorne also notes that Melville "used to ride or drive up, in the evenings, with his great dog, and the children used to ride on the dog's back" (I, 396-397); in 1851 Julian told his father that he "loved Mr. Melville as well as" his father, mother, and sister (I, 422). (2) Smith's second "biographer" is clearly Arthur Stedman, who had written in "'Marquesan' Melville" these sentences—obviously borrowed for Smith's own account: "Mr. Hawthorne . . . had passed a week at Arrow Head with his daughter Una the previous Spring [of 1851]. It is recorded that the friends 'spent most of the time in the barn, bathing in the early Spring sunshine, which streamed through the open doors, and talking philosophy'" (p. 105 above). (3) Smith's term "letter writer" is presumably not an allusion to one of his own correspondents but rather a phrase for the unnamed source of the recorded words "'spent . . . philosophy'" in Stedman's previous account—possibly Theodore F. Wolfe (see p. 70 above, note 13 on p. 210 above, and note 9 on page 221 above). (4) Smith further tangled his references to "biographers" when he reworked this same material for *The Poet Among the Hills* (1895), pp. 32-33 (Appendix D above), where he states that the "intercourse" between Hawthorne and Melville, supposedly founded on Monument Mountain, "extended to the families of the two friends. Hawthorne's biographer tells us that when Melville was approaching the cottage by the lake, a joyous shout went up: 'Here comes Typee!' [*sic*] the pet name they had given him. . . . As we learn from the same biographer [*sic*], one who passed over it [Holmes Road] in 1849-50* [i.e., 1850-51]—might sometimes have enjoyed a rare spectacle. If it chanced to be in summer or early autumn, the great barn-doors of the Arrowhead barn would have been wide open, and if he cast a glance within he might have seen the two friends, reclining on piles of fragrant new-mown hay, and basking in the genial inpouring rays of the sun, while they held high converse on the mysteries and revelations of the world and those who people it."

37. *The Piazza Tales* had drawn Smith's praise shortly after its appearance, in a brief review in the *Berkshire County Eagle,* 30 May 1856, as "decidedly the most readable" of Melville's works "since Omoo and Typee" and "more

uniformly excellent and . . . more free from blemishes" than any of his "later books." As Smith explained, the title alludes to "the piazza on the north of the author's residence and the introduction ["The Piazza"] will be especially interesting to Pittsfield readers for its description of familiar scenery" (*Log*, II, 515).

38. This sentence originated in Smith's reference to Arrowhead in *The History of Pittsfield, 1800-1876*, pp. 7-8. The house, he declares there, "had the good fortune, in 1852,* to be purchased by Herman Melville, then in the freshness of his early fame. Mr. Melville named it Arrow-Head, from the Indian relics found on the estate, and made it a house of many stories; writing in it, besides Moby Dick, and other romances of the sea, the Piazza tales, which took their name from a piazza built by the author upon the north end of the house, which commands a bold and striking view of Greylock and the intervening valley. 'My Chimney and I,' a quaintly humorous essay, of which the cumbersome old chimney—overbearing tyrant of the home—is the hero, was also written here, as well as 'October Mountain,' a sketch of mingled philosophy and word-painted landscape, which found its inspiration in the massy and brilliant autumnal tints presented by a prominent and thickly-wooded spur of the Hoosac mountains, as seen from the south-eastern windows, at Arrow-Head, on a fine day after the early frosts." Slightly different versions of this same passage occur in *Taghconic* (1879), p. 199, and *The Poet Among the Hills* (1895), pp. 29-30, where Smith repeats his inaccurate rendering of the title of "I and My Chimney" and once more refers to another piece called "October Mountain" (Appendix C and Appendix D above). Again Smith's statements have misled later writers, including not only Theodore F. Wolfe in *Literary Shrines*, p. 192, but even Arthur Stedman in his Introduction to *Typee* (1892), p. xxi; Stedman's borrowed reference to "October Mountain" was later corrected by Mrs. Melville (see pp. 154-155 above and note 15 on pp. 240-241 below). That Melville *named* October Mountain—the name is still in use—is affirmed both by Smith in 1895 and by Mrs. Melville in her memoranda, p. 174 above. But Smith is in error when he repeatedly (1876, 1879) attributes to Melville "a sketch" of that same title; what he may have recalled imperfectly is Melville's "Cock-A-Doodle-Doo!" (1853), in which the narrator mentions "a densely-wooded mountain . . . (which I call October Mountain, on account of its bannered aspect in that month)." In "Did Melville Write 'October Mountain'?," *American Literature*, 22 (May 1950), 178-182, I concluded after an examination of the evidence that "Melville never composed a story, sketch, or poem of that title."

39. Seven satirical sketches of New York society by George W. Curtis, originally published in magazines and later collected in book form (1853).

40. In *Taghconic* (1852), p. 13, Smith had first associated Ahab's scar in *Moby-Dick*, Ch. 28, with the Pittsfield Elm (Appendix B above); there is a similar passage in *Taghconic* (1879), pp. 34-35 (Appendix C above).

41. Smith is correct in saying that the source of *Israel Potter* (1855) was a pamphlet: *Life and Remarkable Adventures of Israel R. Potter* (Providence, R.I., 1824), acquired by Melville in 1849 or earlier. The original story may

well have been ghost-written, as the Duyckincks had stated (note 6 on pp. 218-219 above) but there is no known justification for Smith's remark here that "Potter was not the real name of the hero." In *The Poet Among the Hills* (1895), p. 31, Smith again mentions "Potter Mountain" as "a favorite" with Melville (Appendix D above).

42. Melville lectured in "Burbank's hall" at Pittsfield on 14 December 1858, speaking on "The South Seas"; in the *Eagle* three days later Smith reviewed his lecture as "pleasant and instructive," finding it "in the style of Mr. Melville's best books" (*Log*, II, 597). Like Stedman in " 'Marquesan' Melville," p. 106 above, Smith erroneously states here that Melville lectured in San Francisco, adding further misinformation about appearances in Philadelphia and St. Louis. Francis V. Lloyd, Jr., "A Further Note on Herman Melville, Lecturer," *Missouri Historical Society Bulletin*, 20 (July 1964), 310-312, shows that the Mercantile Library Association of St. Louis did in fact extend an invitation to Melville, though he did not appear there. Perhaps there were other overtures as well from Philadelphia and San Francisco—invitations that Melville may have mentioned at the time to Smith.

43. Leaving Arrowhead in December of 1861, the year after his *Meteor* voyage, Melville wintered in New York and Boston rather than at Pittsfield; Smith evidently reckoned his "removal" from that year, although the sale of Arrowhead, as noted in the paragraph following, did not take place until 1863.

44. See " 'Marquesan' Melville," p. 108 above and note 20 on p. 222 above. Smith's ensuing discourse on "the public schools of Pittsfield" reflects one of his long-standing concerns; he had published a pamphlet on the subject, *The Public School System of the Town of Pittsfield Reviewed, 1761-1880, and Public Schools and Berkshire Athenaeum* (Pittsfield: The Pittsfield Sun Office, 1880).

45. Smith, the "friend" accompanying Melville at the time, had reported the accident in the *Eagle* on 13 November 1862 (*Log*, II, 655); see p. 35 above.

46. On Henry A. Smythe and his role in Melville's appointment to the Custom House, see " 'Marquesan' Melville," p. 108 above and note 21 on p. 222 above. Smith's comments here suggest that he learned of the circumstances for the first time from reading Stedman's article rather than from receiving any earlier "intimation" on Melville's part.

47. I have not identified these lines. "What is past is past" occurs in Bulwer Lytton's prose comedy *The Lady of Lyons* (produced in 1838), IV, i.

48. Was Smith recalling the situation of the 1850's as he remembered it, or was he influenced by Stedman's repeated references to the hostile reception of *Pierre?* See "Herman Melville's Funeral," p. 100 above, and "Melville of Marquesas," pp. 112, 114 above.

49. Following the apparent suicide of Melville's son Malcolm in 1867 there had indeed been a succession of deaths among relatives and friends: for example, Melville's cousin Henry Sanford Gansevoort in 1871; his brother Allan, his mother, and his uncle John D'Wolf in 1872; his sister Augusta and his uncle Peter Gansevoort in 1876; his aunt Lucy Melvill Nourse and her husband in 1877; Evert Duyckinck in 1878; Mrs. Melville's stepmother in 1879; his cousin

Robert in 1881; his brother Thomas, his aunt Mary Melvill, and Lemuel Shaw, Jr., in 1884; his sister Frances Priscilla in 1885; his son Stanwix and his brother-in-law John C. Hoadley in 1886; and his sister Helen Maria Melville Griggs in 1888. In the 1897 pamphlet Mrs. Melville let all of Smith's sentence stand except for the final comment, deleting "—sincere . . . symbols."

50. Concerning the sketch of Thomas Melvill, Jr., see the discussion, p. 36 above, and the extract occurring earlier in Smith's biographical sketch, p. 126 above.

51. This paragraph offers Smith's comments on the matter which had so agitated Arthur Stedman: Robert Buchanan's "quest" for Melville in 1884 and his subsequent comments on the supposed neglect of Melville by his fellow authors of New York. In addition to Stedman's " 'Marquesan' Melville," Smith had been reading an editorial in the New York *Times*, 2 October 1891, p. 4, which he quotes above (p. 121): "when a visiting British writer a few years ago inquired [about Melville] at a gathering in New-York of distinctively literary Americans," none could tell him where Melville was living and few had ever heard of him. As for the "intelligent bibliopole" of an earlier day in Pittsfield, Smith was evidently thinking of a story the *New Englander* had carried during Melville's first year in the Berkshires: "Longfellow is known in Pittsfield as 'the man that married Mr. Appleton's daughter,' and Herman Melville as 'the fellow that bought Dr. Brewster's farm' " (*Log*, I, 402). Smith had been a Berkshire correspondent of the *New Englander* at the time.

52. Smith had previously noted, with approval, Stedman's remark in "Herman Melville's Funeral" that Melville "came of patrician blood on both sides of his family"; see pp. 99, 122 above.

53. Mrs. Melville omitted this sentence, with its references to Charles Sumner and Fanny Kemble, from the 1897 pamphlet.

54. The Springfield *Sunday Republican*, 4 October 1891, p. 6, had carried an extended notice of Melville that offers the comment on and quotation of "The Portent" to which Smith alludes here.

55. Smith's discussion of "The College Colonel" was evidently prompted by the *Republican's* observation that the poem "makes one think of Gen. W. F. Bartlett,—Frank Bartlett, the knightly soldier whom Pittsfield counts her hero with pride, and who may well have been in Melville's mind as he wrote. . . ."

56. Here again, Smith appears to be meditating Stedman's repeated remarks about the hostility provoked by *Pierre;* see p. 137 above and note 48 on p. 234 above.

57. Smith is recalling his discussion with Melville of "A Trio of American Sailor-Authors," originally appearing in the *Dublin University Magazine*, reprinted in *Littel's Living Age*, and quoted in the *Eagle* for 8 August 1856; see p. 33 above.

58. "A Trio of American Sailor-Authors," *Dublin University Magazine*, 47 (January 1856), 54, quoted inexactly. This same passage is extracted near the end of the article on Melville in Allibone's *Critical Dictionary*, II, 1265; Smith had made use of Allibone in writing previous instalments of his sketch of Melville.

59. Ulysses' speech in Shakespeare's *Troilus and Cressida,* III, iii; Mrs. Melville omitted the passage and the two paragraphs preceding it from the 1897 pamphlet.

60. "To Greylock's Most Excellent Majesty"; see *Pierre* (1971), p. vii.

61. *Pierre,* Book VII, Ch. 4; see *Pierre* (1971), pp. 131-134.

62. The family portrait "in the Athenaeum" was probably the photograph of Major Thomas Melvill, Jr., mentioned in Smith's letter of 25 October 1871 to Allan Melville (Berkshire Athenaeum): Smith had recently seen "the Major Melville photograph which is a perfect facsimile of the copy. It will be a valuable addition to our cabinet, although I dare say it does no sort of justice to the good looks of the original. I wish we could get a copy of it, and also Mr. Herman Melville, on steel for our history . . ." (see p. 36 above). Smith's reference here to Melville's "maiden aunt," Priscilla Melvill, was retained by Mrs. Melville in the 1897 pamphlet, although she omitted the earlier account of his visit to Miss Melvill in Boston, p. 122 above.

63. Ebenezer Emmons (1799-1863), geologist, physician, and teacher, was on the staffs of various educational institutions near Pittsfield, including Williams College and the Albany Medical School, between 1828 and 1852, when he moved to North Carolina as state geologist. He had earlier compiled a geological map of New York, identifying a system of formations which he named "Taconic." Chester Dewey (1784-1867), clergyman, educator, and pioneer scientist, served on the faculty of Williams College from 1810 to 1827, as principal of the Berkshire Gymnasium in Pittsfield from 1827 to 1836, and subsequently in Rochester, New York, as principal of the High School and Collegiate Institute, 1836-1850, and professor at the University of Rochester, 1851-1861. Among his other interests was the mineralogy and geology of the area near Williams College, a subject on which he published as early as 1819.

64. Without mentioning Melville by name, Smith had previously referred to this same picnic at Balanced Rock in his *Taghconic* (1852), pp. 42-43, and *Taghconic* (1879), p. 84 (Appendix B and Appendix C above). The "cunning priestess" of all three passages was probably Sarah Morewood.

65. From Arthur Stedman's "Melville of Marquesas," *Review of Reviews,* 4 (November 1891), 429; see p. 113 above.

66. In the 1897 pamphlet, Mrs. Melville emended the date of Melville's death to read "Monday, Sept. 28" and changed Smith's "illness of several years" to "illness".

67. Catherine Melville (1825-1905) married John C. Hoadley (1818-1886) in 1853 (*Log,* I, 479); Hoadley had left Pittsfield for Lawrence, but the Melvilles were still local residents. Melville had a high regard for Hoadley, whom he addressed on at least one occasion as "brother" (*Log,* II, 483).

68. Quoted from a letter of 19 April 1867 from Gansevoort to his mother in *Memorial of Henry Sanford Gansevoort,* ed. John C. Hoadley (Boston: Rand, Avery, & Co., 1875), p. 24; the allusion is to Melville's "America," lines 6-7, as printed in his *Battle-Pieces and Aspects of the War* (New York: Harper and Brothers, 1866), p. 160. Both the newspaper text and the 1897 pamphlet fail to distinguish typographically between Gansevoort's enclosing

comments and the lines he quotes from Melville's poem; moreover, both omit altogether the line "With undulating, long-drawn flow," thus blurring the image as both Melville and his cousin employed it. I have corrected the error—whether Smith's or a compositor's—by following the reading of the *Memorial*.

69. Whether Smith is quoting directly from Melville's *Timoleon* (1891) or from Stedman's "Melville of Marquesas" (p. 115 above) is impossible to say. He is clearly following Stedman in speaking of "The Return of the Sire de Nesle" as being Melville's "last poem" and having "a home significance"; see " 'Marquesan' Melville," p. 110 above, where this "last little poem" is said to have been addressed to Mrs. Melville.

70. These paragraphs, printed in the *Evening Journal* as an editorial, are obviously by Smith himself. They show his growing conception of the sketch of Melville's career, "expanding with new sources of information" (primarily Arthur Stedman's " 'Marquesan' Melville" and "Melville of Marquesas"); he may have been thinking as early as 1892 of books on both Melville and Holmes ("Holmes . . . is yet to come."). The unnamed correspondent referred to as "the most eminent of living American literary editors and critics" is very likely Edmund Clarence Stedman, although I have found no record of his corresponding with Smith.

RETROSPECTIVE ESSAYS, 1891-1892:
STEDMAN, IN *APPLETON'S ANNUAL CYCLOPAEDIA*

1. The one emendation: *153.33* Man"] Man

2. Stedman's reference in his second sentence to Melville's great-grandfather derives from the Duyckincks' *Cyclopaedia* (p. 91 above); otherwise, the article to this point follows " 'Marquesan' Melville," p. 103 above, with compression and minor verbal changes.

3. Stedman had not previously suggested that relatives' "stories of travel" influenced Melville's seafaring. Melville had taught school in Greenbush, N.Y., and Pittsfield, as noted in " 'Marquesan' Melville," p. 103 above, but not in Lansingburgh; his quarterly salary is mentioned in "Melville of Marquesas," p. 111 above.

4. The allusion to Dana's influence is from "Melville of Marquesas," p. 111 above; mention of the *Acushnet* and its sailing is taken from " 'Marquesan' Melville," p. 104 above, with the change of "chief romances" to "chief romance".

5. The account of the *Acushnet*'s cruise is from " 'Marquesan' Melville," p. 104 above; "and it may justly . . . edition of 'Typee' " is an addition here.

6. The narrative to this point continues to follow " 'Marquesan' Melville," pp. 104-105 above, with an added reference to the naming of Arrowhead—information either furnished by Mrs. Melville or taken from J. E. A. Smith's *History of Pittsfield, 1800-1876*, p. 7, or his biographical sketch of Melville, p. 130 above. Less space is given here to Melville's friendship with Hawthorne, with no quotations from their respective writings.

7. The account of Melville's lecturing and the references to his three

voyages are from " 'Marquesan' Melville," p. 106 above, with some compression.

8. The references to Melville's family at Pittsfield, his removal to New York, and his Custom House appointment are from " 'Marquesan' Melville," p. 108 above; the reference to Melville's retirement from his inspectorship, an addition, corrects the erroneous date given in "Herman Melville's Funeral," p. 100 above.

9. These three sentences are new to this sketch. Hawthorne and Melville talked at Southport, near Liverpool, in November of 1856; for Hawthorne's full report of their conversation, see *Log*, II, 529. Stedman's reference here is to the abbreviated version printed in *Passages from the English Note-Books of Nathaniel Hawthorne*, 2 vols. (Boston: Fields, Osgood, & Co., 1870), II, 156, which says only that "Melville, as he always does, began to reason of Providence and futurity, and of everything else that lies beyond human ken. . . ." When Stedman adds that in later years Melville's "conversation with friends became chiefly a philosophical monologue," one wonders whether he is reflecting his own experience or that of others such as his father or Dr. Coan.

10. The four sentences on Melville's interest in art, his walks about New York, and his evenings spent with his family are from "Herman Melville's Funeral," p. 100 above; the obligatory refutation of Robert Buchanan and the insistence that Melville's seclusion "was a matter of personal choice" are in the vein of Stedman's earlier articles.

11. The four additional sentences on Melville's later years are from " 'Marquesan' Melville," p. 109 above, modified by some rearrangement and compression; the fifth sentence, on Allan Melville, is recast from "Melville of Marquesas," p. 114 above.

12. The discussion of *Typee* and *Omoo* follows " 'Marquesan' Melville," p. 108 above, with some compression; the reference to Lowell is reminiscent of "Herman Melville's Funeral," p. 99 above.

13. Stedman's treatment of Melville's writing from *Mardi* (1849) through *Pierre* (1852) makes interesting verbal changes in the earlier version in "Melville of Marquesas," p. 112 above, adding the comment on *Moby-Dick* as "perhaps the most graphic and truthful description of whaling life ever written, although it contains some of the objectionable characteristics of 'Mardi,'" and dropping O'Brien's phrase "metaphysical and morbid meditations."

14. This reference to the Harper fire recalls "Melville of Marquesas," p. 114 above.

15. As in "Melville of Marquesas," p. 112 above, Stedman again denigrates *Israel Potter* and *The Confidence-Man*. His comments on *The Piazza Tales* are new here; "The Bell-Tower," now generally regarded as one of the weaker tales of the volume, had been the one prose work by Melville chosen for reprinting in the Stedman-Hutchinson *Library of American Literature*.

16. The comments on *Battle-Pieces* and *Clarel* condense what Stedman had written of these volumes in "Melville of Marquesas," p. 113 above.

17. The sentences on *John Marr* and *Timoleon* are a reworking of "Herman Melville's Funeral," p. 100 above; the words of Clark Russell occur in his

article "Sea Stories," published in the *Contemporary Review* in 1884 (*Log,* II, 785).

18. If the "later Californian romancer" is Bret Harte, Stedman's point is ill taken, since Harte had been unable to maintain his short-lived popularity of the early 1870's.

19. Compare "Melville of Marquesas," p. 112 above, where Stedman cites H. S. Salt in support of his own contention that Melville was basically an autobiographical writer who succeeded "in describing and investing with romance experiences and scenes actually participated in and witnessed by himself" but failed "as an inventor of character and situations."

RETROSPECTIVE ESSAYS, 1891-1892:
STEDMAN, INTRODUCTION TO *TYPEE*

1. *165.39* "Running] Running

2. Lowell had died on 12 August 1891, Melville on 28 September, and Whitman on 26 March 1892. In "Herman Melville's Funeral," p. 99 above, Stedman had briefly associated the careers of Lowell and Melville; in " 'Marquesan' Melville," p. 103 above, he named Melville with Lowell, Whitman, and other writers also born in 1819. Melville's "patrician" heritage, first mentioned in "Herman Melville's Funeral," p. 99 above, is emphasized here in contrast to Whitman's family background, which was familiar to Stedman through his editing of Whitman's *Autobiographia: The Story of a Life* (1892).

3. In " 'Marquesan' Melville," p. 103 above, Stedman had first assembled the information concerning Melville's father and grandfather that is repeated in his article for *Appleton's Annual Cyclopaedia* and again here. The opening sentence of the present paragraph, which comes from the *Cyclopaedia,* p. 150 above, derives ultimately from the Duyckincks' *Cyclopaedia* of 1855. By the time Stedman had composed the full paragraph here he was drawing also on J. E. A. Smith's biographical sketch of Melville: (1) Smith described Major Melvill as "an extreme conservative" (p. 122 above) and Stedman says that he "is reported to have been a Conservative in all matters except his opposition to unjust taxation"; (2) Stedman repeats Smith's error of "Catherine" Gansevoort rather than "Maria" (p. 123 above); (3) Stedman's reference to Burgoyne's campaign of 1777 probably reflects the long discussion in Smith (pp. 123-124 above). Mrs. Melville altered "Catherine" to "Maria" in her copies of the first edition and again in her lists of "Errors corrected in next edition".

4. To his earlier discussion of Melville's birth and education in " 'Marquesan' Melville," p. 103 above, Stedman has added here (1) the quotation from *Redburn,* Ch. 1; (2) the reference to "the family of eight brothers and sisters"; and (3) Dr. West's recollection of Melville's "struggles with mathematics." The last two points may have been picked up from Dr. Coan's " Herman Melville," p. 116 above; the passage from *Redburn* was previously quoted by H. S. Salt in his "Herman Melville," *Scottish Art Review,* 2 (November 1889), 186.

5. The references to Major Thomas Melvill, Jr., and "the 'Van Schaack place' "

may come from J. E. A. Smith's *History of Pittsfield, 1800-1876*, p. 7; see also his biographical sketch of Melville, p. 125 above. In reality, Melville's uncle was less than "successful" as a farmer and was in continued financial difficulties.

6. This paragraph elaborates on what Stedman had written of Melville's first voyage in " 'Marquesan' Melville," p. 103 above.

7. This paragraph corrects the error of "Lansingburg" for "Greenbush" in the *Cyclopaedia* article, p. 151 above, without wholly clarifying the confused chronology of " 'Marquesan' Melville," p. 103 above. Stedman echoes Smith's reference to a rebellion among Melville's students at Pittsfield but notes correctly that while teaching there he had boarded with the families of his students rather than living with his uncle. Compare Smith's biographical sketch, p. 126 above.

8. In both "Melville of Marquesas," p. 111 above, and the *Cyclopaedia* article, p. 151 above, Stedman had mentioned his "fancy" about Dana's influence on Melville's decision to undertake his second voyage. Though Raymond Weaver, *Herman Melville*, p. 131, dismissed Stedman's idea as "an ill-favoured statement," what Melville wrote to Dana on 1 May 1850 about his first reading of *Two Years Before the Mast* (*Letters*, p. 106) lends considerable support to the conjecture.

9. What Stedman says here of the *Acushnet* and its voyage to the Marquesas enlarges upon his earlier accounts; the quotation from *Moby-Dick*, Ch. 24, had been used in " 'Marquesan' Melville," p. 104 above.

10. This paragraph elaborates Stedman's previous references to the Typee Valley in " 'Marquesan' Melville," p. 104 above, and the *Cyclopaedia* article, p. 151 above; the last two sentences are new here.

11. This paragraph recapitulates what Stedman had written of Melville's return from the Marquesas in " 'Marquesan' Melville," p. 104 above, and the *Cyclopaedia* article, p. 151 above, with three additions: (1) the phrase from Dr. Coan's "Herman Melville," p. 117 above; (2) the mention of Melville's clerking in Honolulu; and (3) the reference to Melville's *White-Jacket* as "a narrative of his experiences" aboard the *United States*. Where Stedman learned of Melville's employment in Honolulu is not recorded. He probably did not know that Melville's contract with his employer there had been published in a Honolulu paper in 1873 (*Log*, II, 734).

12. Like the conclusion of the *Cyclopaedia* article, p. 154 above, this paragraph affirms Stedman's belief that Melville was successful in "directly autobiographical" writing but not in his "efforts at creative romance."

13. These three sentences are new in the Introduction.

14. These five sentences rework material of " 'Marquesan' Melville," pp. 104 and 107 above, and the *Cyclopaedia* article, pp. 151 and 153 above.

15. The first sentence of this paragraph is new; the remaining sentences follow " 'Marquesan' Melville," pp. 104-105 above, with one addition from the *Cyclopaedia* article, p. 152 above: the sentence on the naming of Arrowhead. The erroneous date of Melville's letter to Hawthorne remains uncorrected here, but in one of Mrs. Melville's two copies of *Typee* (1892) the

words "another called 'October Mountain' " have been lined out. The attribution of "October Mountain" to Melville originated with J. E. A. Smith; Mrs. Melville's collection of her husband's contributions to magazines and her listing of their titles (both in the Melville Collection of the Harvard College Library) do not include such a sketch. See note 38 on p. 233 above.

16. These two sentences are from " 'Marquesan' Melville," p. 105 above.

17. Smith's "volume on the Berkshire Hills" is *Taghconic* (1879); Stedman quotes here from p. 318, silently changing "review of the Scarlet Letter" to "review of 'Mosses from an Old Manse' " (see Appendix C above). Stedman's authority for the change was evidently one of several corrections in Mrs. Melville's copy of the book, formerly her husband's, which is now in the Melville Collection of the Harvard College Library.

18. The reference to *A Wonder-Book* (1852) and the quoted passage from pp. 252-253 are repeated from " 'Marquesan' Melville," pp. 105-106 above. In the present text, one typographical error, unmarked in either of Mrs. Melville's copies of *Typee* (1892), has been corrected, as it was in subsequent printings of the Preface: *159.12* Taconic] Jaconic (the newspaper text of " 'Marquesan' Melville" reads "Teutonic"). The bracketed identifications are Stedman's: that of G. P. R. James (1799-1860) is in " 'Marquesan' Melville"; that of Catharine Sedgwick (1789-1867) is added here.

19. This paragraph follows the shorter version in the *Cyclopaedia* article, p. 152, of two paragraphs originally appearing in " 'Marquesan' Melville," p. 106, except for changes obviously suggested by Mrs. Melville: substitution of "by way of Cape Horn" for "by the Isthmus route" and addition of "on the Meteor . . . Staten Island, N.Y." Although Mrs. Melville marked "superintendent" for correction in later printings to "governor", she did not challenge Stedman's statements that Melville had lectured in San Francisco and spoken "chiefly . . . of his adventures in the South Seas" while on the lecture platform. "The South Seas" was his subject during only one of his three seasons as a lecturer.

20. This paragraph, including the extract from Coan's letter, is taken over from " 'Marquesan' Melville," pp. 106-107 above, with a few verbal changes, the most significant being Stedman's substitution of "tendency to philosophical discussion is strikingly set forth" for the earlier "fondness for philosophical discussion is interestingly described".

21. The first sentence of this paragraph comes, with minor rephrasing, from " 'Marquesan' Melville," p. 107 above. The second and third sentences rework three sentences of the *Cyclopaedia* article, p. 152 above, dropping "grew as he advanced in years, until his conversation with friends became chiefly a philosophical monologue." in favor of "increased as he advanced in years, if possible."

22. This paragraph is taken over from " 'Marquesan' Melville," p. 107 above, with a change from "Moby Dick, or the White Whale" to "Moby Dick; or, the Whale".

23. This paragraph repeats, with some minor alterations in phrasing, what Stedman had written for " 'Marquesan' Melville," p. 108 above, and retained in the *Cyclopaedia* article, p. 152 above, with the addition there of the final

sentence. Here Stedman has added still another sentence, "This house . . .
Pittsfield." and changed the term of Melville's Custom House service from
"until 1885" to "until 1886"—a more accurate date, since Melville had resigned on 31 December 1885.

24. These two sentences follow the *Cyclopaedia* article, p. 152 above, with
the addition of the six opening words.

25. These three sentences follow the *Cyclopaedia* article, p. 152 above,
which had added to the original phrasing in "Herman Melville's Funeral," p.
100 above.

26. These five sentences combine passages from two of the earlier essays:
(1) "A few . . . Nesle.' " is from " 'Marquesan' Melville," pp. 109–110 above;
(2) "Various . . . success." is from the *Cyclopaedia* article, p. 152 above; (3)
"It has . . . sort." is modified from " 'Marquesan' Melville," p. 109 above; (4)
"His brother . . . accounts." is from the *Cyclopaedia* article, pp. 152-153
above.

27. This paragraph, including Russell's letter, first appeared in " 'Marquesan'
Melville," pp. 108–109 above; there are minor verbal changes here in the
opening sentence.

28. This paragraph was in none of the earlier essays. Stedman's second and
third sentences, comparing the attention given Melville's life and work by the
English and by the American press following his death, draws on Clark Russell's report to Stedman that "the notices in English papers were very meagre
& few," in the words of Stedman's own letter to H. S. Salt, 17 November
1891 (p. 52 above).

29. The paragraph to this point enlarges upon the allusion in "Melville of
Marquesas," p. 113 above, to Stoddard's notice of *John Marr* (1888) (see note
19 on p. 224 above). A survey of Stoddard's writing about Melville between
1866 and his posthumous *Recollections* (1903) appears in my "Melville and
Richard Henry Stoddard," *American Literature*, 43 (November 1971), 359-
370.

30. Stedman's reference to "new movements" means specifically the
Authors Club, founded in 1882: see the discussion, pp. 25–26 above; "Herman Melville's Funeral," p. 100 above; and " 'Marquesan' Melville," p. 109
above. Arthur Stedman, by his own account, "lived for some time" at his
father's residence, 44 East Twenty-Sixth Street, although he is first listed in
the New York City directory for 1890 after the Stedmans had moved to
137 West Seventy-Eighth Street (the directory gives his occupation as "editor"). When Ernest Rhys visited the Stedmans in 1888, as he recalled in his
later Introduction to *Typee* (Everyman's Library, No. 180, 1907), Melville
"was living only a few doors away" at No. 104. "But he had a hermit's reputation," Rhys was told, "and it was difficult to get more than a passing
glimpse of his 'tall, stalwart figure' [Stedman's phrase: pp. 100, 152, 161
above] and grave, preoccupied face." E. C. Stedman first wrote Melville concerning use of material in *A Library of American Literature* on 24 January
1888; another letter of 1 February 1888 refers to a recent conversation in

which Melville had said "much" to him about Walt Whitman (*Log*, II, 805-806). Arthur Stedman's initial visit to Melville may have been made at about this same time, while extracts for the anthology were being cleared, or perhaps later in the year if the idea of obtaining a portrait of Melville came as an afterthought. How often either of the Stedmans called on Melville during his remaining years is unclear. On 20 October 1888, when Melville returned books lent him by E. C. Stedman, he invited the father to "give me the pleasure of dropping in again here when you feel like it" (*Letters*, p. 288); certainly the ice had been broken by that time, for the father and possibly for the son as well.

31. Concerning Melville's last illness and various pronouncements regarding it, including Stedman's, see Mrs. Melville's memoranda, p. 171 above and note 13 on p. 246 below.

32. Stedman's observations on Melville's books and reading are new here; in "Herman Melville's Funeral," p. 100 above, he had said only that Melville "was always a great reader." Melville had long taken "much pleasure" in dramatic literature; Stedman's mention of "the 'Mermaid Series' of old plays" adds to our knowledge of what his reading in that field embraced. His copies of various works by both Schopenhauer and Hawthorne survive, though "fifteen or twenty first editions" is not an accurate tally of what the Hawthornes had actually "inscribed" to the Melvilles. For the titles involved, see Nos. 358, 444-448, and 245-261 in my *Melville's Reading: A Check-List of Books Owned and Borrowed*.

33. This paragraph on the publication of *Typee* departs considerably from passages on the same subject in " 'Marquesan' Melville," pp. 107-108 above, and the *Cyclopaedia* article, p. 153 above. Here Stedman has added (1) Gansevoort Melville's "assurance" to John Murray, (2) the statement that *Typee* was "issued in America . . . in the outward shape of a work of fiction," and (3) the two sentences "Mr. Melville . . . literature."

34. Melville to Nathaniel Hawthorne, 1? June 1851; see *Letters*, p. 130.

35. This entire paragraph is new here.

36. The first two sentences of this paragraph are new here; the next two are taken from "Melville of Marquesas," p. 113 above.

37. The reflections in this paragraph on Melville and the missionaries are an adaptation of two sentences in " 'Marquesan' Melville," p. 108 above; the comments on omission of certain passages from American editions of *Typee* and Stedman's references to his own editorial practice are additions here. Concerning the "written direction" by Melville himself that Stedman claimed to be following (discussed on p. 72 above), the Northwestern-Newberry editors write as follows in *Typee* (1968), pp. 312-313: "The only evidence of such direction now to be found among the Stedman papers at Columbia University is an undated note in Mrs. Melville's hand entitled 'Memoranda for re-issue of "Typee" (made by Mr Melville)'. . . . The fact that the 'Memoranda' note is not in Melville's hand may raise some doubts about the authority to be accorded its directives, but it cannot be lightly dismissed since many changes which are

evidently authorial appear in Melville's manuscripts of the same late years in his wife's hand." Stedman's alterations, as the editors also observe, "went far beyond" the written directive.

38. The first three sentences, with Stedman's praise of Long Ghost as "next to Captain Ahab . . . Melville's most striking delineation," are new here; the statement about the value of *Typee* and *Omoo* to "outgoing missionaries" is repeated from " 'Marquesan' Melville," p. 108 above, and "Melville of Marquesas," p. 113 above.

39. The first two sentences of this paragraph, including the reference to Salt's article, are repeated from "Melville of Marquesas," p. 112 above; the remainder of this paragraph—on *Mardi* as "a splendid failure"—is new here. Stedman's remarks concerning allegory in *Mardi* and the pernicious influence of Sir Thomas Browne upon Melville's style may be indebted to the Duyckincks' discussion of *Mardi* in their *Cyclopaedia* article on Melville (see p. 93 above) and to Fitz-James O'Brien, "Our Young Authors—Melville," *Putnam's Monthly Magazine*, 1 (February 1853), 156-157.

40. This paragraph is new here.

41. The first sentence of this paragraph is repeated from "Melville of Marquesas," p. 112 above, and the *Cyclopaedia* article, p. 153 above; Stedman had quoted Hawthorne more extensively in " 'Marquesan' Melville," pp. 105-106 above, and briefly in "Melville of Marquesas," p. 114 above. The remainder of the paragraph is new here.

42. These two paragraphs, including the references to *Mardi, Pierre,* O'Brien's article, and the Harper fire, come from "Melville of Marquesas," p. 114 above, with slight modifications in phrasing.

43. These two paragraphs on Melville's writing of 1853-1856 restate observations made previously in " 'Marquesan' Melville," p. 110 above, "Melville of Marquesas," p. 112 above, and the *Cyclopaedia* article, p. 153 above. Here Stedman again praises "Benito Cereno" and "The Bell-Tower," omits an earlier reference to "Cock-A-Doodle-Doo!," and takes a slightly more favorable view of *Israel Potter,* which had been mentioned as a possible fifth volume in the 1892 edition of Melville's principal works (p. 55 above). In Stedman's reconsidered view, *Israel Potter* "is hardly worthy of the author of 'Typee,' " and *The Confidence-Man* still "does not seem to require criticism."

44. This paragraph is a shorter version, with some rearrangement, of the section of "Melville of Marquesas" headed "Melville's Poetry," p. 113 above.

45. This paragraph, including the extract from *Moby-Dick,* Ch. 73, is new here.

46. This paragraph is also new here. The observation in the third sentence resembles a remark in " 'Marquesan' Melville," p. 109 above: "had Melville been willing to join freely in the literary movements of New York, his name would have remained before the public. . . ."

47. "A copy of the 1861 Murray *Typee,* marked by Coan with such respellings of native words, is in the Melville Collection in The Newberry Library," as the Northwestern-Newberry editors observe in *Typee* (1968), p. 313, note 17.

48. John La Farge (1835-1910) had accompanied Henry Adams on a trip to Japan, Samoa, and the South Seas in 1886; his references to Melville in letters from the Pacific during 1890 and 1891 appear in *Log*, II, 825, 831, 833.

FAMILY REMINISCENCES:
ELIZABETH SHAW MELVILLE, MEMORANDA

1. The insertion is in pencil.

2. "Bessie" was the Melvilles' unmarried daughter Elizabeth (1853-1908). Rockwood had photographed her parents in October, 1885: see Plate IV above. *The Melville Log*, Plate XV (facing II, 495), reproduces what may be a somewhat earlier photograph of the daughter.

3. The entire entry concerning the bank books is canceled in pencil.

4. The insertion is in pencil. According to the statements of account furnished Mrs. Melville by the United States Book Company and the American Publishers Corporation, she was due a total of $379.06 in royalties by 31 August 1898. After Dana Estes & Company took over the plates she received a total of $117.85 in royalties from that firm at 5 cents per copy (not 5%) between 1900 and 31 January 1906. See G. Thomas Tanselle, "The Sales of Melville's Books," pp. 202-203.

5. The insertion—"1891"—is in pencil. This added date may indicate that after Melville's death his wife either transcribed her original notes of "May 1861" or else reviewed and extended them if they had already been entered in this notebook. In May of 1861, when the country itself was on the brink of civil war, Mrs. Melville's father had recently died, his estate was in probate, and her husband was hoping for a consular appointment abroad.

6. In 1855 Melville's mother had left Pittsfield to live with her widowed brother Herman Gansevoort in Gansevoort, New York. The sentence which follows here, obviously a later addition to the account of Melville's career, is written in ink over the original pencil inscription. Mrs. Melville also refers to erysipelas on p. [230] below, where she mentions that Melville died "after two years of failing health."

7. *Chambers's Encyclopædia: A Dictionary of Useful Knowledge for the People*, 10 vols. (London: W. & R. Chambers, 1868), VI, 397. The article on Melville, after giving the erroneous date of 1860 for the publication of *Israel Potter*, continues: "when he left his farm in Massachusetts and embarked in a whaling vessel on a voyage round the world." One American edition of *Chambers's* (Philadelphia: J. B. Lippincott Co., 1875 and 1891) mentions no such voyage; another (New York, Collier, 1886) reads: "In 1860, he embarked in a whaling-vessel for a new tour round the world" (V, 321).

8. The insertion is in pencil.

9. Hawthorne and his daughter arrived on 13 March 1851, staying for at most three days. For Melville's discussion of the visit with Dr. Theodore F. Wolfe, see p. 26 above and note 13 on p. 210 above. The visit is also mentioned in Stedman's " 'Marquesan' Melville," p. 105 above, and Smith's biographical sketch of Melville, p. 133 above.

10. The account of Melville that follows, pp. ⟦223⟧ - ⟦230⟧, was evidently drafted or transcribed here after Melville's death, presumably for reference purposes. There are especially close parallels in sequence and phrasing with both Arthur Stedman's " 'Marquesan' Melville" and Dr. Titus Munson Coan's "Herman Melville," which sets forth "data, now for the first time fully given," concerning Melville's career (p. 118 above). See pp. 68 and 70 above and Mrs. Melville's reference to Coan on p. 177 above.

11. The insertion is in pencil. Concerning Dr. West, see Arthur Stedman, " 'Marquesan' Melville," p. 101 above; Titus Munson Coan, "Herman Melville," p. 116 above; J. E. A. Smith, biographical sketch of Melville, p. 125 above. Evidently Mrs. Melville reviewed this entry in 1895, when Dr. West was still living; he died on 9 March 1900.

12. With Mrs. Melville's account of the *Meteor* voyage, compare Coan's "Herman Melville," p. 118 above. See also note 7 on p. 245 above.

13. On p. ⟦211⟧ above, Mrs. Melville mentions "two attacks of erisypelas—the last in April 1890—both of which weakened him greatly"; her letters of 1891 to Catherine Gansevoort Lansing trace a further decline during the winter and spring of 1890-1891. He had "not been very well all winter," she wrote on 8 January 1891, and was "pretty ill for the last week or so"; his strength had "gradually returned" but "he has not been out yet or even down stairs" (*Log*, II, 828, 831). By 28 May he was "tolerably well but not strong" and "not well enough to be left alone," though he would be able to accompany her to Fire Island (*Log*, II, 835). Melville's physician, Dr. Everett S. Warner, who began his final attendance in July, gave the cause of Melville's death on 28 September as "Cardiac dilation, Mitral regurgitation . . . Contributory Asthenia" (*Log*, II, 836). Among the biographers, Arthur Stedman wrote in "Herman Melville's Funeral" of Melville's "lingering illness," "the beginning of failing health, some three years ago," and "his final illness" as having set in "last spring" (pp. 99, 100 above). In Stedman's Introduction to the 1892 *Typee* he said only that Melville's "serious illness had lasted a number of months" (p. 163 above), but to Dr. Coan he remarked later that Melville "was confined to his bed for a year before his death" (p. 45 above)—evidently something of an exaggeration. When Mrs. Melville reprinted J. E. A. Smith's biographical sketch of Melville she deleted the phrase "of several years" from his statement that Melville died "after a lingering and painful illness of several years, during which he manifested heroic fortitude, and patience, and also a considerate regard for those who attended him which commanded their admiration as well as their gratitude" (p. 148 above).

14. The date—evidently that of the entry which immediately follows—is canceled in both pencil and ink.

15. (Charles) James Billson (1858-1932) had opened a correspondence with Melville on 21 August 1884. The two volumes that Mrs. Melville mentions here are listed as Nos. 521 and 517, respectively, in my *Melville's Reading: A Check-List of Books Owned and Borrowed: Vane's Story, Weddah and Om-el-Bonain, and Other Poems* (London, 1881) and *The City of Dreadful Night, and Other Poems* (London, 1880).

16. "James Thomson: Poet, Essayist, and Critic," published on 10 February 1885. The clipping is in an envelope inside the front cover of Melville's copy of H. S. Salt's *Life* of Thomson, 1889 (Sealts No. 435).

17. Sealts Nos. 518 and 519: *Essays and Phantasies* (London, 1881), inscribed by Billson on 7 October 1885, and *Satires and Profanities* (London, 1884).

18. Barrs, like Billson, was a resident of Leicester; on 13 January 1890, he wrote to Melville forwarding a copy of his friend Salt's "Herman Melville," *Scottish Art Review*, 2 (November 1889), 186-190, and acknowledging the gift, through Billson, of a copy of Melville's *John Marr* (1888).

19. Sealts Nos. 522 and 393: Thomson's *A Voice from the Nile, and Other Poems* (London, 1884), and a reproduction of a copy Billson had made of the *Rubáiyát of Omar Khayyám* as James Thomson had transcribed it in manuscript. Melville acknowledged the gifts of both Barrs and Billson in writing Billson on 2 April 1886.

20. Sealts No. 520: *Shelley, a Poem: With Other Writings Relating to Shelley . . .* (London, 1884).

21. Sealts No. 435: *The Life of James Thomson ("B.V.") . . .* (London, 1889).

22. A note penciled below the entry by Mrs. Metcalf—"See Malvern Brick— E. M. M."—refers to a souvenir that Melville had evidently acquired while on this expedition to Virginia; the brick is now in the Melville Room of the Berkshire Athenaeum. The battle fought at Malvern in 1862 is commemorated in Melville's poem "Malvern Hill," in *Battle-Pieces* (1866).

23. Inscription on this page is in ink, written over previous inscription in pencil. The entries immediately following concern Melville's paternal grandfather, Major Thomas Melvill (1751-1832).

24. Major Melvill's residence "formerly stood near the easterly corner of Green and Staniford Streets," according to Francis S. Drake; he served forty-seven years as one of the Boston firewards, from 1779 to 1825. See Drake's *Tea Leaves . . . With an Introduction, Notes, and Biographical Notices of the Boston Tea Party* (Boston: A. O. Crane, 1884), pp. cxxix–cxxxv. Mrs. Melville gave her husband a copy of this book in 1886 (Sealts No. 498).

25. Drake's illustrations in *Tea Leaves* include a drawing of the portrait, then "in the possession of his grand-daughter, Mrs. Samuel Downer, of Dorchester" (Nancy Melvill D'Wolf Downer, 1814-1901), and another drawing of the glass vial of tea from the Boston Tea Party, in which Major Melvill had participated, "in the possession of Mrs. Thomas Melvill, [Jr.,] of Galena, Illinois"—Herman Melville's Aunt Mary Ann Augusta Hobart Melvill (1796-1884); George R. Melvill (1826-1899), mentioned above, was her son. The vial of tea, once a feature of the Melvill home in Boston (p. 22 above), had been exhibited at Broadhall when it passed to Major Thomas Melvill, Jr., and his family after the senior Major Melvill's death; Cornelius Mathews and Evert Duyckinck reported seeing it at Broadhall in 1850, although the Duyckincks' *Cyclopaedia* (1855) mentions it as "in possession of Chief-Justice Shaw of Massachusetts" (p. 92 above).

26. Henry Dwight Sedgwick, "Reminiscences of Literary Berkshire," appeared not in 1894 but in the following year: see the *Century Illustrated Monthly Magazine,* 50 (August 1895), 552-568. Sedgwick's article recalls the memorable ascent of Monument Mountain on 5 August 1850, by a group of literati including Melville and Hawthorne; apart from the ladies, as Sedgwick recalled, he himself was "the only one of the party who had not written a book." With his essay appear portraits of Jonathan Edwards, Orville Dewey, Emerson, Thoreau, J. G. Holland, and Melville (p. 563). That captioned "Herman Melville, in 1861" is reproduced here in Plate I. The original ambrotype is No. 6 in "A Checklist of the Portraits of Herman Melville" by Morris Star, *Bulletin of the New York Public Library,* 71 (September 1967), 468-473.

27. All inscription on this page is in pencil. An initial entry concerning gifts to Melville by Peter Gansevoort was later erased and transferred to p. ⟦326⟧ of the memoranda.

28. An old English grandfather clock, given to Melville by his uncle Herman Gansevoort, then given in turn to Melville's daughter Frances Melville Thomas. In *Herman Melville,* p. 265, Mrs. Metcalf recalled seeing the clock in two successive houses where she lived with her parents. Here, on the facing page, ⟦266⟧, is a penciled note by her mother: "at 63"—i.e., at 63 Montrose Avenue, South Orange, New Jersey—with an arrow pointing to the entry concerning the clock; beneath this, Mrs. Metcalf added in pencil: "[to] J[eannette]. O[gden]. Chapin [her youngest sister] after Mother's death [in 1938]."

29. Probably a copy made by the New York photographer of the interior photographed on 5 August 1870, by C. Seaver, Jr.; see *Family Correspondence of Herman Melville,* pp. 68-69, and the reproduction facing p. 64. This photograph is the basis for line drawings used to illustrate Arthur Stedman's "'Marquesan' Melville," p. 105 above, and Mrs. Harriette M. Plunkett's article on Melville and Hawthorne in the Springfield, Massachusetts, *Sunday Republican,* 1 July 1900 (see p. 78 above). The latter specifically identifies the scene as Mrs. Melville does here: "The kitchen of the old farmhouse used by the Melville family as a dining-room."

30. The inscription on this page is in pencil.

31. Major Thomas Melvill's wife was Priscilla Scollay (1755-1833).

32. Inscription on this page is in ink, written over the original pencil inscription.

33. The entire entry is canceled in pencil. General Luigi Palma di Cesnola (1832-1904), author of *Cyprus, Its Ancient Cities, Tombs, and Temples* (1877), became secretary of the Metropolitan Museum in 1877 and served as its director from 1879 until his death.

34. Facing this entry on p. ⟦312⟧ is Mrs. Metcalf's note, in pencil, her references being to herself and her three sisters: to "E[leanor], F[rances], K[atherine], & J[eannette]. each 1 (framed). 2 to Museum of Fine Arts—Boston—".

35. Below this entry on the same page is a note inscribed in ink by Mrs. Thomas: "*I* have given it to Jeannette F. M. T."

36. All inscription on this page is from bottom to top rather than from right to left.

37. "Eagle B. Indian" is partially enclosed by a continuous line.

38. Within this entry, which is canceled in pencil, "C", "C", "M. P.", and "C" are each enclosed by continuous lines. Below the entry is a note by Mrs. Thomas, inscribed in ink and underlined in pencil: *"Lost in box which was stolen";* her reference is to a box of valuables stolen in 1905 from the Metropolitan Safe Deposit Company, 3 East 14th Street, New York (*Log,* I, xiv). Mrs. Melville's entries here and on p. ⟦267⟧ may have been made about 1900: on 27 April of that year she wrote to Melville's cousin Catherine Gansevoort Lansing thanking her for "the memoranda about the tankard and the other old silver" and also mentioning "the old clock" of the entry above (see Mrs. Metcalf's *Herman Melville,* p. 289).

39. The original inscription of this entry is in ink, canceled in pencil; a note by Mrs. Thomas, also inscribed in ink, is written vertically along the left margin of the entry: "Probably in box which was stolen" (see note 38 on p. 249 above). "Minnie" Hoadley was Melville's niece Maria Hoadley Mackintosh (1855-1904).

40. The original inscription of this entry is in ink; the inserted inscription is in pencil; the entire entry is canceled in pencil. I have not identified "Aunt Lucretia."

41. The last two entries, concerning the Staffordshire and the Wedgwood, are inscribed in pencil.

42. The entire entry on pp. ⟦320⟧ and ⟦321⟧ is canceled in pencil. Following it on p. ⟦321⟧ is a note inscribed in ink by Mrs. Thomas, concerning the shaving mug: "Given to M[useum]. of F[ine]. A[rts]. Boston".

43. The insertion is in pencil—evidently after Mrs. Melville had consulted other records.

44. The preceding cancellation and the inscription of the inserted date are both in pencil.

45. The cancellation is in ink.

46. The insertion is in pencil. Mrs. Thurston, mentioned within the original entry, was the mother of Allan Melville's first wife, Sophia (1827-1858); Dr. Hayward's wife, née Caroline Knapp (see p. ⟦336⟧), was Mrs. Melville's aunt; Priscilla Melvill (1784-1862) willed Melville $900 (see p. ⟦350⟧). The Florence apartment house was located at 105 East 18th Street, at the corner of Fourth Avenue, New York City; as Mrs. Metcalf recalled in her *Herman Melville,* p. 288, her grandmother and aunt took meals "at their own table" in its spacious dining room (see p. 65 above). William Charvat, "Melville's Income," *American Literature,* 15 (November 1943), 251-261, clarifies certain financial details concerning the Melville residences in Pittsfield and New York. Melville himself had originally held title to Arrowhead, but in 1860, before embarking on the *Meteor,* he conveyed it to Lemuel Shaw in return for cancellation of all his debts to his father-in-law; Shaw in turn transferred the title to his daughter, Mrs. Melville. Following Shaw's death in 1861 she received as her share of his estate the sum of $15,114.27, paid in three instalments during 1861-1862; it was this legacy that made possible the Melvilles' move to New York in 1863. Records of Conveyance at the Hall of Records in New York, which Charvat consulted, confirm the figures given here, showing that Mrs. Melville—not her

250 Notes to Pages 174-176

husband—bought the New York property from Allan Melville on 25 April 1863 for $7,750 and the Pittsfield house, and that she sold it on 15 April 1892, for $16,250.

47. The inscription of the insertion is in ink. Melville's payment, intended for expenses of the Gansevoort family lot, was sent to Catherine Gansevoort Lansing, his cousin, with a letter of 23 May 1890 (*Letters*, p. 295).

48. Below this entry is Mrs. Melville's broken line, its segments separated by two vertical strokes of the pen—the same device is used to designate chapter divisions in the manuscript of *Billy Budd, Sailor,* with which Mrs. Melville was assisting her husband before his death. The device is represented by a diamond (—— ◊ ——) here and on pp. ⟦338⟧ and ⟦339⟧ of the memoranda.

49. A note below this entry, inscribed in ink by Mrs. Thomas, reads: "I gave it to E[leanor]. M[elville]. M[etcalf]. (F. M. T.)"; the portrait (No. 2.1 in Star's "Checklist") now hangs in the Houghton Library at Harvard University, the gift of Mrs. Metcalf before her death.

50. Shaw, born in 1828, was Mrs. Melville's half-brother.

51. Thomas (1830-1884), Francis Priscilla (1827-1885), Helen Maria (Mrs. George Griggs, 1817-1888), and Augusta (1821-1876), brother and sisters of Melville.

52. Mrs. Hayward and Mrs. Marett were sisters of Mrs. Melville's mother, Elizabeth Knapp Shaw (1784-1822); Josiah Knapp was their father.

53. Both entries on this page are canceled in pencil. Inscribed in ink along the left margin of p. ⟦337⟧ is this note by Mrs. Thomas: "Lost in box which was stolen" (see note 38 on p. 249 above). Below the second entry is this note, inscribed in pencil by Mrs. Metcalf: "Melville folder at Craigie House—" (Cambridge, Massachusetts).

54. Inscribed in pencil along the right margin of this entry is this note (by Mrs. Thomas?): "Gave to A. Putnam [?]".

55. The sculpture is in the Gallery of Statues in the Vatican Museum, which Melville had visited in 1857; the two handbooks cited here may well have been used by him at that time and also in drafting his lecture "Statues in Rome," which he delivered during the lecture season of 1857-1858. (1) Murray's *Hand-Book for Travellers in Central Italy, Including the Papal States, Rome, and the Cities of Etruria* (London: John Murray, 1843), p. 415, lists the statue as No. 414; the account of it, which Mrs. Melville closely paraphrases here, remained unchanged in later nineteenth-century editions. (2) Emil Braun, *Handbook of the Ruins and Museums of Rome. A Guide for Travellers, Artists and Lovers of Antiquity* (Brunswick: Frederick Vieweg and Son; Rome, J. Spithöver, 1856), pp. 217-218, lists the statue as No. 92; Mrs. Melville draws here from the fifth and seventh of Braun's eight paragraphs on the "Ariadne."

56. The inscription on the engraving by Giuseppe Longhi (1766-1831) would appear to be a free rendering of Horace, *Epistles,* II, i (addressed to the Emperor Augustus). This entry is canceled in pencil; along its right margin is this note by Mrs. Thomas, inscribed in pencil: "gave to E[leanor?]." The present location of the engraving is unknown.

57. At the foot of p. ⟦340⟧, with an arrow pointing to this entry, is a note by Mrs. Thomas, inscribed in ink: "Gave to Seaman's Institute New York". The information recorded by Mrs. Melville concerning Ambroise Louis Garnery, or Garneray (1783-1857), apparently derives from one of several reference works by Shearjashub Spooner: both his *Biographical and Critical Dictionary of Painters, Engravers, Sculptors and Architects* (New York, 1853), p. 343, and his *Biographical History of the Fine Arts* (2 vols.; New York, 1855), I, 343, note that the junior Garnery "painted naval battles, and other marine subjects . . . such as the capture of an English frigate by an American . . . ; also the Battle of Navarino. . . . He also engraved and published a pictorial work, entitled, 'Views on the Ports and Coasts of France.'"

In *Moby-Dick,* Ch. 56, "Of the Less Erroneous Pictures of Whales, and the True Pictures of Whaling Scenes," Melville praises as "by far the finest, though in some details not the most correct, presentations of whales and whaling scenes to be anywhere found, . . . two large French engravings, well executed, . . . taken from paintings by one Garneray. Respectively, they represent attacks on the Sperm and Right Whale. . . ." A description of each engraving follows, with the further observation that "Who Garneray the painter is, or was, I know not." Concerning the two prints, see M. V. and Dorothy Brewington, *Kendall Whaling Museum Prints* (Sharon, Mass.: Kendall Whaling Museum, 1969), p. 65: Items 197 ("Pêche du Cachalot," 23 1/2 x 32 inches) and 196 ("Pêche de la Baleine," 23 3/4 x 32 inches); reproductions appear on pp. 64 and 63, respectively.

58. This entry is heavily canceled in pencil. The reference may be to Karl Gustaf Hellqvist (1851- ?).

59. Inscribed in pencil following this entry is a note (by Mrs. Thomas?): "incorrect it was probably by Ezra Ames".

60. This entry is canceled in pencil. Both François Pascal Gérard (1770-1837) and Jacques Louis David (1748-1825) painted Mme Recamier (1775-1849). According to Melville's niece Charlotte Hoadley, "The family tradition has always been that Fanny Fleury [Françoise Fleury (1781-1814)] was an adopted daughter of Madame Recamier and that she was married to Thomas Melville [Thomas Melvill, Jr. (1776-1845)] from Madame Recamier's salon. I have in my possession Fanny Fleury's miniature in an exquisitely carved tortoise-shell box, with her monogram wrought in the carving. I also own the miniature pin painted by Copley of Deborah Scollay. . . . She married John Melville, uncle of the Thomas Melville [Thomas Melvill (1751-1832)] who married Priscilla Scollay." See *Hudson-Mohawk Genealogical and Family Memoirs,* ed. Cuyler Reynolds (New York: Lewis Historical Publishing Company, 1911), I, 64.

61. See p. ⟦350⟧ of the memoranda.

62. The insertion is inscribed in pencil. Willis, who died on 7 May 1900, at his home in Detroit, was a poet, editor, and teacher, brother of the better-known Nathaniel P. Willis and Mrs. Sara Payson Parton ("Fanny Fern"). The opening paragraphs of Coan's "Herman Melville," p. 116 above, mention all of these names except that of Willis, though in a somewhat different sequence.

Having posed the question of which name "will endure the longer as author or artist," Coan singles out *Typee* as being "surer of immortality than any other work by any other name on the list." In view of the differences in phrasing and in the sequence of names between Coan's paragraphs and the present entry, it appears that Mrs. Melville is quoting a letter from him that antedates the essay—possibly one requesting from her the very "data . . . for the first time fully given" that his article claims to be setting forth (p. 118 above).

63. This entry is canceled in pencil.

64. This and the preceding entry are inscribed in ink, both being rewritten over canceled pencil inscriptions—apparently of the same material. The references are to Lucy Melvill Nourse (1795-1877) and Priscilla Melvill (see p. ⟦325⟧ of the memoranda and note 46 above). On 6 November 1878, Mrs. Melville in a letter to Catherine Gansevoort Lansing reported that she had been "spending Aunt Lucy's special legacy to me ($100.00) on our back parlor" (*Log*, II, 770).

65. This second entry concerning the jug was evidently made later in 1897 than that on p. ⟦347⟧. Writing to Catherine Gansevoort Lansing on 5 September of that year, Mrs. Melville acknowledged a letter of 12 July "with the enclosure from Mr. Lemon. . . . I hope you took occasion when in Boston to go out to the 'Wayside Inn' and see the 'old jug'—If so, do write me about it—" (Gansevoort-Lansing Collection, New York Public Library).

66. This entry is in pencil. The reference is to an unsigned article, "Chief Justice Shaw," *American Law Review*, 2 (1867-1868), 47-71; the volume bears the imprint of Little, Brown and Company, Boston, 1868.

FAMILY REMINISCENCES:
ELEANOR MELVILLE THOMAS METCALF, RECOLLECTIONS

1. In her set of the Constable edition of Melville (now in the Brown University Library) Mrs. Metcalf made marginal comments on two passages which are relevant to her observations here. Where Melville in *Mardi*, Ch. 150, wrote of the proud Bardianna: "I stand stiff as a pike and will abate not one vertebra of my stature" (II, 189), she commented: "H. M. stood so"; where in *Redburn*, Ch. 31, the narrator remarks: "My gate was erect" (p. 195), she commented: "Was in old age too".

2. Mrs. Osborne recalls the same custom; see p. 183 above.

3. Mrs. Osborne also remembers the butterfly; see p. 184 above.

4. Compare *White-Jacket*, Ch. 91: " 'Who's Commodore Tiddery-Eye [Tiridates]?' cried the forecastle-man." In *Billy Budd, Sailor*, which Melville was writing during the very years that Mrs. Metcalf was recalling here, there are a number of episodes "so closely resembling passages in Melville's earlier works as to raise the question whether he . . . had read them so recently that he unconsciously echoed even their phrasing." So Harrison Hayford and I observed in our edition of that work (Chicago: University of Chicago Press, 1962), p. 135; the same question pertains to the affectionate phrase Melville addressed to his granddaughter.

FAMILY REMINISCENCES:
FRANCES THOMAS OSBORNE, RECOLLECTIONS

1. J. E. A. Smith observes in his biographical sketch, p. 137 above, that for the Melvilles during the years in New York, "death followed death among their relations and dearest friends in such rapid succession that there was scarcely a year when the family could be said to be out of mourning, . . . although custom did not in all cases require the wearing of its outward symbols."

2. Mrs. Osborne's mother recalled that this episode occurred in 1887 ("Frances aetat 4"; *Log,* II, 804).

3. On Mrs. Metcalf's recollection of the same custom, see p. 178 above.

4. "This bust and two urns were given to the South Orange (New Jersey) Public Library but their present location is not known" [Mrs. Osborne's note].

5. See Elizabeth Shaw Melville's memoranda, p. 176 above and note 57 on p. 251 above.

6. Melville's volumes of Schopenhauer, acquired during his last years, are now in the Melville Collection of the Harvard College Library. See Arthur Stedman, Introduction to *Typee* (1892), p. 163 above.

7. On Mrs. Metcalf's recollection of the butterfly, see p. 178 above.

8. Melville had written a poem for the *John Marr* volume of 1888 entitled "The Aeolian Harp: At the Surf Inn"; see *Collected Poems,* p. 194.

9. Melville's voyage to Bermuda and return took place in March of 1888 (*Log,* II, 806).

APPENDIX B

1. The venerable Pittsfield Elm, which had long been the subject of local anxiety, remained standing until 1861. Smith's quotation is from Ch. 28 of *Moby-Dick;* he alludes briefly to the same passage in the biographical sketch, p. 134 above. Compare *Taghconic* (1879), pp. 34-35 (Appendix C above).

2. Smith applies these same lines to Melville in the biographical sketch, p. 127 above.

3. The "hand which has written many a witty and clever volume" was evidently Melville's; the "cunning priestess" was probably Sarah Morewood. Smith reprinted this passage, with minor variations, in *Taghconic* (1879), p. 84 (Appendix C above), and alluded to the same incident in the biographical sketch, p. 147 above.

4. Smith incorporated this paragraph—including the erroneous spelling "Pynchons" for "Pyncheons"—into an expanded discussion of Melville and Hawthorne in *Taghconic* (1879), p. 318 (Appendix C above).

APPENDIX C

1. Melville's copy of this edition, inscribed in his hand "Kindly presented by Godfrey Greylock, 1879.", is in the Melville Collection of the Harvard College Library.

2. In adapting his earlier passage in *Taghconic* (1852), p. 13 (see Appendix B above), to reflect the fall of the Elm in 1861, Smith retained the quotation from *Moby-Dick,* Ch. 28.

3. Adapted from *Taghconic* (1852), pp. 42-43 (Appendix B above).

4. The second and third sentences of this paragraph condense what Melville himself had written and Smith had adapted for *The History of Pittsfield, 1800-1876,* pp. 398-400; the same material is drawn upon in the biographical sketch, p. 125 above. There on p. 126 and again in *The Poet Among the Hills* (1895), p. 28 (Appendix D above), Smith gives somewhat different versions of Melville's school-teaching at Pittsfield.

5. Smith is adapting in this paragraph —with a correction of "1852" to "1850" —what he had already written for *The History of Pittsfield, 1800-1876,* pp. 7-8, concerning Arrowhead (for the passage, see note 30 on p. 230 above). Some of the same phrasing recurs in both the biographical sketch, p. 130 above, and *The Poet Among the Hills* (1895), pp. 29-30 (Appendix D above).

6. In this account of the friendship of Melville and Hawthorne Smith expands upon his brief paragraph in *Taghconic* (1852), p. 211 (Appendix B above), and adds his initial version of the encounter on Monument Mountain, 5 August 1850, as reported to him by an unnamed informant ("As the story was told to me . . ."). The second and third versions occur respectively in the biographical sketch, pp. 132-133 above, and *The Poet Among the Hills* (1895), pp. 31-32 (Appendix D above).

Smith's informant was of course in error if he stated that Melville had written an earlier review of *The Scarlet Letter* in the *Literary World.* In Melville's copy of *Taghconic* (1879), Smith's reference to a "review of the Scarlet Letter" is changed in Mrs. Melville's hand to read "review of Mosses from an old Manse"; such a reading, however, would place publication of Melville's "Hawthorne and His Mosses" *before* the expedition to Monument Mountain on 5 August when in reality it was not published until 17 and 24 August. Although forgetful of the exact circumstances, Mrs. Melville may well have responded to the essential truth of the Hawthorne-Melville relationship as it developed in 1850 and as Smith, too, evidently grasped it: that the appearance of Melville's essay on Hawthorne did indeed make "two very sensitive men shy of each other" until they had learned "each other's character" more fully, even though this learning took place *after* their first meeting on Monument Mountain.

APPENDIX D

1. Mrs. Melville's copy of this volume, inscribed "Mrs. Herman Melville with the best regards of her friend, J. E. A. Smith.", is in the Melville Collection of the Harvard College Library. Laid in are an advertisement of the book (one leaf) and clippings including a review of it published in the Pittsfield *Evening Journal,* 5 July 1895.

2. Smith's note at this point (pp. 28-29) reads as follows: "In calling this old mansion 'Broadhall' here and elsewhere, we deliberately, for the sake of

convenience and intelligibility, commit an anachronism, rather than change the name with every change of owners, which is the country wont. It was named some three years after Melville, Longfellow, and ex-President Tyler were boarders in it; and in this wise: It had then become the residence of Mr. J. R. Morewood, and at a little party in its parlors—not by any means 'all silent,' it was declared that a mansion with so much character [[29]] ought to have a significant name. The selection of one from the variety proposed was left to chance. Each proposer wrote his proposed name on a slip of paper and dropped it in a basket; the first drawn from it, to be accepted. This chanced to be 'Broadhall,' which was written by Herman Melville. The selection was so 'pat' that it was hailed with unanimous approval; although some serious, or rather merry, suspicion was expressed that chance—lest she might prove Miss Chance—had a judicious adviser in the person of some one of the ladies of the mansion." See the biographical sketch, p. 130 above and note 29 on p. 230 above, for other accounts of the drawing by Smith and a differing version by Mrs. Morewood.

3. The Melvilles had summered at Broadhall in 1850, not 1848, as Smith has it here, or 1849, as in the biographical sketch, p. 129 above.

4. This and the preceding paragraph enlarge upon what Smith had previously written concerning Arrowhead and "I and My Chimney," Melville's fondness for Berkshire excursions, and October Mountain: first in *The History of Pittsfield, 1800-1876*, pp. 7-8, and *Taghconic* (1879), p. 199 (see Appendix C above, and especially note 4 on p. 254 above), and later in the biographical sketch, pp. 131, 133-134 above. In the present passage Smith makes no attribution to Melville of a sketch called "October Mountain," as he had done in 1876, 1879, and 1891.

5. Smith's date is in error; the Hawthornes settled at Lenox in May of 1850.

6. This paragraph constitutes the third of Smith's second-hand accounts of the excursion to Monument Mountain on 5 August 1850. Note that here as in *Taghconic* (1879), p. 318 (Appendix C above), Smith erroneously attributes to Melville the *Literary World*'s review of *The Scarlet Letter;* the biographical sketch mentions only "a most appreciative article upon Hawthorne as an author" (p. 132 above).

7. This paragraph is a reworking of what Smith had written in the biographical sketch concerning the Hawthorne and Melville families and the "philosophical seances" of the two authors (p. 133 above).

Chronology of
Melville's Life

1819   Herman Melvill is born in New York City, 1 August, to Allan and
Maria Gansevoort Melvill.

1825   Herman Melvill enters the New-York Male High School.

1828   Herman Melvill named the best speaker in the High School's introductory department.

1830   Allan Melvill, having suffered business reverses, moves his family
to Albany, New York, where Herman Melvill and his brother
Gansevoort enter the Albany Academy.

1832   Allan Melvill dies on 28 January. Gansevoort and Herman are
withdrawn from the Albany Academy, Herman to work as a clerk
in the New York State Bank.

1834   [?] Herman works on the farm of his uncle, Thomas Melvill, at
Pittsfield, Massachusetts.

1835   Herman joins the Albany Young Men's Association, clerks in his
brother Gansevoort's store, and enters the Albany Classical School.

1837   Gansevoort's business fails. In June, Thomas Melvill moves his
family from Pittsfield to Galena, Illinois. In the Fall, Herman
begins teaching in a district school at Pittsfield.

1838   Herman returns to Albany, becoming president of the Philo Logos
debating society. His mother (now spelling the name "Melville")
moves her family to Lansingburgh, near Albany; in the Fall,
Herman studies surveying and engineering at the Lansingburgh
Academy.

1839   In May, Herman publishes two "Fragments from a Writing Desk"
in the *Democratic Press & Lansingburgh Advertiser*. In June,
having failed to find a position in the engineering department of
the Erie Canal, he sails aboard the merchant ship *St. Lawrence*
from New York for Liverpool with the rating of "boy," spending
five weeks in Liverpool with the ship and returning to New York
on 1 October. In the Fall, he again teaches school, at Greenbush,
New York.

1840   At the end of the school term, unpaid for his teaching, Melville
goes to Galena, Illinois, with his friend James E. M. Fly to visit
Thomas Melvill and his family. In December, with no other work

257

in prospect, Melville goes to New Bedford, Massachusetts, where he signs aboard the whale-ship *Acushnet,* Valentine Pease, Master.

1841   On 3 January, the *Acushnet* sails from Fairhaven, Massachusetts, for the Pacific Ocean via Rio de Janeiro and Cape Horn.

1842   On 9 July, at the Marquesas Islands, Melville and Richard Tobias Greene desert the *Acushnet,* escaping to the interior of the island of Nukuheva. On 9 August, Melville signs on the Australian whaler *Lucy Ann.* On 24 September, at Tahiti, some of the crew, having refused duty, are imprisoned by the British Consul; a few days later Melville too is imprisoned, but in October he and John Troy, a shipmate, escape to the nearby island of Eimeo. In early November, Melville signs as a boat-steerer on the whaler *Charles and Henry,* of Nantucket.

1843   In April, Melville arrives aboard the *Charles and Henry* at Lahaina, Hawaiian Islands, where he is discharged in May. During the summer he works in Honolulu, where in August he signs as ordinary seaman on the American frigate *United States,* homeward bound by way of the Marquesas, Tahiti, Valparaiso, and Callao.

1844   After visiting Lima, Peru, and cruising to Mazatlan, Melville reaches Rio de Janeiro in August and is discharged at Boston on 14 October. Joining his family in Lansingburgh, he begins writing a narrative of his adventures.

1845   Harper and Brothers reject Melville's manuscript. In July, Gansevoort Melville, named Secretary of the American Legation at London, takes his brother's manuscript to England, where in December John Murray accepts it for publication.

1846   On 27 February, Murray publishes Melville's manuscript as *Narrative of a Four Months' Residence Among the Natives of a Valley of the Marquesas Islands; or, A Peep at Polynesian Life;* on 17 March, Wiley and Putnam publish it in New York as *Typee: A Peep at Polynesian Life. During a Four Months' Residence in a Valley of the Marquesas.* 12 May, Gansevoort Melville dies in London. In July, when Toby Greene turns up in Buffalo, New York, Melville sees him and adds "The Story of Toby" to the revised American edition. In December, Harper and Brothers and John Murray accept Melville's second book.

1847   In February, although Melville is already planning a third book, he visits Washington, D.C., as a federal office seeker. On 27 March, Murray publishes *Omoo: A Narrative of Adventures in the South Seas; Being a Sequel to the "Residence in the Marquesas Islands";* about 1 May, the Harpers publish *Omoo: A Narrative of Adventures in the South Seas.* In New York, Melville writes for the *Literary World,* edited by his friend Evert A. Duyckinck, and the humorous weekly *Yankee Doodle.* On 4 August, at Boston, he marries Elizabeth Shaw, daughter of Lemuel Shaw, Chief Justice of the Supreme Court of Massachusetts; after a honeymoon trip to Canada they settle in New York.

1848   Melville works on his third book, which on 15 November the
        Harpers agree to publish.

1849   On 16 February, at Boston, a first child, Malcolm, is born to the
        Melvilles. On 16 March Richard Bentley publishes *Mardi: and a
        Voyage Thither* in London; on 14 April the Harpers publish the
        book in New York. In June Melville completes his fourth book,
        *Redburn: His First Voyage. Being the Sailor-boy Confessions and
        Reminiscences of the Son-of-a-Gentleman, in the Merchant Service,*
        published in London by Richard Bentley on 29 September and in
        New York by the Harpers on 14 November. In August, Melville
        completes his fifth book, *White-Jacket; or The World in a Man-of-
        War,* which is accepted by the Harpers in September. On 11 Oc-
        tober Melville sails for England, carrying the proofs of *White-
        Jacket;* after visiting London, Paris, Brussels, Cologne, and the
        Rhineland he concludes an agreement with Bentley for the pub-
        lication of *White-Jacket* and sails from Portsmouth for New York
        on Christmas morning.

1850   On 1 February Melville reaches New York, where he begins a
        sixth book, about the whale fishery. *White-Jacket* is published in
        London by Bentley on 23 January (though not released until
        about 1 February) and in New York by the Harpers on 21 March.
        In July Melville takes his wife and son to Pittsfield for the summer,
        staying with his cousin Robert Melvill. On 5 August, during a visit
        from Evert Duyckinck, Melville is introduced to Nathaniel
        Hawthorne, then living in Lenox, Massachusetts; on 17 and 24
        August Duyckinck's *Literary World* publishes Melville's "Hawthorne
        and His Mosses." In September Melville buys a farm adjoining the
        Melvill property and moves his family there.

1851   As his friendship with Hawthorne develops Melville continues work
        on his whaling book, which is finally completed in July; on 18 Oc-
        tober Bentley publishes it in London as *The Whale;* by 14 Novem-
        ber the Harpers publish it in New York as *Moby-Dick; or, The Whale.*
        On 22 October a second child, Stanwix, is born to the Melvilles.
        On 21 November the Hawthornes leave Lenox for West Newton.
        Melville begins his seventh book.

1852   Melville's new book is accepted by the Harpers in February but
        later rejected by Bentley. In July he accompanies his father-in-law,
        Lemuel Shaw, to New Bedford and Nantucket. *Pierre,* published in
        late July by the Harpers and issued in London in November by
        their London agent, Sampson, Low, Son, and Co., proves to be a
        financial and critical disaster for Melville. On 2 December Melville
        visits the Hawthornes at Concord and discusses a possible new
        work, the story of Agatha.

1853   On 22 May a third child, Elizabeth, is born to the Melvilles. In the
        Spring Melville takes to New York an unspecified manuscript
        which, in his own later words, he is "prevented from printing";
        his family attempts without success to secure a consular appoint-

ment for him. Melville begins writing for *Putnam's Monthly Magazine* and *Harper's New Monthly Magazine;* on 24 November he proposes to the Harpers a new book on Tortoise Hunting.

1854   *Israel Potter* begins its serial appearance in the July issue of *Putnam's.*

1855   On 2 March a fourth child, Frances, is born to the Melvilles. In early March *Israel Potter* is published in book form by G. P. Putnam & Co., with an English issue in May. Melville is ill with rheumatism in February and with sciatica in June. Late in the year he is planning a collection of the short stories he had published in *Putnam's.*

1856   In May *The Piazza Tales* is published in New York by Dix & Edwards, with an English issue in June. On 11 October, having completed another book-length manuscript, Melville sails for Europe on the steamer *Glasgow* for reasons of health; in Liverpool he sees Hawthorne and stays with him at Southport, leaving on 18 November aboard the *Egyptian* for the Mediterranean. On 12 December he reaches Constantinople and on 30 December he is at Cairo.

1857   Melville spends most of January in Palestine, proceeding in February to Greece, Sicily, Naples and Rome and in March to Florence, Pisa, and Padua. On 1 April *The Confidence-Man* is published by Dix & Edwards, with an English issue later in the month. Melville visits Venice, Milan, Turin, and Genoa, continuing through Switzerland (where he meets Henry A. Smythe), Germany, and the Netherlands to England, reaching London on 26 April. After visiting Oxford and Stratford and seeing Hawthorne at Liverpool he sails for home on 5 May aboard the *City of Manchester,* reaching New York on 20 May. His family has been attempting to secure a place for him in the New York Custom House; on 3 July, Allan Melville signs an agreement for his brother to buy a house in Brooklyn; on 11 August, the agreement is terminated; in the Fall, with the Arrowhead property up for sale, he is accepting lecture engagements, beginning at Lawrence, Massachusetts, on 23 November with "Statues in Rome."

1858   In January and February Melville continues lecturing, in New England, the midwest, and the upper South; in March he is ill in Gansevoort, New York. In December he begins a new lecture season with "The South Seas."

1859   Melville continues lecturing in January, February, and March; in November he introduces a new lecture, "Traveling," but secures only three engagements for the winter season.

1860   Melville lectures twice in February. On 30 May he sails from New York aboard the clipper ship *Meteor,* commanded by his younger brother Thomas, for a voyage around Cape Horn. Left behind is a volume of manuscript poetry, which his family is unable to place with a publisher. On 12 October the *Meteor* reaches San Francisco, where Melville leaves her to return home via Panama, reaching New York aboard the *North Star* on 12 November.

1861 Aided by his family, Melville again tries unsuccessfully for a consular appointment. On 30 March Lemuel Shaw dies in Boston. In December the Melvilles leave Pittsfield for Boston and New York.

1862 The Melvilles remain in New York until April, Melville being ill with rheumatism during much of their stay. Back in Pittsfield, he again offers his farm for sale. On 7 November, having moved temporarily into a house in Pittsfield, Melville is thrown from a wagon and severely injured.

1863 In April the Melvilles buy from Allan Melville his house in New York, selling him the Arrowhead property, to which Mrs. Melville held title. On 26 June Melville attends the semi-centennial anniversary of the Albany Academy. In October the Melvilles move from Pittsfield to New York.

1864 In April, Melville and his brother Allan go to Washington and secure authorization to visit the Army of the Potomac, in which a cousin, Lieutenant Colonel Henry Gansevoort, is serving.

1865 T. B. Peterson & Brothers, Philadelphia, advertise *The Refugee,* by Herman Melville; he disavows the title, but the book is printed from the plates of *Israel Potter.*

1866 Four of Melville's war poems appear in *Harper's New Monthly Magazine,* beginning in February. In August the Harpers publish Melville's *Battle-Pieces and Aspects of the War.* On 28 November he is nominated by Henry A. Smythe as Inspector of Customs at New York, assuming his duties on 5 December.

1867 On 11 September Melville finds his son Malcolm dead of a self-inflicted bullet wound.

1869 On 4 April Melville's son Stanwix sails for China aboard the *Yokohama.*

1870 In May Melville is sitting for his portrait by J. O. Eaton. On 18 July his son Stanwix arrives in Boston from England.

1871 Henry Gansevoort dies on 12 April. Stanwix Melville is in Kansas, returning by December.

1872 Melville's brother Allan dies on 9 February. Maria Gansevoort Melville dies on 1 April, aged 81. Stanwix Melville returns to Kansas. Property owned by Elizabeth Shaw Melville is destroyed in the Boston fire of November.

1873 On 11 February Stanwix Melville is back in New York, having gone from Kansas to Central America; after working briefly as a dentist's assistant he sails for San Francisco on 30 April.

1875 In June Stanwix Melville returns from California, again working as a dentist's assistant. In August Melville's uncle Peter Gansevoort gives him $1,200 to pay for a forthcoming book. Stanwix Melville leaves again for California.

1876 Peter Gansevoort dies on 4 January. Melville's sister Augusta dies on 4 April. On 3 June Melville's *Clarel: A Poem and Pilgrimage in the Holy Land* is published by G. P. Putnam & Sons.

1878 Evert Duyckinck dies on 13 August. Mrs. Melville and the children are remembered in the will of her aunt Martha Marett, who dies in New Haven in August.

1880 Frances Melville marries Henry B. Thomas on 5 April.

1882 Eleanor Thomas, Melville's first grandchild, is born on 24 February. In the Fall Melville declines an invitation to join the Authors Club.

1884 Melville's brother Thomas dies on 5 March.

1885 The New York *Tribune* and the Boston *Herald* of 17 May print a poem by Melville, "The Admiral of the White." Melville's sister Frances Priscilla dies on 9 July. In the summer Melville pays his last visit to Pittsfield. On 31 December he resigns his post as Inspector of Customs.

1886 On 23 February, Stanwix Melville dies in San Francisco. On 21 October, John C. Hoadley dies in Lawrence, Massachusetts.

1887 Melville, walking with his second grandchild, Frances Thomas, on a spring day in Madison Square, forgetfully leaves her behind.

1888 Melville sails to Bermuda, returning in March. On 11 June he writes his will. His privately printed volume of poems entitled *John Marr and Other Sailors with Some Sea-Pieces* is deposited for copyright on 7 September by Theodore L. De Vinne & Co. On 16 November he begins making a fair copy of the new prose manuscript that he was to call *Billy Budd, Sailor.* Melville's sister Helen Melville Griggs dies on 14 December.

1889 On 2 March Melville begins another revision of the *Billy Budd* manuscript.

1890 Melville is greatly weakened by a second attack of erysipelas.

1891 On 8 January Melville is reported as "pretty ill for the last week or so." On 19 April he tentatively ends *Billy Budd,* but continues to revise it. On 16 June another privately printed volume of poems, *Timoleon and Other Ventures in Minor Verse,* is deposited for copyright by the Caxton Press; Melville later arranges the manuscripts of other poems in an unpublished volume entitled "Weeds and Wildings Chiefly: with a Rose or Two." On 28 September Melville dies of cardiac dilation.

Index

263

DESIGNED BY GARY GORE
COMPOSED BY HORNE ASSOCIATES, INC., HANOVER, NEW HAMPSHIRE
MANUFACTURED BY CUSHING-MALLOY, INC., ANN ARBOR, MICHIGAN
TEXT IS SET IN PRESS ROMAN, DISPLAY LINES IN TIMES ROMAN

Library of Congress Cataloging in Publication Data
Sealts, Merton M   comp.
The early lives of Melville.
Includes bibliographical references and index.
1. Melville, Herman, 1819–1891–Addresses, essays,
lectures. 2. Melville, Herman, 1819–1891–Biography–
Sources. 3. American prose literature–19th century.
I. Title.
PS2386.S38   813'.3 [B]   74-5906
ISBN 0-299-06570-7

DATE DUE

PRINTED IN U.S.A.